H Pugsley

Earth Sheltered Community Design
Energy-Efficient Residential Development

Underground Space Center
University of Minnesota

Dr. Raymond Sterling
John Carmody
Gail Elnicky

Funded by:
The Legislative Commission
on Minnesota Resources

VNR VAN NOSTRAND REINHOLD COMPANY
NEW YORK CINCINNATI TORONTO LONDON MELBOURNE

Library of Congress Catalog Card Number 81-11600
ISBN 0-442-28557-4
ISBN 0-442-28558-2 (pbk)

Printed in the United States of America

Published by Van Nostrand Reinhold Company
135 West 50th Street
New York, NY 10020

Van Nostrand Reinhold Limited
1410 Birchmount Road
Scarborough, Ontario M1P 2E7, Canada

Van Nostrand Reinhold Australia Pty. Ltd.
17 Queen Street
Mitcham, Victoria 3132, Australia

Van Nostrand Reinhold Company Limited
Molly Millars Lane
Wokingham, Berkshire, England

16 15 14 13 12 11 10 9 8 7 6 5 4 3 2 1

Library of Congress Cataloging in Publication Data

Main entry under title:

Earth sheltered community design.

Bibliography: p. 249
Includes index.
1. Earth sheltered houses—Design and construction. 2. Dwellings—Energy conservation. 3. City planning. I. University of Minnesota (Minneapolis-St. Paul campus). Underground Space Center.
TH4819.E27E395 711′.58 81-11600
ISBN 0-442-28557-4 AACR2
ISBN 0-442-28558-2 (pbk.)

The financial support of the Legislative Commission on Minnesota Resources is acknowledged, but the authors assume complete responsibility for the contents herein.

preface

At the scale of modern urban life, the ultimate constraints upon the system lie in nature. Energy-balanced development must derive from the main recurrences of heat, light, wind, and water. We must, for example, remember that shadows, representing differential heat gains, are not the same from one season to another. When it is necessary to place hundreds of buildings at a time, not just one, that kind of fact can be taken into consideration. If there is no choice in locating a building, if it must be only here or there, the location becomes a fact and accommodation to the fact takes place as a bigger heating or cooling unit. But if the building can be positioned, if it can be made taller or shorter and on this slope or that, if the packing can be denser on some slopes and sparser on others, a new design freedom can be created that does not totally depend upon the heater or cooler to provide a comfortable range of temperatures. Recognition can be taken of the fact that not only among seasons but at any given instant over the site, the energy gains from the sun are not the same.

Animals and plants have always taken into account such variations in nature. Can we, if we deal with large enough parts of the environment, make arrangements that are as subtly responsive? Once we overcome the attitude that all land increments must be the same size, there is no reason for increments on south slopes to be the same size as the increments on north slopes. These are lessons worth considering, but only if we are able to build in larger increments and only if there is control over more than what we have conventionally defined as a single building. With that lies the possibility of truly responsive form.

Ralph Knowles
Energy and Form

Over the past few years, the rapid growth of interest in and construction of earth sheltered housing has, naturally enough, led to increasing interest in developing earth sheltered communities. This type of larger-scale development is particularly appealing because a number of the environmental and land-use benefits associated with earth sheltered housing can be fully realized in larger projects.

Several communities in the Minneapolis-St. Paul area recently considered developing sites incorporating earth sheltered housing. In observing the planning process, it became obvious that the existence of a few well-designed earth sheltered houses is usually not enough to convince a community to approve a large project using this type of housing. Nor are developers normally willing to risk the large sums of money required for larger-scale development on an untried concept. For the most part, reluctance to proceed with an earth sheltered housing project appears to stem from an inability to envision what form such a community would take—what it would look like, what kinds of densities would be possible, how privacy could be guaranteed. Other factors inhibiting such projects relate to uncertainty about more pragmatic issues such as the costs, relative to those of conventional developments, and marketability of an earth sheltered development.

One of the first things we discovered in attempting to transfer concepts of individual earth sheltered house design to a community development was the difficulty in limiting such a study to earth sheltered housing alone. The type of housing selected for a development is but one element—albeit a very important one—of the total community design. Therefore, we have addressed additional concerns relevant to the planning and design of energy-efficient communities.

Studies do not materialize out of thin air. The Underground Space Center is indebted to the Legislative Commission on Minnesota Resources for funding this study, as well as for their support of both a concurrent study of nonresidential buildings and the previous research that led to the publication of *Earth Sheltered Housing Design*.

We hope this book will pave the way for a better assessment of both the potential for earth sheltered housing communities and the locations in which they are most applicable.

acknowledgments

The Underground Space Center gratefully acknowledges the support of the Legislative Commission on Minnesota Resources, which provided the funding for the research for this book. The authors also greatly appreciate the cooperation of the School of Architecture and Landscape Architecture in allowing Gail Elnicky to participate in this study. Her contribution made it possible to broaden the scope of the work considerably.

Although many people assisted in the study, preparation of this book would not have been possible without the contribution of two people above all. Mark Heisterkamp, a student in landscape architecture at the University of Minnesota, was a member of the project team throughout the study and assisted in virtually all phases of the project, particularly the site analysis, the case studies, and many of the illustrations. Donna Ahrens devoted considerable time and energy to the editing and rewriting involved in producing the finished work.

Such a broad-based study, which explores a number of constantly evolving concepts and technologies, required considerable consultation and review. Two key project consultants who provided thoughtful review and helpful criticism were Peter Herzog of Associated Energy Consultants and Roger Aiken of the University of Minnesota. Many others, too numerous to mention here, provided information and criticism. Some of these individuals and firms are listed in the reference section at the end of the book.

We would also like to thank several members of the Underground Space Center staff who assisted in various ways. The extensive typing and retyping of the book was done primarily by Arlene Bennett with assistance from Andrea Spartz and Penny Bader. Katherine Carmody keylined the study and did some of the graphic work. Several other people, who are listed in the credits, also assisted with the extensive graphics in this work.

Finally, we are grateful to the architects who contributed the drawings and photographs of their work that appear in the case studies chapter of the book. The names of the individuals and firms are indicated in the text describing each project. Of particular importance to the completion of the study was the contribution of Tom Ellison of Ellison Design, Minneapolis, who was primarily responsible for the prototypical housing design in chapter 6.

credits

Dr. Raymond Sterling — **Principal Investigator**
Director
Underground Space Center
Assistant Professor
Department of Civil and Mineral Engineering
University of Minnesota

John Carmody — **Project Coordinator**
Research Coordinator
Underground Space Center
University of Minnesota

Gail Elnicky — **Associate Project Coordinator**
Assistant Professor
School of Architecture and
Landscape Architecture
University of Minnesota

Mark Heisterkamp — **Principal Research Assistant**
School of Architecture and
Landscape Architecture
University of Minnesota

Graphics, layout, and illustrations by John Carmody with assistance from:

Mark Heisterkamp
Katherine Carmody
Tanya Vardoulakis
Rick LaMuro (drawings of prototypical design)

Additional assistance on site analysis:

William Midness
Kevin Keenan

Consultants:

Peter Herzog
Associated Energy Consultants
7505 West Highway 7
Minneapolis, Minnesota 55426

Roger Aiken
Department of Mechanical Engineering
University of Minnesota

Prototypical housing design by:

Tom Ellison
Ellison Design
2001 University Avenue Southeast
Minneapolis, Minnesota 55414

John Carmody

contents

Underground village in northern China. Drawing by Mark Heisterkamp based on a photograph from *Architecture Without Architects* by Bernard Rudofsky (see references).

introduction

The central subjects of this study—the development of new communities and the design of housing within these communities—are in a period of great transition because of significant changes that have occurred in recent years. As energy costs continue to rise, questions about future availability of energy from conventional sources of supply remain unanswered. Other natural resources, such as the supply of pure water, now appear to be limited as well. Moreover, some past development patterns have produced communities characterized by a generally poor quality of life as well as serious destruction of the natural environment.

The energy supply problem is well documented. While energy consumption has been increasing at an exponential rate over the last few decades, the major conventional sources of energy supply in the United States—oil, natural gas, coal, and nuclear fission—all have limitations and associated problems. According to most recent studies, domestic oil production has peaked; thus, foreign imports must increase as consumption increases. The political uncertainties of the Middle East and the constantly escalating prices for oil threaten our entire economic system. Natural gas production is also reaching its limit and will probably not help offset future energy deficits. And, like oil prices, the cost of natural gas undoubtedly will continue to increase, especially as deregulation occurs. Although coal is considered to be abundant and could potentially make a major contribution to future energy supplies, it presents some difficult environmental problems that are likely to hold its development to a relatively moderate pace. Finally, production of nuclear energy, once thought capable of meeting a high percentage of our future needs, is mired in controversy. Political resistance, together with some still unresolved technical problems and higher-than-projected costs, have significantly slowed nuclear plant construction.

Two prominent studies [1.1, 1.2] have concluded that energy conservation—that is, reduced consumption through greater efficiency—is the most cost-effective, politically safe strategy to deal with the energy supply problem and presents the fewest environmental risks. The studies note that reduced consumption need not necessarily result in a lower standard of living or decreased economic activity. The use of renewable energy sources (based directly or indirectly on solar energy) represents another environmentally benign and politically safe strategy that reduces consumption of conventional fuels. Although it is difficult to generalize about the feasibility of these renewable sources because of the wide variety of approaches and differing states of technical development, some systems based on renewable energy sources are certainly feasible today, and more systems will likely become feasible in the future.

Since it is uncertain whether conventional fuels can continue to fulfill the nation's energy needs at the present level of consumption, and because their contribution to these needs is unlikely to increase, maximum conservation efforts—in combination with the use of more renewable sources of energy—appear to be a necessary part of nearly any likely future scenario. Most analyses of potential targets for reduced energy consumption conclude that buildings, particularly housing, are a prime candidate for effective energy conservation. In addition to decreasing the energy actually consumed within the individual housing unit, the entire land development process offers many opportunities for practicing conservation—in overall land-use and transportation patterns, in road and utility layouts, and in materials and construction methods used.

Although the energy supply problem appears to be the predominant reason for changing development patterns and housing design, it is just one component of a larger issue—that of designing our communities to work more harmoniously with the natural systems in the environment. Land development simply cannot continue to pollute clean water and air nor to harm plant life and soils that are vital to maintaining human life. As these natural resources are depleted and natural systems are stressed beyond their capacities, technical solutions to these problems can be developed, but these often require significant amounts of energy to compensate for the lack of healthy, functioning natural systems. Development strategies that include conservation of land, vegetation, and water and careful management of environmentally sensitive areas appear to be the only viable alternative, as they combine the benefits of lower energy consumption with the least cost over the long term.

The energy supply and environmental quality problems clearly form the basis for new goals that must be met in land development and housing design—namely, to reduce energy consumption, to use land more efficiently, and to design to protect the natural environment as much as possible. It should be emphasized that there are other equally important goals in land development and housing design, including reducing costs when possible and providing a properly functioning, socially stimulating, and aesthetically pleasing community environment. Past development practices have primarily emphasized the goals of creating a smoothly functioning community layout with respect to automobile access, and providing uniformly-sized lots and houses placed in a uniform manner based on zoning restrictions. These goals, with their generally repetitive design solutions, have not necessarily resulted in socially stimulating and aesthetically pleasing communities. In addition, as energy and land costs have continued to rise, conventional development practices have ceased to be the most cost-effective approach. In seeking solutions to the more technical goals of reducing energy consumption and providing environmental protection, it is essential that these other goals not be overlooked. Underlying this study is a basic assumption that the goals of energy efficiency and environmental protection are compatible with the aesthetic, social, and economic goals. In fact, designs that respond to the climate and the natural systems on a site can result not only in lower costs, but also in a more varied and stimulating environment.

In response to the goals of designing energy-efficient and environmentally sound communities and housing structures, many approaches have been developed and much experimentation has taken place in recent years. At the scale of individual dwelling design, the earth sheltered house is one emerging solution that attempts to solve some of these problems. Significant energy savings can result from using the earth to protect structures from the surrounding environment. In addition to wind protection provided by earth berms, the more moderate climate below grade and the large thermal mass of the earth contribute to reduced energy consumption for both heating and cooling. Earth sheltered houses are usually designed to take advantage of renewable solar energy as well. Although reduced energy use is a commonly recognized advantage of earth sheltering, many people find the aesthetic and environmental benefits of integrating structures into the earth to be the principal attraction of this type of dwelling. Other advantages associated with earth sheltering include protection from noise, fires, and natural disasters, as well as a more durable structure that requires less maintenance. At the scale of a larger development, the main benefits associated with earth sheltered buildings are the ability to use marginal, steeply sloping land that is unsuitable for conventional development and, in some cases, the ability to increase densities while providing a greener, more natural environment.

Since earth sheltered housing is a housing alternative with some promising benefits, it is useful to examine its application at the scale of an entire community development rather than simply at the scale of individual houses. This examination is one of the main purposes of this study. It is essential, however, to recognize that the problems and solutions involved in the planning and design of a large development are very different from those related to an individual house. For example, the problem of reducing energy consumption is far more complex in a community development than for a single house. In the individual house design, the primary concern is to reduce energy consumed for heating and cooling, whereas considerations at the larger scale include the amount of energy consumed for transportation and in the construction and maintenance of roads and utilities. In fact, according to one study of a typical suburban development, 70 percent of total family energy use was associated with automobile use, and the remaining 30 percent with heating, cooling, and maintenance of housing [1.3]. Thus, such strategies as intermixing of work places, shopping areas, and homes to reduce automobile trips; higher-density developments with mass transit; and more efficient road layouts are likely to have a greater impact on reducing total energy consumption than would the design of the individual housing units.

Like issues related to reducing energy consumption, environmental issues are far different at the scale of a larger development. In fact, very few environmental issues can be dealt with effectively at the individual house scale. On the community scale, however, all of the fundamental issues associated with the environment must be addressed. Environmentally sensitive areas must be protected and managed within the development, and site design related to roads, utilities, and buildings must work with the natural systems.

Another key difference between individual and large-scale housing is that the design of a single house on an individual lot need not address the issue of efficient land use. In some cases a house designed with very efficient heating and cooling systems may have very inefficient lot configuration and associated road and utility system layouts. Thus, design at the community development scale must take into consideration the advantages and disadvantages of all housing types.

Because of these differences between individual house design and large-scale development, the relationship between earth sheltered housing and community design must be examined carefully. It should not be based on the assumption that, since individual earth sheltered houses have many benefits, they will automatically have the same benefits when repeated in multiple-unit structures or when applied to a variety of sites. In order to achieve the broader goal of energy-efficient, environmentally sound communities, alternative strategies at all scales of development must be analyzed, and earth sheltered housing regarded as one of a group of alternative housing types. For this reason the purpose and scope of this study have been broadened from simply multiple-unit earth sheltered housing design to include the larger context of energy-efficient community development. Much of the information in this book therefore applies to various types of energy-efficient development, not just earth sheltered housing. The potential of earth sheltered housing, including design guidelines and examples, is clearly emphasized, however.

Although changes in past development approaches and designs appear inevitable and the potential for better environments is promising, developers, planners, designers, and others in the development process may have difficulty in assessing alternatives properly. Because many new concepts and technologies are constantly evolving, locating the most current information may prove troublesome, and any information may be rendered partially obsolete within a short time. Moreover, few examples of community developments that use alternative planning and design strategies actually exist. Thus, assessing and comparing alternatives and, perhaps more importantly, visualizing these new communities and housing types is quite a difficult task—particularly with regard to earth sheltered housing. To aid in this process, much of the planning and design information in this study is presented by using a prototypical development site. In addition, several case studies of earth sheltered housing developments are included. This information is not intended as a complete or final presentation of these issues, but rather as a collection of relevant information on energy-efficient community design, with an emphasis on earth sheltered housing. The study is organized as a framework that can be modified and expanded as more information becomes available.

The book is organized into seven chapters, beginning with a discussion of traditional planning issues applied to a prototypical development site. In the second chapter, a number of energy-related planning issues are introduced and analyzed with respect to the same prototypical site. This chapter is followed by an assessment of alternative energy-efficient strategies for road and utility systems. Chapter 4 discusses the basic characteristics of various types of energy-efficient housing, including conventional well-insulated housing, solar houses, and different types of earth sheltered housing. The site design implications, including typical layouts and densities, are examined for these housing types in chapter 5. Chapter 6 presents the final development plan for the prototypical site as well as a design for a cluster of earth sheltered houses on the site. This discussion demonstrates many of the concepts covered in the previous chapters. Finally, a series of case studies of earth sheltered housing developments—both proposed and built—comprises chapter 7. The appendices contain supplementary information on alternative energy supply systems, marketability of earth sheltered housing, and the technical criteria for the soils evaluation used for the site analysis in chapter 1. Also included are the direct references and a bibliography.

Proposed earth sheltered townhouse project for site in St. Paul, Minnesota. Design and drawing by Jerry Allen of CRITERIA, inc. (see chapter 7).

1 traditional planning issues

introduction

This chapter presents an overview of the major issues that are traditionally analyzed when planning a community development. These issues, which are part of the typical planning process, are referred to as "traditional" in order to distinguish them from the microclimatological or "energy-efficient" planning issues presented in chapter 2. Aspects of the traditional planning process can be applied to a site to evaluate its potential for energy-efficient building types such as earth sheltered housing as well as for more conventional housing. The ways that these planning issues affect the layout of a community development are illustrated through an analysis of a prototypical site.

The first section of this chapter introduces the traditional development process, indicating the general sequence of events and time required for each phase. This introduction is followed by a description of the prototypical site and a brief assessment of its marketability potential. Then a site analysis is presented, illustrating base data such as topography, percent slope, and vegetation. These physical characteristics of the site are then used as a basis for analyzing the suitability of the site for development. Next, the overlay process is described, suitability for various uses assessed, and a complete development composite presented. Finally, a discussion of how the protection of the natural environment relates to energy-efficient development is accompanied by a presentation of the "natural systems" composite map for the site.

the development process

Generally, the development of any type of housing requires a continuous process involving many phases, including market assessment, land acquisition, various stages of planning and design, construction, marketing, and sales. The exact steps in this process and the time required for each can vary significantly as a function of the individual community and numerous other factors. Figure 1-1 presents a general overview of the sequence of activities and approvals typically experienced in development, based on a chart developed by Robert Engstrom and Marc Putnam to show the sequence of events and estimated time for town house and condominium development [1.4].

Obviously, a great deal of time and investment are necessary before a project is finally approved. These factors can work against the development of more innovative concepts such as solar or earth sheltered housing because marketability and, therefore, loan approval are less certain, thereby increasing the risk for the developer. These issues are discussed in greater detail in appendix B.

1-1: the development process

1. market analysis/land

market demand and awareness developer commitment	choose development team	identify site locations	buildable land area schematics	option site market research initial program
1-4 weeks		2-5 weeks		1-2 weeks

2. concept planning and design

concept plans and designs	developer review revisions	local govt. staff discussion local community input	preliminary legal documents prepare final concept plans	local govt. staff review revisions	planning and zoning commission review revisions	local govt. zoning approval local govt. plan approval non-local govt. approvals
2-5 weeks	0-2 weeks		2 weeks	6 weeks-??		

3. preliminary planning and design

ongoing market research program refinement	feasibility decision revisions	buy land	preliminary plans and designs	developer review revisions	local govt. staff discussion local community input	prepare legal documents prepare preliminary drawings	local govt. staff discussion revisions	planning and zoning commission review revisions	local govt. zoning approval local govt. plan approval non-local govt. approvals
1-6 weeks			2-8 weeks	0-1 week		1-2 weeks	6 weeks-??		

4. final planning and design

ongoing market research program refinement	feasibility decision revisions	buy land	final planning design and specifications	feasibility decision revisions	legal documents construction plans and specifications
0-3 weeks			1-8 weeks	0-2 weeks	3-16 weeks

5. construction and marketing

negotiated contractor or bids revisions	financing final feasibility decision permits	develop merchandising program pre-sales model home construction site development construction	model center grand opening	home sales home buyer reaction	closing service home construction program and design modification
4-10 weeks		10-20 weeks	total: 33-88 weeks		

the prototypical site

The site chosen to illustrate the planning issues discussed in this chapter comprises approximately 143 acres (57.2 ha) of county park land in central Minnesota. As shown in the adjacent maps (fig. 1-2), the site is located within the Minneapolis-St. Paul metropolitan area, in the township of Apple Valley in Dakota County. The Apple Valley township, easily accessible from both Minneapolis and St. Paul, has a tremendous potential for growth between now and the year 2000. The geological character of Dakota County is distinctive in that it is characterized by glacial overlay of the bedrock with transported soils, creating rolling land forms (moraines) and kettle lakes. These features are clearly present on the site, which has two bodies of water and a rugged sandy terrain.

In determining the potential for marketing a housing development on a particular site, a number of features and services must be assessed, including proximity to schools, churches, shopping centers, and various natural and man-made amenities. As indicated in figure 1-3, the prototypical site has many of these features, most notably a large zoological garden, extensive parkland, lakes, and golf courses located immediately adjacent to the site. In addition, the site is reasonably close to schools and churches as well as to regional and local shopping centers.

Another factor in assessing the marketability of a site is the future development plans of the surrounding community. It is important to be aware of future plans that might adversely affect a development—such as industrial uses—as well as plans that may positively affect it, such as housing or compatible types of commercial development. Although the land-use plan for Apple Valley is not shown here, the parkland to the west and north of the site and the golf course to the east can be regarded as permanently dedicated to those uses. The land to the south is agricultural at present, but future plans indicate low- to medium-density housing.

Thus, the prototypical site would be a desirable location for housing.

This parkland site was chosen because it offers an excellent opportunity to compare the suitability of conventional housing with that of earth sheltered housing. Due to the steep terrain, this parcel of land was not suitable for development of conventional housing. It has been legally dedicated as parkland. If it were available, however, the site could be developed for earth sheltered housing, which can be built into slopes steeper than 15 percent if soil conditions permit. In the past, many sites like this have been overlooked because their potential for conventional development was considered marginal. Through the appropriate construction of earth sheltered housing, land can be used more efficiently by developing such marginal sites.

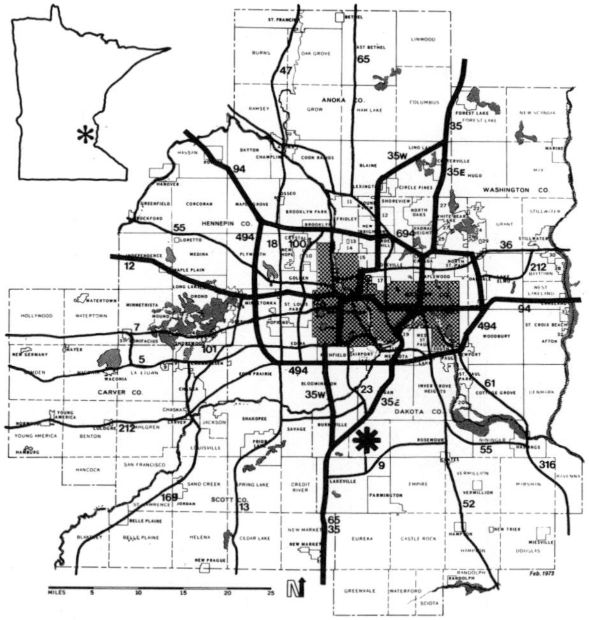
ANOKA CO.
HENNEPIN CO.
WASHINGTON CO.
CARVER CO.
DAKOTA CO.

1-2: site location

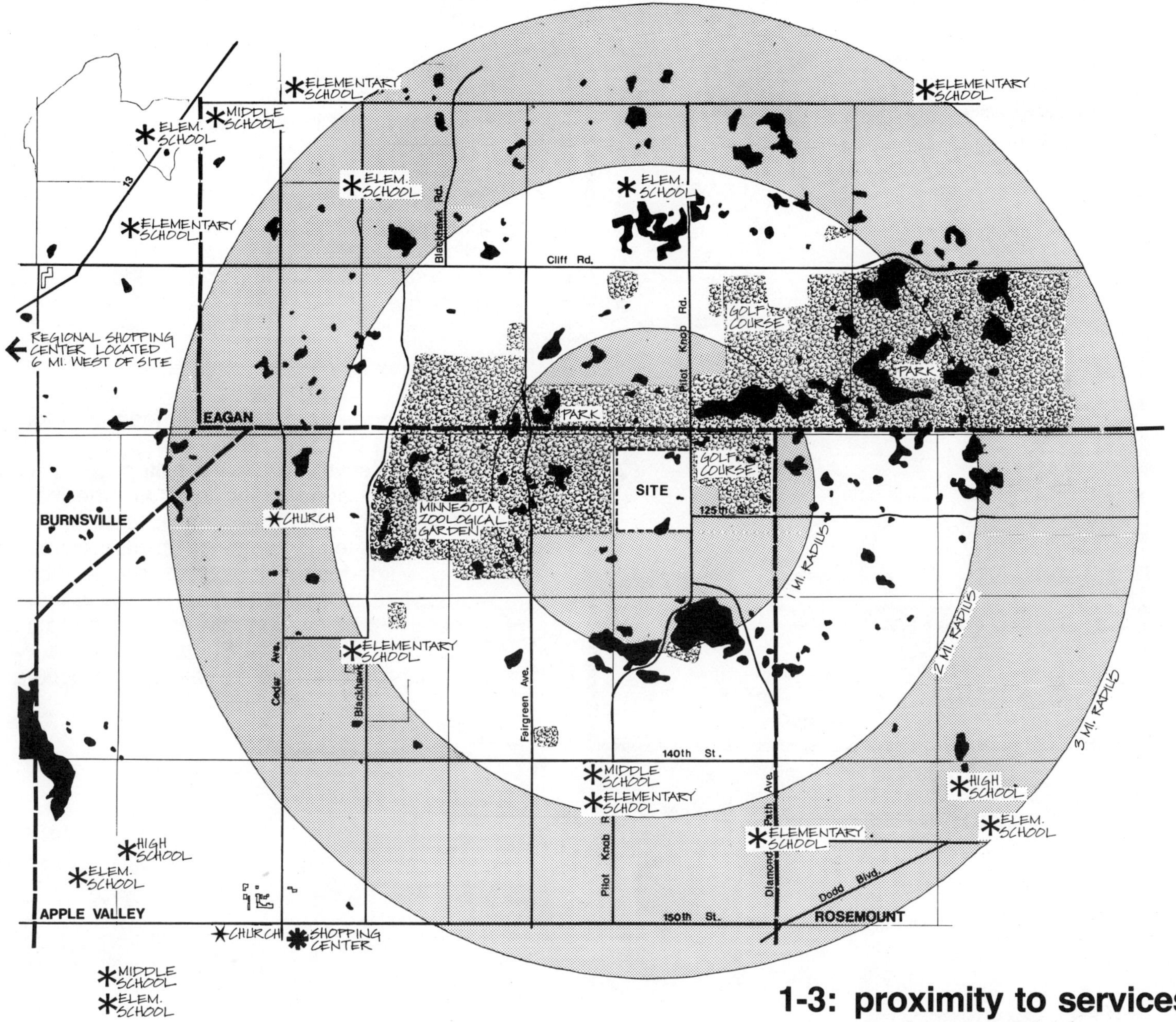
ELEMENTARY SCHOOL
ELEMENTARY SCHOOL
MIDDLE SCHOOL
ELEM. SCHOOL
ELEM. SCHOOL
ELEM. SCHOOL
ELEMENTARY SCHOOL
13
Blackhawk Rd.
Cliff Rd.
REGIONAL SHOPPING CENTER LOCATED 6 MI. WEST OF SITE
GOLF COURSE
PARK
Pilot Knob Rd.
PARK
EAGAN
GOLF COURSE
SITE
125th St.
BURNSVILLE
CHURCH
MINNESOTA ZOOLOGICAL GARDEN
1 MI. RADIUS
2 MI. RADIUS
3 MI. RADIUS
ELEMENTARY SCHOOL
Cedar Ave.
Blackhawk
Fairgreen Ave.
140th St.
MIDDLE SCHOOL
ELEMENTARY SCHOOL
HIGH SCHOOL
ELEM. SCHOOL
ELEMENTARY SCHOOL
Diamond Path Ave.
Pilot Knob Rd.
Dodd Blvd.
HIGH SCHOOL
ELEM. SCHOOL
APPLE VALLEY
150th St.
ROSEMOUNT
CHURCH
SHOPPING CENTER
MIDDLE SCHOOL
ELEM. SCHOOL

1-3: proximity to services and amenities

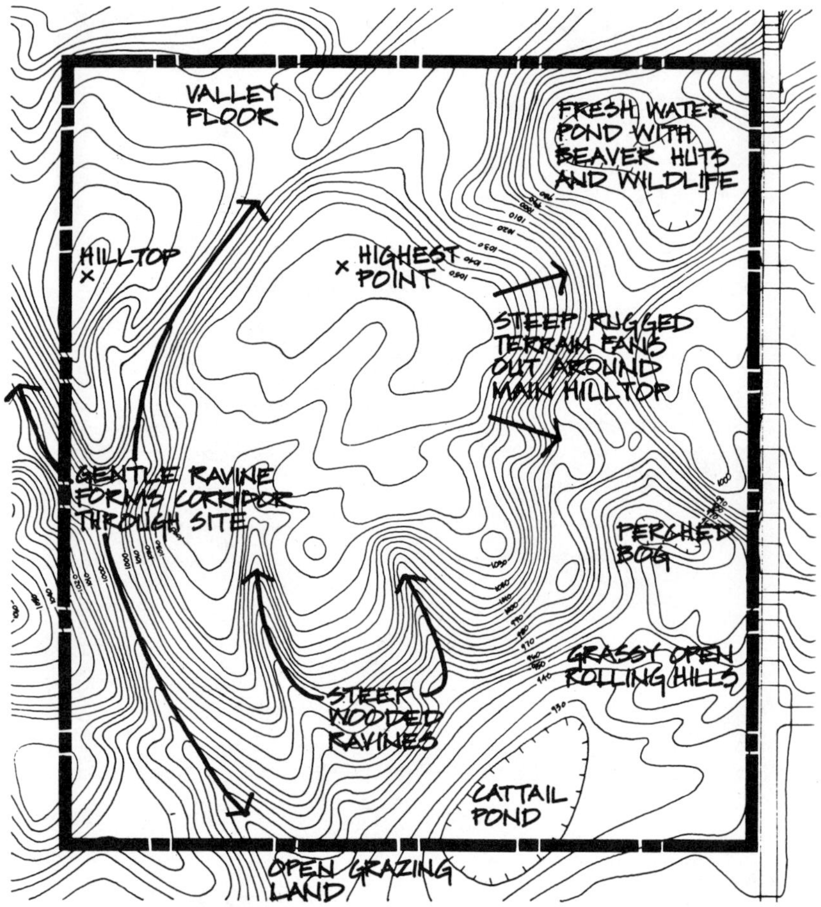
VALLEY FLOOR
FRESH WATER POND WITH BEAVER HUTS AND WILDLIFE
HILLTOP
HIGHEST POINT
STEEP RUGGED TERRAIN FANS OUT AROUND MAIN HILLTOP
GENTLE RAVINE FORMS CORRIDOR THROUGH SITE
PERCHED BOG
GRASSY OPEN ROLLING HILLS
STEEP WOODED RAVINES
CATTAIL POND
OPEN GRAZING LAND

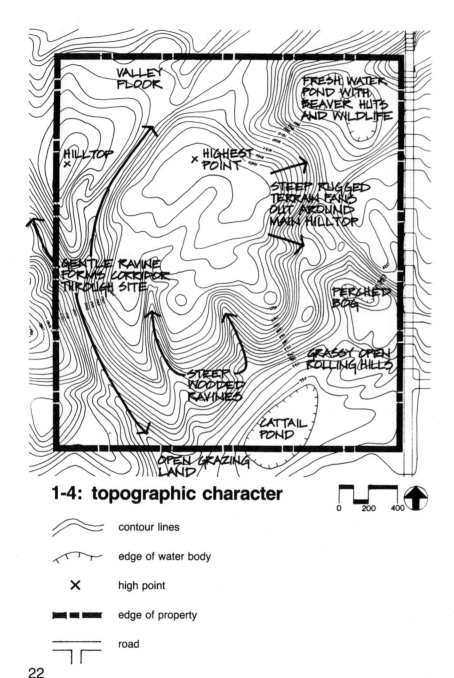

1-4: topographic character

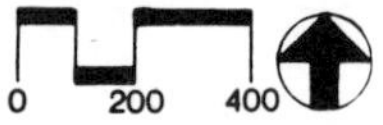
0 200 400

contour lines

edge of water body

× high point

edge of property

road

In the traditional method of site analysis, information pertaining to land topography, percent slope, surface hydrology, and interpreted vegetation (based on aerial photographs) is collected. This information provides the basis for assessing the potential of the site for development of housing. For the prototypical site, this information is shown in figures 1-4 through 1-7 on the following pages. The major implications and limitations of these maps are summarized in the paragraph adjacent to each map.

topography

The site consists mainly of rugged land forms fanning out around a major central hilltop. On-site water bodies and the relatively large, flat hilltop, which offers extensive views of the surrounding land, are the major visual assets of the site. Topographic features that are potentially useful for energy-efficient development are the steep, south-facing slopes that are protected from winter winds. The topographic map shown in figure 1-4 is a general representation interpreted from aerial photography by the U.S. Geological Survey. On-site surveys would be required to determine its validity and accuracy.

percent slope

The flat hilltop and extremely steep terrain surrounding it result in a variety of slope gradations. A relatively small portion of the site has a slope of less than the 8 percent that is preferred for conventional development. On the other hand, a relatively high proportion of the site can be developed for earth sheltered houses, since slopes of 8 to 25 percent are preferable and even steeper slopes may be usable. The data in figure 1-4 are based on the topographic map; on-site surveys would be necessary to determine the validity of the data.

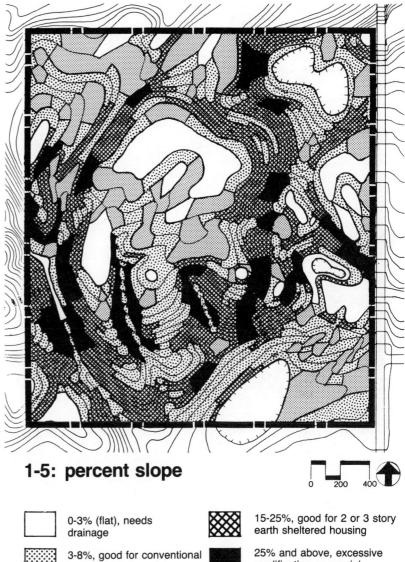

1-5: percent slope

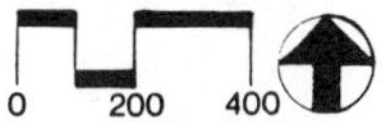
0
200
400

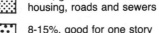

- 0-3% (flat), needs drainage
- 3-8%, good for conventional housing, roads and sewers
- 8-15%, good for one story earth sheltered housing
- 15-25%, good for 2 or 3 story earth sheltered housing
- 25% and above, excessive modification or special building technology needed

Photograph by Mark Hurd Aerial Surveys, Inc., Minneapolis, Minnesota
Date flown: April 26, 1977

1-6: aerial photograph of site

vegetation interpreted from aerial photograph

As shown in the aerial photograph in figure 1-6 and the interpreted vegetation map in figure 1-7, the site is densely covered with unmanaged, second growth, mixed understory and overstory tree vegetation, with the exception of small open fields scattered along the base of the hilltop and adjacent to the site boundaries. For both conventional and energy-efficient development, the main feature is the dense vegetation throughout the hilltop area, which will aid in wind protection and add visual interest via its diverse plant communities. The vegetative data are interpreted from aerial photography, surface hydrology, and soil interpretation data (see appendix C). Current aerial photographs as well as site visits would be needed to check the accuracy of these data.

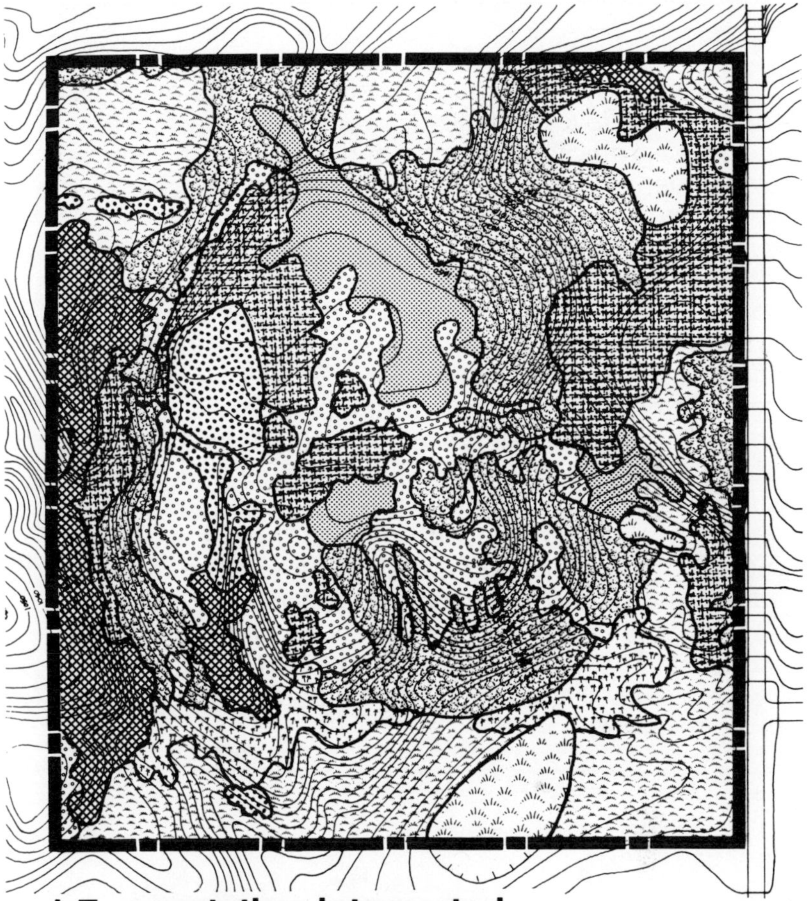

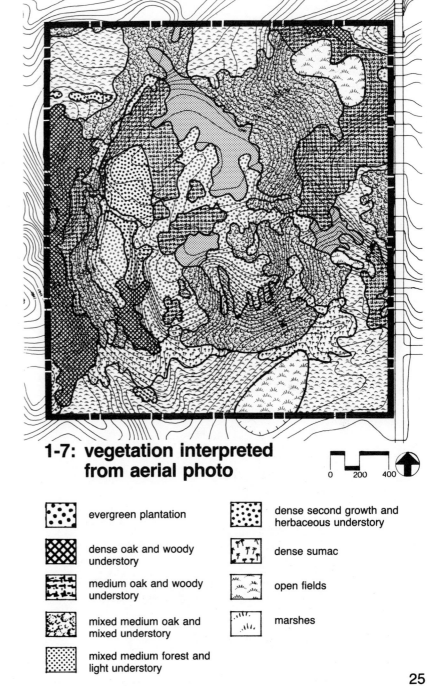

1-7: vegetation interpreted from aerial photo

0 200 400

- evergreen plantation
- dense oak and woody understory
- medium oak and woody understory
- mixed medium oak and mixed understory
- mixed medium forest and light understory
- dense second growth and herbaceous understory
- dense sumac
- open fields
- marshes

the development composite

A number of physical characteristics of a site affect its feasibility for development. Since these characteristics differ in degree of importance and affect various kinds of development in different ways, a technique known as the overlay process is used to determine a site's development suitability. This process is widely used to aid in preparing and interpreting site conditions for their potential use. Key environmental conditions are indicated on base maps that clearly define the opportunities and constraints with regard to the site. By overlapping two or more characteristics from different base maps, a composite map indicating various degrees of suitability for one intended use is derived. For example, the diagram in figure 1-8 indicates the base maps required to develop a suitability composite for conventional or earth sheltered housing. This information can then be used to resolve conflicting physical demands for the site, within the limits of the site. In order to illustrate this process, which will result in a development composite for the prototypical site, four suitability composites for the site are presented on the following pages.

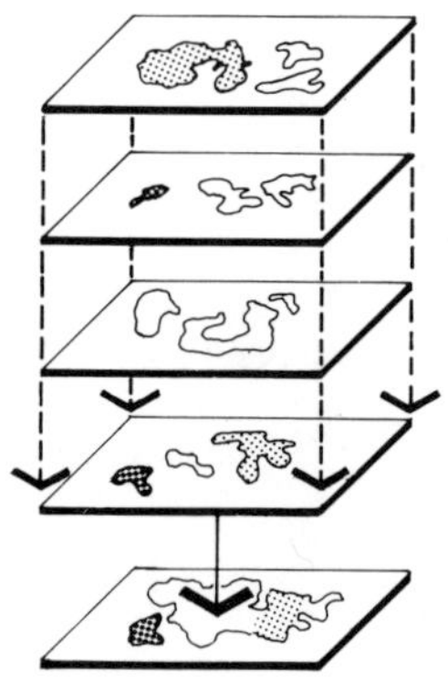
soils
percent slope
geology
surface hydrology
suitability for
housing development

1-8: the overlay process

suitability for conventional housing

Figure 1-9 shows the suitability of the prototypical site for conventional housing. The cross-hatched pattern covering a large portion of the site represents severe limitations caused by steep slopes and extremely erodible or heavily organic soils; the medium tone represents areas of moderate limitations. The best areas for conventional development are indicated by the relatively few white areas. The darker-toned areas, which represent areas of empondment, steep slopes, and poorly drained soils, could be developed by major restructuring of the slopes and the soils. These high-technology solutions are costly and energy intensive, however, and involve considerable environmental risks.

suitability for earth sheltered housing

Figure 1-10 shows the suitability for earth sheltered housing on the prototypical site. The resulting map is different from figure 1-9 because earth sheltered houses are well suited to steeper slopes and the soil characteristics found on this site. In fact, earth sheltered housing that is carefully integrated into the land can actually better protect the site against erosion than if the site remained in a natural, unmanaged state. As indicated on the map, the majority of the site is very suitable for earth sheltered housing, with the exception of minor restricted areas at the base of the hill. Development would not be restricted in the white area of the map; however, the toned areas would require moderate to severe alteration of the soils in order to be suitable for earth sheltered housing development.

The remarkable difference between these two suitability maps emphasizes one of the great advantages of earth sheltered housing: its feasibility for development on sites considered marginal for conventional development. Both suitability maps are based on maps of the geology,

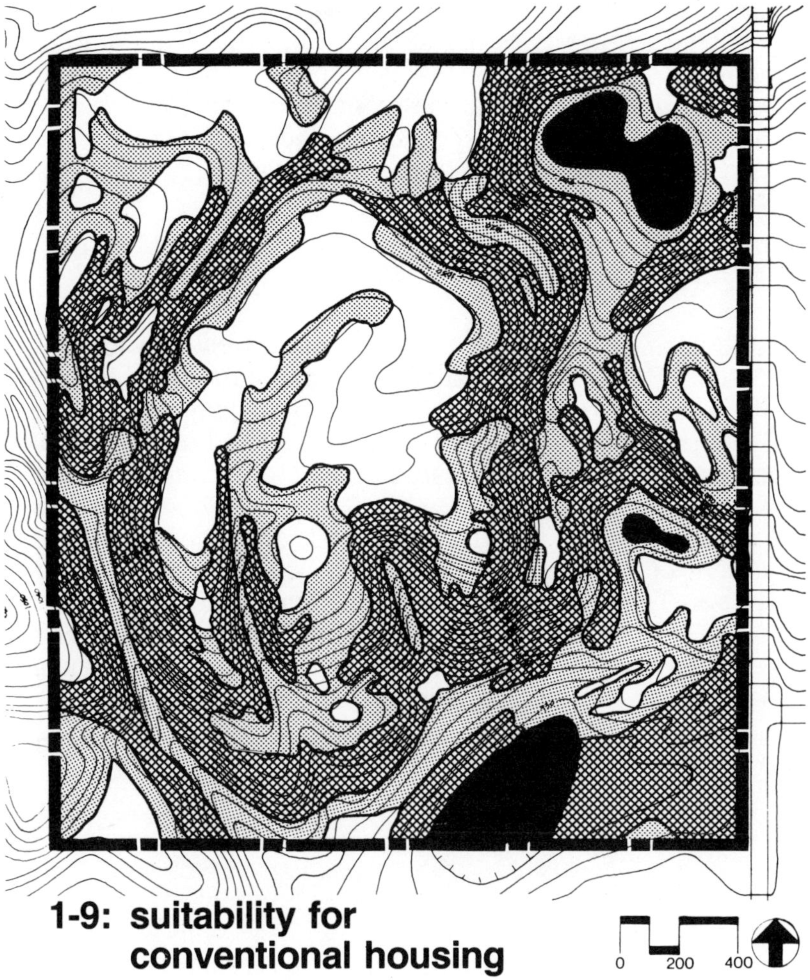

1-9: suitability for conventional housing

- best suited (30 acres)
- moderate limitations by % slope and soil type (48 acres)
- severe limitations by % slope or soil type (58 acres)
- emponded areas (7 acres)

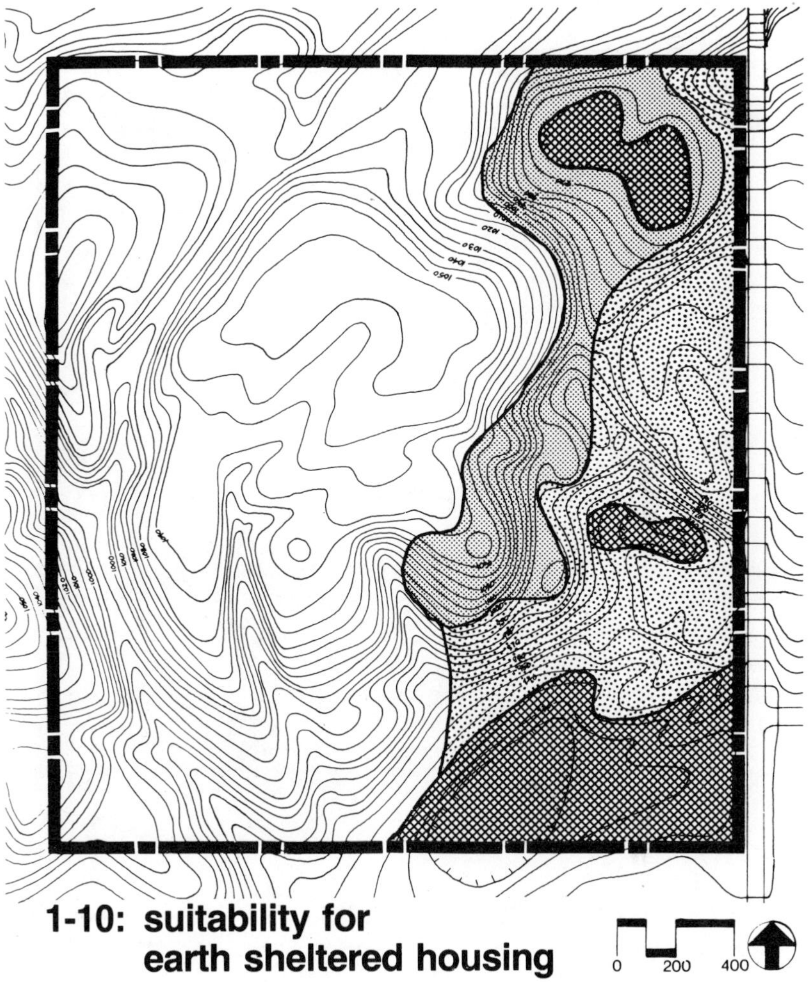

1-10: suitability for earth sheltered housing

- best suited (91 acres)
- some restrictions at base of hills against slippage (16 acres)
- clayey; wet but low organic content, tends to have high frost action (17 acres)
- severe wetness (19 acres)

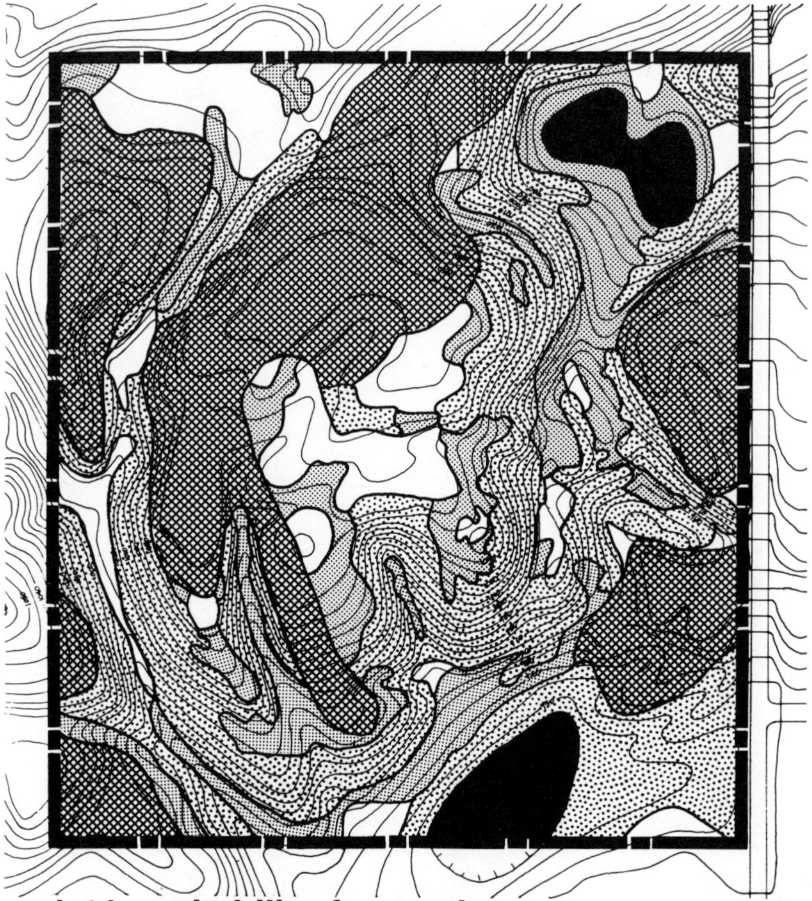

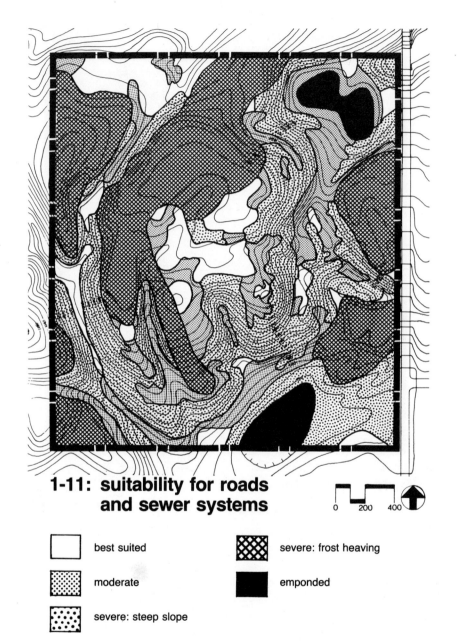

1-11: suitability for roads and sewer systems

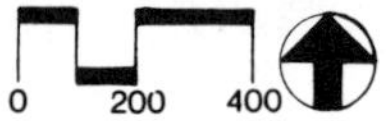

0
200
400

- best suited
- moderate
- severe: steep slope
- severe: frost heaving
- emponded

surface hydrology, soils, and percent slope (see fig. 1-5). The characteristics of the soils are based on general soil interpretation sheets (available from the Soil Conservation Service) for the various soil types found on the site. Current soil borings would be needed to determine the validity of these profile sheets. Soil rating information is presented in appendix C.

suitability for roads and sewer systems

In addition to assessing the suitability of the site for housing, it is useful to determine its suitability for roads and sewer systems to ensure that development is feasible. The map shown in figure 1-11 is based on the percent slope and soil characteristics of the site. The development of roads is directly related to percent slope. For example, roads must be limited to a slope of 10 percent or less to be acceptable in icy Minnesota winters. The majority of the map, represented in darker tones, is unfeasible for development of roads and sewer systems. Only the lighter areas on the hilltop and around the base of the hill are feasible for these purposes.

suitability for agriculture and recreation

The overlay process can also be used to assess the suitability of the site for agriculture and recreation. Like the other suitability maps, this one is based on percent slope of the land and various characteristics of the soils. Relatively flat land composed of easily drained, rich soil types is desirable for both agriculture and intense recreation uses. It is very useful to identify these areas within the boundaries of a potential housing development. Allocating a portion of this land for use as community open space is desirable. As shown on the map in figure 1-12, all the toned areas are classified by soil suited for agricultural use and/or intense recreation use. The values of the various components used in the suitability composite are subjectively rated.

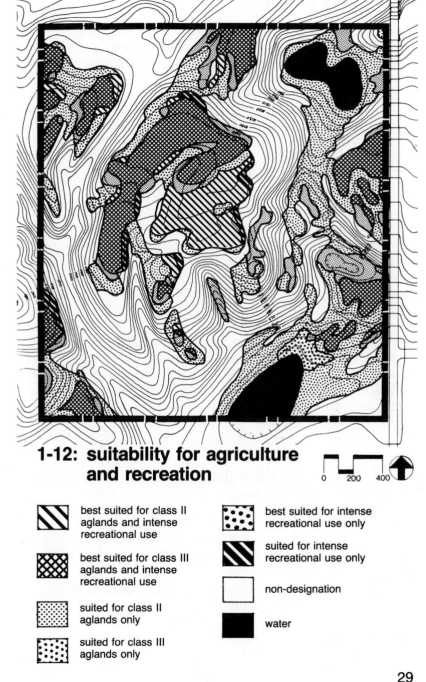

1-12: suitability for agriculture and recreation

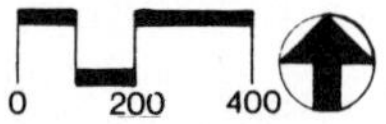
0
200
400

- best suited for class II aglands and intense recreational use
- best suited for class III aglands and intense recreational use
- suited for class II aglands only
- suited for class III aglands only
- best suited for intense recreational use only
- suited for intense recreational use only
- non-designation
- water

development composite

The development composite shown in figure 1-13 indicates the areas that are suitable for earth sheltered and/or conventional building on the prototypical site. The base information has been organized, rated, and combined to indicate the best possible locations for each use. The composite map comprises the following base maps: suitability for conventional housing (fig. 1-9), suitability for earth sheltered housing (fig. 1-10), road and sewer system suitability (fig. 1-11), agricultural/intense recreational suitability (fig. 1-12), and the interim watershed/erosion map (not shown).

The cross-hatching on the map indicates areas where only earth sheltered housing could be developed. The light-toned areas on the east side of the site represent prime locations for conventional housing development only. The majority of the site is covered with a dark tone that represents an intermixture of sites suitable for both earth sheltered and conventional housing. When considered as individual parcels of land, certain sites within this dark-toned area are more suitable for earth sheltered housing; others are more suitable for conventional housing. A letter symbol inside an area indicates that the area contains very wet soils, which must be considered in planning and design. While both earth sheltered and conventional housing are feasible in these wet areas, the letter symbol indicates which type of housing is the most suitable.

The white areas on the map represent zones that should be preserved as open space because they are characterized by soil types that severely limit development. The heavy dashed line represents a geological barrier (i.e., an edge of a moraine with normal bedrock parent material underlying the morainal surface geology) associated with severe erosion problems. For development to occur in this area, land-management techniques would be required. A more complete analysis of natural systems and environmentally sensitive areas on this site is provided in the following section.

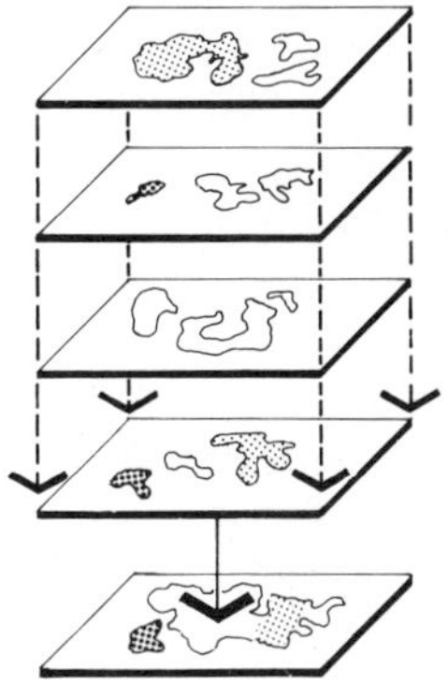
suitability for agriculture and recreation
suitability for roads and utilities
suitability for earth sheltered housing
suitability for conventional housing
development composite

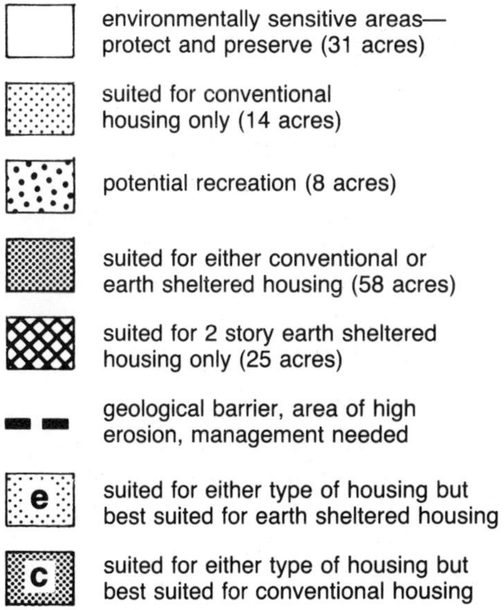
environmentally sensitive areas—protect and preserve (31 acres)
suited for conventional housing only (14 acres)
potential recreation (8 acres)
suited for either conventional or earth sheltered housing (58 acres)
suited for 2 story earth sheltered housing only (25 acres)
geological barrier, area of high erosion, management needed
e
suited for either type of housing but best suited for earth sheltered housing
c
suited for either type of housing but best suited for conventional housing

1-13: development composite

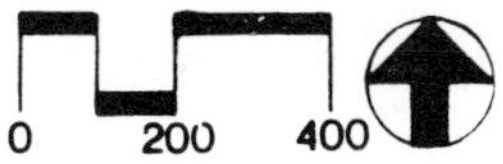
0
200
400

Protection of the natural environment is not only a desirable goal in community development, but a legal requirement as well. Because of the consequences of past practices in which open space and natural systems were not preserved in development, many communities now have legal requirements for protection of the environment. The zoning ordinance for Apple Valley, Minnesota, where the prototypical site is located, states:

> *Site planning and development shall show due regard for all natural terrain features, such as trees or vegetation, water courses, historic areas, slopes, soil conditions, ponding areas and wet lands and similar existing physical features in order that development of any type will not have an adverse or detrimental effect upon the ecology or natural character of an area [1.5].*

In order to maintain a harmonious relationship between the natural environment and our use of it, the locations, design, and construction of all buildings, roads, and utilities must be based on proper management of the environment. The impact of all new developments on natural systems should be assessed, and appropriate changes should be made in the development plan. In general, each state regulates its own variation of the Environmental Assessment Worksheet/Environmental Impact Statement (EAW/EIS) process and lists the various categories of development that require an EAW/EIS report. The three basic guidelines that help determine whether or not an optional EAW/EIS report should be prepared are:

- Is the project in or near an area that is considered to be environmentally sensitive or aesthetically pleasing?
- Is the project likely to have disruptive effects, such as generating traffic and noise?
- Is there public question or controversy concerning the envrionmental effects of the proposed project?

Some people consider the EAW/EIS process a roadblock to development. Only one in five hundred cases requires an EIS report after the environmental assessment worksheet (EAW) has been prepared, however. Because both processes involve time and money that could be used elsewhere, the developer should prepare a composite map of the natural systems on the site. This map provides a number of benefits to the developer, since the areas indicated for environmental protection are also the areas that require the greatest monetary expenditures and the most energy-intensive development. Thus, while helping the developer comply with environmental protection laws, the map also has the potential to indicate the worst areas for development from both economic and energy points of view.

natural systems composite

The natural systems composite map, shown in figure 1-14, for the prototypical site comprises the following base maps: the interpreted vegetation map (fig. 1-7), the interpreted soil data information (see appendix C), and the interim map of water domains (surface hydrology and precipitation; not shown here). Before these maps were combined, they were rated as equal based on a subjective assessment of critical environmental issues affecting development.

The very few isolated white areas on the map represent prime locations where development will have no impact on the natural systems. The light-toned areas represent areas where vegetative and wildlife management principles should be applied if development is to be undertaken. The majority of the site is covered with a sparse dot pattern, which represents those areas in which erosion management principles should be applied to the site if development is to take place. The cross-hatched pattern represents areas that are highly sensitive but still buildable if vegetative, soil, and water

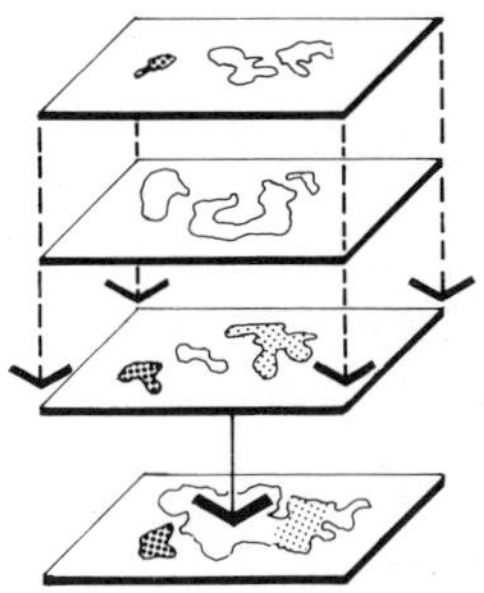
water domains
vegetation interpreted from aerial photograph
soils
natural systems composite

best suited for development no restrictions (13 acres)

vegetation and wildlife management should be considered if development occurs (37 acres)

effects of water hydrology should be considered if development occurs (58 acres)

environmentally sensitive areas which are still buildable (21 acres)

environmentally sensitive areas which should be protected (7 acres)

reserved water bodies (7 acres)

1-14: natural systems composite

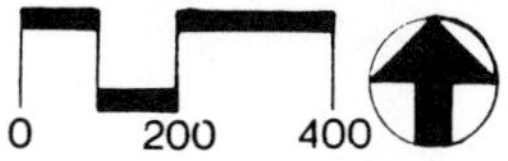
0
200
400

management principles are applied. Based upon the most restrictive characteristics of the base maps listed above, the black-striped/black-toned portions of the map represent the areas that are most environmentally sensitive to development and, hence, should be protected. In this case nearly the entire site is developable as long as proper soil, surface water, and vegetative management principles are applied.

It is important that the reasons behind environmental protection are well understood. The following quotation from *Performance Controls for Sensitive Lands* explains some of these reasons.

> *When we talk about the destruction of environmentally sensitive areas we do not mean just the possible loss of some "intrinsic" environmental values or benefits, but also loss to the social and economic welfare of a community. Environmentally sensitive areas are land areas whose destruction or disturbance will immediately affect the life of a community by either (1) creating hazards such as flooding and landslides, or (2) destroying important public resources such as water supplies and the water quality of lakes and rivers, or (3) wasting important productive lands and renewable resources. Each of these threatens the general welfare of a community and results in economic loss. The direct costs of not protecting these areas can be high. In the private sector, costs may include the reduction of property value or the actual destruction of property; in the public sector, they include finding alternative sources of water or installing expensive storm sewers and water purification systems.*
>
> *Local regulation is needed not only because of the public character of the resources, but also because the real estate market does not adequately consider the costs and benefits of protecting these resources. The functions of these environmentally sensitive areas are what economists call public goods—if they benefit one person, they benefit all. A wetland, for example, filters sediment and traps nutrients from upland runoff, thus cleaning water before it enters adjacent water bodies. These are important functions, but the landowner cannot sell this filtering capacity of his land. If the land is providing a cleaner lake for one man, it is providing it for all the people who use and enjoy the lake. Thus in terms of maximizing his own profits, he may be better off to drain and fill the wetland so he will have more land to sell, but the larger community will then have to absorb the cost of lowered water quality.*
>
> *Because protecting these land areas involves important public costs and benefits which are inadequately considered by the normal market mechanism, it is logical that communities would turn to their police powers [i.e., the Environmental Assessment Worksheet, commonly called the EAW, and the Environmental Impact Statement, commonly referred to as the EIS report] to ensure a balance between the public interest—the health, safety, and welfare of the community—and the landowner's desires to use his property [1.6].*

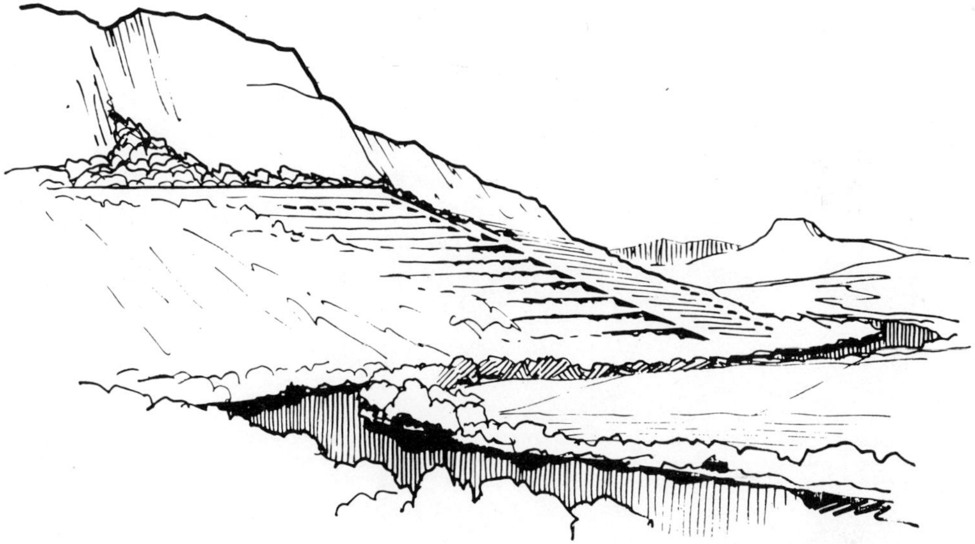

Proposed underground community.
Drawing by Malcom Wells from
his book *Underground Designs*
(see references).

2 energy-related planning issues

introduction

In addition to the traditional base data used in large-scale planning illustrated in the previous chapter, a number of energy-related factors can be analyzed for a specific site. The most commonly recognized site characteristic for energy-efficient development is the orientation of land forms with respect to the sun. The generally greater potential for maximizing the benefits of solar heating for buildings on south-facing slopes is increasing the value of such land and should be an important factor in large-scale planning of housing developments. In the first section of this chapter, the prototypical site is analyzed with respect to solar orientation.

In addition to considering the solar orientation of the land forms, other environmental factors that would affect energy-efficient layout of the land can also be analyzed. These include the relative radiation, or heat gain, on different portions of the site; the heat loss on other portions, caused by shading and the effects of the winds; and the effects of the other thermal phenomena, such as the movement of cool and warm air. Environmental factors are not only experienced directly, in terms of human comfort, but also affect the amount of energy required for mechanical heating, cooling, and ventilation in order to provide comfortable living environments.

In this chapter each of these environmental factors is discussed and its effect on the prototypical site illustrated by a series of maps. By using the traditional overlay process described in the previous chapter, these energy-related factors are combined into a composite map that indicates the areas best suited for development from an energy-efficient point of view. Although each environmental factor is discussed and illustrated separately, only the composite analysis should be used in making decisions to select more energy-efficient alternative sites. The environmental factors should be considered as a total system, rather than separately. In chapter 6 the composite map of energy-related factors presented at the end of this chapter is combined with the traditional development composite and the natural systems composite from chapter 1 to form a final energy-efficient development composite for the prototypical site. This total composite is used as a basis for the planning and design of the site, which is presented in chapter 6 together with designs for prototypical clusters of housing.

The intention in presenting this analysis of energy-related factors is to establish a framework in which they can become part of the planning process for development. The relative importance of each factor and the criteria used to rate the factors may vary considerably and will continue to be refined in the future—particularly as more research is done on the specific impact of these effects on energy use. To quote from *Landscape Planning for Energy Conservation:*

> *. . . the essence of all landscape development for energy conservation [has been] to modify the aspects of our temperature, humidity, radiation and air movement in such a way as to bring existing or unpleasant conditions as closely as possible into the climatic conditions which are comfortable to specific persons on a precise site at a particular time [2.1].*

It is important to go beyond the concept of simply modifying the environment to include a better understanding of these factors. By incorporating them into comprehensive energy-efficient planning, designs can capitalize on the potential for passively heating and cooling buildings and thus reduce reliance on energy-consuming mechanical systems.

In most cool and temperate areas, solar orientation of housing units is the single most important factor in reducing energy use for heating. Thus, it is desirable in energy-efficient development to provide access to the sun for as many units as possible and to provide optimal southerly orientation for these units whenever possible. Although houses can be oriented in any direction with equal facility on flat land, on sloping sites the unit is usually oriented in the direction that the slope faces. While this is not an absolute restriction—there are, in fact, a number of design opportunities on any site—orienting the house in the direction of the slope is usually the most natural solution for providing views and can result in planning units at higher densities. This is particularly true with earth sheltered structures, which are more frequently built into the sloping hillside than are conventional structures.

For these reasons south-facing slopes are considered best for energy-efficient housing. Southeast and southwest slopes are also quite desirable, since considerable solar gain can still be achieved by orienting units in these directions. Land sloping directly to the east or west is less desirable, since winter heat gain is not as substantial from these directions as it is from the south and the large summer heat gain causes cooling problems.

The actual layout of lots for energy-efficient housing involves a number of considerations. The optimal lot shape and placement of the building on it relates to the specific design of the house and the surrounding structures. In addition, housing developments must be integrated with efficient street and utility layouts. Energy-efficient strategies for roads and utilities are discussed in chapter 3, and energy-efficient housing types and their site design implications are covered in chapters 4 and 5.

Although the variations in solar design are numerous and complex at a more detailed scale, the implications for large-scale site analysis are relatively simple. Moreover, sites can be rated according to their relative potential for solar orientation. The map in figure 2-1 shows the prototypical site broken down into sections. Those planes of land that offer opportunities for southern orientation are represented in black; those that offer the next best opportunities are shown in the darkest diagonal tones for southeastern orientation and in the cross-hatched tone for southwestern orientation. The areas toned in the dot pattern are oriented more directly to the west. These sites would require careful design to offset the late afternoon summer heat.

The map is created by first connecting the points that define the ridge and valley lines. Then the land forms are divided into planes that reflect sixteen different directional orientations. Divisions between the planes are determined by geometric calculation. Abrupt changes in the points of tangency indicate a change in direction for the plane. On the map in figure 2-1, some of the sixteen compass directions have been combined for the sake of simplicity; the southerly orientations are shown in five basic divisions, and the northerly orientations are combined into one area.

The map could be used for siting either conventional housing or alternative housing types. The information is limited in that the land has not been divided into buildable lots based on their total development suitability. In order to assess the number of sites having a good orientation, this map should be combined with the development composite.

It is important to note that the land has been evaluated as if it were cleared of all vegetation. The shading effects of vegetation can significantly reduce cooling demands. The cooling and sheltering effects that the vegetation provides are evaluated on page 157. It should also be noted that this interpretation applies to climates in the 44° latitude range, where a slight correction for the compass toward the east is accounted for in the positive rating of east-facing areas of land.

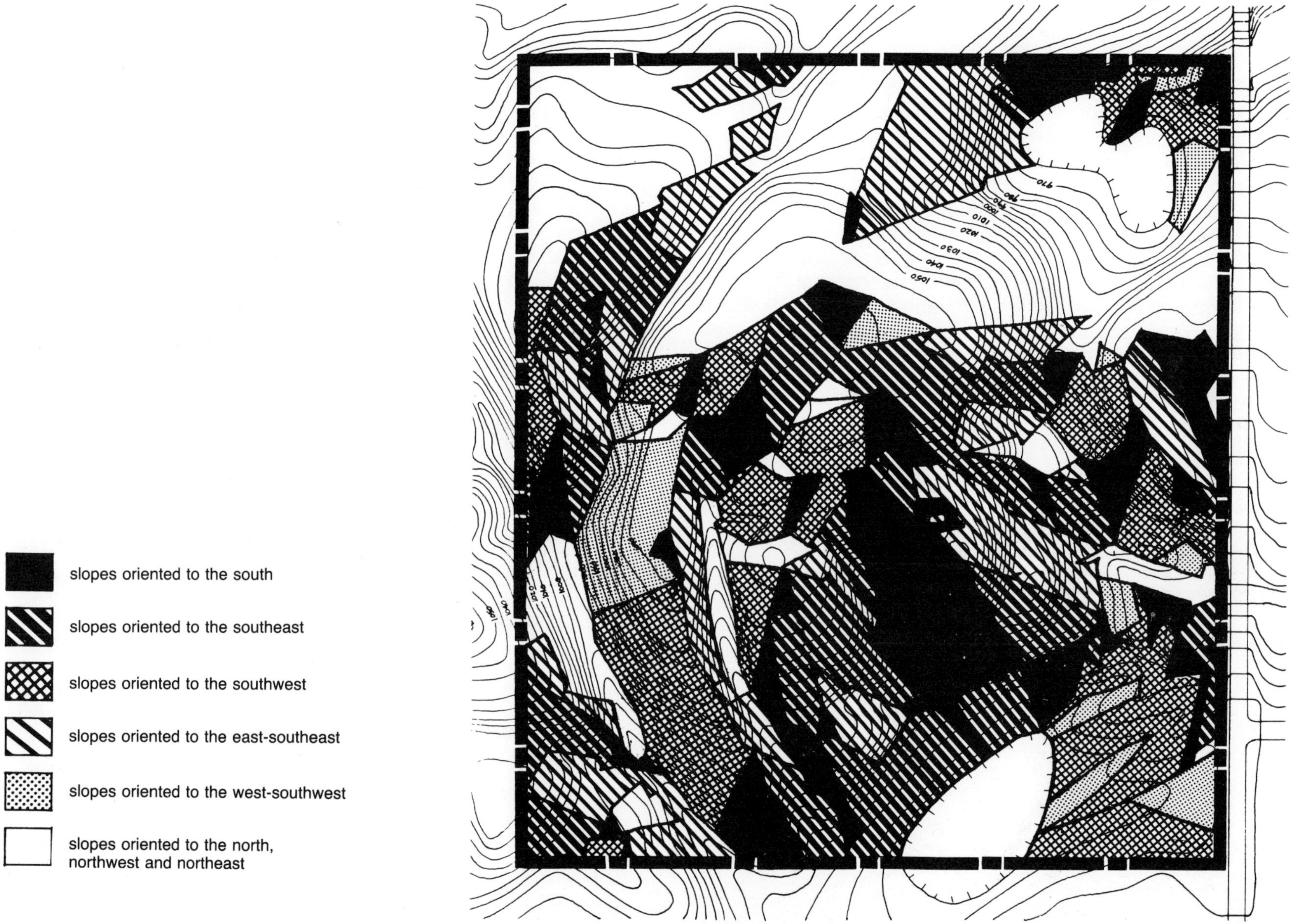
slopes oriented to the south
slopes oriented to the southeast
slopes oriented to the southwest
slopes oriented to the east-southeast
slopes oriented to the west-southwest
slopes oriented to the north, northwest and northeast

2-1: solar orientation

radiation: slope exposure and albedo

Perhaps the most significant influence of the variety of land forms and their covers on designing with natural environmental factors for energy efficiency is in the different amounts of radiation given off as heat is absorbed into the soils. For this discussion, the term radiation generally refers to the total incident radiation that falls on a point of land, as distinguished from the separate effects of insolate radiation, which falls directly from the sun, and global radiation, which is bounced off the clouds and other objects in the environment. Furthermore, this discussion concerns only the significant heat-producing daytime periods when shortwave radiation is broadcast; it does not deal with the additive effects of nighttime global radiation.

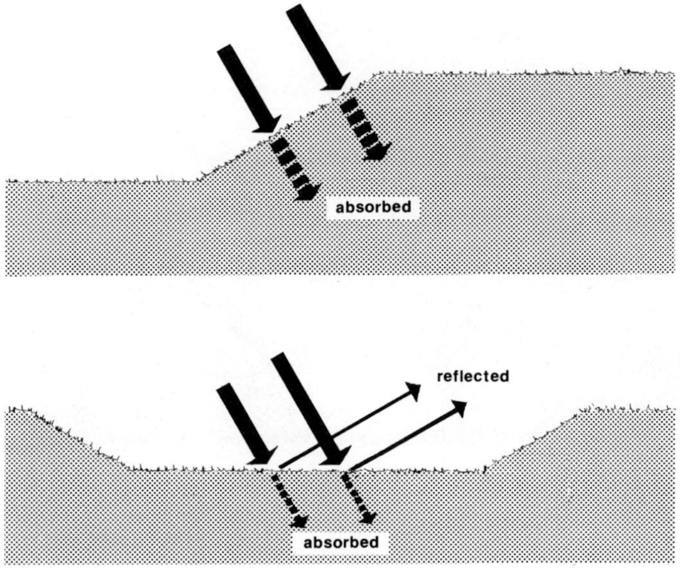
absorbed
reflected
absorbed

2-2: solar radiation on sloping and flat land

The total incident radiation is either transmitted into the soils, absorbed by the ground cover and used for evapotranspiration, or reflected back into space, as shown in figure 2-2. Because transmission is a complex issue relating soil types, moisture transfer, and ground and air temperatures, and because a complete evaluation of these relationships is not yet available, it will not be discussed in this text. The potential for siting earth sheltered structures in different soil types to maximize heating or cooling effects from the earth should be explored as more information becomes available.

2-3: direct radiation for March 21

time of day	orientation of slope	radiation for 33° slope (langleys/hour)	radiation for 10° slope (langleys/hour)
noon	north	40	50
	east/west	50	55
	south	60	55
10:00AM	north	20	40
	east/west	55	45
	south	65	50

Source: *The Climate Near the Ground [2.2].*

2-4: direct radiation for December 21

time of day	orientation of slope	radiation for 30° slope (langleys/hour)	radiation for 10° slope (langleys/hour)
noon	north	5	0
	east/west	15	5
	south	25	15
10:00AM	north	12	5
	east/west	15	8.9
	south	20	10

Source: *The Climate Near the Ground [2.2].*

slope exposure

Given two south-facing slopes, the steeper slope gives off significantly higher values of radiation than the gentler slope for the same time of year and same time of day. The charts in figure 2-3, extracted from information in Rudolph Geiger's *The Climate Near the Ground* [2.2], show measured comparisons of radiation reflected by different slopes for different times of day on March 21. For colder climates it is significant to compare the total radiation for similar slopes at the same times on a winter day (fig. 2-4). The total amounts of radiation are significantly lower, especially for gentler slopes, in winter. In both winter and spring, the east and west slopes become important second choice areas for optimizing radiation gains when selecting areas for potential energy-efficient siting. On March 21 the total radiation for these slopes was equal to that for south-facing slopes, and on December 21 the total was relatively close. It should be pointed out that this information is limited in that only insolate radiation (i.e., both longwave and shortwave radiation that falls directly on the site) was accounted for in the measurement, while global radiation (i.e., the additional radiation that hits a site because of reflection off the clouds) was not included. Minnesota's topography and, more specifically, that of the site, is typically more similar to the 10° slope used in the chart.

The amount of radiation (heat) available for transmission into the soil is affected by the boundary conditions, i.e., the angle of inclination (slope) of the surface relative to the angle of incidence; what the surface material is and how much that surface absorbs energy for evapotranspiration; and to what degree that material causes the radiation to be reflected back into space (referred to as the albedo of the material). In evaluating the land for energy-efficient layout alternatives, these boundary conditions can be classified into zones that offer relative opportunities or constraints for development. The results of the effects of the different slopes on total radiation or heat available are described on the slope exposure map shown in figure 2-5. The albedo of the

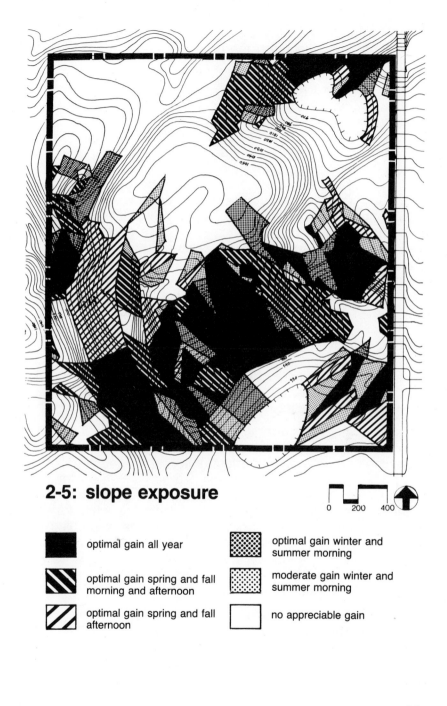

2-5: slope exposure

0 200 400

- optimal gain all year
- optimal gain spring and fall morning and afternoon
- optimal gain spring and fall afternoon
- optimal gain winter and summer morning
- moderate gain winter and summer morning
- no appreciable gain

various materials on the site is discussed and a map indicating their effects on the prototypical site is shown later in this section.

Although an analysis of slope exposure appears to be similar to the analysis of solar orientation in the previous section, it is more complex in that it takes into consideration the degree of slope and the changing conditions of incident radiation at different times of the year. The slope exposure map illustrates the evaluation of the southeasterly and southwesterly areas, where slope will improve the total radiation available on the site. (Note: on a site that is not as hilly, the evaluation and comparison might be meaningless.) Those areas represented in black would be the areas of highest total radiation: in all seasons they are steep, or very steep, south-facing slopes. The southeasterly slopes that are shaded in the darker diagonal tone would be the next best areas for total radiation gains because of the steepness of their slopes. The steeper southwesterly slopes are rated as next best, followed by the less steep easterly slopes. In these areas the angle of slope is at best equal to the angle of incidence for winter morning sunlight gains, which are significant when compared to winter noontime ratings of available radiation.

This evaluation is significant for conventional or alternative types of housing and is perhaps more meaningful than a simple orientation map because it provides a numerical comparison. As suggested earlier, during heating periods earth sheltered housing would benefit from increased absorption of radiation, while for cooling periods increased reflection would be desirable. Because radiation levels are highest in the summer when cooling is desired—particularly on east-facing slopes very early in the morning—design solutions such as vegetative screening are needed to mitigate these effects.

This information has limitations, however. The detailed site topography is composed of complex forms that interact with each other in ways that affect the measurements of microclimate for each site differently. Moreover, as stated above, the microclimatic effects represent the total response to all the environmental factors acting together and have little validity sectored out of this system. For example, the total radiation may be radically affected by thermal factors or by counterbalancing effects of the winds. Most significantly, the type of ground cover and its relative reflectivity (albedo) versus absorption (specific heat) are direct determinants of how much of the total radiation cast on the site is reflected back for heat gain.

albedo

As direct solar radiation strikes a surface, a portion of radiation is absorbed and a portion is reflected. Different surfaces have widely varying degrees of reflectivity. The degree of reflection of solar radiation off a given surface is referred to as the albedo rate. As shown in figure 2-6, albedo is expressed as the percentage of both direct solar radiation and the diffused radiation from the sky vault.

2-6: albedo of various surfaces for total solar radiation with diffuse reflection

fresh snow cover	75-95%
old snow cover	40-70%
light sand dunes, surface	30-60%
brick	23-48%
dirty, firm snow	20-50%
sandy soil	15-40%
meadows and fields	12-30%
densely built-up areas	15-25%
woods	5-20%
asphalt	15%
dark, cultivated soil	7-10%
water surfaces, sea	3-10%

Sources: *The Climate Near the Ground [2.2].*
Design With Climate [4.2]

Albedo is an important component in modifying the microclimate. For example, urban settings are often characterized by many light concrete surfaces, which reflect a relatively high amount of radiation. In the winter this reflectivity can prove beneficial in warming the adjacent building surfaces—an effect that is maximized if the buildings are fully protected from cold winds. In the summer, when the high reflectivity of concrete surfaces is undesirable, vegetation in the form of shade trees and vine-covered walls can be used to control the degree of reflectivity by lowering the albedo rate.

In a more natural, undeveloped setting, such as the prototypical site, the albedo is relatively low. The four different albedo levels shown on the map in figure 2-7 are all relatively low, since most of the heat is absorbed by the woods, dense ground covers, and meadows. Development of the site, which will introduce more hard surfaces, is also likely to increase total albedo levels. Thus, it will be most important to design the environment to keep reflected radiation as low as possible for summer comfort. High albedo levels will generally be a greater problem for conventional housing than for earth sheltered structures with grass-covered roofs and earth-bermed walls. In analyzing albedo it is important to remember that relative comfort on a site is significantly influenced by other interrelated factors, particularly wind.

2-7: albedo

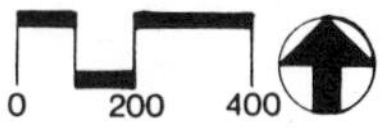
0
200
400

- .03-.05, bogs and dense woods
- .12, medium thick woods
- .20, low woods, dense ground cover
- .23, grassy meadow and planted fields

shadows cast by land forms

The heat gain from increased radiation on sloping land can be offset by the natural variation, or reticulation, of the topography, which causes some areas to be shaded longer than others. By establishing the maximum angles and the altitudes of the sun for different times of the year and day, the patterns of shadows cast by one land form on another can be determined. Figure 2-8 illustrates how the same land forms may cast shadows at one time of the day or year but not at others, depending on the altitude of the sun. Similar analyses can be done for different times of day and year to develop a shadow zone map. On the prototypical site, shadows are only cast from the land forms during winter mornings and evenings. These patterns are illustrated in figure 2-9 for 8:00 am and 4:00 pm on December 21. Because cold, shaded areas have very low design-location appeal as well as low energy efficiency, this type of information affects planning for all types of housing. Moreover, the shading effect is not limited to the edges that these tones represent, since the actual topography would be more complex.

In a more built-up urban environment, the shading effect of existing buildings on potential sites should be evaluated. In addition, a comprehensive shadow plan for proposed buildings should be developed and locations refined either to accommodate unavoidable shading or to provide suitable uses for shaded areas.

2-9: shadows cast by land forms

0 200 400

free of shade at all times

shaded during winter (morning and/or evening)

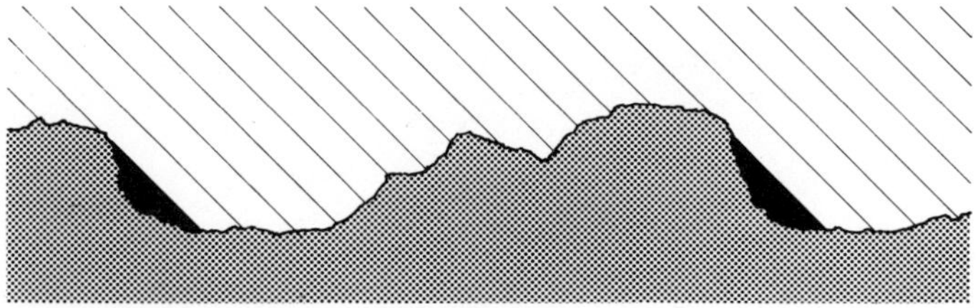

2-8: shading by land forms

winds

The interrelationship of the environmental factors of heat gain through radiation and heat loss in shaded areas is complicated by the effects of the winds on the site. The following five major effects created by the wind will ultimately affect selection of proper location for buildings in order to optimize for energy efficiency:

- the direction and intensity of the prevailing winds for the different seasons
- the mixing effect of prevailing winds with winds from other directions
- the effect that different land forms have on distribution of the winds across the site
- the bubble effects that result from the mixing of thermal and prevailing winds
- the thermal effects of winds

In this section these five effects and their influences on the prototypical site are discussed. The limitation of dealing with each of these phenomena in turn is that, in reality, they cannot be sectored out and measured separately because they interact with one another to produce a total effect.

Although it is generally acknowledged that the effect of wind has a substantial impact on home energy use, additional research and measurement are needed to accurately assess this impact. For conventional houses heat loss resulting from infiltration (which is increased by winds) can represent 25 to 75 percent of the total heating load. Significant energy savings would be realized if housing could be located in areas that are protected from the negative effects of winds as well as in areas that are exposed to the cooling benefits that winds offer. It should be emphasized that small-scale site design, which includes the proper location of fences and vegetation, would have a greater effect on the heating and cooling loads of an individual building than would locating the house in a generally protected zone. The large-scale interpretations that these maps provide can be considered relevant only in identifying one part of the composite analysis, which takes into account all environmental factors.

In considering alternatives for site selection and building design criteria, the first and second of the five effects listed above concern the relationship between direction and intensity of prevailing winds, and the mixing of winds. Wind directions and speeds are typically measured and recorded by state climatological personnel; wind roses, which graph the directions, intensities, and frequencies of winds on a month-to-month basis, are commonly available. Figures 2-10 through 2-13, which illustrate the wind roses for Minnesota in December, March, June, and February, represent the average graphs for five years of data collection.

These four diagrams illustrate several essential points relevant to building design. The rosette form of the graph shows the phenomena of the mixing of winds. The graph for December (fig. 2-10) illustrates the predominance of intense, cold winds of 12, 15, and 18 knots that come from the northwest and north, as compared to intense warming winds carried in from the south and southeast. Winds of 12 knots and more tend to be hard-driving winds that are not easily broken up by currents eddying off buildings and ground surfaces. It is essential to design against these winds in order to reduce infiltration. Sites that are exposed to the assault of such winds will be harder to protect than those in locations where the land form blocks or shelters against them. Although the southerlies tend to be warmer winds, they are also intense, thus complicating design solutions that would protect only against the northwesterlies.

The rosette for March (fig. 2-11) illustrates a shifting of the intense prevailing winds to the north. The representation of the frequency of winds, which are 12 knots and greater measured in all directions, indicates an increased windiness during this month. Hence, design strategies must aim to compensate for the extension of the cold period into late spring because of the frequent, cold, intense north winds. More alternatives for designing to block against these northerly winds should be developed.

By June the intense winds have shifted to the southeast (fig. 2-12). In this case design considerations need to compensate for these wet, rainy winds while capitalizing on their potential for providing natural ventilation. Shutters and awnings may be necessary components of design against these winds.

The February rosette (fig. 2-13) is included to call attention to another factor that complicates designing to protect against adverse winds while creating natural ventilation. In December the southerlies were frequently intense enough to balance the northwesterlies, and the air was mixed. This mixing phenomenon combats

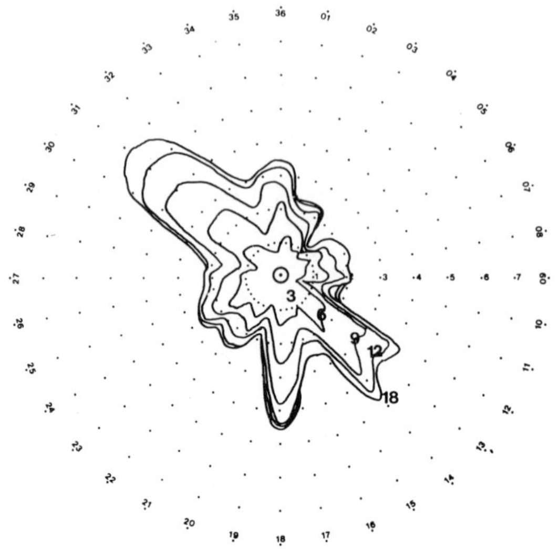

2-10: wind rose—December

2-11: wind rose—March

3
6
9
12
15
18
21
24

2-12: wind rose—June

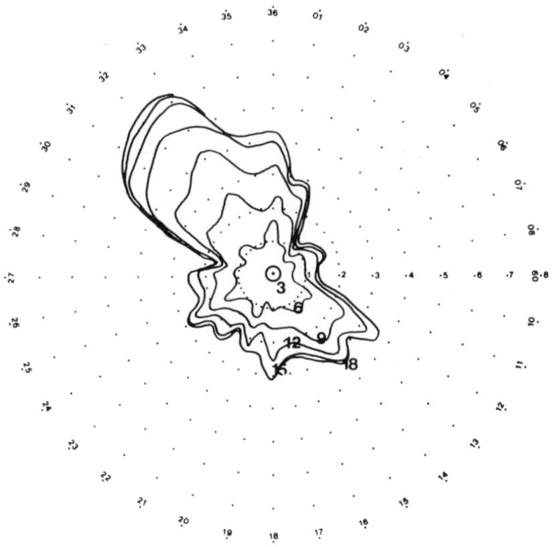
3
6
9
12
15
18

2-13: wind rose—February

SOURCE: Annual, Monthly and 10-Day Wind Rose for Minneapolis-St. Paul, Minnesota 1963-1974

stagnation. In February, however, frequent and complicated inversions occur, in which upper atmosphere warm air masses sit on top of and trap cold air masses. Hence, during this month stagnation occurs. Moreover, at the same time that these inversions are taking place, the frequency of winds from southerly directions is at its lowest, so that the northwesterlies clearly dominate. Appropriate design should deflect these winds to recirculate into spaces so as to help create fresh air movement despite the inversions. Although a total design solution is never simple and priorities must always be established, the more of these phenomena that are taken into consideration, the more energy efficient a design solution will be.

The distribution of these predominant winds over the naturally rolling land has been studied in wind tunnels and has been modeled, as shown in figure 2-14. After receiving some uplift from the warmth of the earth and the eddying of less intense winds across the surface, intense winds of 12 knots and more travel across the land for a distance of twenty times the height of the land. In a zone just over the crest of the hill, a mixing of winds—called a bubble effect—can occur. This bubble effect is caused by the updrafts of warm air and downward flows of cold winds, which tend to create a turbulence area just in front of a relatively calm area located at a distance ranging from five to twenty times the height of the crest of the hill (i.e., 5h to 20h). This

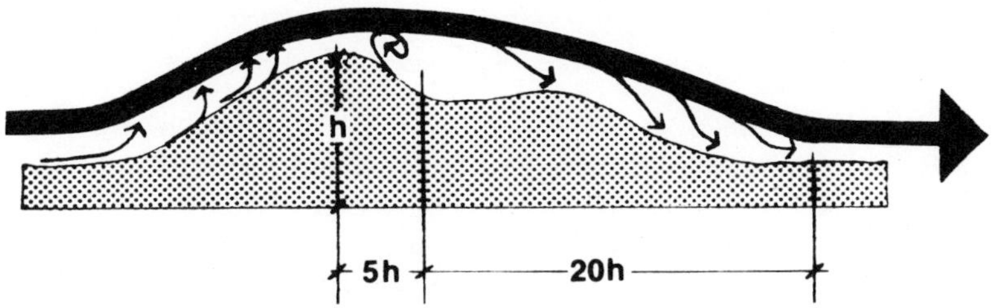
h
5h
20h

2-14: zones of influence

area of calm is commonly referred to as the windshed area. These drafts, called thermals, are illustrated for the prototypical site in the next section. Other land forms within the zone will tend to have this same uplift effect and will create turbulence that may cause the wind to dissipate before it reaches the 20h windshed. This is a generalization extrapolated from modeling rather than an exact model of the effects of the winds.

To best incorporate this information, housing should be located in the exposed area when ventilation is the primary consideration and in the 20h windshed when avoidance of the wind is most desirable. The exposed areas and windsheds for the prevailing winds on the prototypical site are displayed in figures 2-15, 2-16, and 2-17. Exposed areas are white; turbulent areas are toned with dark cross-hatching; and quiet zones are toned gray. In Minnesota, for example, the ideal sites would be in the 20h zones of the northwest windsheds and in the exposed areas of the southerly winds to receive the natural ventilation benefits of these winds during the humid summers. The eddying of winds around the sides of the land forms tends to cause the angled pattern formation of the 20h zone.

More exact wind roses can be produced for individual sites. In some cases additional wind roses for immediately adjacent areas are helpful in providing a more accurate assessment of wind effects for a particular topography and location. For other parts of the country, different factors that affect human comfort—such as excessively high humidity or unrelieved dry periods—should be considered when ideal locations are designated.

The effects of existing and proposed structures on wind patterns can be significant. Modeling of these wind-related effects, similar to modeling of solar access and shading effects for proposed buildings, could help properly locate buildings in relation to each other, as well as indicate potential problems and opportunities for the design.

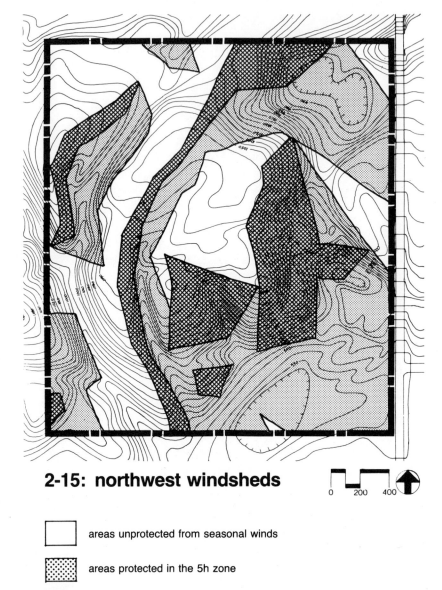

2-15: northwest windsheds

0 200 400

areas unprotected from seasonal winds

areas protected in the 5h zone

areas protected in the 20h zone

2-16: southwest windsheds

- areas unprotected from seasonal winds
- areas protected in the 5h zone
- areas protected in the 20h zone

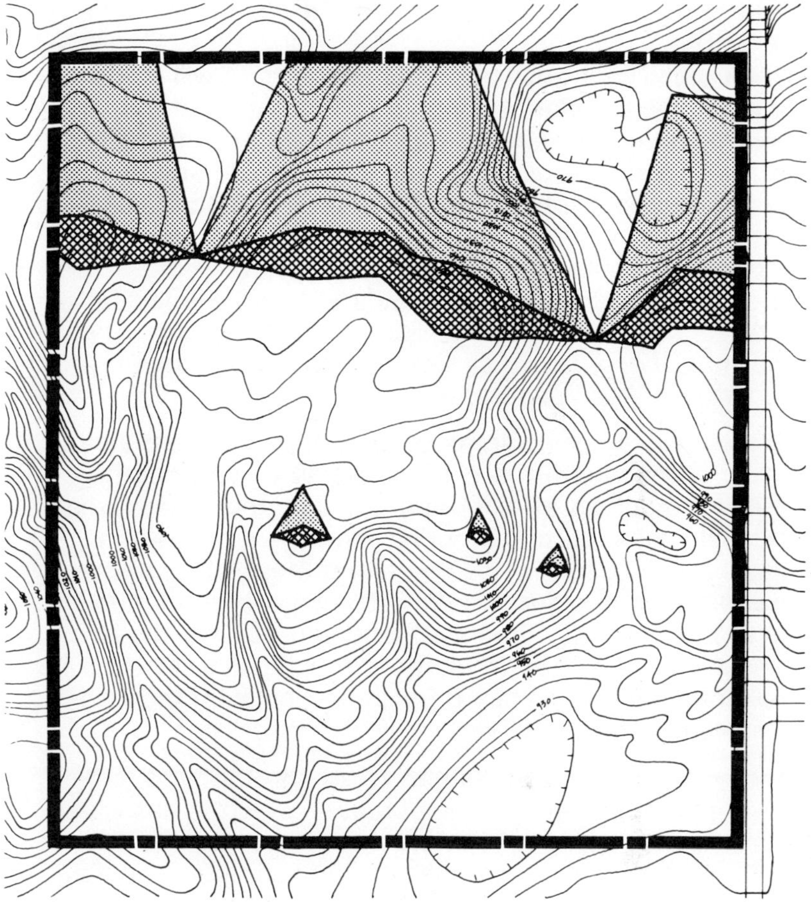

2-17: south windsheds

- areas unprotected from seasonal winds
- areas protected in the 5h zone
- areas protected in the 20h zone

other thermal effects

Other significant environmental factors that will influence energy-efficient planning relate to the shape of the land. The movement of air can be accelerated or obstructed by land forms, resulting in a modification of any energy gains from solar radiation. These phenomena include the flow of air in valleys, the effects of radiation and convection frosts, ambient air temperature changes due to significant changes in elevations, and the effects of radiation gains on leeward sides of water bodies. The site map (fig. 2-19) illustrates how these phenomena occur on the prototypical site.

The diagonally lined areas on the map represent the valley areas where the cold air drains down from the higher elevations at night and flows up the valleys from the low protected areas during the day, as shown in figure 2-18. Locating housing along these air drainage areas allows designs to take advantage of the natural ventilation provided by this phenomenon. The middle ranges of the slopes would be the optimal zones for development, since they offer protection from the cold in winter and from the warm air flows in summer.

Another thermal phenomenon related to the land forms on a site is ambient air temperature, which is associated with significant changes in elevation. For each 1,000 feet (303 m) of vertical decrease in elevation, the temperature rises approximately 3.5°F (1.9°C). While this temperature change is not as significant on flatter topography, the complexity of the reticulation of forms and the relatively significant drops in elevation do contribute to an observable change in temperature from the top to the bottom of the hills. For the prototypical site, this change has been interpolated to be roughly .35° to .45°F (.19° to .25°C) for every 100-foot (30-m) drop (signified on the map by the heavy dark lines). As a design strategy, the top of the hill should be avoided in order to protect housing from the extra cold assault of lower temperatures there.

Still other thermal phenomena that contribute to these significant changes in air movement on the site are called convection and radiation frosts, which create frost pockets. These phenomena—which occur more frequently during those times of year when cold air masses sit on top of an area held down by continental air pressure systems—are common in the depressed, enclosed valley areas of hilly topography. In summer these areas would be hot and humid because warm, moist, stagnant air is trapped in these areas, unrelieved by prevailing cool winds (which, in Minnesota, come from the northwest). Mechanical cooling and ventilation systems would have to be designed to counteract this effect if buildings were to be placed in these locations on the site. In addition, earth sheltered housing would probably be inappropriate

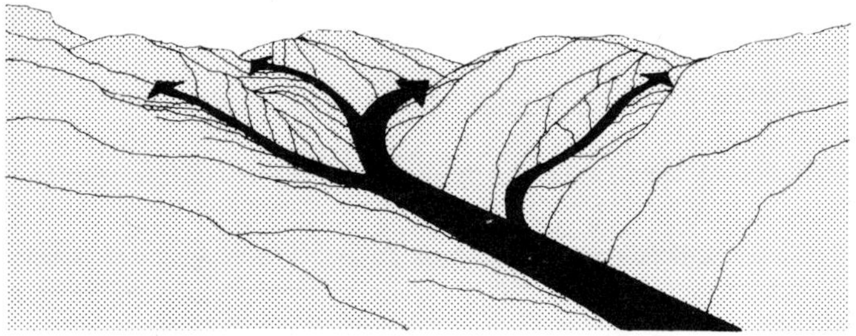

2-18a: daytime cold airflow

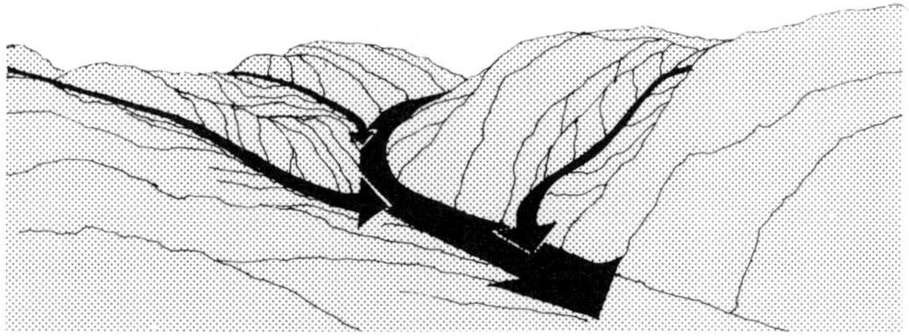

2-18b: nighttime cold airflow

in these areas because of the poor air circulation. Although these areas, which are marked by a gray-dotted tone on the map, are warm in winter, the stagnatary effects may offset the benefits of a warmer climate.

Finally, land located on the leeward, or downwind, side of water bodies receives the benefits of cooling breezes in the summer and warmth from reflective radiation off the frozen, snow-covered mass in winter. Areas of the site that are located immediately leeward of water bodies (represented on the map by a cross-hatched tone) should be considered for site selection in energy-efficient planning. The beneficial effects of this thermal phenomenon would suggest that empondment designs for natural drainage of stormwater can have still another energy-saving effect in addition to the recycling of water on-site.

In planning for energy efficiency, all of these thermal phenomena should be interrelated with the other environmental factors. They should be equally important in siting conventional and alternative styles of housing. The limitation in using this information is that, because the actual site topography is more detailed and complex, not all the appropriate zones are completely represented on the map. It should be noted that the division between two thermal conditions is not a distinct line, as shown on the map; in reality, the two conditions would gradually blend together in a transition zone. As with all the other environmental factors, more information should be monitored and collected to understand the magnitude of these effects on actual energy use in buildings.

2-19: other thermal effects

0 200 400

- no thermal effect
- high precipitation zone
- leeward zone
- valley air drain pocket
- change in ambient air temperature zone by .35°F

shadows cast by vegetation

While the major environmental factors—orientation, exposure/radiation, windsheds, and thermal comfort zones—are important, they must be considered at a more detailed level than the larger interpretation provides. The detailed investigations of environmental factors should take into account the relative effects of different locations, densities, and types of vegetation on-site as well as the albedos of all existing and proposed materials. Human comfort is perceived on this detailed scale. Figure 2-20 illustrates an analysis of the relative densities of existing on-site vegetation. The areas marked with an S are either exposed in the summer or need shading or protection in the winter.

An analysis of the relative merits of total versus selective clearing of the site could be enhanced by combining information regarding type, age, and special character of the vegetation. No decision aimed at achieving energy efficiency would, however, include total clearing of the site. The cost of restoring a cleared site far outweighs the cost of selectively protecting the desirable vegetation, especially when the restored planting required to provide shelterbelts and masses that can deflect the wind necessitates dense plantings to produce immediate results. Additional information on vegetation used for wind control, and other more detailed site considerations, are provided in chapter 5.

S
S
S
S
S
S

2-20: shadows cast by vegetation

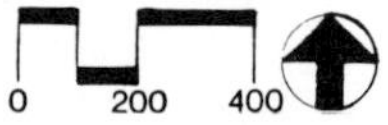
0
200
400

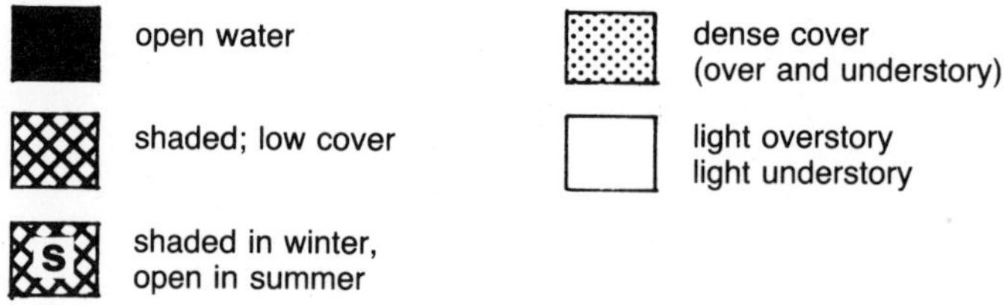
open water
shaded; low cover
shaded in winter, open in summer
dense cover (over and understory)
light overstory light understory

composite of energy-related factors

The composite map of energy-related factors is optimized for the winter season because most energy is consumed during the cold Minnesota winter. The most energy-efficient areas in winter will generally provide the best locations for energy-efficient houses. Conversely, the areas that are least energy efficient in winter are the least desirable for development. The composite map represents a combination of all of the energy-related factors previously presented in this chapter. Obviously, not all of these factors have an equal impact on energy efficiency. In order to present these factors in appropriate balance, the various base maps were combined into three interim composite maps, which were then assembled into a final composite. The components of the three interim maps—orientation factors, land-related factors (other than orientation), and land-management factors—are shown in the adjacent chart (fig. 2-21). In the final composite, orientation factors are weighted three times as heavily as land-management factors, while land-related factors are weighted twice as heavily as land-management factors. It is important to note that the three interim maps from which the composite was formed were developed using a subjective rating system for the various energy-related factors.

2-21: components of energy-related composite map

1. orientation factors

solar orientation (fig. 2-1)

South-, southeast-, and southwest-facing slopes are rated positively. These are the most favorable orientations for passive solar gain.

2. land-related factors (other than orientation)

northwest windshed (fig. 2-15)

Areas within the 5h and 20h zones are rated positively. These are the most favorable areas for protection from cold winter winds.

south windshed (fig. 2-16)

Areas within the 5h and 20h zones are rated negatively, as they are not exposed to warm southerly winds in the winter.

slope exposure (fig. 2-5)

Slopes with optimal gain in morning and afternoon for spring and fall, slopes with optimal gain in morning for winter and summer, and slopes with optimal gain year-round are rated positively. These areas trap and absorb heat all year.

shading by land (fig. 2-9)

Areas shaded by natural land forms are rated negatively, since they are the areas of least heat gain in winter.

air drainage/ambient air (fig. 2-19)

Areas in valleys or ravines and areas of lowest elevation are rated positively. These areas constitute warm air pockets.

leeward zone (fig. 2-19)

Areas in the leeward zone adjacent to water bodies are rated positively. In winter these areas are warmer because of reflection off of the snow cover.

snowdrop zone (fig. 2-19)

In early spring, areas adjacent to water bodies rate negatively because they lose heat from high snow melt.

3. land-management factors

relative albedo (fig. 2-6)

Areas of 20-23% albedo are rated positively. These areas diffusely reflect heat.

shading by vegetation (fig. 2-20)

Open areas are rated negatively because they have no protection from cold winter winds.

shading by land (fig. 2-9)

Areas shaded by land forms in winter are rated negatively, as they are areas of least heat gain.

other thermal effects (fig. 2-19)

In winter, snowdrop zones rate positively because they reflect light and heat into adjacent buildings. Also, the ground in these areas is well insulated by the snow cover.

On the energy composite map in figure 2-22, the cross-hatched pattern represents the best areas for development based upon all of the positive factors considered beneficial for energy-efficient planning. The majority of the site is covered with a dark tone that represents the next best areas for development based primarily on the positive factors of orientation and slope exposure. The lightly toned areas represent a moderate number of energy-related benefits based upon all factors except slope exposure. The areas with the sparse dot pattern, located mainly along the northern edge of the site, are considered to have few such benefits based on the positively rated land-management factors only. The white areas throughout the site represent the worst areas for development based on all negative energy-efficient factors related to planning for energy efficiency.

Basically, the prototypical site is very favorable for energy-efficient development. Various levels of energy-conserving benefits are indicated on the majority of the site; only the white areas—which are exposed to the cold northwest winter winds—are considered totally undesirable. Based on this analysis, these white areas should be considered energy-consumptive were development to occur within them.

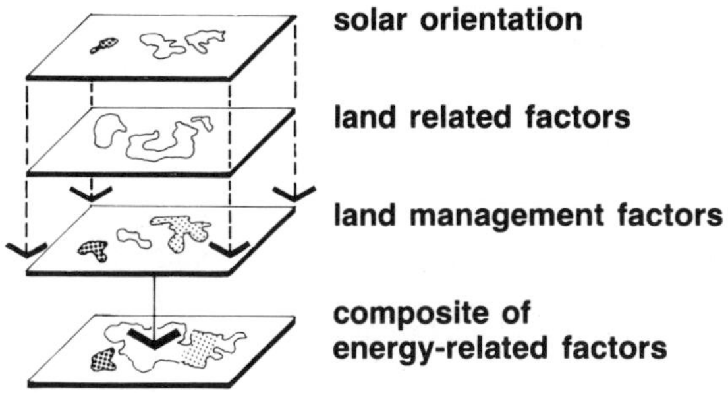
solar orientation
land related factors
land management factors
composite of
energy-related factors

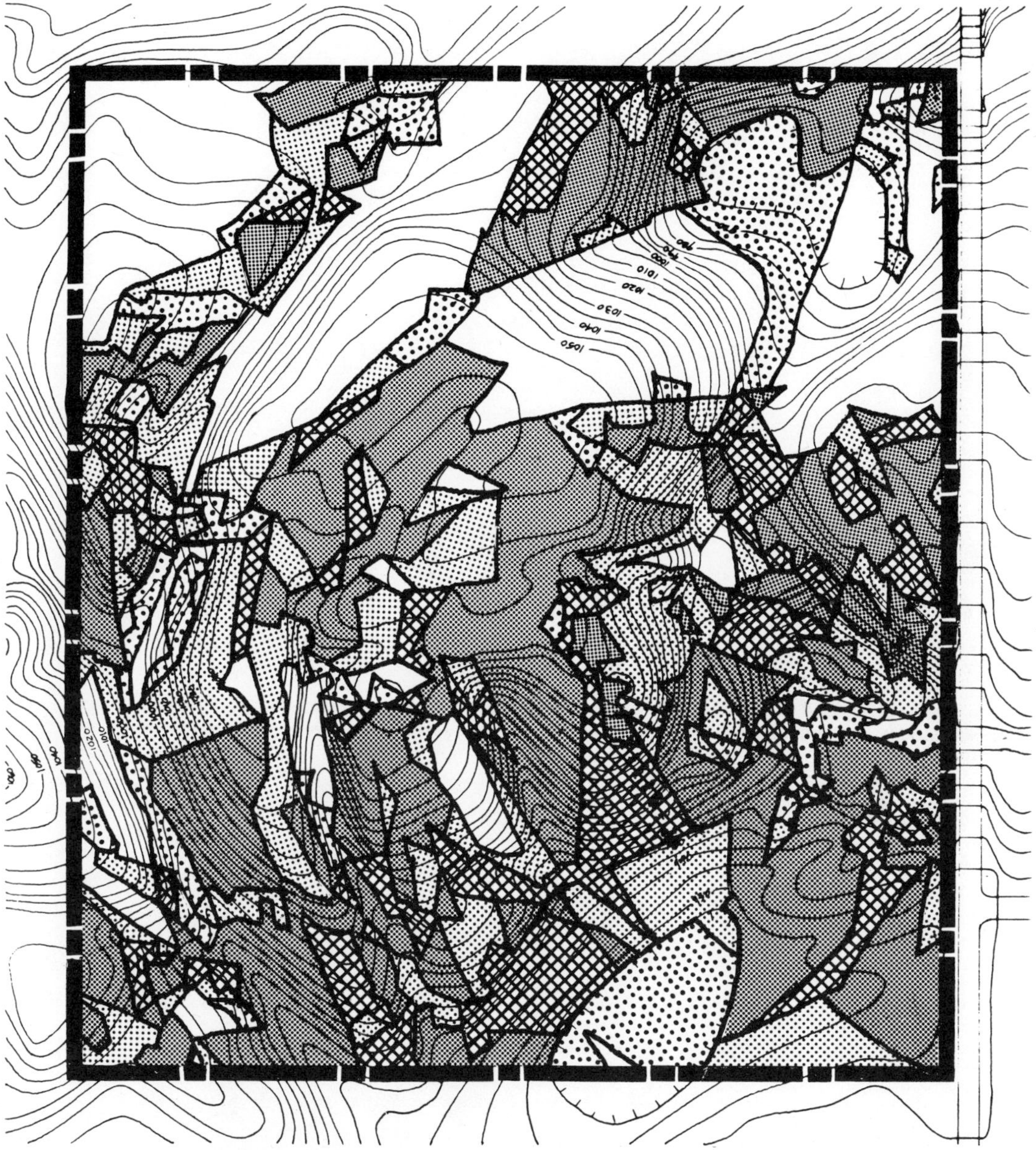

- optimal areas for all energy benefits (24 acres)
- next best areas for energy benefits based on orientation and slope exposure (45 acres)
- moderate areas for all energy benefits except slope exposure (27 acres)
- marginal areas for energy benefits (10 acres)
- worst areas for energy benefits (37 acres)

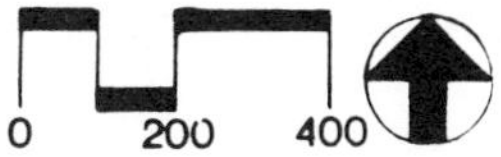
0
200
400

2-22: composite of energy-related factors

Proposed earth sheltered housing project for site in Minneapolis, Minnesota. Design by Mark Dohrmann, Mike Joyce, and Jack Snow (see chapter 7).

3 roads and utilities

introduction

New roads and utility systems that are extensions of larger, existing systems must be provided for any housing development. The utilities required are sanitary sewer, potable water supply, stormwater collection, electricity, telephone, and sometimes natural gas and cable television. As the desire for energy efficiency and conservation of natural resources has resulted in new design strategies for buildings, it has created a need for more efficient approaches to the design of conventional road and utility systems as well. It would seem shortsighted and ineffective to build innovative, efficient housing structures while continuing to use costly and inefficient systems to service the houses.

Because the material presented in this chapter is intended for use mainly by developers, planners, and designers, the first four systems discussed are those for which the developer must arrange the design and underwrite the cost—i.e., sanitary sewer, water supply, roads, and stormwater collection. The other systems—electricity, telephone, natural gas, and cable television—are typically designed and installed by the utility companies and have little effect on the layout of the project. In the near future, however, the supply of electricity and natural gas and/or other forms of heat supply may be the developer's concern; hence, a survey of potential electrical and heat supply systems is included in the last section of this chapter. One additional service system not previously mentioned is solid waste collection and disposal. At present, the most efficient strategy for dealing with solid waste is for people to separate waste into different types at home and have each type collected separately.

The systems discussed in this chapter vary both in the degree of potential for change and the degree of difficulty involved in changing because of the different natures of the systems. For example, while the efficiency of current sewage systems can certainly be improved, alternatives to conventional sanitary sewers must be carefully scrutinized in order to preserve health standards and control costs. On the other hand, water supply systems are relatively efficiently designed, so that the major energy savings in this case are associated with conservation of water use rather than system design. Roads have great potential for saving energy, costs, and land, with more efficient road sizes and layouts that require no new technology. Although the collection and distribution of stormwater has potential for change that is more energy efficient and ecologically sound than past practices, such change will require careful design on a site-by-site basis. Information for each system is presented in a slightly different way to reflect the different issues involved. In general, however, for each system a performance standard is stated, followed by a presentation of conventional physical design criteria, energy-efficient strategies and, finally, a discussion of any special implications of the system design for earth sheltered housing.

Of course, the design of any road or utility system is strongly related to the conditions of the particular site. Natural features such as topography and soils are important, as are the existing road and utility networks available in the community. Typically, considerable information on existing systems must be compiled to assess the feasibility of a site and to later design the systems. For the prototype site in Apple Valley, Minnesota (described in chapter 1), the existing road and utility information is shown in figure 3-1. It must be emphasized that, in designing any system, consideration of compatibility of the proposed system with local environmental conditions is paramount. Some sites present so many environmental constraints that they are cost-prohibitive for development, even if the structural building systems would be compatible with the soil, technical, and geological conditions.

It should also be noted that the efficient design of roads and utilities must be integrated with the efficient design of housing units for various densities and layouts. In this chapter the basic patterns and strategies associated with road and utility systems are discussed separately; they are also integrated into the discussion of site and building design in chapter 5.

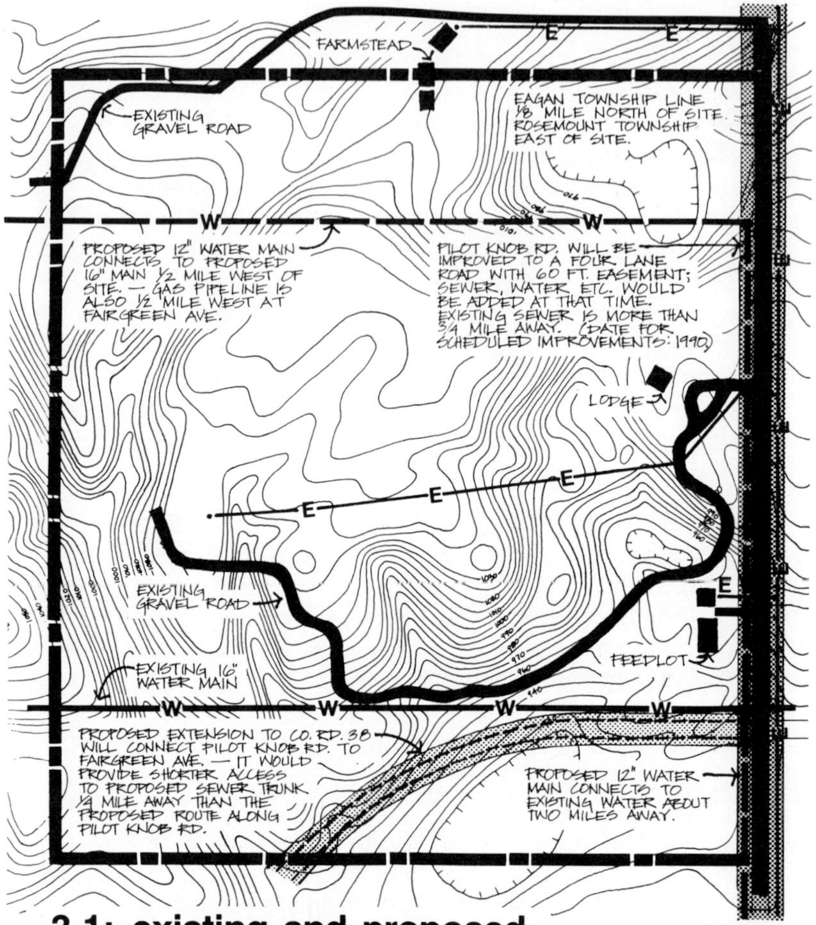
FARMSTEAD
E
E
EXISTING GRAVEL ROAD
EAGAN TOWNSHIP LINE 1/8 MILE NORTH OF SITE. ROSEMOUNT TOWNSHIP EAST OF SITE.
W
W
PROPOSED 12" WATER MAIN CONNECTS TO PROPOSED 16" MAIN 1/2 MILE WEST OF SITE. — GAS PIPELINE IS ALSO 1/2 MILE WEST AT FAIRGREEN AVE.
PILOT KNOB RD. WILL BE IMPROVED TO A FOUR LANE ROAD WITH 60 FT. EASEMENT; SEWER, WATER ETC. WOULD BE ADDED AT THAT TIME. EXISTING SEWER IS MORE THAN 3/4 MILE AWAY. (DATE FOR SCHEDULED IMPROVEMENTS: 1990)
LODGE
E
E
E
E
EXISTING GRAVEL ROAD
FEEDLOT
EXISTING 16" WATER MAIN
W
W
W
W
PROPOSED EXTENSION TO CO. RD. 38 WILL CONNECT PILOT KNOB RD. TO FAIRGREEN AVE. — IT WOULD PROVIDE SHORTER ACCESS TO PROPOSED SEWER TRUNK 1/4 MILE AWAY THAN THE PROPOSED ROUTE ALONG PILOT KNOB RD.
PROPOSED 12" WATER MAIN CONNECTS TO EXISTING WATER ABOUT TWO MILES AWAY.

3-1: existing and proposed roads and utilities

0
200
400

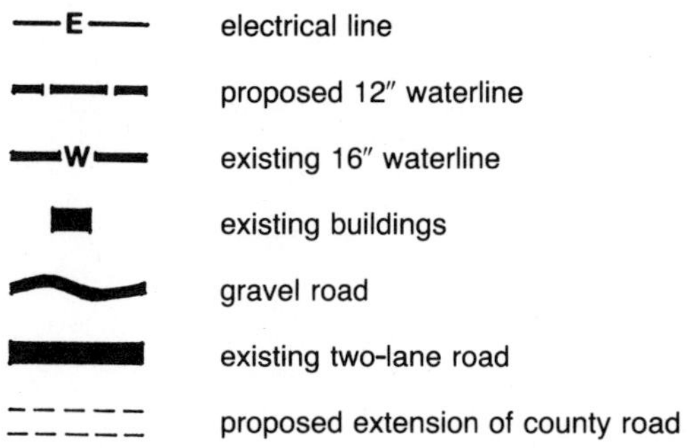
E
electrical line
proposed 12″ waterline
W
existing 16″ waterline
existing buildings
gravel road
existing two-lane road
proposed extension of county road

introduction

Conventional gravity sewer systems are a very important component in the development of land for housing. A basic sewer system not only represents a high percentage of the total cost of developing land, but also has an impact on the actual layout of the development. According to recent figures for the Minneapolis-St. Paul metropolitan area, approximately $80 per front foot of lot is spent in providing this service. Costs of continued maintenance and operation programs can also play a major part in a community's decision to permit a development at a particular time and/or in a particular location. The rigidity of the traditional grid system layout, the pressure for equal lot size (which means equal absorption of the cost of installing the utilities), and the obvious economics of clustering are all conditions that are closely related to the requirements of gravity sewers and water delivery systems. (The need for access for automobiles, which has a comparable influence on layout, is discussed in a following section.)

Conventional gravity sewer systems have remained at the same basic stage of development for many years. Current concerns over energy supply, water supply, and environmental degradation are causing a reexamination of these systems. Conventional gravity systems require energy to pump sewage as well as treat it at the plant. In addition, energy is required to manufacture the extensive networks of pipes and place them in the ground. The energy required and the cost of development for gravity systems are increased for sites with poor soils, rugged topography, or remote access. In all cases considerable amounts of fresh water are required to transport the sewage to the treatment plant, and extensive treatment is required to ensure that the water is not returned to the environment in a polluted form. The increasing awareness of the scarcity of water resources—especially pressing in the dry southwestern areas of the United States—is already motivating refinements of conventional gravity sewer systems.

In response to these problems, several experimental alternatives have been developed in recent years. One of the most publicized examples is the dry, or composting, toilet. Not only is the extensive amount of water used for flushing toilets (approximately 40 percent of the total water used in the household) completely eliminated, but the solid waste is converted into a natural fertilizer requiring neither a network of pipes nor energy-intensive treatment methods. Another concept is the use of already dirty water from sinks, baths, and washing machines to flush toilets. Although this type of system would also eliminate the use of fresh water for flushing toilets, conventional sewerage systems and treatment plants would still be required.

Although these experimental systems do work in many individual dwellings, they represent a radical departure from conventional systems. They also have certain drawbacks that are unacceptable to many people, making application on a wider scale questionable at this time. Individuals from various agencies and departments concerned with sewerage systems (e.g., the Minnesota Pollution Control Agency and Department of Natural Resources, Metropolitan Waste Commission, local officials, etc.) have expressed the opinion that, to many people, dry and chemical toilets in particular represent a step backwards in quality of service, and therefore—at least in their current states of development—they simply will not be acceptable alternatives to the general public. These alternative systems are considered a step backwards in quality of service because they require the individual home owner to take on additional tasks in management and handling of wastes, and because the systems are not odorless. A related problem is that, since these alternative systems often require a great deal of owner care and involvement, information about proper care may not be passed on from owner to owner upon sale of the home. The need for more frequent pumping and removal of wastes with some of the systems also implies the need for more energy expended for transportation, which may make the overall energy efficiency of the system questionable.

Because of these drawbacks and uncertainties, most developers do not consider the existing alternative systems marketable. Stating these concerns is not meant to imply a total rejection of all these new systems, nor should these concerns discourage proponents of alternative systems. On the contrary, investigation of alternatives that require the use of less energy and less water becomes increasingly necessary as these resources become more scarce. Typically, the first, innovative systems are designed to solve one major technical issue without concern for secondary issues. Only after the general suitability of the system is assured do refinements begin. Moreover, refinements of the design are often slow in coming and comparatively more costly, particularly if their adaptation fulfills no compelling need.

Because of the concerns about most of the more radical departures from conventional systems that exist today, the following information is based on the assumption that viable alternatives are based on refinement of conventional systems. Rather than address all parts of the sewerage and water delivery systems—i.e., home service, the delivery networks, and the types of treatment plant—this text focuses on energy-efficient solutions that relate to home service and delivery networks (transportation agents). Alternative plant types are not evaluated, since the home connection and delivery network components of the system are those that most directly affect design layout.

In this section minimum performance standards are presented as a starting point, followed by physical design criteria, design considerations, and general strategies for energy conservation related to sewerage systems. This information is followed by a discussion of several energy-efficient alternatives—both at the home site and in the delivery network. Finally, the compatibility of earth sheltered design with the more energy-efficient sewer system designs is considered.

performance standard

". . . to provide each living unit with a water carried sewerage system adequate to collect, treat and dispose of waste water in a manner which will not create nuisance (including odor) or endanger the public health" [3.1].

physical design criteria

The physical design criteria listed below typically apply to gravity sewerage systems. All alternative systems should have complete detailed plans and engineering analysis to support the contention that their performance standards are equal to those listed here, particularly when the systems do not depend upon water (and gravity) for transportation.

- The system should be separated from the clear water supply by a minimum of 10 inches (25 cm) and the top of the sewer should be 18 inches (46 cm) below the bottom of the water main and sealed to prevent seepage into the groundwater.
- The lines should be capable of a minimum flow of 2 inches (5 cm) per second and should have a minimum diameter of 8 inches (20 cm) (unless local conditions allow a minimum of 6 inches—15 cm).
- The minimum capacity of the line should be 75 gallons (285 l) per day per capita (100 gallons—380 l—is a typical minimum); laterals and submains should be capable of carrying four times the average daily flow (when full).
- The design period of the system should be adequate for the life of the residents it serves, and service should be continuous.

design considerations

The design and feasibility of sewer systems are affected by the proximity of the development to existing systems and the density of the development. It has been stated that when a new development is greater than 1,000 feet (303 m) from a currently available access to a trunk line, it is only marginally cost-effective to connect them. It has also been suggested that with densities of 2 units per acre and less, public sewer hookup becomes marginally cost-effective because of the additional costs of carrying the lines over the distances between units, i.e., the frontage costs. Access for a low-density development on flat land that covers long distances requires either deeper trenching to ensure gravity flow or the addition of energy-intensive pumping systems.

Another design consideration is the volume and strength of sewage to be added to the system and the degree of treatment required for the connection. It has been proven that sewage in more concentrated form can be treated more effectively. Although one case in Marin County, California, resulted in savings of up to 30 percent in treatment costs, the operating costs and the need for extra clean-out of the line somewhat offset that benefit. Other conditions that affect design are the local climate, the soil, groundwater, geology, and the type of terrain found on the site. Steeper terrain provides for steeper pipe gradients and, hence, higher capacities for the same size of pipe.

The types of ground cover and slope orientation are also important, since they affect ground temperature. The pipes can often be located in shallower trenches when sewers are located on warm slopes in soil types that allow heat to transfer to the pipes; where the ground cover is grassy and provides insulation, or where snow cover is allowed to accumulate to provide insulation.

Design is also affected by the character and capacity of the stream to receive the outflow from the sewage treatment plant as well as by costs for installation, operation, and maintenance of the system.

general energy-efficient strategies

- The amount of water used for transporting sewage should be reduced.
- Water-saving appliances and other devices should be used to reduce the amount of water required for transporting sewage.
- Portions of the water should be recycled. Black water (toilet wastes) should be separated from gray water (other wastes) so that the gray water can be reused. This method should only be used with on-site disposal systems, for a maximum of ten houses. Efficiency is not increased with a larger system, since two separate systems must be constructed in place of one.
- Total dependence on electrical/mechanical equipment that runs constantly (such as pumps) should be reduced or the efficiency of the equipment improved where possible.
- The amount of materials embodied in the system (e.g., in terms of pipe lengths and sizes, frequency of clean-outs, etc.) should be reduced.
- The sizing of systems should be based on the drainage area served and the local soil conditions rather than on current planned growth patterns. This sizing technique will result in larger trunk systems suitable for higher-density and/or infill development in the future.
- Initial construction practices and material selection should be of high quality to ensure lower maintenance and replacement costs over time.
- Regulations should be redefined where local soil conditions permit alternatives.
- Lines and mechanical components should be more accessible for maintenance and replacement; mechanical components should be simple to maintain and operate.
- Existing systems should be reused when redevelopment occurs, and inefficient components of existing systems should be replaced.

- Infill housing sites should be developed to bring existing systems up to capacity.
- In industrial areas that may be part of a mixed-use development, intermittent rather than continuously running systems should be used when appropriate. On-site separation of hazardous wastes should be required so that they can be treated efficiently and not force oversizing of common collection systems.

home connection alternatives

Listed below are alternative methods of increasing the efficiency of the sewage system at the home site. These include conservation practices, water-saving appliances and chemical or dry toilets. The specific energy-saving strategies associated with each alternative are listed, followed by constraints to utilizing the systems and considerations in implementing them.

conservation practices

energy strategies: These include voluntary reduction of the total amount of water used and voluntary change from concentrated use at peak times. With water use increasing each year at a rate of one gallon (3.8 l) per person per day, these strategies have significant potential.

constraints: In general, all of these alternatives involve substantial changes in lifestyle patterns. Education and information about these alternatives are inadequate at present.

implementation: First, the consumer must be provided with adequate information concerning water conservation. Second, economic incentives could be provided, such as special conservation rates for water. If these methods do not work, ordinances can be created that help incorporate these changes into lifestyle patterns (e.g., watering bans). The city of Davis, California, has developed some ordinances that are considered prototypes.

water-saving appliances and fixtures

energy strategies: Water conservation is incorporated into new appliance and plumbing fixture design, and water control valves can be added to existing appliances. This can be done for all fixtures, including toilets, sinks, and showers, as well as for such appliances as dishwashers and clothes washers. These strategies can result in greater concentration of sewage, thereby making it easier to treat.

constraints: At present, costs are greater for energy-efficient appliances and fixtures than for conventional ones. Adaptation of existing appliances and systems should be explored as an alternative to the higher first costs and the considerable energy embodied in the manufacture of new appliances.

implementation: As with all conservation measures, education and economic incentives are useful to encourage the use of water-saving appliances. In addition, building codes should encourage these alternatives.

alternative appliances and fixtures

energy strategies: This category refers primarily to chemical or dry toilets, which save water or eliminate it altogether.

constraints: As stated in the introduction to this section, there is cultural resistance to the radical change these appliances represent. Although a dry toilet eliminates the water required for flushing and the piping necessary to carry solid wastes from a conventional toilet, a conventional system is still required for the remaining wastes from baths, sinks, and other appliances (referred to as gray water). This means that greater initial costs are incurred for a dry or chemical toilet, although long-term savings of 20 to 40 percent are possible. The success of these appliances is unproven when applied to a larger development.

implementation: Performance standards would have to be changed in most cases to allow for these alternatives.

delivery network alternatives

Energy-efficient strategies applied to conventional systems, as well as some unconventional alternative systems, are described below. The conventional systems include the septic tank and drainfield, septic tanks connected to a gravity system, and the conventional gravity systems; the alternative systems are the pressure, vacuum, and gray water systems. Energy-efficient strategies are listed for each alternative, together with a discussion of constraints and implementation.

septic tanks and drainfields

energy strategies: Septic tanks with drainfields are generally appropriate on lots of 1 acre (0.4 ha) or more and in areas where there will be no community sewer system. If these conditions exist, serving each house separately is usually more efficient than clustering and sharing drainfields. When septic tanks and drainfields are appropriate, careful location of lines to ensure a managed flow through smaller pipes by adequate change of grade rather than use of larger pipes increases efficiency. Systems should be sited to eliminate the need for lifting the sewage between the septic tank and the drainfield. Pipes should be located to optimize solar access and insulation by snow cover in winter.

constraints: One drawback with respect to energy and land-use efficiency is the need for larger lots. In addition, maintenance and replacement are more frequent than in closed systems. The extensive land requirements make adaptation of this system to medium- and high-density developments difficult. This type of system is not an acceptable solution for infill housing developments.

implementation: Evaluation of soils is necessary to establish the suitability of this system. Specific building codes and zoning plans are required for its implementation.

septic tanks, pumps, and pressure lines connected to conventional gravity systems

energy strategies: In some cases sewage can be collected in a septic tank and then pumped into a trunk line of a conventional gravity system rather than using a drainfield. This system would be useful on sites that require lifting to reach the conventional sewer system. One advantage of this system is its ability to work with a gray water separation system. With respect to energy and land-use efficiency, the most important characteristics of this system are that houses can be clustered (ideally in groups of four to six) and lot sizes can be smaller than those required for drainfields (as small as 1,000 square feet—90 ca).

constraints: This type of system depends on electrically powered pumps and places considerable wear on mechanical components, which require continual maintenance. Although it is costly to install and operate, it serves larger developments more effectively than do drainfields.

implementation: Building codes and zoning regulations need to be changed in order to implement this system.

conventional gravity systems

energy strategies: In these network systems, sewage is transported by water and gravity (for minimum standards, see physical design criteria, above). Because this is a known system, it is cost-effective and conveniently links with other systems requiring no extra conversion stations. Although conventional gravity is not an alternative system, many energy-efficient strategies can be applied to it. A conventional gravity system should be audited to ascertain critical tolerances so that it can be designed more efficiently. The amount of water used to carry the sewage should be reduced to allow the sewage to be more concentrated. The specific location on the site should be carefully chosen so that gravity flow is utilized, thereby allowing reduction in sizes of pipes and minimizing the use of pumps. (Note: 4-inch—10-cm—

pipes to houses and 8-inch—20-cm—pipes for trunk lines are absolute minimums.) To lower costs and improve efficiency, houses should be clustered and smaller lots or long, narrow lots should be used so that access is concentrated and frontage is reduced. In addition, the efficiency of pumps, valves, and lift stations should be improved, and the system should be designed to reduce the total number of manholes required. Construction and maintenance costs can be reduced if all utilities are placed in one trench rather than in several separate trenches.

constraints: Lack of or excessive topographic relief can contribute significantly toward making these systems more costly and energy intensive. Designing a layout for energy efficiency with this type of system would be more time-consuming than normal. One constraint to reducing pipe sizes is the absolute minimum size required to move the sewage.

implementation: More information is required to help in the local governmental review process. Standards defined by building codes should be refined so that they can be applied to the differing conditions in urban and rural areas.

pressure systems

energy strategies: In this system effluent is clarified at the home site and then carried by pressure to a central gravity sewer station. The layout of piping is more flexible, since this system does not depend on gravity for flow and the pipes can be laid parallel to the surface, just under the frost line. This flexibility is particularly advantageous in areas of rugged topography that are not suitable for gravity systems. Energy-efficient strategies include the use of smaller pipes than are required for gravity systems and the ability to place houses close together. In fact, this system works most efficiently with small clusters of houses.

constraints: Because this system is relatively unknown, the approval process takes longer, design is more complex, and installation may be more expensive. In addition, the system is heavily dependent on additional mechanical components, and because the system depends on electrical energy, it may be subject to failure or overload at peak periods (i.e., power brownouts). Maintenance is generally more demanding, and preventative maintenance is essential. The cost is higher when compared to the other two main types of systems (i.e., gravity and vacuum) except on completely flat or very steep sites. Generally, this system does not work efficiently for large developments.

implementation: Changes in performance standards and local building code regulations may be necessary.

vacuum systems

energy strategies: This is a system in which sewage is transported by an absence of pressure, or vacuum, in the line. Usually appropriate for industrial sites, it does not depend on water as a transporting agent. The layout and grade of piping can be more flexible, although it is not as flexible as the pressure system in hilly areas. In addition, smaller pipes can be used. Because an individual pump at each home is not required, this system is not as dependent on mechanical systems as are pressure systems. The system combines conveniently with gray water separation systems and black water treatment equipment. Neither manholes nor pumps are required. Vacuum systems work best with clustered housing.

constraints: Because the power demand of the whole system is continuous, it may require more energy than the maximum allowable pressurized system. The length of line is more limited because of the method of transportation, and the cost per lineal foot is higher than for pressure systems. The central station, which includes the vacuum pumps, is expensive. In poor soils infiltration is a problem, since leaks are hard to locate and repair. Frequent maintenance is necessary, and because the system requires a trained operating staff, operating costs are especially high.

implementation: Changes in performance standards and building code regulations would be required.

gray water recycling systems

energy strategies: This is a secondary system that can be combined with the septic systems described above to separate and recycle gray water. This system's great advantage is that it cuts back on water use by approximately 50 to 70 percent.

constraints: Gray water recycling systems are appropriate mainly at the scale of individual houses, and the technology is new and experimental. Although the system requires additional mechanical and electrical equipment (i.e., circulation pumps), the long-term savings may offset these costs. The additional plumbing required also increases costs.

implementation: Changes in performance standards and building codes are necessary.

conclusion

Although some of the alternative systems may appear to be more efficient than existing systems because they are waterless, they are generally more costly in terms of additional electrical power, maintenance, and labor required for operation. Gravity systems that are more effectively laid out, in combination with water-saving features and appliances, may be the most realistic strategy for energy conservation for the short-term future. This strategy should be coupled with a community-wide audit to determine locations within the system that could accept expanded sewage loads. These recommendations are not meant to preclude adjustment for future changes in technology. Experimentation with different systems (always with the assistance of a qualified engineer) should be encouraged in anticipation of future competition for power and water resources.

implications for earth sheltered housing design

All developers of earth sheltered housing share the problem of public resistance to change in building design, especially since the form of earth sheltered houses can appear to be even more radical a departure from conventional housing than is housing designed simply for passive solar gain or use of active solar systems. Furthermore, a somewhat common public misconception is that earth sheltered designs would require more radical and expensive sewer system designs.

In an informal survey of earth sheltered housing developers in the Midwest (Minnesota, Ohio, Illinois), all but 2 of the 173 houses built by those developers to date have required no alternative design of sewer and water systems to provide service. One house required an additional pumping system because it was an atrium-style house placed completely below existing grade on a low, flat lot. The other house was built into a site on which the soils were totally unsuitable for development. Most of the existing houses are on remote, large lots and are served by septic tank and drainfield systems. Houses located in developed areas have been easily connected to the existing gravity systems, without requiring additional pumping, however.

In fact, the suitability of steeper sites for earth sheltered housing is totally compatible with gravity sewer systems and actually permits more efficient design, since steeper slopes allow for smaller pipes. The depth of the trenches can also be reduced. In some cases, however, earth sheltered housing design requirements may force consideration of other systems if either extensive pump systems or excessively deep trenches would be required to link the buildings to an existing gravity-flow system. For these marginal sites, pressure systems have distinct advantages over vacuum systems.

Water supply and sewerage systems are closely related and, in fact, could be considered as two components of one large supply and disposal system. In both cases the central concern is maintaining an unpolluted supply of fresh water. With respect to energy efficiency, water supply systems have many of the same characteristics as conventional sewage systems. Energy is required to manufacture and install the pipe network, to pump water to maintain pressure, and to treat the water. Within the house, water heating is a large component of energy use. Water supply systems are quite different from conventional sewerage systems in that gravity is not required for movement of the water, treatment costs are not as high, and pipes are much smaller since solid wastes do not move through them. These factors make water supply systems more adaptable to varying topography and generally account for the relatively efficient design of these systems. They can be improved, however, particularly with respect to conserving the water supply. In this section a typical performance standard is given, followed by physical design criteria, energy-efficient strategies, and implications of water supply systems for earth sheltered housing.

performance standard

"Every building equipped with plumbing fixtures and used for human occupancy or habitation shall be provided with a supply of potable water, which meets the standards of the State Board of Health in the amounts of pressures specified. . . . For permanent residences or buildings in which people are employed, hot water shall be provided to all plumbing fixtures requiring hot water for proper use" [3.2].

physical design criteria

All information in this section is based on the *Plumbing Code* and *Recommended Standards for Water Works* [3.3,3.4]. More complete information can be found in these references.

fixtures and building supply system

- Pipe should be one piece or jointed; joints should be kept to a minimum.
- Minimum pipe should normally have a 3/4-inch (2-cm) diameter.
- There should be a minimum 10-foot (3-m) horizontal separation between water pipe and the sewer.
- Pipes can be placed in the same trench as the building drain.
- The bottom of the water pipe should be at least 12 inches (30 cm) above the top of the sewer line at its highest point.
- The pipe should meet minimum fixture branch-line sizes.
- The pipe should meet minimum flow pressures and flow rates, as required by fixture type as shown in the chart below.

location	flow pressure (pounds per square inch)	flow rate (gallons per minute)
Sink faucet, 3/8″ (.95 cm)	8	4.5
Sink faucet, 1/2″ (1.3 cm)	8	4.5
Bathtub	8	6.0
Shower	8	5.0
Ball cock for closet	8	3.0
Flush valve for closet	15	15-35

- Fixture should meet minimum design criteria for total daily water requirements. For single-family houses, the requirement is 75 gallons (285 l) per day per person; for multiple-family housing, the requirement is 60 gallons (228 l) per day per person.

- Calculation for fixtures must provide for peak demand and for pressure loss per gallon and friction loss per 100 feet (30 m).

It should be noted that a gray water recycling system, discussed in the previous section on sewerage systems, is also related to the water supply system. Wastes from sinks, bathtubs, and washing machines are recirculated as supply water for toilets and are sometimes used directly for irrigation. This system requires departures from the normal system of supply piping and must be designed and installed carefully in order to protect against interconnection of waste and supply lines.

supply network: well system

The location of a well system relates to the size of the lot, contour of the land, slope of the water table, rock formation, porosity and absorbency of the soil, and local groundwater conditions. Physical design criteria for such a system are listed below.

- The well should be placed a minimum of 5 feet (1.5 m) from the property line for an individual well and 50 feet (15 m) from the property line for a community well.
- The well should be located at the following minimum distance from potential contaminant sources:
  —150 feet (45 m) from chemical storage
  —100 feet (30 m) from a feed lot
  —75 feet (22.7 m) from cesspools, leaching pits, or dry wells
  —50 feet (15 m) from sewer, septic, subsurface disposal field, grave, etc.
  —25 feet (7.6 m) from buried sewer constructed with cast-iron pipe, plastic pipe, or a sump pump
  —Distance from the landfill depends on local soils and geological conditions
- The well system should be placed at least 3 feet (.9 m) from the house (it may be closer to a pumphouse).
- The well system should be located at least 15 feet (4.5 m) from gaslines or an overhead electric distribution line and at least 25 feet (7.6 m) from a transmission line greater than 50kV.
- The well system should be placed out of the flood zone (unless in casing and 2 feet—.6 m—above flood level).
- The well should be located at least 50 feet (15 m) from the high-water mark of a permanent body of water.
- The system should be sited 2 feet (.6 m) above ground level of the surrounding area.

supply network: closed systems

- The development supply system must connect to the main supply pipe at a point where the static pressure within the development will not exceed the main supply pressure. The normal pressure should be not less than 35 nor more than 60 pounds per square inch.
- Bedding depths depend on soil types, local frost conditions, and width of the trench.
- The system must have a minimum cover of 2 feet (.6 m) if it is located under a body of water. Special treatment is necessary when the system is located more than 15 feet (4.5 m) under a body of water.
- The pressure main is connected to one of the following:
  —Directly to a community well (i.e., one that serves more than fifteen units or twenty-five people for more than six months)
  —A reservoir that is connected to a well system (service of fifty or more houses required)
  —A storage tank that is connected to a well system (service of fifty or more homes required)
  —A water treatment plant
  —Other systems, such as surface water treatment systems

hydrants

- Hydrants should be spaced at 350- to 600-foot (106-to 182-m) intervals.
- Hydrants should be placed at intersections and at intermediate points as recommended.
- Hydrants should not be located within 10 feet (3 m) of a sanitary sewer or storm drain.

energy-efficient strategies

The design of water delivery systems has been refined over the years to be very efficient. Although some savings could result from clustering several houses around a common well, shared ownership has many potential problems. The greatest possibility for energy conservation is in the design of the treatment plants and through conservation of water use at the home site. Energy-efficient strategies for treatment plants are not discussed here, since they are not the concern of the developer and do not affect design.

- Water conservation strategies that will improve energy efficiency are education of the public to reduce water use in general and during the peak demand periods in particular, along with the use of energy-efficient appliances and fixtures—especially energy-efficient hot water tanks. In one evaluation of all home conservation strategies, improvements in efficiency of hot water tanks represented the second most significant gain (following insulation of the home).
- Systems should be planned so that each house is fully metered, rather than allowing either flat rates or block rates. In this way each user pays directly for the amount of water used.
- For cases in which water is extremely scarce, increased block rate charges should be applied or flow restriction devices should be used.
- Wells should be properly sited to provide the best source at the shallowest aquifer location.
- The quality of the water supply should be protected by enforcing a fixed limit on the number of private wells permitted.
- Individual developments should be connected to larger community systems whenever possible to save on long-term operation and maintenance costs.
- In areas where the supply of good-quality water is low, gray water systems should be explored but only at the individual dwelling scale.

implications for earth sheltered housing design

Since water supply systems, unlike conventional sewer systems, are not greatly affected by steeply sloping topography or the relationship of the house to the street, they present no special considerations for earth sheltered housing.

introduction

Another major portion of the cost of developing land is the money the developer must invest in the design, layout, and construction of roads. Unlike sewer systems, which have received little attention regarding their energy efficiency, road systems have been studied rather thoroughly to determine more energy-efficient criteria for their design and layout. This information has been applied to some road systems and is documented in several studies referred to throughout this chapter.

The various strategies for energy-efficient design of roads may be classified into three groups: those that relate to the resultant effect on land-use patterns and, therefore, transportation costs; those that affect the configuration of lots; and those that relate to the construction costs and the energy embodied in the road system materials.

The effect of road layouts on land-use patterns and transportation costs demands that conventional road layout be seriously reconsidered. Studies published by the Environmental Law Institute note that the single most effective strategy for saving transportation costs is not to drive smaller cars or improve bus systems, but rather to reconsider land-use patterns and to select those that reduce our dependency on automobiles, especially for running daily errands [3.5].

The studies suggest that multiple-use zoning be created at the neighborhood scale to provide stores and office spaces that are accessible to pedestrians and bicyclists. This recommendation need not imply the abandonment of the inner city or of large "satellite" shopping centers. These shopping centers have proven very effective in reducing transportation because housing has built up around them, making them convenient for many people. Shoppers can accomplish all of their errands in one area rather than in many separate areas. The inner city will have to offer sufficient and desirable housing in order to achieve a similar energy effectiveness. To abandon the city totally, however, would represent a great waste in energy because of the energy embodied in the systems and buildings already there. Hence, adaptive reuse in inner cities will be an essential energy-effective strategy, as will development of infill lots.

The typical intensely automobile-oriented land-use pattern is reflected in the actual construction of roads. Current road construction provides a system of equally fast, wide, and energy-intensive streets that allow through traffic at countless intersections on the grid. A more efficient system in terms of transportation patterns, land use, and construction costs provides a hierarchy of narrow roads leading to a few fast and intensively used vehicle collectors. (A study by the Bucks County Planning Commission presents an analysis of how to adapt current performance standards for residential streets to a hierarchical system [3.6].) Residential streets (as opposed to arterials or expressways) comprise 60 to 80 percent of all roads constructed. Thus, if the conventional concept of road construction (which is identified with wider roads) were changed, the amount of materials required for construction would also be altered. Such a change would radically decrease the total cost of road development while simultaneously reducing the total energy expended both in transportation and energy embodied in the materials. A change in land-use concepts and a corresponding change in the pattern of streets into a hierarchical system would mean a significant energy savings at a time of escalating gasoline and oil costs.

The second group of energy-efficient strategies for road layout concerns the ways in which alternative layouts of streets affect the configurations of buildable lots. Historically, lot configurations have been determined by the major issues of the times, which traditionally have centered on providing equal cost and opportunity for all potential lot owners. The grid system most directly provides equal lot sizes and frontage requirements. The development of culs-de-sac offered an alternative that allowed lots to conform to varied topography without sacrificing equal costs (based on frontage) to supply utilities to the separate parcels of land.

The current issue in determining lot size is equal opportunity for energy-efficient layout. This concept implies that lots should be configured to provide the same opportunities for energy-efficient building strategies, e.g., optimized solar access for each house or cluster of houses. These issues are quite complex and do not necessarily imply one set of optimal lot and road layouts. For example, the spacing of houses to provide clear solar access is based on many variables, such as latitude, building heights, and topography. In addition, there are many strategies for solar collection in a house, all of which have somewhat different implications with respect to building and lot configuration. These issues are discussed in greater detail in chapters 4 and 5.

It has been stated that a reduction in the width of residential streets is not only energy efficient for a number of reasons, but is cost-effective as well. By using less land, narrower streets allow a greater percentage of the land to be used for buildable lots. The larger building area is particularly advantageous for the more complex lot configurations required for solar houses or closely clustered conventional houses. It permits more flexibility in the placement of buildings so that solar gain can be optimized, and it allows for clustering of buildings on smaller lots, thereby reducing utility costs.

Several studies have compared the land-use efficiencies of various street configurations. In one such study, prepared for a development in Davis, California, a hierarchical system using narrower roads and culs-de-sac is compared to conventional wider roads on a grid pattern. As shown in figure 3-2, the amount of land used for roads is reduced from 25 percent to 8 percent with the hierarchical system, and costs are reduced as well.

3-2: street system comparison

streets	conventional	Village Homes (Davis, California)
width	44 ft (13.3 m)	23 ft (7 m)
configuration	grid pattern	culs-de-sac
length of culs-de-sac	about 200 ft (61 m)	about 400 ft (121 m)
percent of land	25%	8%
cost per unit	$4,800-5,500	about $4,000 (includes parking bays, bike paths, landscaping, and drainage)
sidewalks	adjacent to street	adjacent to common areas
parking	off- and on-street (up to 4 spaces per unit)	off-street only (2 spaces per unit)
drainage	storm sewer carries runoff	channelized, landscaped areas hold runoff

Source: *Residential Street Design [3.7].*

The third type of strategy to promote energy-efficient development through appropriate road design involves proper selection of building materials and alternative detail design layouts. Narrower roads require less energy expenditure in the production of materials. Furthermore, because narrower streets that conform to the topography tend to work more effectively with the natural dynamics of the varying soil and water relationships of the land, they require less frequent and less radical maintenance.

One important consideration is that changes in road surface area and types of materials can affect the microclimate, which in turn affects the heating and cooling loads in buildings. Generally, building materials such as concrete and asphalt radiate more heat than do natural ground covers. Regardless of the material used, wider streets produce more heat than narrower streets. One disadvantage of using asphalt, rather than concrete, is the greater frequency of total replacement required in a normal maintenance cycle. Asphalt is flexible, however, and in colder climates with longer freeze-thaw periods and diurnal temperature variations or in more expansive soil, may even require less frequent maintenance than does concrete. Other flexible materials that require less energy embodiment should be explored and developed. Plantings that shade streets and surface lots should also be considered an integral factor for energy-efficient development rather than a simple design amenity. According to a study done in Davis, California,

> *. . . Even greater energy cost can be attributed to the adverse effect of streets on the microclimate during the summer. The surface temperature of asphalt on a 90° day can reach 140°. This increase in temperature can increase energy use in several ways. First, this hot surface increases the maximum air temperature by 10°F or more and increases the heat load on home air conditioners. A 10°F difference in air temperature may not sound like much; yet if the difference between outside and inside (75°F) air would be 20° without wide streets but is 30° because of them, then the 10° increase represents a 50% increase in thermal load on structures and a 55% increase in energy use (50% + efficiency loss). The use of narrower streets makes shading easier; shading can in many cases completely eliminate the temperature rise and may in fact produce a reduction in ambient temperature.*
>
> *Streets also increase the temperature at night because they have collected a great deal of energy during the day and reradiate it at night. This increases the use of air conditioners at night when natural ventilation might otherwise suffice [3.7].*

The combined effect of implementing all three of these types of strategies for road layout will be significant in terms of both initial construction costs and energy-efficient development. In order to illustrate this point, a comparison between a residential street of standard width and a narrower alternative street is shown in figure 3-3. Although the cost and land-use figures are based only on assumptions for Davis, California, the relative savings in land, materials, and initial investment would hold true for other communities.

3-3: comparison of residential streets

	conventional	**alternative**
street width	34 ft (10.3 m)	16 ft (4.8 m)
land use in streets	6,800 sq ft (612 ca)	3,200 sq ft (288 ca)
percentage of lot area	21%	10%
land cost $1/sq ft	$6,800	$3,200
construction cost		
street $ .50/sq ft	$3,400	$1,600
curb $8/sq ft	$3,200	$3,200
sidewalk $8/sq ft	$3,200	—
total	$9,800	$4,800

Source: *Residential Street Design [3.7].*

These strategies will provide immediate benefits to the developer as well as to residents and the entire community. That is, the developer who pays for less road can offer more desirable lots at a lower cost per lot. The residents will have quieter, safer streets, alternatives to total dependence on their automobiles, a higher-quality environment, and fewer long-term maintenance and operation costs for their roads.

All decisions concerning changes in road layouts must be based on a complete understanding of three major issues.

1. *Basic safety criteria cannot be neglected in favor of an alternative that solves another problem.* Roads must meet standards that ensure adequate visibility and safe speeds on curves as well as function for emergency vehicles and other services (e.g., snow removal). The minimum visibility distances as they relate to speeds should be used as guidelines in any road design. Furthermore, lane widths originally were coordinated with the operating speeds of the vehicles and the relative hilliness of the terrain or density of development. Hence, if lane widths are reduced, speed limits should be lowered correspondingly [3.6].

   Maximum percent grades should be maintained as standards for narrower streets, since they most often reflect performance under local climatic conditions. While a 10- to 12-percent grade is acceptable in some parts of the country, 8 percent is a more acceptable maximum in Minnesota. Emergency and snowplow vehicles can be accommodated by providing alternative designs of the edge and curb type, and height at the edge, without having to keep the road surface wide. Figure 3-4 illustrates a design adaptation that allows accommodation of snowplows without needless widening of the right-of-way. Through careful examination of design details, energy-efficient standards can be developed without sacrificing safety, service, or maintenance.

2. *The energy-efficient layout of utilities is interrelated with road design and configuration, especially with respect to choices for types of stormwater collection systems and water lines, and should be integrated in design solutions.* The most energy-efficient way to provide utilities is to locate all services in trenches that are buried beneath the road surface and accessible either from the road (on a street that is not heavily traveled) or in an adjacent easement area. Placing all utilities in one trench minimizes damage done to the site during the trenching for installation and increases the efficiency of operating and maintenance. Figure 3-5 illustrates a typical cross-section showing the utilities (either an open drainage system or a storm sewer with curbs and gutters) encased under the road system. A cross-section with the utilities in separate trenches would require a wider easement to meet plumbing codes, as described in the sections on water and sewer systems, and to provide adequate room for street trees to shade the pavement.

Although the issues related to efficient collection of stormwater are discussed in the next section, it is important to mention here that the cross-sectional design of the road depends on the type of stormwater collection system available. Roads that are cross-sloped work in conjunction with open channel drainage collection systems. These roads provide the most energy-efficient system because they generally require the least site alteration and the least amounts of cut-and-fill. With enclosed collection systems, this cross-sectional design requires fewer inlets and manholes than do crowned roads. On roads with lower speed limits and low average daily traffic counts, the likelihood of pollution of the roads is also low, so that

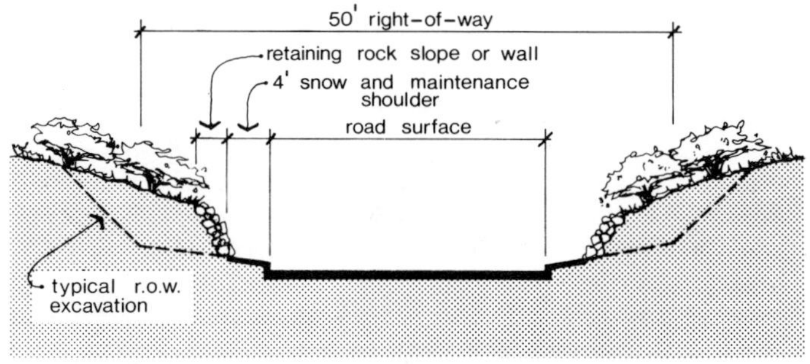

50' right-of-way
retaining rock slope or wall
4' snow and maintenance shoulder
road surface
typical r.o.w. excavation

3-4: alternative road section for maintenance

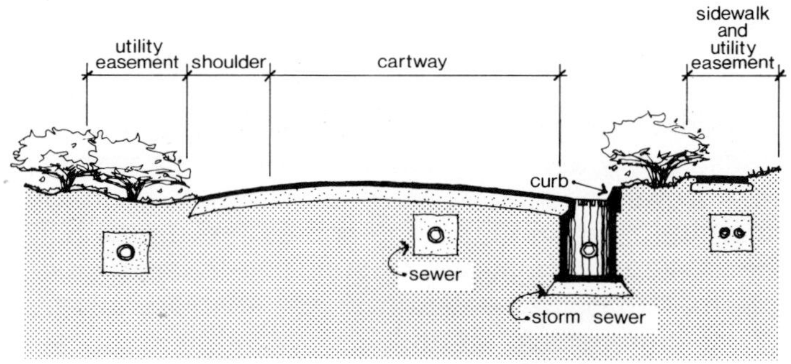

utility easement
shoulder
cartway
sidewalk and utility easement
curb
sewer
storm sewer

3-5: alternative road section for utilities

pollution probably can be adequately handled by drainage channels. On roads with higher speed limits and more traffic, however, the use of closed systems should be considered in light of the environmental degradation caused by pollution. Standards for closed systems should be adapted to make them feasible for less intensive use conditions. To make this adaptation feasible, smaller collection manholes must be developed and mass-produced. The only units currently available are oversized for these conditions.

3. *Energy-efficient design solutions should show a concern both for the total design experience and for pedestrian, bicycle, and alternative vehicle circulation needs.* Whether or not it can be statistically verified, it is generally acknowledged that the higher the quality of experience while driving, the lower the stress experienced and, therefore, the lower the speed attempted by the driver. Designing energy-efficient environments should take into account the quality of experience they provide for the people who live in them. Provisions for separated pedestrian ways and bicycle paths should be incorporated into a master plan that optimizes the experience of traveling by each mode of transportation and yet provides for safety at roadway intersections.

   Although the reasons for designing and building narrower streets are compelling, changing conventional standards will most likely meet resistance. Objections to narrow streets may be raised by fire department officials, who understandably wish to maintain ease of travel. By eliminating street parking, however, the travelway will in many cases be increased, thereby facilitating fire response rather than hindering it. A second objection concerns the loss of parking on the street. With narrower streets driveways will be used more, and parking bays can provide extra parking for visitors. If car sizes continue to be small, parking might be added to what are now considered narrow streets. Pedestrian safety concerns are another issue related to narrower streets. Research in Britain has shown a very clear relationship between safety and narrow streets: wider streets have low impedance and result in high speeds, making them more dangerous, whereas narrow streets have high impedance and result in low speeds [3.7]. The study noted that careful demarcation of street type will further increase safety and that the use of T intersections can reduce the accident rate considerably.

In the remainder of this section, the general performance standard for the design of residential roads is given, followed by the standard physical design criteria and energy-efficient strategies for each of the three major categories of roads and for related road features (e.g., driveways, intersections, parking). Finally, the implications of road layout as it pertains to the design of earth sheltered housing developments are discussed. It should be noted that arterials and expressways are not included in this study because they are designed to serve higher volumes of traffic as efficiently as possible and are financed with federal and state funds rather than by the developer.

performance standard

To establish appropriate standards for the design of streets in residential subdivisions that will (1) promote the safety and convenience of vehicular traffic, (2) protect the safety of neighborhood residents, (3) minimize the long-term costs for the maintenance and repair of streets, (4) minimize crime in residential areas, (5) protect the residential qualities of neighborhoods by limiting traffic volume, traffic speed, noise and fumes, (6) encourage the efficient use of land, (7) minimize the cost of street construction and thereby restrain the rise in housing costs, and (8) minimize the construction of impervious surface, thereby protecting the quantity and quality of the municipality's water resources [3.6].

collectors

Collectors are the highest order of residential street. Designed to carry traffic volumes of 3,000 ADT (average daily trips), a collector generally connects approximately 150 dwelling units each or connects a neighborhood and an activity area. No residential lots front directly onto these streets and parking on them is usually prohibited. Generally, it is considered desirable for collectors to run north/south whenever possible to allow for maximum solar lot configurations off local east/west streets. As shown in chapter 5, however, local north/south streets can work efficiently for solar access under certain conditions.

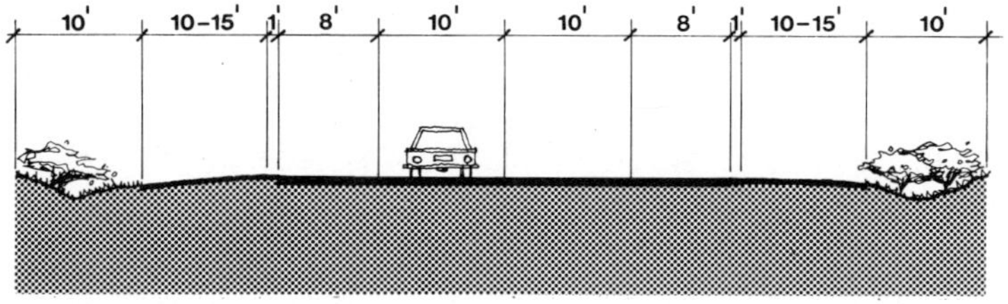
10'
10-15'
1'
8'
10'
10'
8'
1'
10-15'
10'

3-6: standard road section

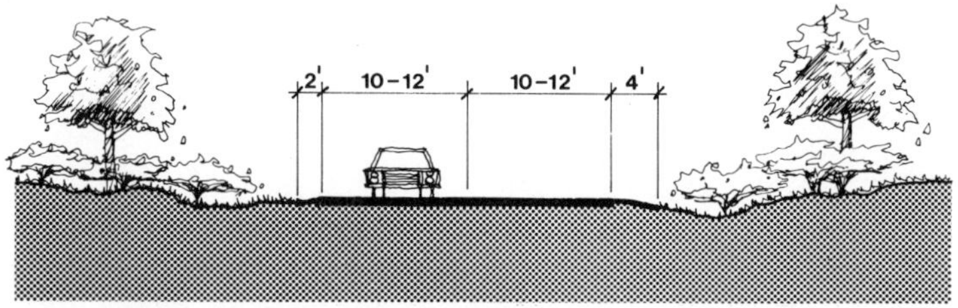
2'
10-12'
10-12'
4'

3-7: road section—alternative a

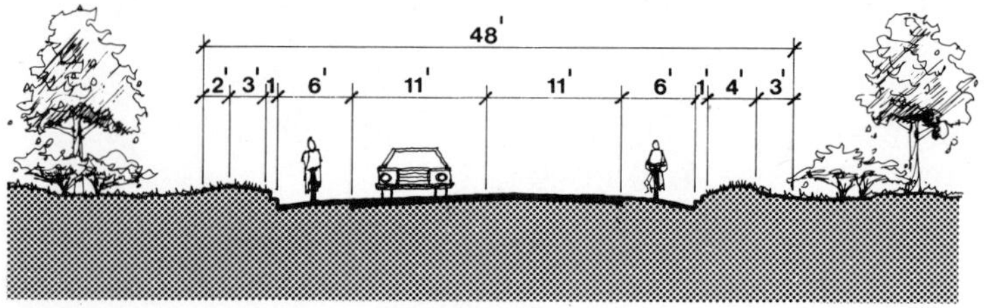
48'
2'
3'
1'
6'
11'
11'
6'
1'
4'
3'

3-8: road section—alternative b

3-9: standard criteria for collectors

	ordinary terrain	rolling terrain	hilly terrain
right-of-way width	60 ft (18 m)	60 ft (18 m)	60 ft (18 m)
pavement width	36 ft (11 m)	36 ft (11 m)	36 ft (11 m)
type of curb	vert. face	vert. face	vert. face
sidewalk width	5 ft (1.5 m)	5 ft (1.5 m)	5 ft (1.5 m)
sidewalk distance from curb face	10 ft (3 m)	10 ft (3 m)	10 ft (3 m)
minimum sight distance	250 ft (76 m)	200 ft (61 m)	150 ft (45 m)
maximum grade	4%	8%	12%
minimum spacing along major route	1300 ft (394 m)	1300 ft (394 m)	1300 ft (394 m)
design speed	35 mph	35 mph	25 mph
minimum centerline radius	350 ft (106 m)	230 ft (70 m)	150 ft (45 m)

Note: These figures are for medium-density development (2-6 units per acre).
Source: *Performance Streets [3.6]*.

3-10: energy-efficient criteria for collectors

	alternative a	alternative b
right-of-way width	60 ft (18 m)	48 ft (14.5 m)
pavement width		
with curb	22-24 ft (6.7-7.3 m)	36 ft (11 m)
without curb	20-22 ft + 4-ft shoulder (6-6.7 m + 1.2-m shoulder)	34 ft (10.3 m) (includes 12 ft—3.6 m—for bike path)
sidewalk width		2 ft (.6 m)
sidewalk distance from curb		2 ft (.6 m)
minimum sight distance	250 ft (76 m)	
maximum grade	8%	
minimum spacing along major route	300 ft (91 m)	¾ mile (1200 m)
design speed	35 mph	25 mph
minimum centerline radius	350 ft (106 m)	
maximum superelevation	.08 ft/foot	
maximum grade at intersection	3% for 100 ft (30 m)	

Sources: *Performance Streets [3.6]* for alternative a
Residential Street Design [3.7] for alternative b

subcollectors

Subcollectors are access streets that may provide frontage for residential lots. Designed to carry traffic volumes of 1,000 ADT, subcollectors collect from smaller residential access streets while excluding external traffic. Sidewalks and parking may be included. Wider streets are usually required for multifamily development.

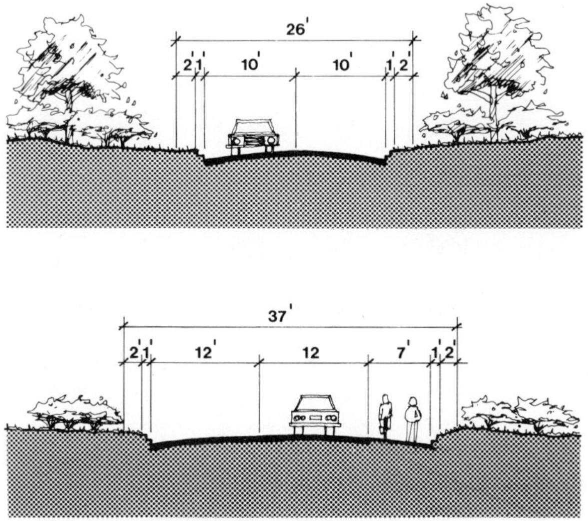
26'
10'
10'
37'
12'
12
7'

3-11: road sections—alternative b

3-12: standard criteria for subcollectors

	ordinary terrain	**rolling terrain**	**hilly terrain**
right-of-way width	60 ft (18 m)	60 ft (18 m)	60 ft (18 m)
pavement width	32 ft (9.7 m)	34 ft (10.3 m)	34 ft (10.3 m)
type of curb	vert. face	vert. face	vert. face
sidewalk width	5 ft (1.5 m)	5 ft (1.5 m)	5 ft (1.5 m)
sidewalk distance from curb	6 ft (1.8 m)	6 ft (1.8 m)	6 ft (1.8 m)
minimum sight distance	200 ft (61 m)	150 ft (45 m)	110 ft (33 m)
maximum grade	4%	8%	15%
maximum cul-de-sac length	500 ft (151 m)	500 ft (151 m)	500 ft (151 m)
minimum cul-de-sac radius (right-of-way)	50 ft (15 m)	50 ft (15 m)	50 ft (15 m)
design speed	30 mph	25 mph	20 mph
minimum centerline radius	250 ft (76 m)	175 ft (53 m)	110 ft (33 m)

Note: These figures are for medium-density development (2-6 units per acre).
Source: *Performance Streets [3.6]*.

3-13: energy-efficient criteria for subcollectors

	alternative a	**alternative b**
right-of-way width	50 ft (15 m) minimum	26-30 ft (7.9-9 m)
pavement width		
with curb	22-26 ft (6.7-7.9 m)	
without curb	20 ft (36 ft w/parking) (6 m—11m w/parking)	20-24 ft (6-7.3 m)
sidewalk width		2 ft (.6 m) on one side
sidewalk distance from curb		0 ft (0 m)
minimum sight distance	300 ft (91 m)	
maximum grade	8%	
maximum cul-de-sac length	1000 ft (303 m)	
minimum spacing	125 ft (38 m)	
design speed	30 mph	
minimum centerline radius	140 ft (42 m)	
maximum grade at intersection parking	5% for 50 ft (15 m) none permitted	
driveways	permitted from 40-100 ft (12-30 m) apart	

Sources: *Performance Streets [3.6]* for alternative a
Residential Street Design [3.7] for alternative b

residential access roads

Residential access roads are intended to carry the least amount of traffic at low speeds while providing immediate access to homes. Designed for 200 ADT, residential access roads may permit parking if twenty to twenty-five dwellings are served and front on the street. The standard criteria for subcollectors and residential access roads do not differ. It is generally considered desirable for residential access roads to run east/west to allow for maximum solar lot configuration. As shown in chapter 5, north/south local roads can work efficiently for solar access in some cases.

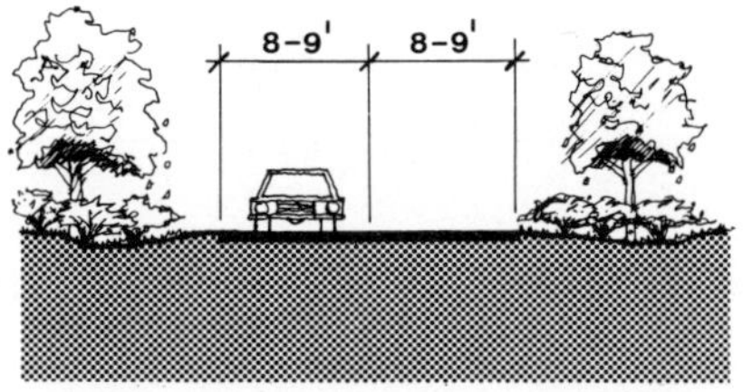
8-9'
8-9'

3-14a: road section—alternative a

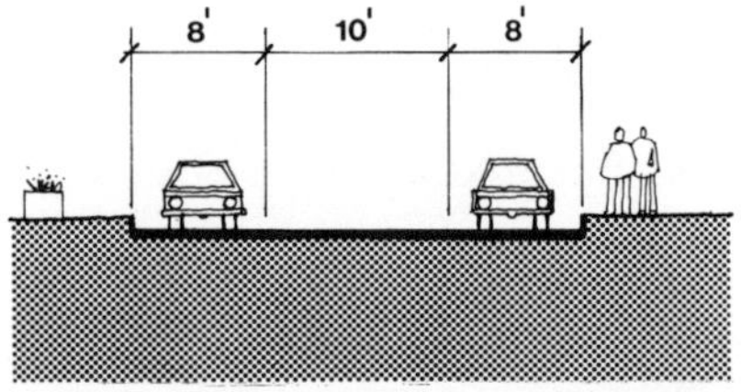
8'
10'
8'

3-14b: road section—alternative a

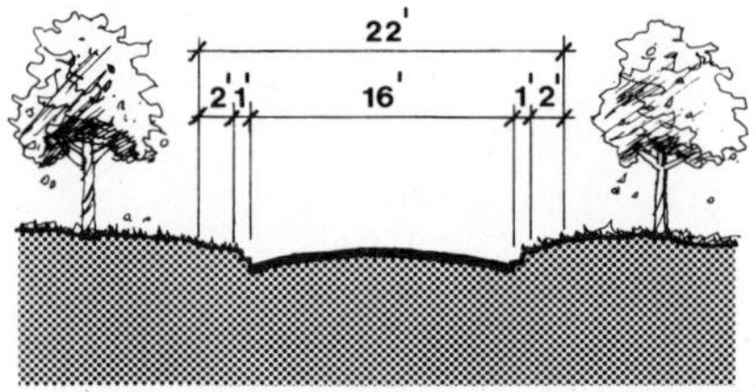
22'
2 1
16'
1 2

3-15: road section—alternative b

3-16: standard criteria for residential access roads

	ordinary terrain	rolling terrain	hilly terrain
right-of-way width	60 ft (18 m)	60 ft (18 m)	60 ft (18 m)
pavement width	32 ft (9.7 m)	34 ft (10.3 m)	34 ft (10.3 m)
type of curb	vert. face	vert. face	vert. face
sidewalk width	5 ft (1.5 m)	5 ft (1.5 m)	5 ft (1.5 m)
sidewalk distance from curb	6 ft (1.8 m)	6 ft (1.8 m)	6 ft (1.8 m)
minimum sight distance	200 ft (61 m)	150 ft (45 m)	110 ft (33 m)
maximum grade	4%	8%	15%
maximum cul-de-sac length	500 ft (151 m)	500 ft (151 m)	500 ft (151 m)
minimum cul-de-sac radius (right-of-way)	50 ft (15 m)	50 ft (15 m)	50 ft (15 m)
design speed	30 mph	25 mph	20 mph
minimum centeline radius	250 ft (76 m)	175 ft (53 m)	110 ft (33 m)

Note: These figures are for medium-density development (2-6 units per acre).
Source: *Performance Streets [3.6]*.

3-17: energy-efficient criteria for residential access roads

	alternative a	alternative b
right-of-way width	50 ft (33 ft minimum) (15 m—10 m minimum)	22 ft (6.7 m)
pavement width		
with curb	18 ft (5.4 m)	18 ft (5.4 m)
without curb	16-18 ft (4.8-5.4 m)	16 ft (4.8 m)
with parking	26 ft (5.4 m)	
sidewalk width		0-2 ft (0-.6 m) on one side
sidewalk distance from curb		0 ft (0 m)
minimum sight distance	250 ft (76 m)	
maximum grade	10%	
design speed	25 mph	10-20 mph
minimum centerline radius	100 ft (30 m)	
stopping distance	175 ft (53 m)	
maximum grade at intersection	5% at 50 ft (15 m)	
parking	8 ft (2.4 m)	none or 7 ft (2.1 m)

Sources: *Performance Streets [3.6]* for alternative a
Residential Street Design [3.7] for alternative b

culs-de-sac

physical design criteria

Culs-de-sac, or turnarounds, are a type of access road designed to permit free turning for the largest service vehicles regularly servicing a neighborhood. The turning radius of trash collection vehicles is 28.5 to 35 feet (8.6 to 10.6 m), suggesting that the minimum diameter of the cul-de-sac would be 70 feet (21 m). Other standards for cul-de-sac diameters range from 70 to 80 feet (21 to 24 m). Planted islands in the center reduce the total paved area of the cul-de-sac, as shown in figure 3-18. The traffic lane is usually 14 feet (4 m) wide. Recommended lengths for culs-de-sac range from 400 to 1,000 feet (121 to 303 m); a 500-foot (151-m) length typically would serve 0.25-acre (0.1-ha) lots. Shorter culs-de-sac help reduce traffic.

A number of alternatives to culs-de-sac are possible, depending on the lot sizes, configurations, and total number of lots served by the road. The T-type turnaround shown in figure 3-19 requires less pavement area and space than a cul-de-sac, but it also usually serves fewer lots. Another alternative is the loop road, which is used either when more lots are to be served or when a conventional cul-de-sac does not fit the topography. A smaller loop road can simply have a central green space with lots surrounding it; a larger loop street with lots in the central space is shown in figure 3-20.

energy-efficient strategies

- The cul-de-sac should use the smallest radius possible while still providing adequate space for service vehicles.
- The cul-de-sac should protect the easement space for use as an overhang area for occasional larger vehicles but should not have an excessively large radius.
- Mountable curbs should be used.

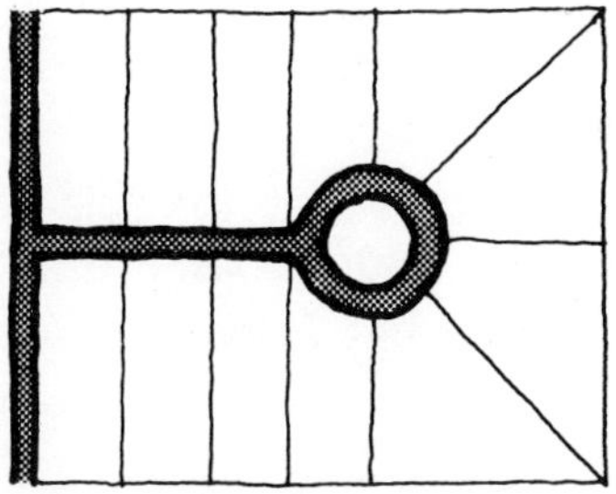

3-18: cul-de-sac

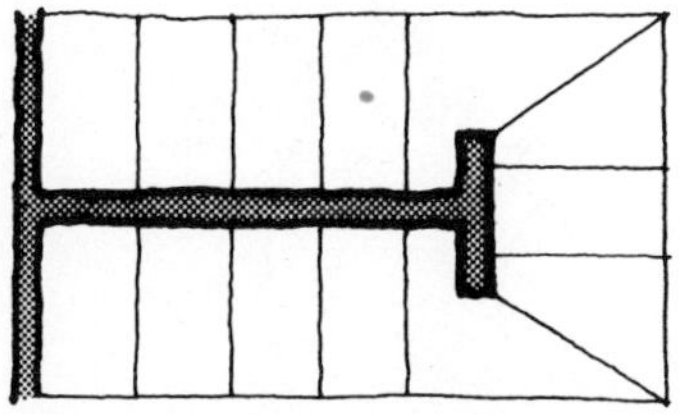

3-19: T-type turnaround

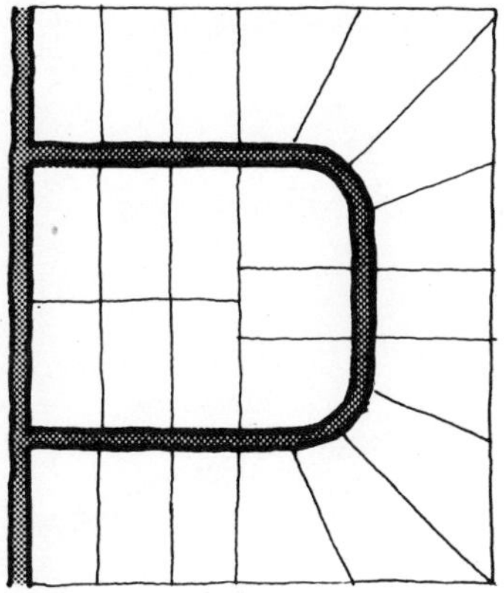

3-20: loop road

- The cul-de-sac should include a central planting strip to reduce the total amount of pavement.
- Designers should reconfigure the shape of the cul-de-sac to allow for service vehicles, such as snowplows, while reducing the total radius to 30 to 35 feet (9 to 10.6 m), as shown in figure 3-21.
- As shown in figure 3-22, service roads for culs-de-sac should be extended by adding intermediate turnarounds rather than by using looped access roads.

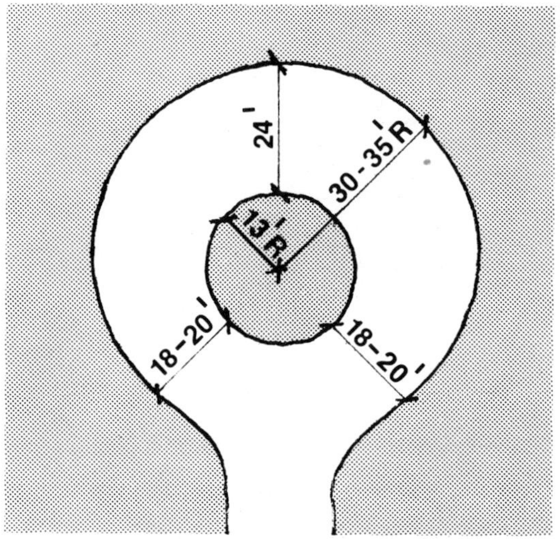

24'
30-35'R
13'R
18-20'
18-20'

3-21: alternative cul-de-sac dimensions

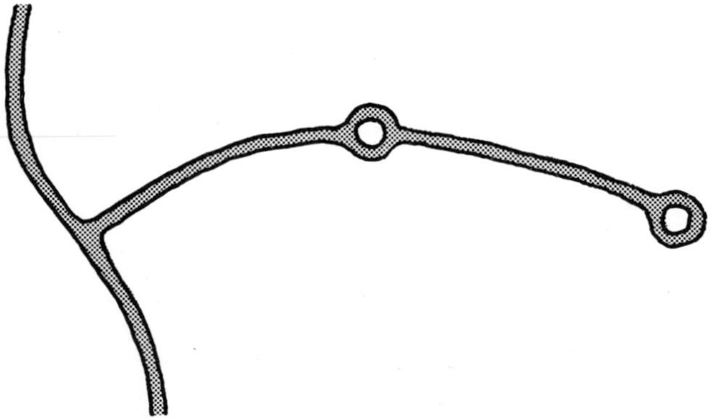

3-22: intermediate turnaround

intersections

physical design criteria

Intersections should be carefully engineered according to design speeds, visibility, and terrain requirements.

3-23: standard criteria for intersections

	ordinary terrain all densities	**rolling terrain** all densities	**hilly terrain** all densities
approach speed	25 mph	25 mph	20 mph
clear sight distance along each approach leg	90 ft (27 m)	90 ft (27 m)	70 ft (21 m)
vertical alignment within area	flat	2%	4%
minimum angle of intersection	75° (90° preferred)	75° (90° preferred)	75° (90° preferred)
minimum curb radius			
1. local-local	20 ft (6 m)	20 ft (6 m)	20 ft (6 m)
2. local-collector	25 ft (7.5 m)	25 ft (7.5 m)	25 ft (7.5 m)
minimum centerline offset of adjacent intersections			
1. local-local	150 ft (45 m)	150 ft (45 m)	150 ft (45 m)
2. local-collector	150 ft (45 m)	150 ft (45 m)	150 ft (45 m)
3. collector-collector	200 ft (61 m)	200 ft (61 m)	200 ft (61 m)

Source: *Performance Streets [3.6]*

3-24: minimum intersection spacing

major road type intersected	**spacing (ft)**	**(m)**
higher-order street	1,000	303
residential collector	300	91
residential subcollector	125	38

In order to prevent dangerous jogs and turning movements, intersections are required to be either aligned directly opposite one another or offset by a minimum distance. The 125-foot (38-m) offset shown in figure 3-25 is considered a minimum by some sources; adjustments may be required to suit local conditions. It is also unacceptable to allow streets to intersect at a narrow angle. As shown in figure 3-26, streets should intersect at a 90° angle for a minimum of 50 feet (15 m) from the intersection.

energy-efficient strategies

- The total number of gridded intersections should be reduced by using street layouts that are arranged in hierarchies.
- When appropriate, properly designed jogged intersections should be used to discourage through traffic.

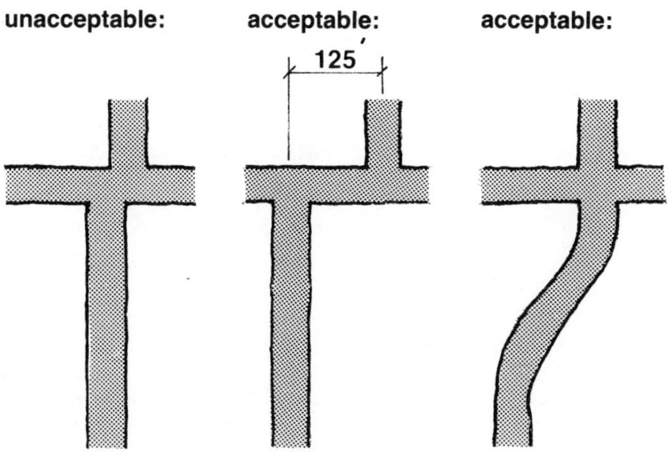
unacceptable:
acceptable:
125'
acceptable:

3-25: intersection spacings

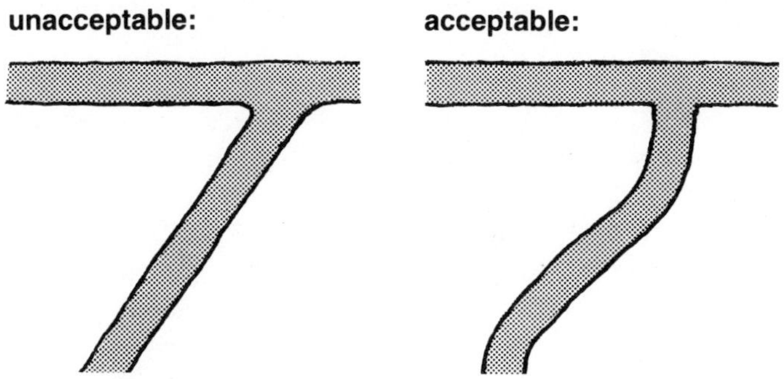
unacceptable:
acceptable:

3-26: intersection angles

driveways

physical design criteria

Driveways are typically 10 to 20 feet (3 to 6 m) wide. Usually a setback distance of 40 feet (12 m) between an intersection and a driveway is established as a safety factor designed to avoid traffic conflicts at intersections.

energy-efficient strategies

- Shared driveway access should be promoted where possible to reduce the total paved area and the numbers of intersections with subcollectors, and to provide less expensive common utility access. Although a maximum of four units per driveway has been recommended by the Bucks County Plan as shown in figure 3-27, utilities could serve six to eight units adequately.
- Narrow driveways are recommended—10 feet (3 m) for one house, 16 feet (4.8 m) for multiple-house service.
- Pervious materials should be used wherever possible, and drainage designed to be collected in small collection service systems or surface drainage channels.

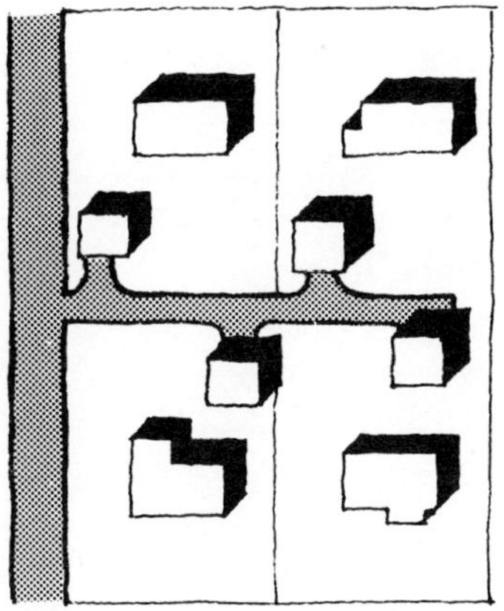

3-27: common driveway

parking

physical design criteria

Parking has typically been provided on the street with an 8-foot (2.4-m) lane out of the flow of moving traffic. The number of available off-street parking spaces is usually defined in the zoning regulations. One to two spaces per unit is typically required for residential developments. The size of these spaces is usually approximately 10 by 20 feet (3 by 6 m) in surface lots and 8 by 23 feet (2.4 by 7 m) for street parking. Smaller cars require smaller spaces: 9 by 18 feet (2.7 by 5.4 m) for surface lots, 8 by 20 feet (2.4 by 6 m) for street parking.

energy-efficient strategies

- Street parking should be eliminated in order to reduce the total road surface required to service residential neighborhoods. Occasional surface lots should be provided in higher-density areas.
- On-street parking should only be retained in areas with lot widths of less than 100 feet (30 m). Two parking lanes with one moving traffic lane should be used for developments with narrower lots, resulting in a 26-foot-wide (7.9-m-wide) road, including curbs.
- Sizes of parking spaces for smaller vehicles should be reconfigured rather than enlarged.
- Cross-sloping to open drainageways should be used whenever feasible.
- At least half of all large parking surfaces should be covered with tree canopy within fifteen years of the granting of the construction permit.
- Lighting of parking areas should be designed to reduce total energy demand while still maximizing lighting coverage appropriate to the character of the neighborhood.
- Tier parking surface areas, if they are required, should blend as closely as possible into the land contours to reduce the total cut-and-fill required to prepare the lots.

street lighting

Streetlights are required for all residential developments, particularly medium-to high-density developments with relatively heavy traffic and clustered parking areas.

energy-efficient strategies

- A variety of more efficient lamps, such as the sodium vapor lamp, should be used.
- If individual needs and circumstances allow lower lighting levels, the number of lights should be reduced or lamps of lower wattage should be used.

traffic lights

Traffic lights are required at major intersections in some developments. Although some electrical energy is required in their operation, a much more serious energy concern is the fact that traffic lights cause automobiles to waste fuel in stopping and idling.

energy-efficient strategies

- Traffic signals should be synchronized by computer to minimize stopping and idling time. Ironically, although this strategy saves time as well as fuel, it may also make driving more attractive and thus increase the number of miles traveled.

implications for earth sheltered housing

In general, most of the standards and recommendations for road systems apply equally to all types of housing. The layouts of both solar and earth sheltered housing do, however, require special modifications of the road system under some circumstances. For example, earth sheltered housing on steep slopes of 30 to 50 percent presents some unique problems for vehicular access and parking. This type of situation and other issues related to road systems for earth sheltered housing are discussed in chapter 5.

Stormwater collection and distribution is another important aspect of housing development. The various means of collecting and distributing stormwater to protect buildings and roads from destructive forces can be costly to the developer and, like all utility systems, can affect energy efficiency. If the design of the buildings and roads in a development results in large areas of hard surface, then greater reliance on larger storm sewer systems may be necessary. Such systems are more energy intensive in the manufacture of materials as well as in their installation. Although the technical knowledge to deal with many different design approaches exists, designs that are harmonious with natural drainage patterns, soils, and other site conditions not only cost less and require less energy to construct and maintain, but generally also result in less environmental damage.

In this section, a performance standard for stormwater management is given, followed by physical design criteria for a number of surface and subsurface collection systems, energy-efficient strategies for these systems, and finally, the implications of these systems for earth sheltered housing.

performance standard

". . . must prevent significant loss of life and property due to runoff of unforeseeable rainfall and . . . provide an acceptable degree of convenient access to property following frequent rainfall . . . provides for maximum convenience at an individual site by the most rapid possible elimination of excess surface water after a rainfall and the containment for the disposal of that water as quickly as possible through a closed system" [3.8].

physical design criteria

In this discussion stormwater collection and distribution systems are divided into two major categories—surface collection systems and subsurface drainage systems. Surface collection systems are further classified into three types—storage systems, open collection systems, and closed collection systems. The type of system required on a particular site depends on the type of soils, the amount of water, and the specific code requirements of the area.

surface collection systems

storage systems: These are reservoirs designed to collect rainwater.

open collection systems: Open collection systems consist of some or all of the following four components:

1. Grading to promote sheet drainage away from the house, especially at points of access or entry.
2. A series of open channels (ditches and swales) to collect and redistribute the water over a larger area of land, allowing immediate infiltration and/or exfiltration of groundwater. The various types of control are:
   - Portland cement, asphaltic concrete, or soil cement paving. Although this type of channel is permanent if carefully constructed and maintained, it accelerates runoff and is very costly.
   - Drop structures across the channel at intervals so that the slope of the channel between drops keeps drainage velocities below the allowable velocity for turf. This method is satisfactory if drops are designed and built well. It does not speed up runoff, but it is unsightly if natural materials are not used and may have maintenance problems.
   - Lining with graded crushed rock or gravel. A well-designed channel using this type of lining can harmonize with the landscape and allow for both

infiltration into permeable soil and exfiltration of groundwater. This type of lining can be costly if the rock or gravel selected is not available locally.

- Riprap. Although this type of lining is permanent if it is carefully installed and maintained, it can be both costly and unattractive.
- Rock enclosed in galvanized wire baskets (gabions). This type of lining generally requires wide, shallow channels so that drops will not be overridden and channels destroyed during unusually extreme flow events. This type of lining can be permanent if it is carefully installed, can allow infiltration into permeable soil, and can be aesthetically pleasing. It can be costly, however [3.8].

3. A series of open channels (curbs) to collect and redistribute the water to an internal collection system. The various types of control used for the design of street cross-sections are:
   - Normal crown with curb and gutter. In these types of roads, the center lane remains clear during minor storms, and the curbs serve as traffic barriers on both sides. Driveway ramps behind the curb and gutter increase assessment costs, however. Since these streets must have longitudinal grade to assure proper drainage, they tend to concentrate water and increase downstream flooding.
   - Cross-slope with curb and gutter. Cross-sloped roads reduce the number of inlets and manholes, decrease earthwork required, fit into the natural topography well, and create a traffic barrier on both sides of the road. One drawback, however, is that water from streets intersecting on the high side must be collected, as the system will tend to overflow the intersection. Such a system also increases the maximum width of sheet flow, is hazardous if sheet flow from rain or snow melt freezes, and can achieve flow capacity in only one gutter.
   - Asymmetrical crown. This type of road has no cross flow until the crown is overtopped, lessens the hazard of icing, integrates well with the natural topography, and creates a traffic barrier on both sides. The flow capacity is limited on the upper side, however, and automobiles tend to ride somewhat differently on these roads.
   - Drainage swales. Where drainage swale systems are usable, they are the least expensive collection system. They allow for infiltration of runoff in channels; no water is confined on pavement, permitting freer movement of traffic during storms. Drainage swale systems can be merged with the natural topography and they they have fewer underground storm drains. Moreover, they slow down the runoff because of the much lower velocities in the grass-lined channel and the considerable storage that must be filled before overflow occurs. Drainage swale systems are not advisable in cases where small lots require frequent driveway culverts, however. The shoulders and channels require more maintenance. These systems may require a wider right-of-way to accommodate flat-side slopes on drainage swales, and they are less adaptable to sidewalks (although they are compatible with off-street walk systems) [3.8].
4. A series of retention or detention ponds, which concentrate water to a greater degree than do ditches but still allow percolation to occur.

closed collection systems: Through round conduits made of reinforced concrete, clay, or corrugated steel, water is collected and delivered to the nearest allowable natural water body for release. The minimum standard for slope is 1 foot per 100 feet (.3 m per 30 m) and a velocity of 2 feet (.6 m) per second (the maximum velocity has been set at 20 feet—6 m—per second). Pipes are sized for 82-percent capacity at peak period to compensate for hydraulic action at the joints of two pipes. The minimum pipe size is 4 inches (10 cm). Laterals are laid at the greatest slope possible, while submains follow natural drainage lines and interceptors enter at angles across the slope. Deeper systems are more effective because they reduce hydraulic pressure. The best designs compensate for heavy flow by paying critical attention to the staggered times of concentration of the various interceptors.

subsurface drainage

In a subsurface drainage system, drain tiles are laid adjacent to the foundations of buildings to draw the water away from the buildings and the surrounding soils. In poorer soils where critical design conditions require more protection of the building—as would be the case for earth sheltered homes—interceptor drain systems are included to collect the rapid and excessive overland flow. These interceptor drains can be designed simply as a system of gravel- or sand-filled trenches that divert water under more extreme conditions, e.g., when the property line is close and the adjacent slope is severe or when soils are highly expansive or highly susceptible to erosion. The trenching includes a subsurface drain tile system that redistributes the water to another empondment area or closed system collection point. In some cases the interceptor system is tied into the outflow pipe of the foundation system. It should be noted that soils that require subsurface drainage systems simply to make them developable are not very suitable for earth sheltering and are, in fact, very limited for all types of conventional housing that include a sub-entry-level floor (basement).

energy-efficient strategies

- Sites should be designed for zero runoff in all areas, permitting polluted runoff from salted streets, for example, to be collected in a closed system while all unpolluted runoff is redistributed or retained on-site. Collection of water should be confined to areas where salting of streets creates a problem. Clustering helps to optimize the efficiency of the zero-runoff approach by allowing a common area of collection and redistribution rather than having to provide these services on a house-by-house basis. On flat sites to be developed for earth sheltered housing, the ground modeling should be conceived as a way both to integrate the houses and to design the runoff to attain zero-runoff conditions.
- In areas where the design storm and design period can be reassessed and intermediate remedial changes made, those changes should be effected instead of switching to a more energy-intensive and expensive new system.
- Open rather than closed systems should be used wherever possible for surface water in order to reduce use of—and energy embodied in producing—closed systems. Natural materials such as bentonite, rather than energy-intensive plastics, should be used for empondment.
- Subsurface systems needed for earth sheltered housing should be connected to outflow systems that are part of the open surface redistribution system. By determining the building site location ahead of time, the system can be planned to work collectively regardless of the variety of housing designs that is finally built.
- When closed systems are mandatory, the possibilities of redesigning layouts to optimize the efficiency of using smaller pipes, fewer pumps, etc., should be considered. In addition, the design of smaller, standardized collection systems should be promoted.

- The total amount of impervious surface area should be minimized. More porous materials should be used for paving whenever possible, and grasses should be used to line the ditches and channels.
- Natural drainage channels should be used whenever possible.
- Surfaces and grading should be used to handle redistribution of water.
- Where soils are highly susceptible to erosion, runoff should be carefully controlled (one way of determining the likelihood of erosion is to measure the quantity of water, Q, before and after development).
- Road design in cross-section should take the needs of the drainage system into consideration. Where possible, cross-slope and drainage design should be used to reduce the need for inlets and manholes. The total lengths of curb and gutter should also be reduced.

implications for earth sheltered housing

The development of sites for earth sheltered housing should be planned with special sensitivity to designing for the management of stormwater runoff and the movement of water through the soils or available groundwater. Although in some ways it would seem expedient to remove all water from the site through closed systems, this strategy would directly conflict with the energy-efficient strategies enumerated above. On some sites, especially those with individual homes infilled among other types of housing, contained systems may be essential to collect the water before it runs off onto adjacent sites. Furthermore, contained systems are the only feasible system of collection for housing designs where the steepness of the slope required to berm the building can accelerate the runoff. It should be noted that the relative steepness of slope is the factor that most radically affects the design time of water concentration. When buildings are sited downhill on continuing slopes composed of sandy soils, the use of swales is recommended. Interceptor drainage systems are recommended on drier soils or highly erodible soils.

Planning that takes into account the entire development can also assure the provision of areas for drainage ditches or swales that feed retention and detention ponds. If such ponds are lined with native materials (i.e., plants that generally grow in those environmental conditions), the collection areas can also serve as designed amenities and provide open space. Ponds must be located in soils that allow for natural percolation. When the ideal design condition is to deliver water off-site as quickly as possible, thick, manicured grasses or rock-lined channels, rather than more native plantings, should be used.

If subsurface drainage foundation systems are necessary, they should be discharged into collection ponding areas whenever possible rather than carried to public collection systems. The sizes of ponding areas are calculated in relation to the time of concentration and design storm. More than is true for other utilities, this strategy is extremely useful to earth sheltered community layouts in maximizing the effectiveness of the building system. Soils that are excessively wet and/or subject to severe slippage under pressure should be avoided as possible building sites rather than drained by subsurface drainage, particularly when these types of soils are located at the foot of a hill. For multiple-unit developments of earth sheltered housing that step down hillsides, the structures may act to retain the soils and actually make the slope more buildable. In these cases an engineer must be consulted for assistance.

In addition to the systems that normally must be provided and paid for by the developer—sanitary sewer, water, roads, and stormwater drainage—other systems must directly supply energy to housing units for such needs as heating, cooling, lighting, and power for mechanical and electronic devices. In the past, these needs were met by conventional supply systems of fuels and electricity provided by large companies with large distribution networks. Typically, the developer did not pay for the initial cost of the distribution system. Today this may no longer be the most energy-efficient means of supplying energy. Just as it is necessary to explore alternatives for the design of buildings, roads, and the utility systems normally paid for by the developer, it is also necessary to consider alternatives that can provide more efficient, reliable, and environmentally acceptable systems of energy supply.

Most housing must be designed for a lifetime of thirty to one hundred years, yet there is great uncertainty over future energy use patterns and systems of supply. It is, of course, impossible to predict the future or recommend optimal systems. Nonetheless, many decisions made in planning and developing housing communities are based on assumptions about energy supply. In some cases these decisions will place unnecessary limits on future options. This section identifies some of the basic characteristics of various supply systems and summarizes physical planning and design considerations. The intention is to establish a framework through which alternative systems can be understood and included in the planning process. (A more complete description and discussion of the basic characteristics of these systems appears in appendix A.) Obviously, the goal of providing efficient, reliable, and environmentally acceptable systems of energy supply is applicable not only for earth sheltered housing but for any housing development.

In order to understand and make choices concerning energy systems for housing communities, it is first necessary to examine some basic characteristics of energy use. The energy-use patterns to be considered here are the actual end uses of energy in the housing unit (relative magnitudes of the end uses are shown in fig. 3-28). These uses do not include the energy required to transport, generate, or distribute the various fuels, but represent only the amount consumed in the housing unit. It is interesting to note that the great majority of energy is required in the form of heat. Almost 90 percent of the total energy use comprises space and hot water heating, cooking, and clothes drying. The remaining needs require energy in the form of light and power for mechanical and electrical devices.

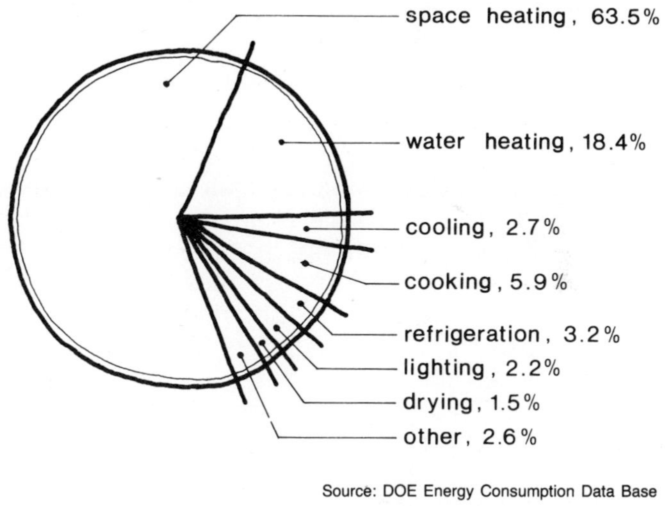
space heating, 63.5%
water heating, 18.4%
cooling, 2.7%
cooking, 5.9%
refrigeration, 3.2%
lighting, 2.2%
drying, 1.5%
other, 2.6%
Source: DOE Energy Consumption Data Base

3-28: residential energy consumption by end use (U.S.—1974)

The conventional sources of energy to supply these needs in housing are electricity, natural gas, and oil. Electricity, the only form of energy currently used for lighting and various appliances, accounts for about 10 percent of the total energy used in an average residence. It is highly unlikely that gas lamps and motors would ever displace electricity for these requirements. The predominant requirement of heating, however, can be met by any of the available fuel sources. It is important to distinguish between different fuel sources because they have different overall efficiencies. For example, 3.45 units of primary energy (coal, oil, gas, or nuclear) are required to deliver 1 unit of electrical energy to the building. This means that over two-thirds of the primary energy is lost in fuel extraction, transportation, power generation, and electricity distribution. The amount of primary energy is much lower for electricity generated by hydropower, because no fuel is consumed. Petroleum refining and distribution results in an overhead of 1.11 units for oil, while long-distance pumping of natural gas in pipelines adds 15 percent to its end use for an overhead of 1.15 units [3.9].

The relative amounts of the various fuels used in the entire residential sector, including their primary energy inputs, are indicated in the pie chart (fig. 3-29). Electricity accounts for the largest portion, since it requires such a high amount of source fuel to provide a unit of energy for a home. The percentage of electrical use in the residential sector for 1977 (45 percent) is considerably higher than the 26 percent used in 1960 or the 37 percent used in 1970 [3.10]. This dramatic increase in the use of electricity over the last twenty years indicates that an increasing portion of the energy required in the form of heat is being supplied by electricity. From an energy-efficiency point of view, this trend has been counterproductive, since electricity is only one of many ways to provide heat and is the least efficient from the viewpoint of total energy expended in the system.

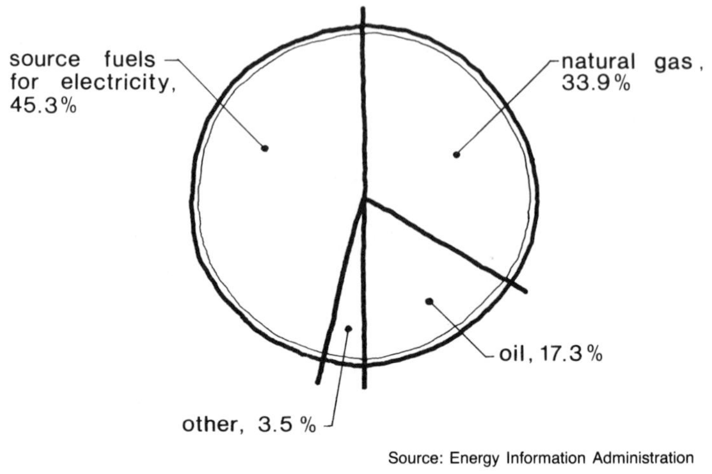

source fuels for electricity, 45.3%
natural gas, 33.9%
oil, 17.3%
other, 3.5 %
Source: Energy Information Administration

3-29: source fuels for residential sector (U.S.—1977)

Many of the problems related to continued reliance on these conventional systems of supply are widely documented. The conventional energy supply systems all have many positive characteristics, which have accounted for their widespread development. In times of reduced supply, however, they must be used more prudently, their inefficiencies minimized, and new sources found to supplement the old ones in meeting future needs. The strategies applicable to systems of supply can be classified into the following five categories:

increases in efficiency: Devices such as heat pumps, which are more efficient than electric furnaces, can increase the efficiency of energy supply. Efficiencies may also be increased by district heating, which can burn fuels more efficiently and generate electricity and heat at the same time. An important key to efficient systems is designing them at appropriate, economic scales.

appropriate matching of end use and fuel source: This strategy refers mainly to the use of high-quality energy (e.g., electricity) only for a task that requires energy in a lower quality form, such as heat. Although electricity is essential and flexible, it is wasteful to use it for space heating if a lower-quality source is available.

replacement of fossil fuels with renewable sources: Renewable sources, based on solar energy, range from direct solar heating to indirect sources such as wind and biomass fuels.

flexibility of fuel source: To ensure reliability despite potential shortages and interruptions of conventional supply, design strategies to provide for future flexibility are essential.

local control: The lack of community and individual control over energy supply can have negative political consequences. Ownership of systems by groups and individuals and participation in their operation can have political and social benefits but may cause management and control problems if not well supported, maintained, and operated.

In order to properly plan a housing community for the rather uncertain energy future, both the level of consumption and the systems of supply must be considered. The importance of the relationship between the level of energy consumption and the type of system and fuel source cannot be overemphasized. Certain systems, such as district heating, may be economically feasible with a certain level of consumption but totally unjustifiable if consumption is reduced. Although conservation has the potential to reduce all energy loads by enormous amounts, a minimal level of supply in the form of heat, light, and power for mechanical and electrical devices will always be required; thus, some type of supply system will always be necessary. As indicated in previous sections of this chapter, there is a link between energy supply requirements and the consumption and efficient disposal of water as well as solid waste generation and disposal. These systems not only consume energy but can also provide alternative fuel sources.

basic characteristics of energy supply systems

The identification and selection of appropriate energy supply systems is often oversimplified. Generalizations about sources or systems must be regarded with caution, since the feasibility of most systems depends on some very specific conditions related to climate, site, energy demand, and scale of project. Despite the relative uncertainty surrounding many of the alternatives, they do represent solutions to some of the serious problems with conventional energy systems. Figure 3-30 presents basic characteristics of the conventional systems of heat and electrical supply and of several alternative systems. A more complete evaluation of each of these systems appears in appendix A. Alternative systems may represent a change in the manner energy is generated and distributed, a change in the basic source of the energy, or both. The alternative systems included here do not include every theoretically possible source or manner of energy supply. Rather, they represent a selection of systems that are currently available or have sufficient potential to be an option in the near future.

In examining the potential for including alternative systems in development, the developer must first assess the technical state of the art for each system. As indicated in the chart, the on-site alternatives of electrical generation by wind or by combustion of biomass or fossil fuels are adequately developed from a technical point of view. Photovoltaic systems do work but technical breakthroughs to mass-produce them at a reasonable cost are still in the future. The alternatives for heat supply with active and passive solar heating and with district heating using a variety of renewable and nonrenewable sources are also technically developed to the point that they can be implemented.

After assessing the state of the art of the systems, the developer must determine their economic feasibility. Although it is difficult to generalize about economic feasibility, there appear to be three basic types of systems with different economic implications. The first type of system must be located near sources of otherwise wasted energy—i.e., district heating systems located near existing power plants or industries with waste heat. Such a system is likely to be feasible only for relatively high-density areas that have a substantial number of units to justify the capital investment of the system. A large, high-density development could benefit greatly from such a system, since the source of energy is basically free.

The second group of systems comprises district systems that are completely on-site and use fossil or biomass fuels to generate electricity and/or heat. These systems also require relatively high densities and a large enough number of customers to justify the initial capital expense of a central generation facility and distribution system. Unlike the district systems that use "free" wasted heat from existing power plants, a completely on-site system must import its own fuel, which represents an additional cost (an exception is a system that uses solid waste, which can provide a free fuel source).

The systems in the third group are those that use the sun and wind available on-site. These systems have greatly reduced fuel costs and do not require high densities or large numbers of units for the system to function efficiently. At this time, neither solar collectors for heat and electricity nor wind generators are generally considered economically competitive with conventional sources because of their high initial cost. The borderline economic feasibility of these systems may improve rapidly, however, with predicted rises in conventional fuel prices and predicted cost reductions accompanying the mass production of alternative systems. The simplest forms of passive solar heating, which do not necessarily involve large capital investment, appear to be feasible now.

3-30: basic characteristics of conventional and alternative systems of energy supply

system	type of energy supplied	source of energy	scale of system	limiting factors to development	key design and planning implications
conventional gas & oil furnaces	heat	• non-renewable fossil fuels	• heat generation in individual unit • fuel distribution regional scale	• rising prices & uncertain supply	• development must be located within existing distribution network
conventional electrical power grid	electricity	• non-renewable fossil fuels & nuclear reaction • renewable hydropower	• regional scale generation and distribution	• inefficiencies of generation, high cost of new plants	• none-available almost everywhere
district heating	heat	• non-renewable fossil fuels • renewable biomass & solar • waste from other processes	• on-site or off-site generation of heat • distribution at single development scale or larger	• uncertain economics: high density, large scale developments probably required to justify costs	• medium to high densities required • near source of waste heat or existing district system preferable
cogeneration	heat & electricity	• non-renewable fossil fuels • renewable biomass fuels	• on-site or off-site generation of heat • distribution at single development scale or larger	• uncertain economics: high density, large scale developments probably required to justify costs	• medium to high densities required
wind energy conversion system	electricity	• renewable wind	• generation and distribution at scale of single development or individual unit	• relative cost of initial equipment • economic methods of storage	• locate and preserve best areas on site for wind
photovoltaic solar system	electricity	• renewable solar	• collection and distribution at scale of single development or individual unit	• technical and economic break-throughs required in mass production • economic methods of storage	• preserve solar access for each unit or in a community area
active solar	heat	• renewable solar	• collection and distribution at scale of single development or individual unit	• relative cost of initial equipment	• preserve solar access for each unit or in a community area
passive solar	heat	• renewable solar	• collection at scale of individual unit	• none except for better under-standing	• preserve solar access for each unit
solar pond	heat	• renewable solar	• collection and distribution at scale of single development	• research at an early stage	• large water body must be available or created on site

In summarizing the physical planning implications of the alternative energy supply systems, it is important to emphasize that the plan should be based not only on the systems that are economically and technically feasible today but also on systems that may be feasible in the near future. The general priorities for physical planning are:

- Designing for passive solar systems—and for the potential future feasibility of active solar collectors for heat and photovoltaic cells for electricity—requires maximum solar access for each unit. If such access cannot be provided, then suitable areas within the development should be preserved for shared collection systems.
- The best sites for wind generation should be selected and incorporated into the community open space.
- District heating systems require higher densities and clustered units for economic feasibility. District systems will be most feasible when located near and coupled with existing sources of waste heat, such as power plants or industry.

Earth Sheltered Town Houses
Minneapolis, Minnesota.
Developer: Seward West Redesign
Architect: Close Associates

4 types of energy-efficient housing

introduction

One of the primary purposes of this study is to clarify the opportunities and limitations in building multiple-unit developments of earth sheltered housing. In particular, it is important to understand the kinds of building configurations that are possible with earth sheltered houses, the types of sites on which they can be built, and the potential densities of the various configurations. This is a complex task, since building and site design for earth sheltered housing can vary considerably. It is made even more complex because these variations include a number of building design features associated with solar and other energy-efficient types of houses as well as site design features employed in more conventional housing. In order to simplify this examination, the basic characteristics of energy-efficient housing are presented in this chapter and the site design considerations for energy-efficient housing are presented in chapter 5.

Since there is some overlap among earth sheltered, solar, and more conventional energy-efficient houses, exploring the building and site design characteristics of each type separately will help clarify their similarities and differences. It is important to remember that this is an artificial categorization; aspects of all three types of housing are often combined in one design. Nevertheless, this comparison is useful in identifying the critical design issues and most appropriate applications for each type of housing. The building and site design techniques shown in this chapter are based on generally accepted patterns for balancing human comfort requirements with climatic conditions in the cool and temperate areas that cover most of the United States. Although many of these patterns may also apply in warmer regions, local climatic conditions must always be understood in order to apply these concepts and techniques appropriately.

Earth sheltered, solar, and conventional well-insulated houses represent three general approaches to conserving energy used in heating and cooling a structure. The intent of this chapter is not to compare the actual energy-use performance of these different types of houses. With proper design and construction, any of the housing types can be built with exceptionally low heating and cooling requirements. The next chapter, however, will demonstrate that the physical characteristics of these energy-efficient units result in certain building configurations and site layouts that may or may not be efficient in other ways. For example, the benefits of building a certain type of unit—particularly an earth sheltered housing unit—should be considered in terms of its efficiency of land use as well as the road and utility layouts characteristic of that housing type.

This chapter is divided into four sections that discuss the basic characteristics of the following types of energy-efficient housing units:

- conventional energy-efficient housing
- solar housing
- earth sheltered housing—type 1: elevational
- earth sheltered housing—type 2: atrium

Earth sheltered housing is a general term that applies to a relatively new and still evolving type of housing. Although this innovativeness makes exact definitions difficult, two basic types of earth sheltered housing—elevational and atrium designs—will be considered here, since they are commonly recognized and have fundamentally different characteristics. In addition to defining the four housing types listed above, this chapter will evaluate the basic physical characteristics, general land-use implications, and critical design issues and variations related to each.

conventional housing

A number of architectural and site design strategies can be applied to conventional housing to make it more energy efficient. Since solar energy and earth sheltering are treated separately in following sections of this chapter, conventional housing as discussed here includes energy-efficient techniques that do not depend on solar access or use of earth. Primary among these are increased insulation, extremely well-sealed structures, decreased window area, and nighttime insulation. In recent years improvements in standards for insulation have brought about a corresponding reduction in energy required for heating. More effective caulking and sealing of structures to reduce infiltration has also been implemented, although such measures are more difficult to describe and control than insulation values.

The most dramatic reductions in heating energy that have been achieved by these methods have been reported in several so-called superinsulated houses. Such houses use very substantial quantities of insulation (perhaps R-30 in the walls and R-60 in the roof) along with meticulous sealing against infiltration. These strategies have proven very effective in reducing energy used for space heating—so much so that some superinsulated houses have heating requirements that are equivalent to those associated with the best solar and earth sheltered houses [4.1]. In the most successful superinsulated houses, the windows are mainly oriented to the south for passive solar gain. The basic energy-conserving characteristics of these houses do not seem to depend on this southern orientation, however, but rather on the very well-insulated envelope. Thus, for purposes of comparison in this study, the conventional energy-efficient house is defined as a completely above-grade structure with no particular orientation toward the sun.

This conventional approach to energy-efficient housing results in basic architectural and site design characteristics similar to those of most existing housing. Housing units can be designed in a wide variety of configurations, although compact shapes and two-story houses in particular are more efficient, since less exterior surface is exposed to the weather for a given volume of space. Because solar gain is not an integral part of a conventional house, window orientation is based on factors such as view and room arrangement (fig. 4-1).

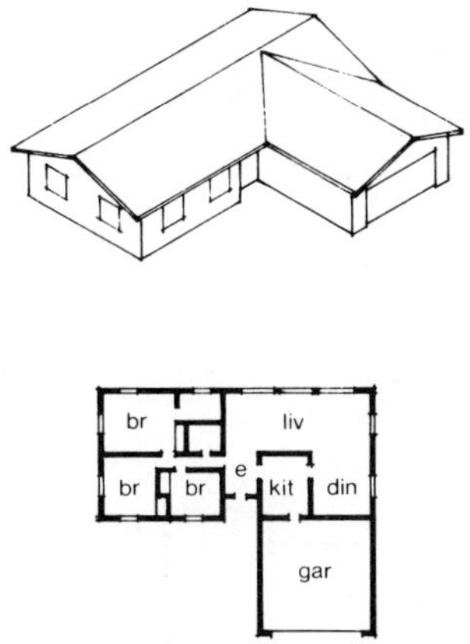

br
liv
e
br
br
kit
din
gar

4-1: conventional single-family detached housing

Conventional houses are usually arranged so that the entry side is relatively close to the street and a private outdoor space is at the back of the house. A final basic characteristic of conventional housing is that it is normally limited to slopes of less than 15 percent. This slope limitation is typically used as a guideline for conventional development, since road and house siting and construction become more difficult and costly on slopes exceeding 15 percent. Although certain variations of conventional housing—such as walk-out basements and split-level designs—can be adapted to slopes in some cases, conventional houses are defined as completely above grade in this study to simplify the comparison with earth sheltered housing. Conventional well-insulated housing with these basic characteristics is generally appropriate and acceptable to the housing market in all parts of the country that have a heating requirement.

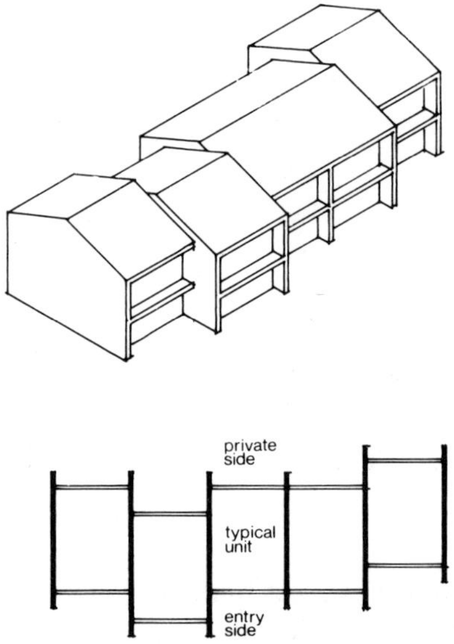
private side
typical unit
entry side

4-2: conventional single-family attached housing

The fact that conventional housing is restricted to slopes of less than 15 percent is one important land-use implication of this type of housing. While it is, of course, possible to build houses on steeper land through extensive grading and retaining of the earth to form flatter areas, site preparation costs more, and additional land is usually required. A principal advantage of conventional housing is that, because the shape and spacing of the units are not as physically restricted as they are in solar and earth sheltered houses, a number of very efficient land-use strategies—for both detached and attached units—can be employed. These techniques are discussed in chapter 5.

Conventional well-insulated housing units can be attached in a number of configurations that contribute to both energy- and land-use efficiency. Typically, single-family attached units are combined into duplexes, triplexes, quadplexes, or town houses. The duplex units may be side by side or atop one another, whereas triplexes—similar to town houses—are generally attached in rows with common side walls (fig. 4-2). Although windows in town houses are usually limited to the two exposed walls, the room layout and general relationship to the outdoors are similar to those of detached houses. Normally, each town house unit has a separate exterior entrance, and one side of the house is a public entry while the other opens to a private outdoor space. One important design consideration with town house units is the individual identity of each unit. The potentially monotonous and somewhat dehumanizing effect of long rows of units is often eliminated by staggering units and providing varied facades and roof shapes. The exterior surface area of a town house unit is 20 to 50 percent less than the area of a comparable detached unit.

Housing units can also be attached into multiple-unit structures such as low- and high-rise apartment buildings. The units are stacked vertically and are usually arranged along both sides of a central corridor, resulting in a single window wall in each unit (fig. 4-3). This type of arrangement results in units that have an exterior surface area 50 to 80 percent less than that of a comparable detached unit. Because they lack separate entrances and private exterior spaces, units in multiple-unit buildings differ considerably from town house units.

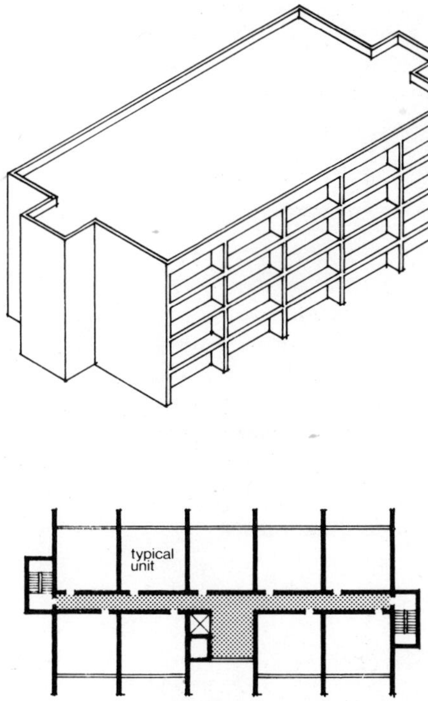
typical unit

4-3: conventional multiple-unit housing

solar housing

Generally, solar houses can be defined as dwellings that use the radiant energy from the sun to provide space heating and, in some cases, hot water heating. They are commonly divided into two categories: houses that employ passive systems and those with active systems. Completely passive systems collect, store, and distribute heat by natural means without the use of mechanical equipment such as blowers and ducts or separate collector panels. This usually means that the structure, spaces, and windows of the house are part of the system. Active systems, on the other hand, generally consist of collector panels, storage tanks, and pipes or ducts for distribution of heated fluids. Solar houses frequently have hybrid systems, which combine active and passive features. A number of designs and systems are classified as passive. As shown in figure 4-4, the basic types of systems are:

direct gain: In this system the building itself acts as the collector. The windows admit sunlight, which is stored in massive floors, walls, or ceilings. Houses that utilize direct gain—the most common approach to incorporating passive solar features—generally look more like conventional housing than do those houses that incorporate the other passive systems listed below. Proper orientation, a careful balance of window sizes, thermal mass, and the use of nighttime insulation over the windows are all required to maximize the solar gain. It is also possible to benefit from direct gain simply by placing more windows on the south side of the house. Although such a solution will not maximize energy performance, it generally will improve it.

thermal storage wall: In this type of system, the sunlight strikes a massive wall of masonry or water located inside the glazing, between the sun and the living space. Heat is stored and transmitted to the space by convection and radiation.

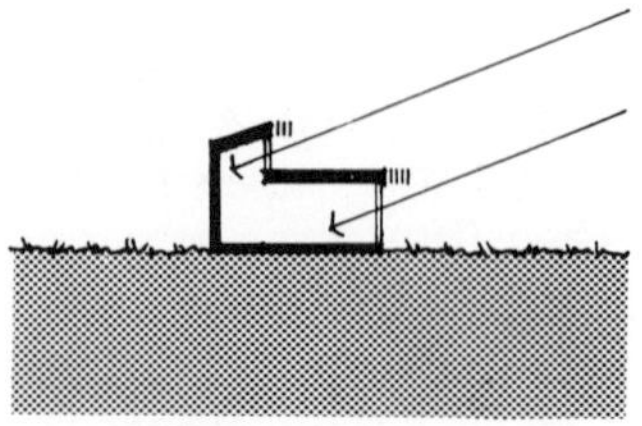

direct gain

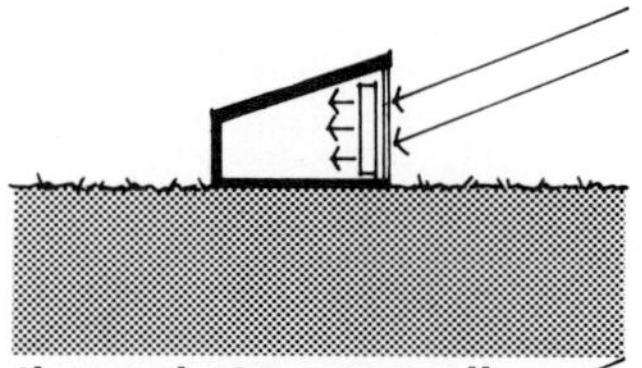

thermal storage wall

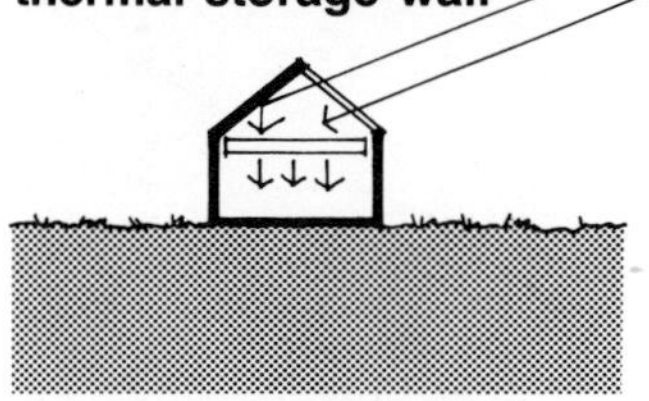

thermal storage roof

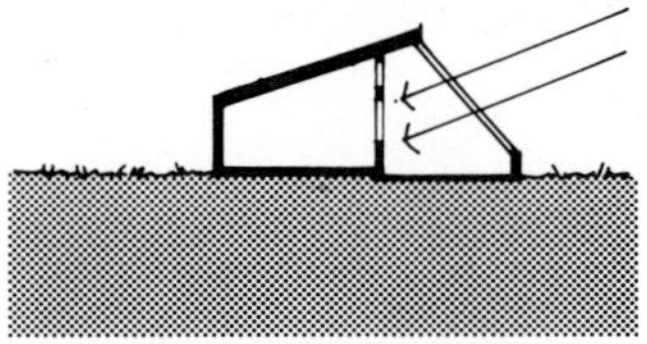

sunspace/greenhouse

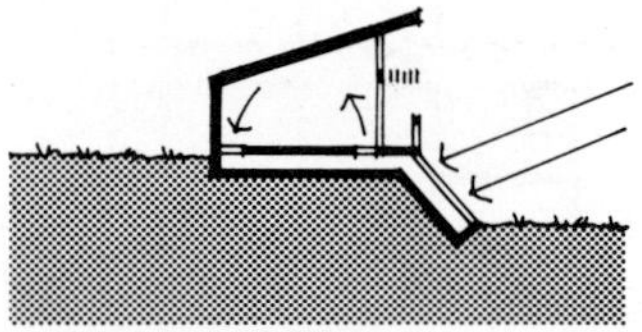

convective loop

4-4: basic types of passive solar systems

thermal storage roof: This passive solar feature acts much like a thermal storage wall. Sunlight strikes the massive roof, which is usually covered with water-filled bags, and the heat is transmitted to the space by radiation. Insulation must be placed over the mass at night to prevent heat loss to the night sky. In more northern latitudes, reflectors should be used, as shown in figure 4-4.

sunspace/greenhouse: Here, the passive solar feature is a glass-enclosed space, attached to a house, that collects a great amount of heat during the day. The sunspace/greenhouse can effectively be used to contribute to heating the house when warm air collected in the space is circulated into the house during the day. Heat is stored in a massive wall between the sunspace and the house. An attached sunspace or greenhouse has great potential for passive heating, since it can be attached at any time and the extra capital investment results not only in reduced energy, but in an attractive and marketable extra space as well.

convective loop: This type of system is not very different from an active system of solar collectors. As a result of the location of the collectors relative to the house and storage mass, heat is transferred by natural convection rather than by mechanical means.

Passive solar houses using one or a combination of these systems can obviously be built in a variety of configurations. In the simplest and most efficient design, all of the windows are placed on the south wall, and the house is elongated in an east-west direction to provide direct solar access to all living spaces (fig. 4-5). The interior spaces are arranged with storage areas, utilities, and garage on the north side of the house and living spaces on the south. Although entries facing prevailing winter winds should be protected, the house can be entered from any side. Another configuration, a two-level house with all spaces facing south, results in a more compact shape. Although this layout appears applicable only to a direct gain approach, it may be characteristic of any of the other systems, which may be used in combination with direct gain.

A direct southern orientation is generally considered optimal for the maximum amount of incident solar radiation on a vertical surface. There is some variance in optimal orientation, however, depending on the type of passive solar system employed and the specific climate. The orientation of many passive solar houses utilizing direct gain is adjusted toward the southeast, to warm the house with sunlight earlier in the day and—in climates with prevailing winter winds from the northwest—to protect the open side of the house. According to Victor Olgyay in *Design with Climate,* the optimal orientation for a house in a cool climate (e.g., that of Minneapolis) is 12 degrees east of south [4.2]. For passive solar houses with thermal storage walls, however, the optimal orientation in many locations is slightly west of south. This is because the solar radiation received later in the day is more easily stored for use during the night when it is needed. In the *Passive Solar Design Handbook,* Douglas Balcomb suggests that the orientation of the solar glazing should lie between 20 degrees east and 32 degrees west of true south [4.3]. This range is based on

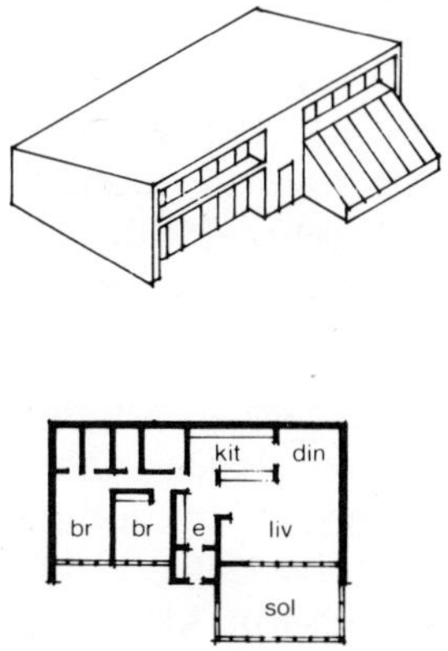

kit
din
br
br
e
liv
sol

4-5: passive solar housing unit

calculations for thermal storage walls in several cities, each with a different optimal orientation.

It is important to note that the orientation can be varied considerably to the east or west of south with little change in performance. Based on Balcomb's calculations, there is only a 20 percent decrease in the optimal performance of thermal storage walls at 42 degrees east or 54 degrees west of south [4.3]. Even greater possible variations to the east or west still provide solar radiation in particular spaces in the morning or evening and substantial heating during the spring and fall months. The drawback of east/west window orientation is the undesirably large summer heat gain, which must be blocked in some manner.

Houses that employ active solar systems are not quite as restricted in design as passive solar houses, since they need not be integrated into the structure of the house. Although there are many different types of collectors, the design implications are generally the same for almost all of the systems. Collectors are usually mounted on the roof or south wall of the structure, and the general orientation of the houses is very similar to the orientation for passive houses (fig. 4-6). Almost any shape and layout, however, is acceptable for an active solar system, assuming that it is not combined with passive gain. Another important characteristic of active systems is that the collectors do not have to be attached directly to the house, but may be placed elsewhere on the site (e.g., on a garage or on the ground). In some cases active collectors for several houses could be combined; heat could then be distributed from a central collection and storage area. This type of system would be similar to district heating.

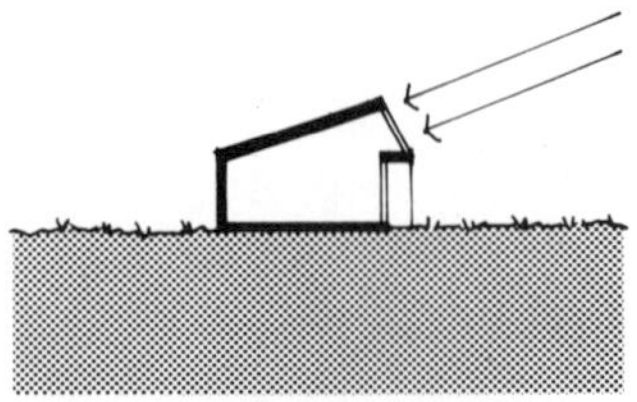

attached solar collector

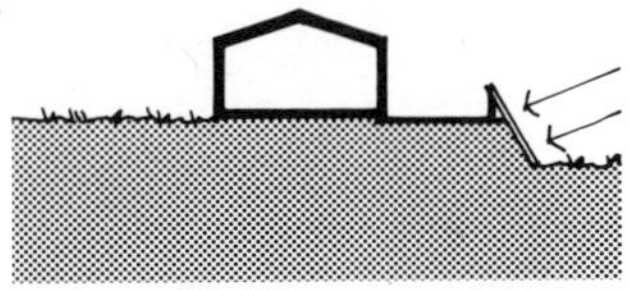

detached solar collector

4-6: active solar systems

Although the designs of passive and active solar houses differ in many ways, they also have many general similarities. In order to compare conventional, solar, and earth sheltered housing, a few basic characteristics of both passive and active systems will be assumed. Generally, solar houses must be oriented to the south, and the entire south wall and roof must be exposed to the sun at all times of the year. This restriction would allow any of the passive systems to function efficiently (with the possible exception of the convective loop, which may require an unshaded south yard as well); it would also allow for an active system to be mounted on the house. Houses with detached collectors are not included here, since their basic characteristics are similar to those of conventional housing. In this chapter it is also assumed that solar houses are completely above grade, since combination solar/earth sheltered houses are discussed in chapter 5. Thus, like conventional above-grade houses, solar houses are restricted to slopes of 15 percent or less.

The land-use implications of solar houses are quite different from those for conventional housing. In order to provide solar access for each house, the houses can either be spread out on rather large lots that ensure flexibility in house placement without interfering with solar access for neighboring structures, or they can be placed somewhat closer together in a coordinated manner with restrictions on building heights and setbacks. Because the houses can be placed closer together on south-facing slopes (i.e., slopes less than 15 percent), they can make much more efficient use of land than those that face north.

Although the efficiency and appropriateness of passive solar and active solar systems vary considerably in different parts of the country, solar houses in some form appear to be a reasonable concept nearly everywhere. Only in hot areas with virtually no heat requirement or in extremely cloudy areas would their design be a disadvantage. It can be argued that some solar systems are economically unfeasible in colder regions and, therefore, that only conservation measures are warranted in those climates. It can also be argued that some passive systems have only been developed and tested in more moderate climates. Nevertheless, designing houses for solar access is still important because of the great future potential for technical breakthroughs and changes in economic feasibility of solar systems.

Housing with passive and active solar systems can be attached in the same basic configurations as conventional housing, including duplexes, rowhouses, and low-rise—or even high-rise—multiple-unit structures. Single-family attached housing units designed to receive solar energy directly into each unit differ from conventional attached units in two basic ways. The primary difference is in orientation: rows of town houses must extend east-west so that each unit has a south-facing window wall. Moreover, the units themselves may be more elongated in the east-west direction than are typical town houses so that most of the rooms in each unit include south-facing windows. This type of room arrangement may not be essential, however, if the heat can be transferred from the rooms on the south side to the rooms on the north.

Multiple-unit structures present a more difficult challenge in designing to provide solar exposure for each unit. If typical apartment buildings with double-loaded corridors are placed on an east-west axis, half the units have complete southern exposure, while the remaining units—which face north—receive no direct southern exposure. If these same buildings are placed on a north-south axis, the direct east and west orientation of the units provides limited solar gain in the winter, when it is needed, and excessive gain in summer, when it is undesirable. In larger buildings the transfer of heat from units on the south to units on the north is difficult because the fire walls prevent air movement. In addition, central heating systems decrease the effectiveness of solar input in reducing the building energy load, since tenants are not billed individually for their energy consumption. The simplest solution is to provide direct access to all units by extending the building along the east-west axis and placing units only on the south side of the corridor. Unfortunately, buildings utilizing such single-loaded corridors are more costly to construct because of the increased space devoted to corridors. It is possible to compromise by facing the majority of the units to the south, southeast, or southwest and a few units to the north, as shown in figure 4-7. Another solution is to use more complex unit arrangements, e.g., two-story units that reduce total corridor space. The two-story units also allow for cross-ventilation, which often is a problem in typical double-loaded corridor buildings.

With town house and multiple-unit structures, it is possible to use only active solar collection systems and to ignore the passive gain for each unit. These buildings would not be restricted in orientation, since only the rooftops may need exposure to the sun.

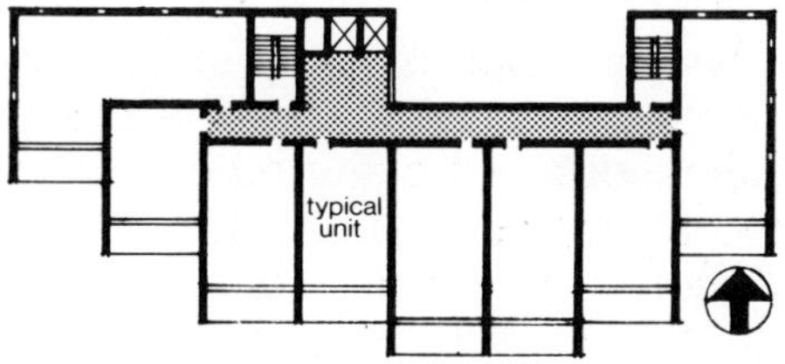
typical unit

4-7: multiple-unit solar housing

earth sheltered housing: elevational

Earth sheltered housing is a general term referring to structures that use the earth to reduce both heating and cooling requirements. The superior energy performance associated with earth sheltering is due in part to the use of earth berms, which provide protection from wind, thus reducing infiltration. Moreover, the surfaces of the structure are exposed to more moderate temperatures below grade than occur on the surface. In addition, the mass of the earth creates a seasonal time lag, resulting in warmer winter temperatures and cooler summer temperatures. Finally, many earth sheltered structures are designed to take advantage of either passive or active solar energy. Although there is a wide variety of earth sheltered designs—all of which have different design and site planning characteristics—it is convenient for the purposes of this study to divide these designs into two basic categories: the elevational and the atrium.

By far the most common type of earth sheltered house is that which is bermed with earth on three sides, leaving one exposed elevation (fig. 4-8). Sometimes referred to as an elevational house, it may be covered with earth on the roof or have a conventional, well-insulated roof. The site planning considerations are basically the same regardless of whether earth covers the roof. In most parts of the country, the optimal orientation for an elevational house is with the window wall to the south or southeast to maximize the passive solar heat gain. The earth berms completely protect the house from northwest winds, which are the prevailing winter winds in Minnesota and many other northern states. The shape of the house is usually elongated in the east-west direction to increase exposure to the sun and provide adequate light and ventilation to all rooms. The most important difference between conventional and earth sheltered elevational houses is the relationship of the house to the surrounding earth. Although they can be

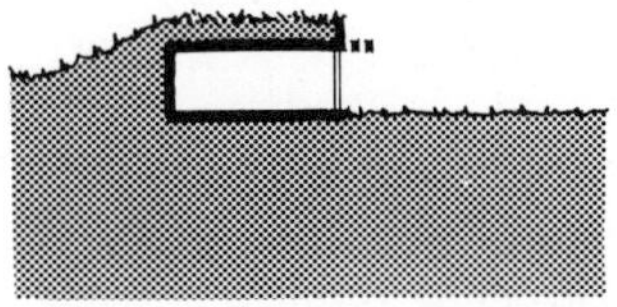

section—bermed and covered

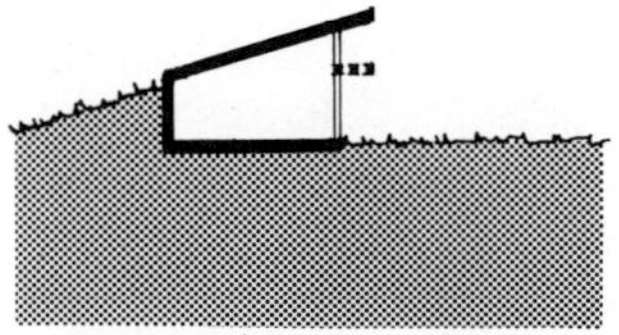

section—bermed only

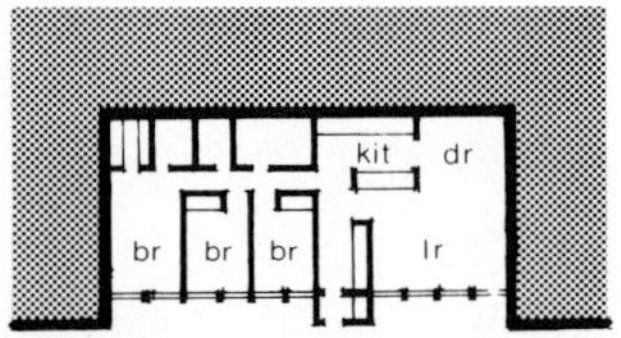

kit
dr
br
br
br
lr

plan

4-8: elevational housing unit

built on flat land with berms formed around the house, elevational houses are more suited to sloping topography where they can be set into a hillside. Under the right conditions, they can be built on slopes of up to 50 percent.

With respect to overall land use, elevational houses have both advantages and disadvantages. In general, the elongated geometry, area required for berms and drainage, and spacing required for solar access contribute to a need for larger lots and a more spread-out arrangement than is the case with clustered conventional houses, particularly for homes built on flat land. The ability to build on steeper slopes is, however, a definite advantage, and the density can be increased as the slope increases. Thus, elevational houses can use more of the available land on a given site than can conventional housing, which is limited to slopes no greater than 15 percent. For steeper slopes, however, only south-, southeast-, and southwest-facing slopes are suitable if the houses are to be oriented for passive solar gain.

Although little research has been done relating the performance of earth sheltered structures to specific climates, they are apparently applicable in a variety of climates because of the potential benefits during both cooling and heating seasons. Since earth sheltered structures are also appropriate in hot climates where cooling is the predominant concern, orientation to the south for maximum solar gain is not always a necessary characteristic. In cooler areas orientation to the south may not always be possible or desirable because of amenities or topography. Energy-saving benefits from earth sheltering can be achieved with other orientations, although the passive solar performance of the house is diminished in comparison with a southerly orientation. Since it is desirable to combine passive solar with earth sheltering in most parts of the country, an orientation generally to the south is assumed in the following discussion of architectural and site planning considerations unless otherwise noted.

As with conventional and passive solar houses, elevational units can be combined to form various attached configurations. Two-level or side-by-side duplexes, as well as longer rows of attached town-house-type units, can be built as elevational designs. Attached units of any type generally save on construction costs, land, and energy. Since elevational units would generally be attached on the shorter east-west wall, the energy savings may not be as dramatic as for conventional units that are attached on the longer wall. Construction costs, however, would still be affected considerably as a result of the reduced amount of heavily reinforced and waterproofed exterior wall required. Attached elevational units also require less land for berms.

It seems unlikely that the elevational concept would be applied to larger multifamily structures that are similar to conventional low-rise apartments. Although the units could be single-loaded as with passive solar buildings, a completely vertical, multiple-story bermed building would be difficult and costly to build. Retaining an earth berm height of 30 feet (9 m) or more would incur high structural costs, and a site with a very steep slope would be required. A far better and more likely solution would be housing units that step up the hillside; such a development would be easier and less expensive to construct. Although these hillside units could be detached dwellings or rowhouses, large multifamily buildings with enclosed corridors and vertical circulation are also possible. Examples of attached units on slopes of up to 50 percent are shown in chapter 5.

The basic design for an elevational unit shown in figure 4-8 can have many variations. Some of these variations affect the shape and orientation of the unit as well as the lot size and site planning. For example, while a two-story elevational house results in a more compact, less elongated plan, it often requires larger berms or a steeper slope to build on than does a one-story structure (fig. 4-9). Elevational units also may have different means of providing more natural light and ventilation, such as skylights or window openings that penetrate the berms (fig. 4-10). Some designs provide an almost continuous row of small windows along the north side of the house for cross-ventilation—a design feature that reduces the size of the berms, as shown in figure 4-11. If the berms are diminished considerably or even eliminated, a house with well-insulated walls and an earth-covered roof can still provide summer cooling benefits. Very small berms are associated with architectural and site planning implications more similar to those for conventional or passive solar houses, rather than typical earth sheltered elevational designs.

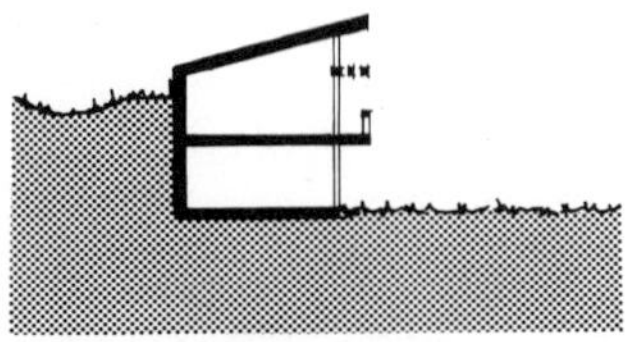

4-9: section

One very important design consideration for elevational houses is the entry. Although the house is typically entered through the single exposed elevation, a separate entry can also be created through the berm on the north side of the house or from the east or west end. All of these variations can be designed to work successfully, but each has advantages and disadvantages. For example, an advantage of entering through the exposed south side is the simplicity of construction and the protection of the house from winter winds. A disadvantage is the problem of having the public entry on the same side as the private outdoor spaces. Thus, a house located on the north side of a street with a south entry may have less yard space and privacy than a house that has a north entry and is located on the other side of the street.

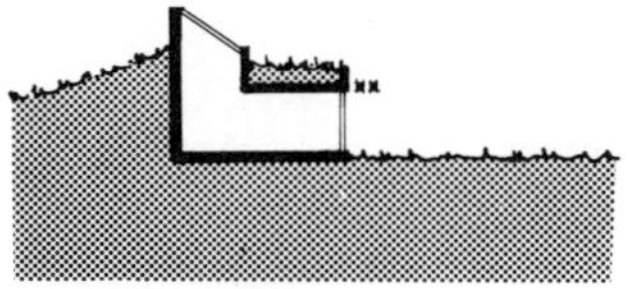

4-10: section

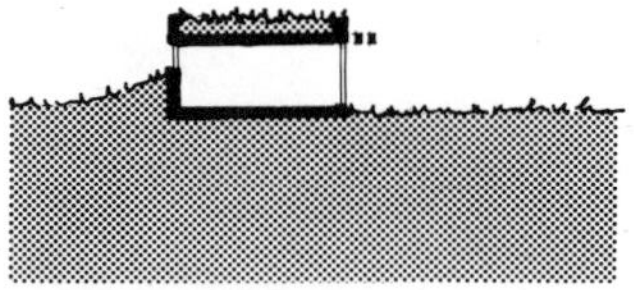

4-11: section

Designing a successful entry is complicated by the relationship of the house to the garage. Although an attached earth-covered garage is often desired, it is more expensive than a conventional garage. In addition, driveway access can be difficult if the floor level is below street level. An alternative is to place a conventional garage—which may or may not be attached to the house—at street level. Although it solves the access and cost problems, such a garage may appear too prominent next to a house that is recessed into the earth. This architectural problem deserves special attention, since a development of several houses could result in an environment dominated by garages. If the houses are bermed and have conventional roofs, the situation is not as problematic. These related concerns of entry and garage design, which obviously affect site design for the individual lot as well as for an entire cluster of houses, are discussed more fully in chapter 5.

A final design consideration with elevational houses is the stark and uninteresting architecture that can result from a single, long, flat facade. This is an even greater concern with attached units, where there is a tendency to create long, uninterrupted rows of this type of housing to prevent units from casting shadows on each other and to simplify earthwork and structural systems. Unfortunately, this tendency can result in buildings that lack variety or a sense of individuality, as in figure 4-12. Conventional town houses are often intentionally designed with staggered facades and varying roof heights to alleviate this problem. Although these same techniques may not be as practical for earth sheltered buildings, the design concepts of variety and individuality must be maintained. Greenhouses, decks, sunshades, and rooms extending out from the exposed wall, as shown in figure 4-13, can add variety without complicating the basic structure. Detached garages can also define outdoor space and relieve monotony. Some flexibility can also be exercised in orienting windows and allowing some shadows to be cast from building projections. Figure 4-14 illustrates how variety can be achieved with southeast and southwest orientations without creating an overly complex structure.

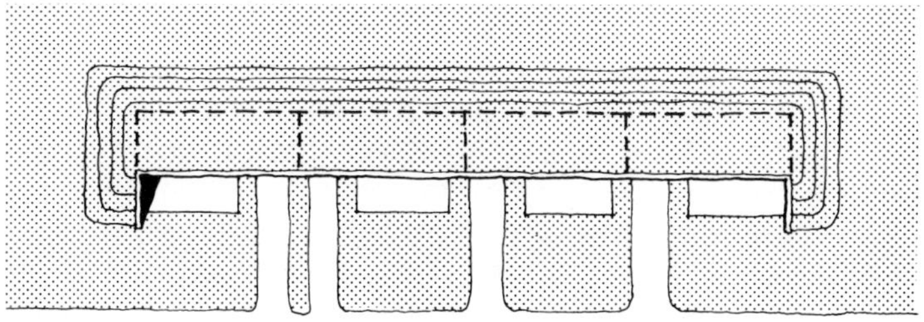

4-12: site plan—attached units

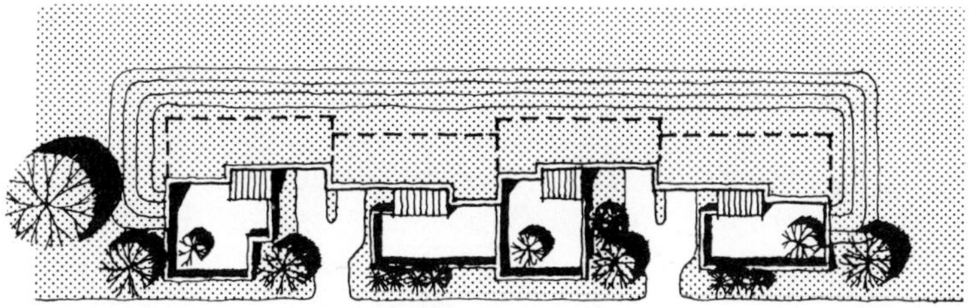

4-13: site plan—attached units

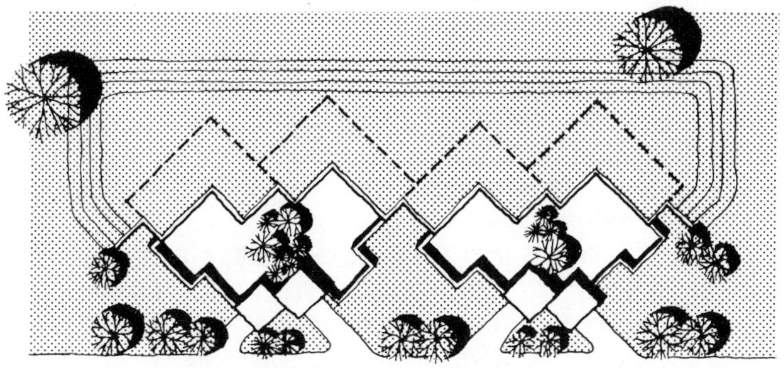

4-14: site plan—attached units

The second commonly recognized type of earth sheltered house is the atrium house, in which rooms are arranged around a courtyard. In its simplest form, all of the spaces have windows opening onto the atrium, and the outside walls and roof are completely covered with earth. The resulting shape is close to a square. If it had no other openings, the house would be entered through a stairway in the courtyard; it is more typical, however, for entry to occur on an outside wall, as shown in figure 4-15. The surrounding earth berms protect against winter winds from any direction and almost completely eliminate air infiltration. As with the elevational house, the large amount of contact with more moderate earth temperatures assists in reducing both heating and cooling loads. One key difference between an atrium and elevational design is that the atrium does not depend on any specific orientation. It is possible, nevertheless, to benefit from passive solar gain by making the courtyard large enough to allow sunlight to strike the walls, and by placing the most active living spaces on the north side of the atrium (where the windows face south). A typical one-level atrium house with a large, square shape is most easily constructed on flat land, although slopes of up to 15 percent can be used.

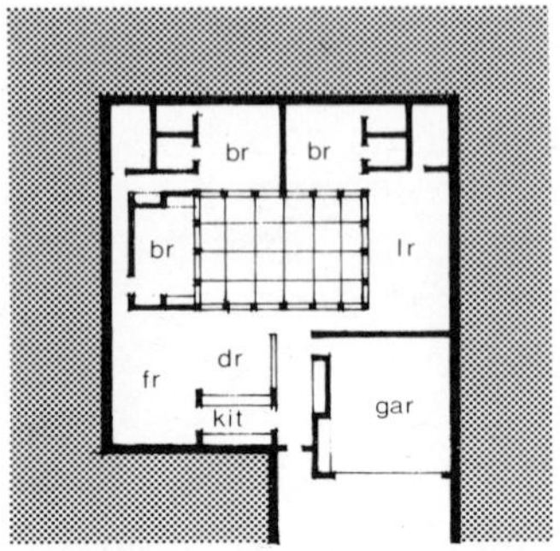
br
br
br
lr
fr
dr
kit
gar

plan

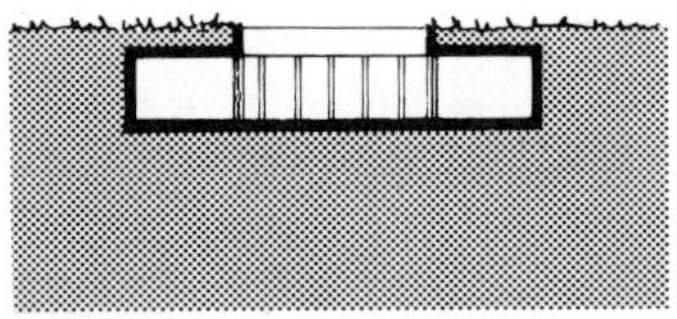

section

4-15: atrium housing unit

The land-use implications of individual earth sheltered atrium units are similar to those of elevational units in that relatively large lots are usually necessary to provide an adequate area for earth berms and drainage around the houses. Even though lot sizes can be reduced somewhat by completely submerging an atrium house below the existing grade so that no berming is necessary, mininum lots for atrium houses are still likely to be larger than the smallest lots for conventional housing. Two potential advantages of earth sheltered units compared to above-grade units are the additional outdoor space available on the roof and the appearance of a less dense, built-up environment. Although both of these advantages could contribute to more efficient land use with atrium houses, it is not clear that efficient land use would always take place. Nor is it clear to what extent rooftop open space and a greener appearance would compensate for increased densities. A final overall land-use implication for earth sheltered atrium houses relates to the inability, as in conventional housing, to use slopes greater than 15 percent for these types of house. On the other hand, since atrium designs do not depend on a southerly orientation in the same way that passive solar houses do, all slopes under 15 percent are equally usable for atrium houses. In fact, an atrium design may be a very effective solution on a 10-percent, north-facing slope.

Atrium-type houses can generally be considered appropriate in most regions of the country. The wind protection afforded by an atrium design is a definite benefit in colder climates, and the protection from desert heat by courtyard designs has long been recognized in hot, arid regions. Here again, the substantial amount of earth contact and the surrounding mass have both heating and cooling season benefits. In the more hot and humid areas of the country, atrium houses may be less appropriate unless they are carefully designed to maximize natural ventilation. An important difference between atrium houses in different regions is that, in warm climates, atriums can be larger and may be used for circulation between spaces throughout the year, whereas in colder climates, open courtyards are unusable in winter, so that circulation must be enclosed in corridors around the atrium. This limitation can render the design of an atrium house in a cold climate complex and inefficient. One possible solution—a glass cover over the courtyard—will increase the temperatures in and usefulness of the open space in the winter but may introduce fire exit problems from sleeping areas if the atrium space is relied on for escape purposes.

As with the other housing types, atrium units can be combined into a variety of attached configurations. Two or more units could be attached along common walls, resulting in the energy, cost, and land-use efficiencies associated with any attached units. A few basic patterns for attached atrium units are presented in chapter 5. The basic shape of the unit and the need for light and privacy in the individual courtyards makes vertical stacking of this type of unit unfeasible. Thus, multiple-unit atrium structures similar to conventional apartments are not possible. The atrium concept could, however, be applied to a multiple-unit structure in a different manner so that several units faced into a much larger atrium that served as common open space. In such a case, the design of the individual units would be very similar to that of elevational units.

Unlike earth sheltered elevational houses, which can easily provide exterior views, the basic atrium house (fig. 4-15) is oriented almost exclusively inward. This type of design is most appropriate in an area without attractive views and, perhaps, on sites with undesirable or noisy surroundings. Disadvantages associated with the basic atrium house include the difficulty of arranging rooms around a single courtyard, the need to provide a public entry that is not through the private court, problems in providing adequate natural ventilation, and the difficulty of creating a good relationship of the house to roads, parking, and/or garages.

To alleviate these problems, a number of design variations can be used that make the design more complex but result in more livable and accessible houses. For example, opening one side of the courtyard to the outside (fig. 4-16) and placing the floor only a few feet below grade creates a partial view out and a better

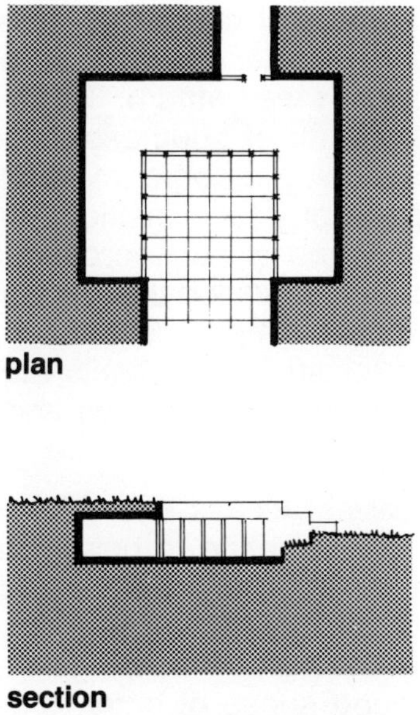
plan
section

4-16: open atrium design

transition to the outdoors. A separate public entry could also be built into the berm to keep the courtyard private. Another variation is the use of two or more courtyards. This type of design makes room arrangement easier, especially for larger houses. In figure 4-17 one atrium is open as an entry court, and the second is a fully enclosed private space. Opening up the courtyards to the surrounding landscape affects the orientation and allowable slope characteristics somewhat. In most parts of the country, it is desirable to orient the open side of the courtyard to the south or southeast for maximum solar gain and wind protection. Building on a sloping site, rather than a completely flat one, may also be slightly more desirable.

A more radical change from the basic atrium scheme is the opening of one complete side of the house so that it is a combination of an atrium and an elevational design (fig. 4-18). This design solves many of the view and entry problems cited above. Because the basic characteristics of elevational houses are more restrictive, however, they will definitely affect the orientation and allowable slope for this type of design. A large, exposed elevation presents much greater opportunity for passive solar heating than does a small atrium. Thus, orientation toward the southwest, south, or southeast becomes important. In addition, sloping topography is more desirable than flat topography for elevational houses in order to prevent large berms or sunken courtyards with no view. Combined atrium/elevational units would generally be deeper than a simple elevational unit. The greater depth required for such units limits their use to slopes of 10 percent for detached houses and up to 20 percent for attached units.

A final variation that solves access and view problems is the addition of above-grade space to below-grade spaces around an atrium (fig. 4-19). This is particularly effective for defining space on the site, relating the structure aesthetically to other above-grade buildings such as garages, providing a good sense of entry, and providing access to the earth-covered roof. As with other design

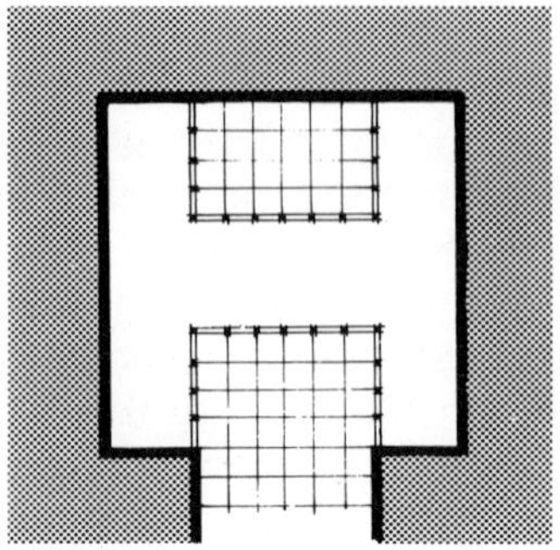

plan

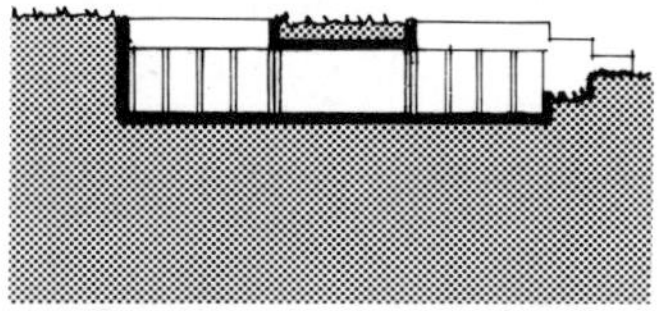

section

4-17: two atrium design

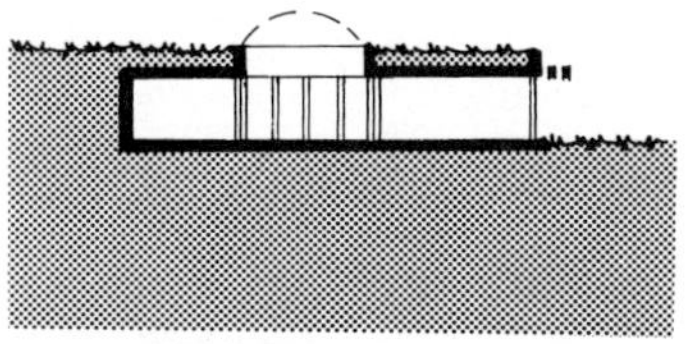

4-18: section

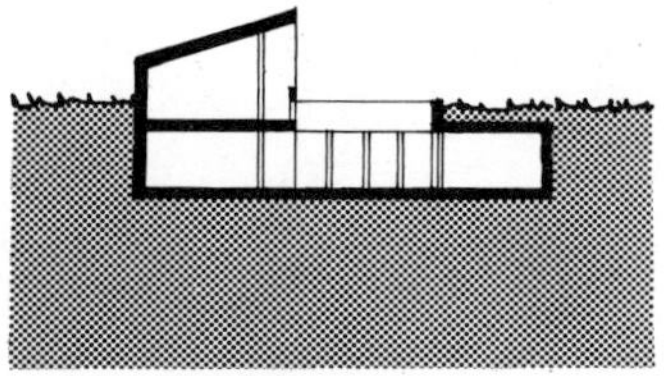

4-19: section

variations, orientation is affected by an aboveground element. The second-story portion of the building should be placed on the north side of the atrium so that it does not shade the courtyard. Placement on the east or west sides is less desirable but may be an acceptable compromise in some cases. In a warm climate, of course, the emphasis on passive solar orientation may be less critical.

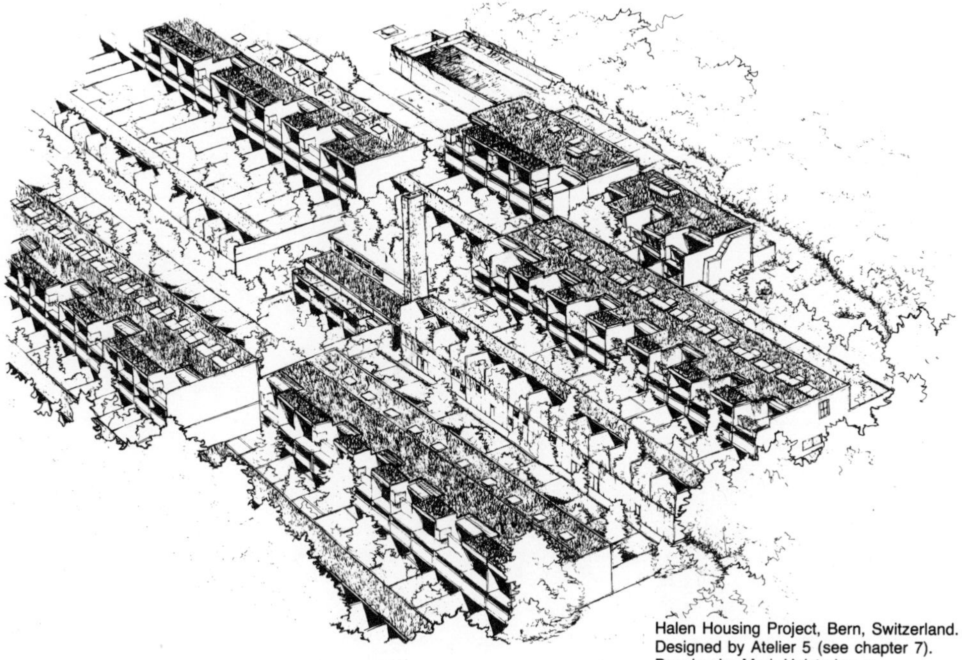

Halen Housing Project, Bern, Switzerland.
Designed by Atelier 5 (see chapter 7).
Drawing by Mark Heisterkamp.

5 site design for energy-efficient housing

introduction

This chapter examines site design implications, including typical lot sizes, layouts, densities, and various site design issues, for the four types of housing—conventional well-insulated, solar, earth sheltered elevational, and earth sheltered atrium—described in chapter 4. Each housing type is examined first in terms of detached units and then in terms of various attached configurations. Some of the key characteristics of each housing type are compared in the summary near the end of the chapter. Finally, this chapter includes a number of additional energy-efficient site and building design considerations that were not mentioned in the previous chapter because they apply to all of the energy-efficient housing types.

The site design discussion that follows is based on generalized housing types with generalized site characteristics. The many possible variations in housing unit size and design can modify the layouts and densities illustrated in the examples provided in this chapter. Moreover, these designs are mainly based on responses to the Minnesota climate. In Minnesota, where winters are the predominant concern, protection from cold winds from the north and west and maximization of solar gain are primary goals. Although these characteristics are generally appropriate in much of the northern United States, local climatic variations must be considered.

A number of factors shape site design for conventional residential buildings. Principal among these are the layout of roads and utility systems (discussed in chapter 3) and the zoning regulations of the community, which specify the size, shape, and placement of units. Although each community zoning ordinance has its own definitions and classifications of housing types, most ordinances have at least three categories, which correspond to low-, medium-, and high-density housing. The lowest density is associated with single-family detached housing, the medium density usually includes attached units such as duplexes and town houses, and the higher densities include apartment buildings, sometimes in combination with town houses. Within each classification specific requirements for lot area and width as well as building setbacks from the lot lines are given. Most community zoning ordinances also include provisions for Planned Unit Developments, for which the typical zoning requirements can be modified in order to provide a mix of land uses, housing types, and densities that will result in a more creative and efficient approach to land use.

In considering the development of more energy-efficient housing types, two potential problems arise with regard to community zoning ordinances. First, since solar and earth sheltered houses often have some physical characteristics basically different from conventional housing, they are likely to require different lot sizes, shapes, and setbacks in order to be placed efficiently on the site. These needs may conflict with present zoning requirements. Fortunately, the Planned Unit Development approach provides a method for modifying the typical requirements. Second, site planning for solar and earth sheltered houses is more complex than for conventional houses because of spacing for solar access, land required for earth berms, and variations in topography. Site planning is a problem for the developer in particular because potential densities and layouts for these alternative housing types are difficult to conceive when few examples and no guidelines exist.

This discussion, then, is intended to provide a general understanding of building and site design for energy-efficient housing. A special effort has been made to convey the broad range of interrelated energy-efficient strategies as well as the wide variety of approaches in building and site design. It should be emphasized that examples of building designs and site layouts in this chapter are diagrams for illustrative and comparative purposes. The assistance of skilled professionals is required to adapt and develop these concepts into designs for an actual site. It should also be noted that the design issues and variations for earth sheltered housing are more fully developed than for the other housing types, since the focus of this study is earth sheltered housing and the design considerations for more conventional types of housing are well known.

Two points require clarification in connection with the illustrative layouts that follow. The first concerns the relationship of individual lots, or lots for multiple-unit structures, to the street layout. It is impossible to show the many variations in clustering and attaching units for all the different types of road arrangements. In most cases, therefore, a cluster of eight or more units is shown along a straight section of street. This type of layout would be directly applicable to a through street, a segment of a loop road, or a driveway without a turnaround that serves several units. It is assumed that similar layouts with similar densities could be developed for culs-de-sac or curving segments of roads.

A second concern is the manner in which density is calculated. Housing developments are usually discussed in terms of gross density, which is the total number of units divided by the total acreage of the site. Thus, all roads, parks, and other common space are included in this gross density figure. Even with the same lot sizes, gross densities can vary considerably, depending on the amount of developable land, the natural features, and the efficiency of the road layout. Since one purpose of the illustrative layouts is to provide a direct comparison of the potential densities for four different housing types, including road areas and open space in the density calculations would only obscure this comparison. Thus, all densities given in this chapter are calculated using the building lots only. Estimates of road areas and open space would have to be added to these lot areas in order to calculate a true gross density.

detached units

The layout of conventional detached housing is based on equal access to utilities and roads as well as on generally equal-sized lots. Typically, the houses all have a similar relationship to the street, with a public front yard and a private back yard. One of the most typical patterns for conventional detached housing is the familiar grid system. Rectangular blocks, usually from 1,200 to 1,400 ft (364 to 424 m) long, contain two rows of lots and are surrounded by streets on all four sides. Sometimes an alley is provided through the middle of the block. A pedestrian walkway that crosses the block may be required for very long blocks. Houses must be placed on the lot within setbacks that are typically 30 feet (9 m) for front and rear yards and 10 feet (3 m) for side yards (except on corner lots, which may have a larger side yard setback).

Most single-family detached housing in this country has been built at densities of 4 units per acre or less. Larger lots often result in extended utility systems and large road areas, both of which are costly and waste land. A number of site planning techniques can enhance the energy efficiency of conventional, well-insulated houses while increasing the efficiency of street and utility systems. These techniques, which have been partially discussed in chapter 3, do not include site planning for solar or earth sheltered houses, which are discussed in subsequent sections of this chapter.

One technique for site planning of conventional housing that is particularly appropriate in cool climates is clustering. When detached units are placed closer together, the units protect each other from winter winds, contributing to a lower heat loss and conserving energy. In addition, clustering reduces development costs by reducing roads and utilities and preserves more of the natural landscape. Figure 5-1 shows a typical cul-de-sac that illustrates a number of efficient techniques for conventional housing. When a cul-de-sac is used, the street can be narrower and less pavement per house is required. Similarly, utility runs are shortened by the cul-de-sac and the proximity of the homes to the street. In a cluster such as this, the lots are smaller than 0.25 acre (0.1 ha) and are shaped so that the narrow dimension of the lot is parallel to the street.

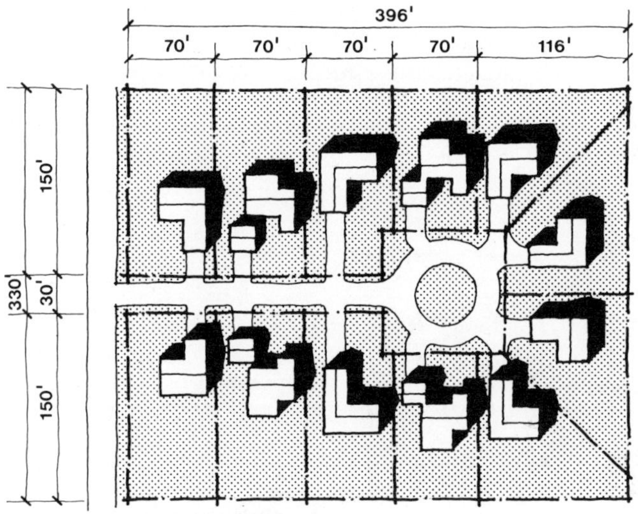
396'
70'
70'
70'
70'
116'
150'
330
30'
150'

5-1: site plan

Another technique for clustering houses more closely together is the use of zero lot-line siting, in which units are placed exactly on the lot line, leaving no side yard on one side. This technique, illustrated in figure 5-2 for units along a public street, often requires walled courtyards or fences to define outdoor spaces. The densities for figures 5-1 and 5-2 are 4.3 and 5.8 dwelling units per acre respectively. By reducing spaces and increasing the emphasis on these techniques, detached conventional units can be built at densities up to 8 units per acre [5.1]. It is important to note that for conventional houses built without regard for solar orientation, densities are unaffected by gentle topography, in contrast to the significant effect of topography on densities for solar and earth sheltered houses.

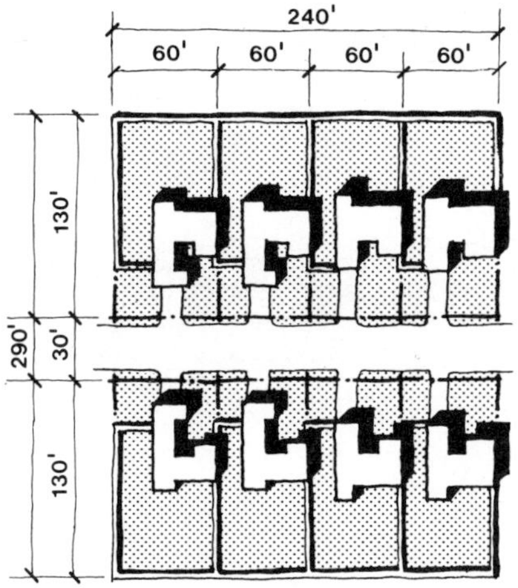

240'
60'
60'
60'
60'
130'
290'
30'
130'

5-2: site plan

attached units

Attached units can enhance all of the advantages of clustering single-family detached units while reducing construction costs. The general site planning implications for duplex, triplex, quadplex, and town house units are similar to those for closely clustered single-family detached units. Conventional town houses are usually arranged with an entry side facing a street or parking area and a private side facing open space. On sites with natural amenities such as surrounding forests and open space, the units are in clusters facing outward, whereas on sites without natural amenities the units often face inward toward a landscaped area with parking on the periphery. One important difference between town houses and detached housing is that direct vehicular access to each town house unit is not always necessary. Eliminating vehicular access to each unit reduces road area and permits more freedom in the building layout. Large parking lots and garages must be carefully designed, however, so that they do not result in a bleak environment. Because of the wide range of town house unit sizes, as well as acceptable amounts of open space surrounding town house units, these unit developments can result in densities ranging from 5 to 15 units per acre. Under special circumstances densities for these units may be even higher.

Conventional multiple-unit apartment buildings also can improve energy- and land-use efficiency. Unlike town houses, however, they represent a significant change from detached units in many ways that affect site planning. For example, the individual units do not have separate entrances or separate outdoor spaces (except for balconies), and cars must be grouped together in garages or relatively large lots. Typically, conventional multiple-unit buildings are separated by open spaces and landscaped parking areas to preserve privacy and, as much as possible, to provide equitable views. The densities for these low- and high-rise structures may be high in comparison with any other form of housing, since theoretically the buildings can be many stories high and spaced rather close together. Maximum densities are normally imposed by zoning restrictions, rather than by the physical limitations of the structures.

The critical concern in site planning for solar housing units is simply to provide clear access to the sun so that sunlight is not blocked by other buildings or trees. In order to provide this access, the length of the shadows cast by buildings and trees must be calculated for the winter solstice (December 21 or 22), when the sun is at its lowest point. If buildings that require solar access are sited so that no shadows are cast on them during the solstice, i.e., when the shadows are longest, they will have adequate access throughout the year. Solar access is sometimes discussed in terms of "skyspace" rather than shadows. Skyspace is the area to the south of a structure that must be kept clear of buildings and trees, whereas shadow calculations indicate the area that is unbuildable to the north of a structure. Basically, skyspace and shadows are calculated from the same sun angles and result in the same spacing of buildings for solar access.

The shadow pattern cast by an object depends on the height of the object and the altitude and azimuth angles of the sun. The altitude and angular sweep of the sun both vary with the latitude for which the calculations are made. The shadow patterns used for illustration purposes in the remainder of this chapter are based on the recommended solar skyspace angles shown in figure 5-3.

When the figures for 40° north latitude are used in determining the shadow pattern for a one- and two-story building on a flat site, they result in patterns like those in figure 5-4. For more southerly latitudes, shadows would be shorter, resulting in the potential for closer spacing of units and higher densities. For more northerly latitudes, such as the 45° latitude in which Minneapolis, Minnesota, is located, the shadows would be longer than those shown in figure 5-4. However, in *Site Planning for Solar Access,* it is recommended that altitudes and azimuths very similar to those for 40° north latitude be used for more northerly latitudes, since radiant energy below 12° in altitude must pass through a great deal of

5-3: recommended skyspace angles for winter solstice

n.latitude	AM/PM position* azimuth	AM/PM position* altitude	noon altitude	percent radiation***
25°	45°	25°	42°	76%
30°	45°	20°	37°	80%
35°	45°	16°	32°	85%
40°	45°	12°	27°	90%
45°**	(50°)	(12°)	22°	88%
48°**	(50°)	(12°)	18°	87%

Source: *Site Planning for Solar Access [5.2]*

* The AM/PM angles presented in this chart are the same for both east of south and west of south. For example, if the skyspace azimuth is 50°, then the protected area extends from 50° east of south to 50° west of south.

** The 50° azimuths are not based on the winter solstice, but rather are suggested as a compromise to assure solar access during the entire heating season exclusive of the winter solstice period. Similarly, the 12° altitudes apply only to those months when the sun's path is 12° above the horizon and within 50° azimuth angles.

***Radiation is based on the percentage of total available radiation falling on a horizontal surface during the winter solstice. Example: If the skyspace between 45° east of south and 45° west of south is protected at 30° latitude, then 80 percent of the available radiation will strike the collector.

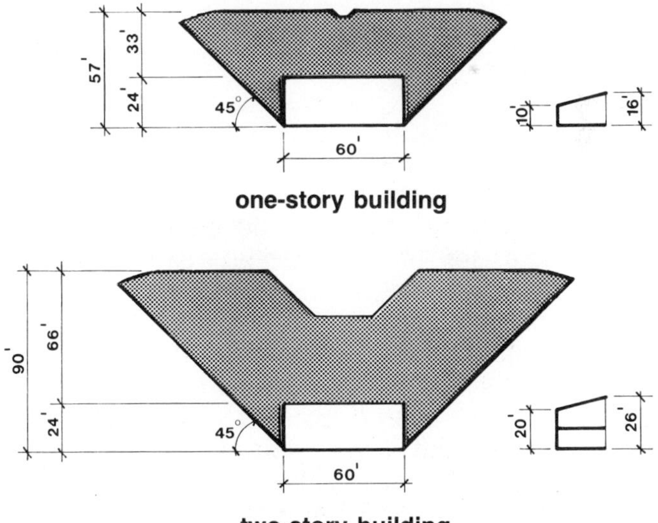
57'
33'
24'
45°
60'
10'
16'
one-story building
90'
66'
24'
45°
60'
20'
26'
two-story building

5-4: shadow patterns

the earth's atmosphere [5.2]. Attempting to space houses so that very low-altitude sunlight (below 12°) is available to them is considered inefficient because the solar radiation is less intense and the shadows are extremely long; hence, much lower densities are required to capture a marginal amount of energy.

Obviously, buildings are not the only objects that cast shadows and interfere with solar access—trees and any steep land forms must be considered as well. Deciduous trees present a unique problem for solar access. It is often assumed that adequate solar gain is available in the winter when deciduous shade trees drop their leaves. Actually, the bare branches of these trees can block from 20 to 80 percent of the sunlight, depending on the type of tree. Thinning the branches may be a solution in some cases. For the purposes of this study, the effects of vegetation are not included in illustrative layouts so that building placement alone can be examined with respect to solar access. It can be assumed that the layouts and density calculations that follow are valid only if trees are placed either where they do not interfere with buildings or where they can be regarded as relatively transparent without their leaves in the winter.

detached units

In comparing various layouts in this chapter, the criterion for solar access is the provision of complete access for the south wall of every unit in the development, based on the sun angles for 40° north latitude (which also apply to 45° north latitude, as discussed above). Although site planning to provide this access is restricted by these requirements, many different approaches are still possible. For single-family detached housing, solar access can be guaranteed if lots are large enough so that an individual house never casts a shadow on a neighbor's property. Because this siting approach requires lots of at least 0.5 acre (0.2 ha) if there is to be some flexibility in building shape and placement, it causes inefficient land use. Such an approach is unnecessary if lot layouts and building placement can be coordinated so that adequate solar access is provided, even if houses cast some shadows onto adjacent properties. If lots remain relatively large (i.e., 0.25 to 0.5 acre—0.1 to 0.2 ha), solar access can be provided for a variety of street layouts and lot shapes by carefully siting each building so that its shadows do not interfere with the solar exposure of another house. This type of siting is shown for a typical cul-de-sac in figure 5-5. Although the street pattern and lots are conventional, the relationships of the houses to the road, the varied entrances, the varying distances to utility hookups, and the setback requirements in general are all very unconventional. Achieving such a layout requires not only flexibility in typical regulations such as setbacks, but also great coordination or a rigid master plan whereby all the houses are sited at once because they are so interdependent.

In order to determine maximum potential densities with solar houses as well as illustrate some limitations and opportunities in site planning, a few basic layouts for single-family detached houses are presented in the

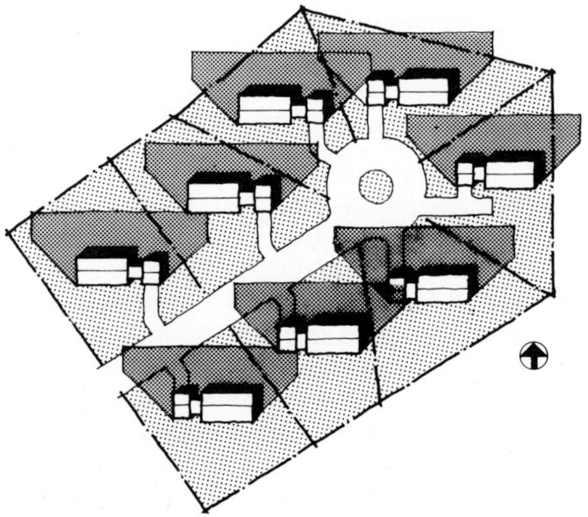

5-5: site plan

following pages. The first two layouts are for one-story houses that are elongated in the east-west direction (24 by 80 feet—7 by 24 m—including double garage). Although this prototypical layout ensures solar exposure to all living spaces in the house with no interference from projections, such a long house is not very compact and requires careful building and site design to avoid a monotonous appearance. In figure 5-6, the one-story prototype is shown on flat land with east-west streets. In addition to providing adequate spacing for solar access, these lot sizes and shapes are based on 20-foot (6-m) minimum setbacks for front and rear yards and 10-foot (3-m) minimum setbacks for side yards. The resulting density is 6.7 units per acre, ignoring the area for streets and community open space. The density could actually be increased if solar access were the only criterion for spacing, since the shadows do not reach the houses.

Three potential drawbacks of the plan in figure 5-6 are apparent. Because one-level solar houses can be spaced closely together, the yard spaces are not only small, but largely unusable as well, since they exist mainly to satisfy setback requirements. By placing buildings exactly on the lot lines, more usable yard spaces can be created while maintaining the same density. A second drawback is the difference in the entrances and the private outdoor yard spaces for houses on opposite sides of the street. Since the interior living spaces face south, placing the outdoor living spaces on the south side of the house is preferable. This layout, however, results in private yard spaces being located in the back yard in some cases and in the front yard alongside the entry in others. For houses on the north side of the street to be acceptable, extensive landscaping and perhaps a walled courtyard would be necessary to separate the private yard space from the street and entry. A final concern with the plan in figure 5-6 is the relatively large area required for streets and utilities with east-west streets and lots elongated in the east-west direction.

An alternative layout for the one-story prototypical solar house is shown in figure 5-7. While the lot sizes are

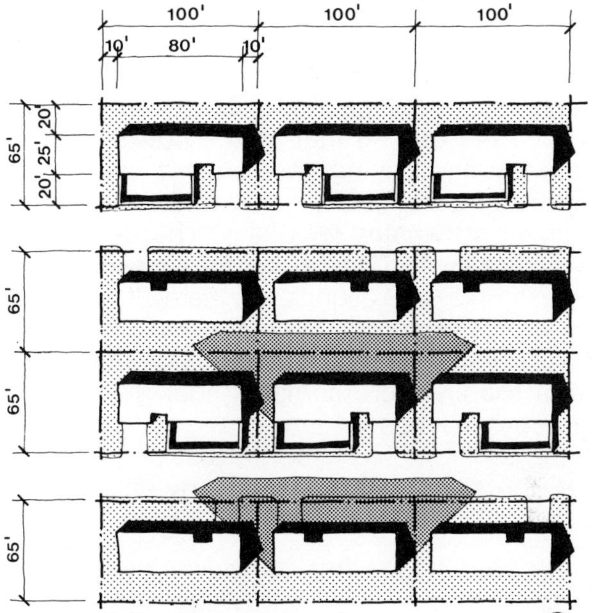

100'
100'
100'
10'
80'
10'
65'
20'
25'
20'
65'
65'
65'

5-6: site plan

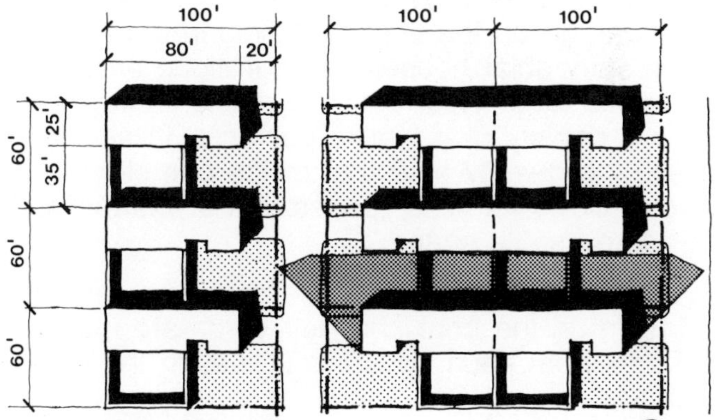

100'
100'
100'
80'
20'
60'
25'
35'
60'
60'

5-7: site plan

actually smaller than in the previous example, all three problems mentioned above have been solved. First, the north-south street layout reduces the area required for streets and utilities for each lot. Second, the houses are entered from the end so that all the houses have a separate entry and private yard. Finally, attaching some units and using zero lot-line siting makes the yard space more usable and wastes less land. The density is increased from the 6.7 units per acre provided in the previous example to 7.3 units per acre. It should not be assumed from this comparison, however, that north-south streets are always superior for one-level houses. For example, a slightly more compact floor plan and a slightly more generous lot size may produce square lots when there is little difference in street orientations. Moreover, the siting situation is clearly different for two-story houses.

A two-story solar house has the advantages of being more compact than a one-level house and of appearing similar to a conventional two-story house. Of course, because a taller structure casts a longer shadow, two-story houses must be spaced further apart. For the purpose of comparisons with one-story houses, the prototypical two-story house is assumed to be the same size (24 by 40 feet—7 by 12 m—on two levels, including a double garage on the first level). Figures 5-8 and 5-9 show two-story solar houses laid out along east-west streets on flat land. This relatively efficient street layout results in a density of 8.1 units per acre. In addition to increasing the density over that of the one-story layouts, this layout allows for yard spaces that are larger and have a more usable shape.

In this layout very conventional setback requirements of 30 feet (9 m) in the front and rear yards are met and the distance from each house to utilities in the street is approximately equal. But, assuming that most of the windows and living spaces face south, the houses on the north side of the street are less desirable because of the smaller, less private yard space to the south of the house. In addition, the large yard to the north of the house would be in shadow, and few windows would look

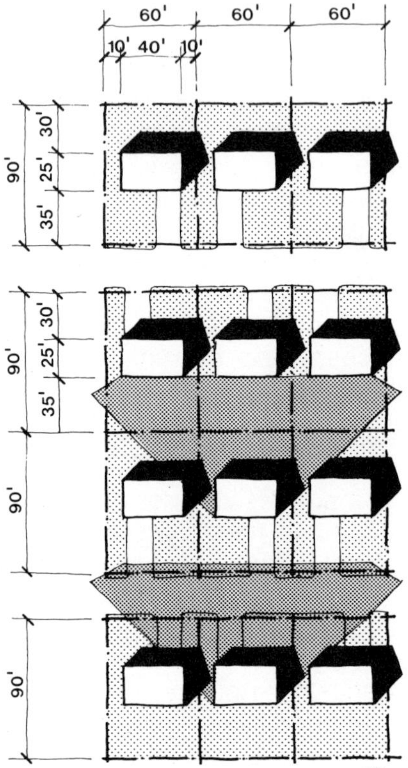
60'
60'
60'
10' 40' 10'
90'
30'
25'
35'
90'
30'
25'
35'
90'
90'

5-8: site plan

out on it. If these houses were moved to the north side of the lots, the south yard would be larger but the driveway and utility hook-ups would be longer. Apparently, no optimal layout exists in which solar access is provided for each unit, cost efficiency is maximized, and other design considerations are resolved.

Topography influences the spacing of solar houses significantly. The shadows cast on a south-facing slope are shorter, allowing for increased densities; the shadows on a north-facing slope are longer, resulting in lower densities. As shown in figure 5-10, the density on a 10-percent, south-facing slope for two-story detached units is 10.4 units per acre, not counting the area required for streets. Conversely, the density on the north-facing slope is reduced to 5.4 units per acre. Because houses on slopes greater than 10 percent would have to be set into the hillside, they are discussed in the following section on earth sheltered housing.

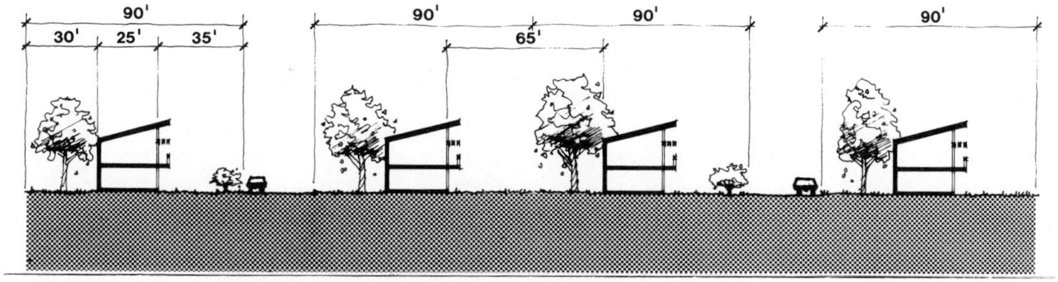

90'
30'
25'
35'
90'
65'
90'
90'

5-9: section—two-story houses on flat site

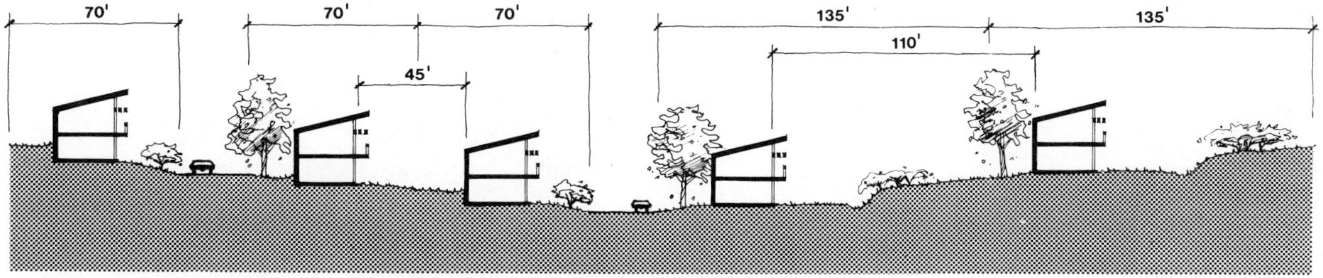

70'
70'
45'
70'
135'
110'
135'

5-10: section—two-story houses on 10 percent slope

Since the two-level layout presented in figure 5-8 has the drawbacks of unequal and, in some cases, undesirable entries and yard spaces, it may be useful to show variations in layout that have different features. In figure 5-11, detached garages are used for lots on the north side of the street, creating improved entry and yard space for these houses. In addition, houses are sited on the lot lines and some are attached as duplexes, resulting in more useful side yard spaces. The lots in this case are longer and the density is reduced to 6.6 units per acre. Two-story solar houses may also be built along north-south streets, as shown in figure 5-12. The separation of the entry and the private yard on the south side of each house is clearly an improvement; however, since the lot sizes are unchanged from 60 by 90 feet (18 by 27 m), the streets and utilities for the same number of houses would have to be longer. In both examples the house sizes are actually larger than in figure 5-8 because the garage is not included in the 40- by 24-foot (12- by 7-m), two-story mass.

The lot sizes and densities indicated in these illustrations represent a very restricted and controlled situation. For complete access to be provided, the houses must be built to meet very strict setbacks and regulations, which in turn define the size and shape of each house. This type of rigid layout not only requires extensive regulation and coordination, but offers little opportunity for variety in site and building design. For these reasons and because the prototypical houses in the examples are relatively small, larger lots and lower densities of 2 to 4 units per acre seem likely for single-family detached solar houses. As shown in some of the previous examples, many of the problems involved in siting detached solar units are resolved more easily with attached units.

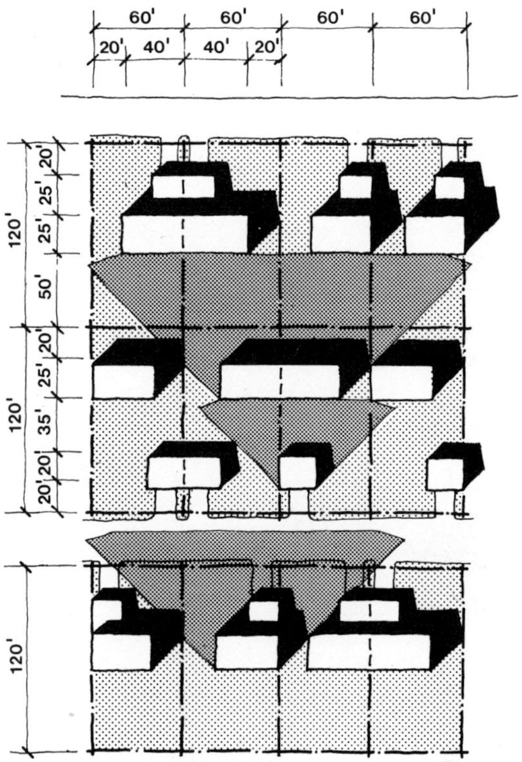
60'
60'
60'
60'
20'
40'
40'
20'
120'
20'
25'
25'
50'
120'
20'
25'
35'
20
20'
120'

5-11: site plan

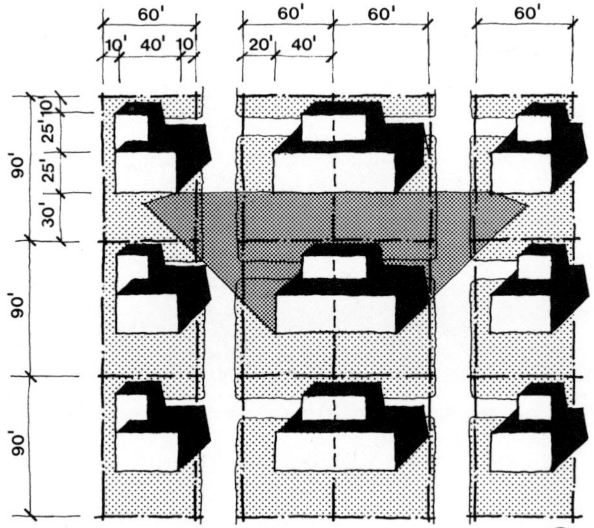
60'
60'
60'
60'
10'
40'
10'
20'
40'
90'
10
25'
25'
30'
90'
90'

5-12: site plan

attached units

Attached solar housing units in the form of duplexes, rowhouses, or multiple-unit buildings present siting considerations very similar to those for single-family detached houses. Basically, building heights and topography determine the spacing between buildings. The reduction in heat loss associated with attached units can be supplemented by other advantages when attached units are designed for solar access. Because town houses are designed and built by one party, they offer more control and thus more opportunity to design efficiently. This type of unit allows the developer to maximize densities while simultaneously providing solar access to each unit.

One of the most obvious ways of attaching solar housing units is to build town houses that extend along an east-west axis. In order to provide a comparison with the detached housing layouts, the same 40- by 24-foot (12- by 7-m), two-level unit is shown in an attached configuration in figure 5-13. The resulting increase in density to 10.8 units per results from the elimination of the almost useless side yards. The use of town houses could yield even greater densities, especially if direct vehicular access to each unit was not required.

The layout in figure 5-13 presents a design conflict similar to that which arises with single-family detached units with solar access. Again, the units on the south side of the street have an entry and garage on the north, while the windows and private outdoor spaces face south toward open space. This desirable arrangement cannot be provided in the same manner for the units on the north side of the street. The units must be designed so that the south-facing glass and outdoor space can be separate from the garage, entry, and parking area. One solution, as illustrated in figure 5-13, is to place the living spaces on the second level and elevate the outdoor space above street level on a deck. While this reduces sunlight to the first floor, the deck is important, since the marketability of the units on the north side of the street may be adversely affected if they lack that area or some other attractive, private outdoor space. In both town houses and larger multiple-unit buildings, detached garages or more remote parking lots are acceptable options. This alternative may be particularly beneficial in allowing more flexibility in layout for solar units and more equal access by all units to open space on the south side.

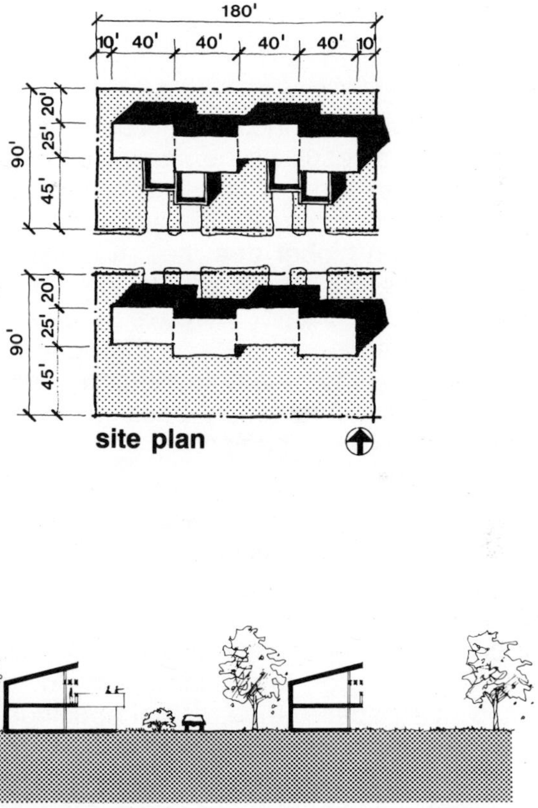
180'
10' 40' 40' 40' 40' 10'
90'
20'
25'
45'
90'
20'
25'
45'
site plan
section

5-13: attached solar housing units

In order to establish the maximum possible densities for various attached configurations of solar housing units, minimum spacings for one-, two-, four-, and eight-story buildings are shown in figure 5-14 for both flat land and a 10-percent, south-facing slope. In all cases it is assumed that individual housing units are attached continuously and have an area of 1,440 square feet (130 ca) arranged on either one or two levels. These units, then, have the same features as the prototypical units used in previous examples except that these lack garages. Actual densities would be less than those calculated here, since land area at the ends of the buildings is not included in the calculations.

One notable aspect of this comparison is the approximately 30-percent increase in density for each building height as a result of the sloping topography. On south-facing slopes, shadow length is reduced as the degree of the slope increases; therefore, steeper slopes would result in even higher densities. It is also interesting to note the increase in density due to the stacking of units. Although much greater increases certainly are possible with conventional buildings that ignore solar access, in this case the steady increase in density with the taller buildings occurs simply because less ground is covered by the buildings themselves.

Although it is theoretically possible to achieve the densities shown in figure 5-14 while still providing complete solar access for each unit, in practice such densities may either be difficult to achieve or result in an undesirable environment. In the case of the one- and two-story buildings, the spaces between the buildings do not appear large enough to include space for roads, parking, and open space; thus, actual spacings would probably be larger. For the four- and eight-story buildings, the spaces between the buildings present difficult problems. Although these areas may be large enough for open spaces, they may be rather undesirable for that purpose because they are substantially shaded in the wintertime. These spaces are, however, acceptable for roads and parking.

In summary, it appears that a variety of configurations in and types of solar housing units can be built at densities that are not significantly less than densities for conventional housing developments. For single-family detached houses at 40° north latitude, densities up to 8 units per acre can be achieved on flat land that has a fairly rigid layout of buildings and roads. Developments of solar houses that allow for some flexibility in site and building design are likely to require larger lots, however, and therefore result in densities of 2 to 4 units per acre. It also appears that single-family attached and multifamily units with complete solar access for each unit can be built at densities in the range of 10 to 20 units per acre. For all types of solar housing, topography has an important impact on the density that can be achieved. On a 10-percent, south-facing slope, densities can be increased by 20 to 30 percent, whereas they are reduced by a similar amount on a 10-percent, north-facing slope. Slopes steeper than this, which produce even greater increases or decreases, are discussed in the following section on earth sheltered houses.

In examining the lot sizes and layouts presented here, it is important to remember that they are based on very basic and conventional passive solar house design. The buildings are rectangular and oriented directly toward the south; sunlight striking the entire south wall all day is the criterion for solar access. Although all of these characteristics are reasonable and easily understood, the need for solar energy can be met with more complex building forms that receive sunlight from a variety of directions rather than just through a vertical south wall. In addition, sunlight may be necessary for only part of the day rather than all day. For example, in order to optimize solar gain for housing units on east- or west-facing slopes, walls may be angled so that windows face southeast or southwest, and clerestory windows on the roof may face directly south. Arranging buildings in a more staggered layout rather than in rigid rows would also allow at least partial exposure to all units while keeping densities relatively high. For these reasons simple generalizations concerning solar building design and site planning should always be examined in light of the assumptions on which they are based.

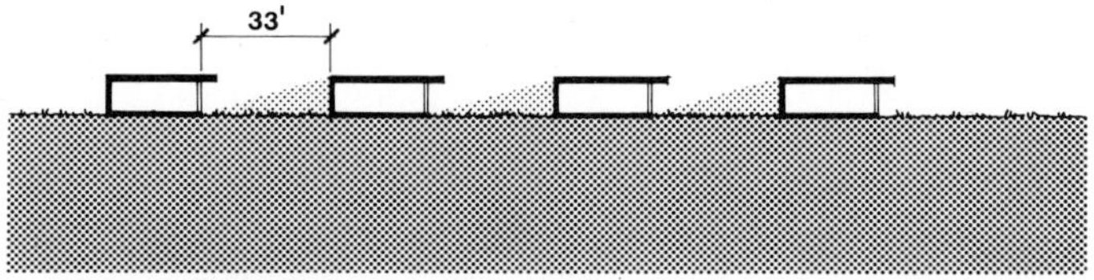
33'

one-story buildings on flat land
12.1 units per acre

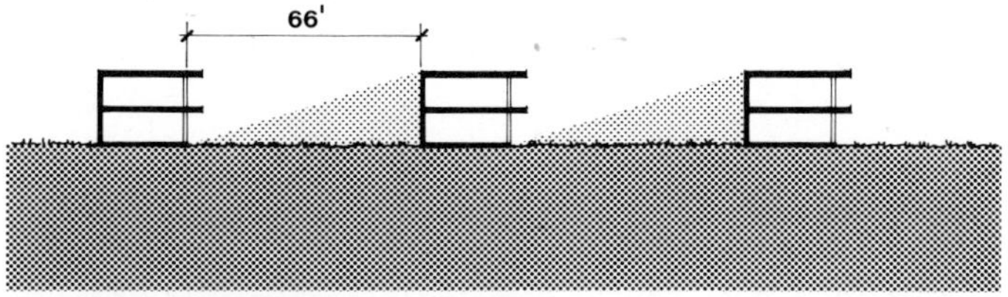
66'

two-story buildings on flat land
16.1 units per acre

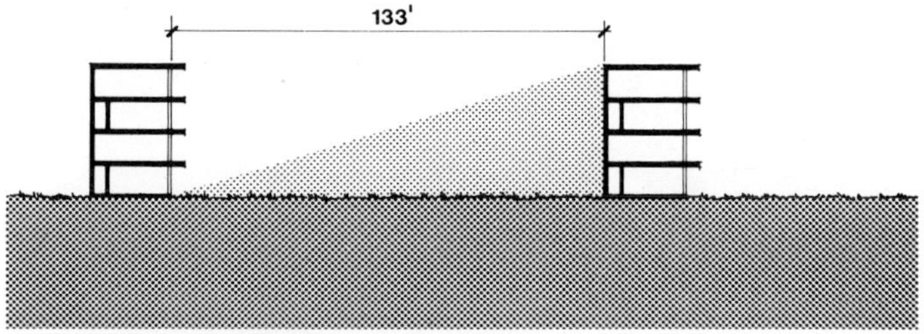
133'

four-story buildings on flat land
18.1 units per acre

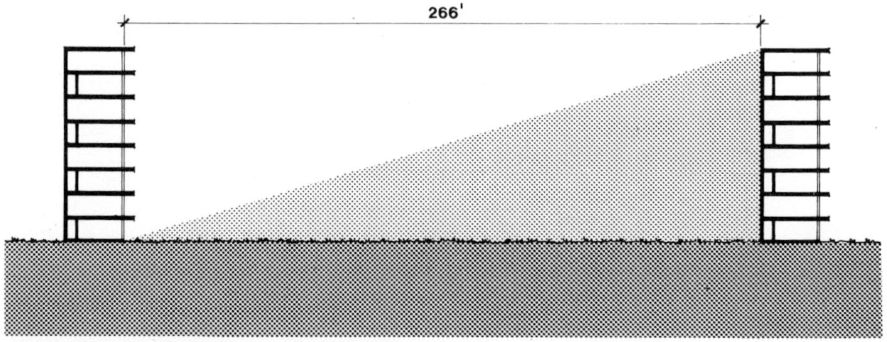
266'

eight-story buildings on flat land
20.0 units per acre

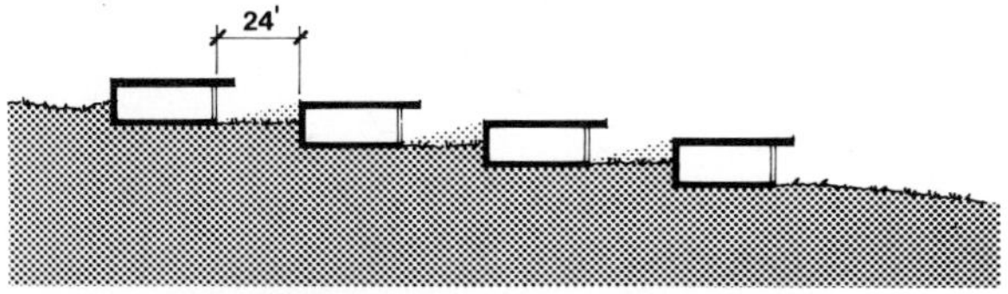
24'

one-story buildings on 10 percent slope
16.1 units per acre

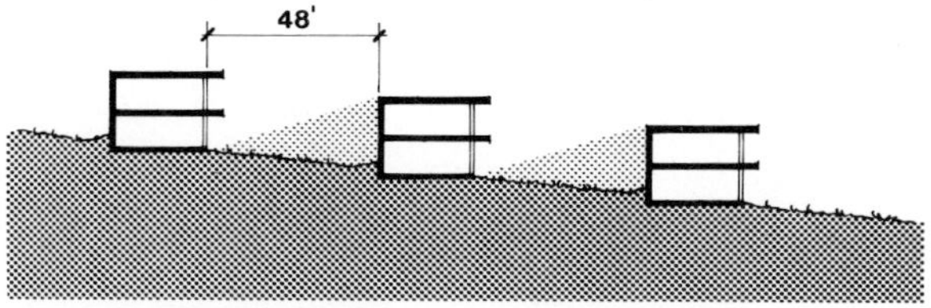
48'

two-story buildings on 10 percent slope
20.7 units per acre

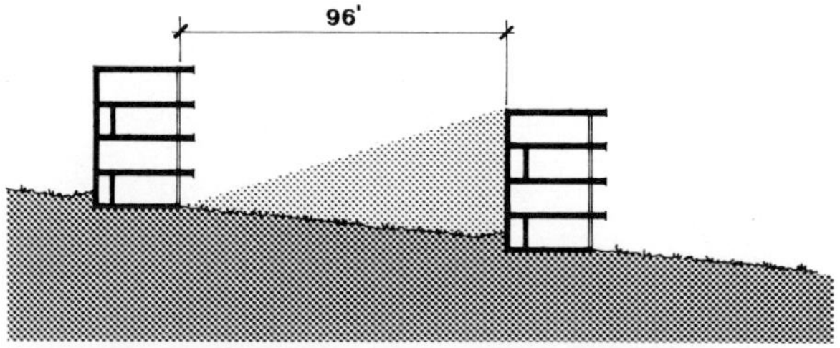
96'

four-story buildings on 10 percent slope
24.2 units per acre

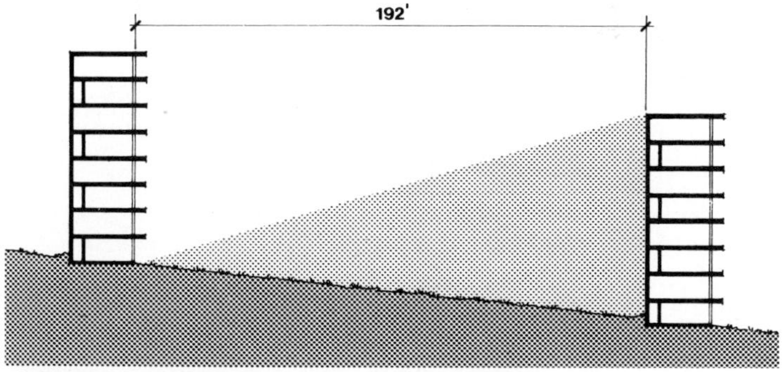
192'

eight-story buildings on 10 percent slope
26.4 units per acre

5-14: comparison of multiple-unit solar buildings

detached units

A number of variables affect lot size and shape of single-family detached elevational units with passive solar orientation. The most critical of these are the size and shape of the unit, the slope of the land, and the manner in which the house is set into the site. The relative effect of these key variables can be illustrated by examining some prototypical units. For a relatively small, 24- by 80-foot (7- by 24-m), one-story elevational house (including garage) built on a flat site, a lot of nearly 0.5 acre (0.2 ha) is required, as shown in figure 5-15. This rather large lot size results not from solar access requirements, but from the significant area required to create earth berms around the house together with an adequately sized outdoor living space to the south, since the berms are unsuitable as yard space. In addition, the berms are large because the floor level of the house is at existing grade. Another problem with this type of design is that earth would probably have to be transported onto the site, making the design costly and somewhat unrealistic. The berm sizes are based on maintaining a 1:3 slope and providing enough space around them (10 feet—3 m) for drainage within the site boundaries, since berms cannot cause water to run onto adjacent properties. The resulting 45-foot (13.6-m) setbacks far exceed typical setback requirements.

Designing the floor level at the existing grade eases vehicular access and entry. Although a south entry is shown in the plan, entrance would be possible through the berm on the north side or at either end without changing the lot size. As with solar houses, a drawback to the south entry is that the private yard space is on the same side of the house as the entry. Separating these two features by building forms, landscaping, or a walled courtyard would be desirable.

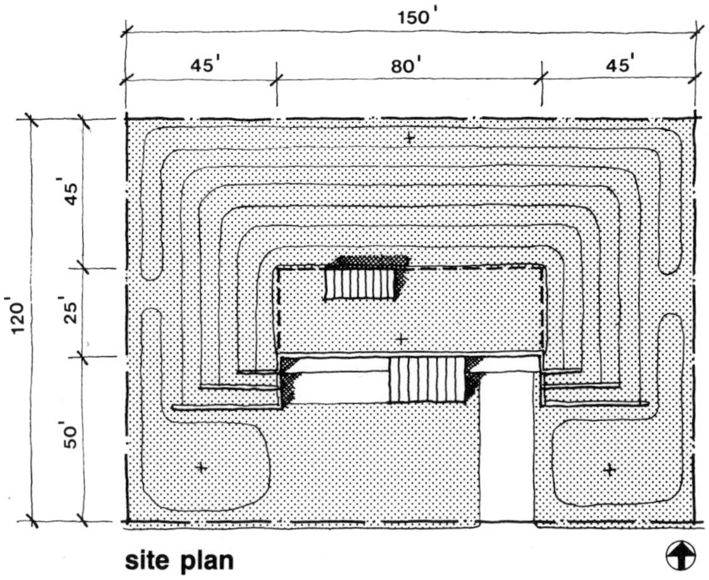
150'
45'
80'
45'
120'
45'
25'
50'

site plan

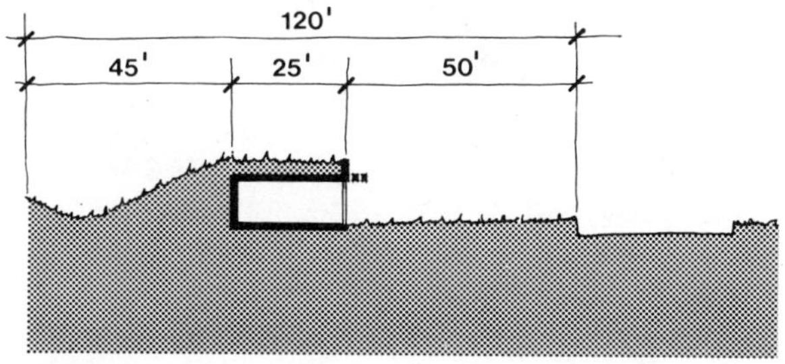
120'
45'
25'
50'

section

5-15: elevational house on grade

A two-story elevational house can be placed into a flat site by creating a sunken courtyard for the lower level (fig. 5-16). With this type of design, the cut-and-fill of the earth could be more easily balanced on-site. A two-story design would not require a larger lot than a one-story house and may, in fact, work on a lot that has a smaller east-west dimension. This conclusion is based on the assumption that a two-level house would be 20 to 40 feet (6 to 12 m) shorter than a comparable one-level house, and thus would require a lot no longer than 150 feet (45 m).

On a completely flat site, one important adjustment that affects the sizes of the berms is the level of the house floor relative to the existing grade. Lowering the floor level and creating a sunken courtyard in front of the house reduces the height of the berms and reduces or eliminates the need to transport earth onto the site (fig. 5-17). The lot size is not reduced in the north-south direction since extra space is required for the sunken courtyard. The smaller berms allow a reduction of 20 feet (6 m) in the east-west dimension, however, resulting in a lot size of slightly over 0.4 acre (0.16 ha). As with the one-story example, the 35-foot (10.6-m) setbacks still exceed typical requirements. This 150-by 120-foot (45- by 36-m) lot is the basis for some of the density calculations that follow.

Two problems that arise with a semirecessed design are vehicular access and drainage. The illustration in figure 5-17 shows that the floor level is only 4 feet (1.2 m) below the surrounding grade, making it possible to slope the driveway down to enter the earth-covered garage even from the north side. A more deeply recessed house would require either a larger lot and longer driveway or an above-grade, and possibly detached, garage. In addition, sunken courtyards must be properly drained. Incidentally, this plan clearly illustrates the separation of entry and private yard space that results from a north, east, or west entry.

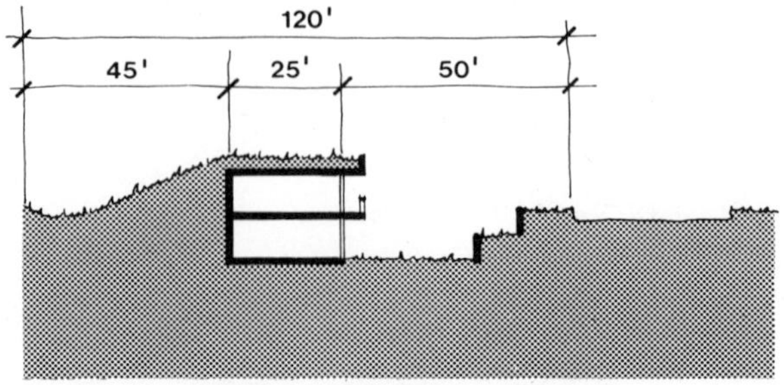

120'
45'
25'
50'

5-16: section—two-story design

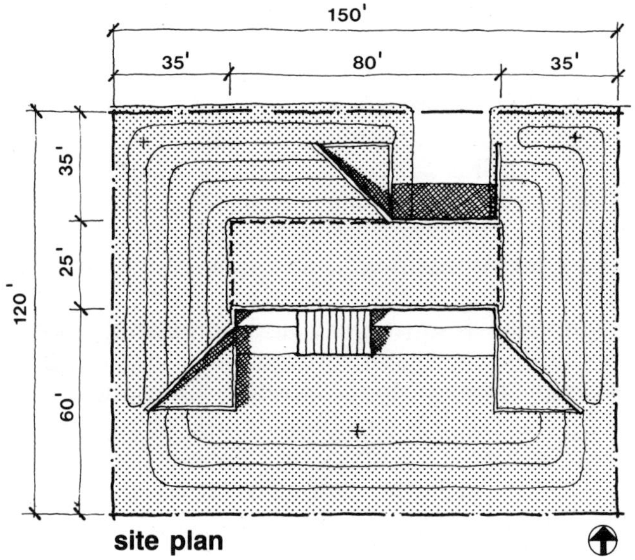

150'
35'
80'
35'
120'
35'
25'
60'

site plan

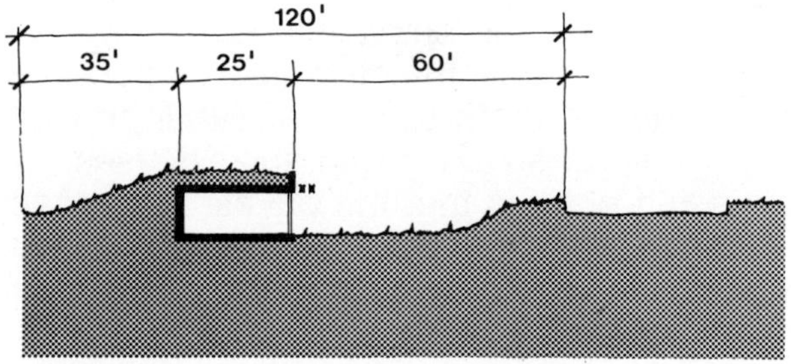

120'
35'
25'
60'

section

5-17: semi-recessed elevational house

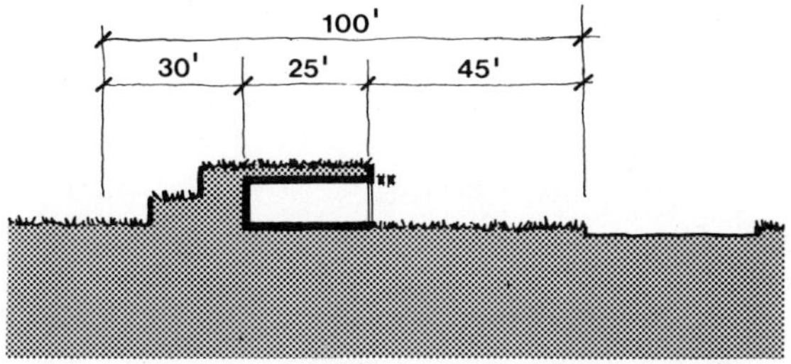
100'
30'
25'
45'

5-18: section—use of retaining walls

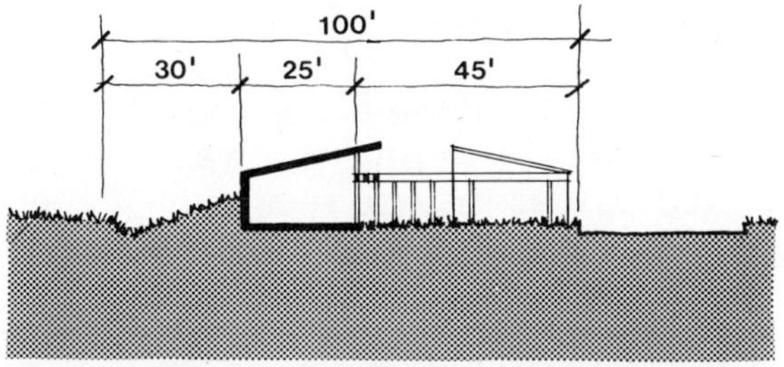
100'
30'
25'
45'

5-19: section—partially bermed walls

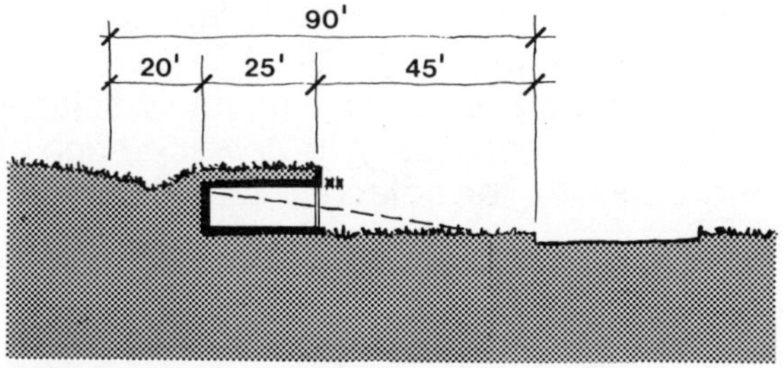
90'
20'
25'
45'

5-20: section—10 percent slope

An even smaller lot on flat land is possible with variations in the landscape and architectural design. For example, the area devoted to berms can be reduced by using retaining walls that, in effect, create a steeper berm (see fig. 5-18). Steeper berms can also be created without retaining walls if proper soils and plant materials are used to prevent erosion. The area required for earth berms is also diminished for houses with earth against the walls but not covering the roof. As shown in figure 5-19, because the berm need not be as high, less area is required for a 3:1 slope. Another advantage of conventionally roofed structures is that detached above-grade garages can be more easily related to the house in an aesthetic sense. Reducing the area required for berms—whether by creating steeper berms or using a conventional roof—results in lot sizes of 140 by 100 feet (42 by 30 m), or 0.32 acre (0.13 ha).

One of the most important factors that affects lot size and overall design for elevational houses is the topography. For example, the same prototypical house discussed in previous examples requires 35 percent less land when placed on a 10-percent slope. In this case, as shown in figure 5-20, the area required for berms is eliminated on the north side, resulting in a 90-foot-deep (27-m-deep) lot. It is assumed that the lot width is also reduced to 130 feet (39 m) because not as much space is required for berms and drainage on a sloping site. The resulting setbacks on the ends are 25 feet (7.6 m), which is an adequate distance, but only 15 feet (4.5 m) on the back wall—a setback distance that may not meet typical requirements. In order to more fully understand the effect of topography on density and layout, the layout of clusters of lots and units must be examined.

Earth sheltered elevational houses can be combined in many patterns, both as detached and attached units. The layout of lots and buildings is affected by many factors, such as the specific topography of a site and the limitations of road and utility systems. In the following examples, simple layouts of units are presented in order to determine maximum possible densities with elevational units and to identify some of the key design issues. It should be noted that these layouts are not intended to represent complete designs.

Based on the prototypical lot developed in the previous section for a semirecessed house (120 by 150 feet—36 by 45 m), a simple cluster on flat land is shown in figures 5-21 and 5-22. The houses, all oriented toward the south for passive solar gain, are placed along east-west streets with both north- and south-facing entrances. If the land required for roads and open space is ignored, the density for the housing alone is 2.4 units per acre. Two-story units could be substituted on these flat lots without changing the density.

To illustrate the impact of topography on single-family detached units, houses are shown on both north- and south-facing slopes in figures 5-23 and 5-24. For both the 10-percent and 20-percent slopes, it is assumed that vehicular access to every unit is required; thus, the roads run in an east-west direction parallel to the slope. On the south-facing, 10-percent slope, many of the problems

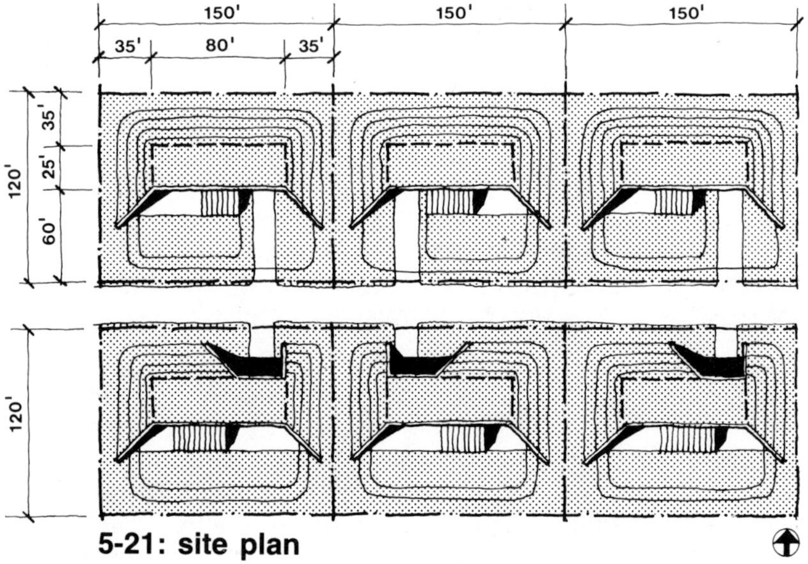
150'
150'
150'
35'
80'
35'
120'
35'
25'
60'
120'
5-21: site plan

associated with passive solar elevational houses—large land area devoted to berms, limited views—are reduced considerably. The resulting density of 3.7 units per acre is a considerable improvement over densities possible with flat sites. Two-story units could work as well as one-story units on a 10-percent slope; in fact, in some cases they may be essential in order to provide vehicular access to an attached garage. If elevational houses oriented toward the south are built on north-facing, 10-percent slopes, the minimum lot sizes are much larger because of the requirements for solar access. As shown in figure 5-23, in this case the needs for more extensive earthwork and carefully handled drainage result in a density of 1.5 units per acre.

The density can be increased to 6.9 units per acre on a south-facing slope of 20 percent. The steepness in combination with the requirement for direct vehicular access results in two-story designs limited by some very tight restrictions. To fit the houses so closely together, zero-lot lines, extensive retaining walls, and the use of rooftop yard spaces may be required. Of course, some of these problems can be resolved by using larger lots and lower densities. Similarly, higher densities can be achieved more easily on steep slopes through the use of attached units and more remote parking. A truly elevational passive solar house cannot be built on a north-facing, 20-percent slope. But a design combining earth sheltering, solar, superinsulation, and a windbreak—as shown in figure 5-24—could work on such a slope. Compromises in the amount of solar access will most probably be necessary to develop such slopes. Lot sizes and densities for detached elevational units on various slopes are summarized in the following chart.

topography	**lot size**		**density**
	(ft)	(m)	(units/acre)
flat	120 × 150	(36 × 45)	2.4
10%, south-facing slope	90 × 130	(27 × 39)	3.7
10%, north-facing slope	160 × 180	(48 × 54)	1.5
20%, south-facing slope (two-story units)	70 × 90	(21 × 27)	6.9

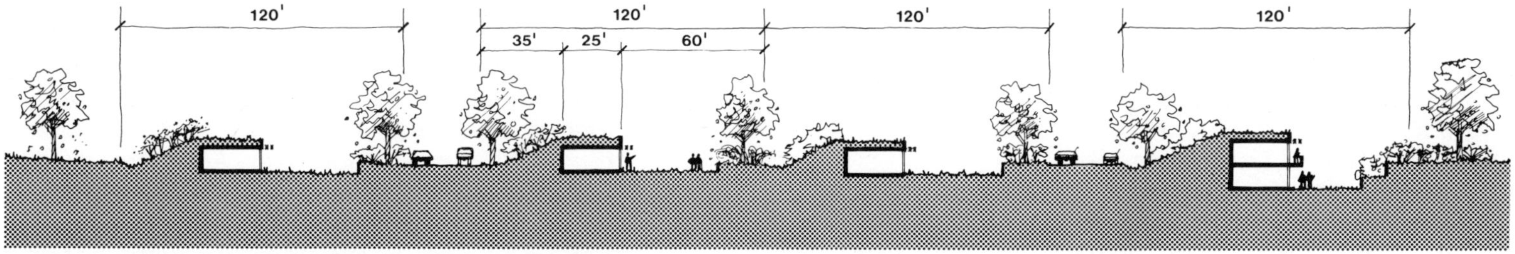

120'
120'
35'
25'
60'
120'
120'

5-22: section—elevational houses on flat site

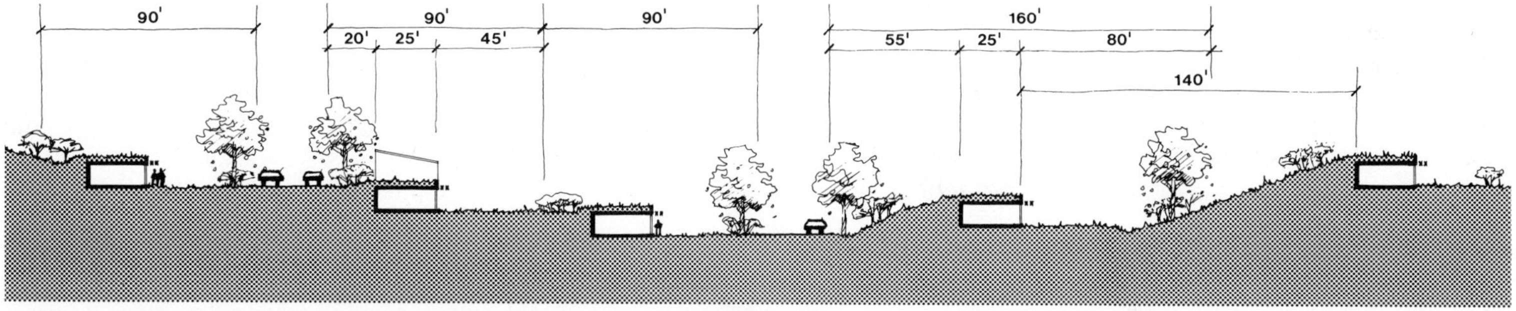

90'
90'
20'
25'
45'
90'
160'
55'
25'
80'
140'

5-23: section—elevational houses on 10 percent slope

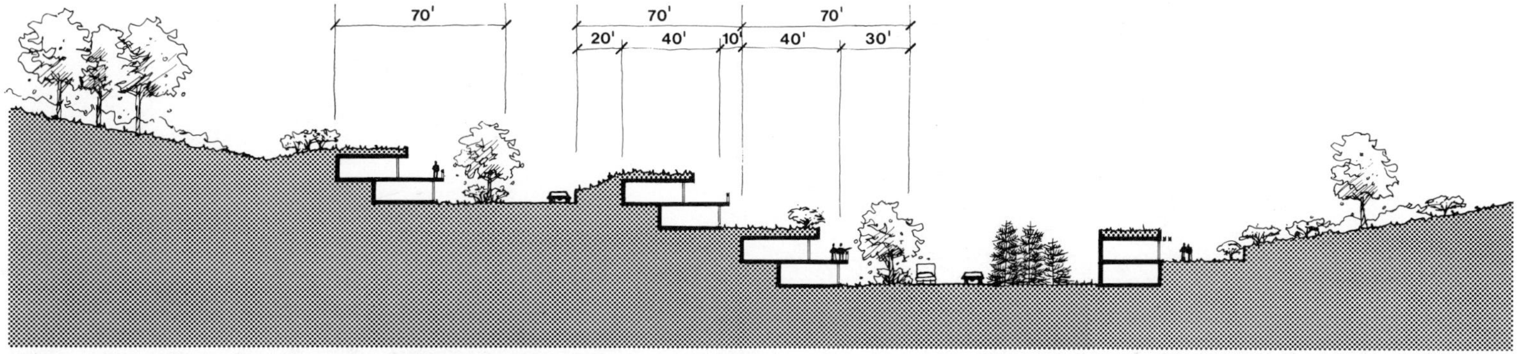

70'
70'
20'
40'
10'
70'
40'
30'

5-24: section—elevational houses on 20 percent slope

Another adjustment that can be made to affect lot size is the extension of berms onto more than one lot, as shown in figure 5-25. Using the prototypical south-facing elevational unit on flat land, a continuous east-west berm could be created between houses, resulting in a density of 3.2 units per acre. By leaving 20 feet (6 m) between units, conventional side yard setbacks of 10 feet (3 m) could be met. On a south-facing, 10-percent slope, this density would be increased to 4.5 units per acre. In addition to increased densities, underground units that are placed close together—such as these are—may result in a greater storage of heat in the earth in winter and a greater cooling surface for the house in summer. Assuming the berm is not an existing land form, the houses would have to be designed to work together and built at the same time, and adjustments in normal regulations would be required. The resulting design does not appear to be very different from attached housing, which is less expensive to build and allows for even higher densities. On the other hand, detached units may be more marketable.

All of the layouts in the previous examples are shown with east-west streets. Because the prototypical elevational lot is elongated in the east-west direction, longer roads and utility systems are required than is the case with conventional lots. An alternative lot layout with north-south streets is shown in figure 5-26. Although the lot sizes differ little from the east-west layouts (which have a density of 2.4 units per acre), the street area and length of utility lines per housing unit is shorter. In this layout all units would have either an east or west street access, which would provide each unit with an identical entry and private yard. The separation between the public entry at the end of the unit and private yard space is an advantage of this design. Drawbacks include less earth berming for wind protection and the inability to attach more than two houses if vehicular access to each unit is required. Moreover, on sloping sites the roads would not run parallel to the incline, thus limiting potential slopes to those at less than a 10-percent grade.

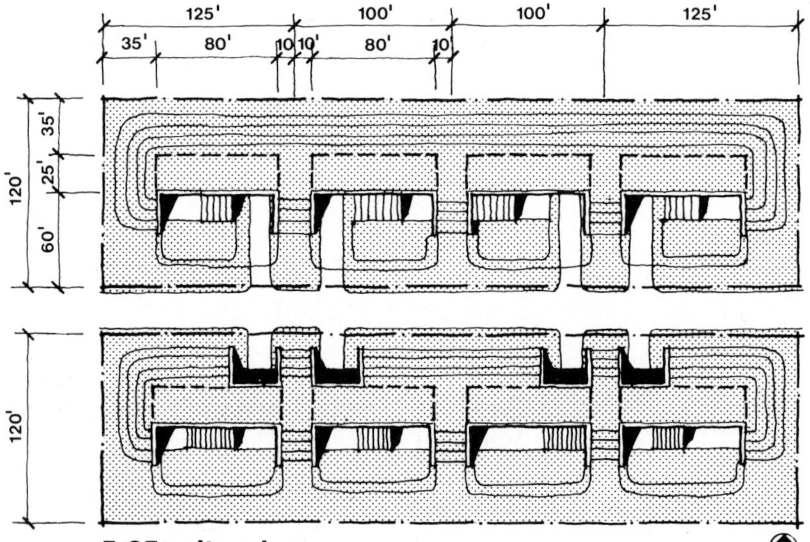
125'
100'
100'
125'
35'
80'
10
10'
80'
10
35'
25'
60'
120'
120'

5-25: site plan

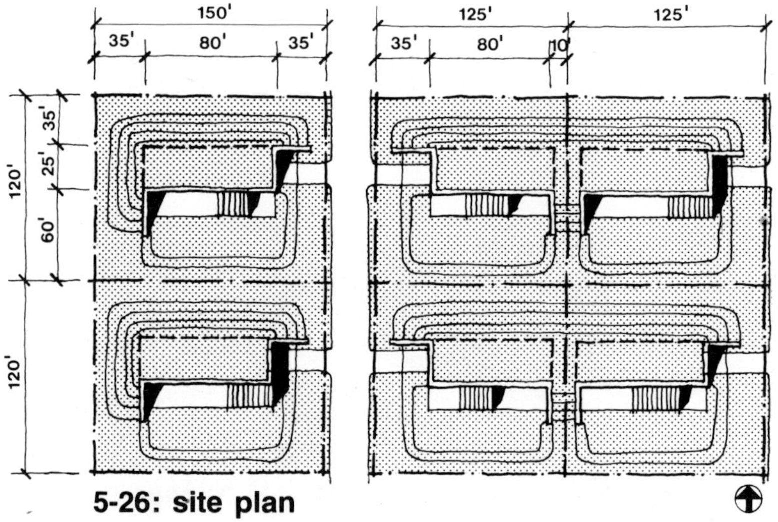
150'
35'
80'
35'
125'
125'
35'
80'
10'
35'
25'
60'
120'
120'

5-26: site plan

Obviously, a major characteristic of elevational houses with passive solar orientation is that they are best suited to south-facing slopes. Some degree of variation is acceptable, and there are many ways in which even houses on north slopes can be designed for solar orientation, although at much lower densities. An earth sheltered house with one exposed elevation does not, of course, always require passive solar gain. One primary reason for ignoring solar orientation is location of a house in a warm climate where the cooling effect of the earth is beneficial but solar access is not as important. Other reasons might include the desire to orient the house toward amenities or reliance on a community or district heat supply system in place of solar collection at each house.

The site planning and layout implications for elevational houses that ignore solar orientation are somewhat different from those for south-facing units. Generally, the lot sizes and densities should not differ from those of solar units, since the berm sizes and topography—rather than solar access—determine unit spacing. Nonetheless, many natural land forms, such as north-facing slopes, could be used at higher densities without concern for maximizing solar orientation. If solar orientation is ignored, units can also be placed back to back, resulting in a density of 5.5 units per acre (fig. 5-27). This layout has the advantages of working very well on flat sites and reducing the land area normally devoted to berms. Although this type of arrangement suggests the potential for achieving higher densities, it also requires units to be designed and built as one project. Obviously, attached as well as detached units could be built in this manner.

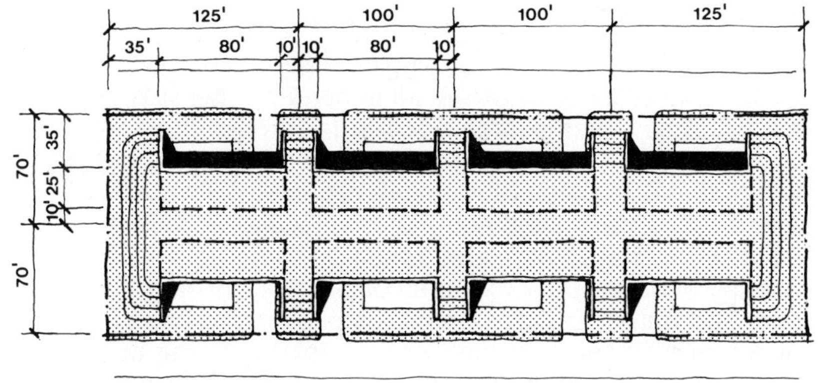
125'
100'
100'
125'
35'
80'
10'
10'
80'
10'
70'
35'
25'
10'
70'

site plan

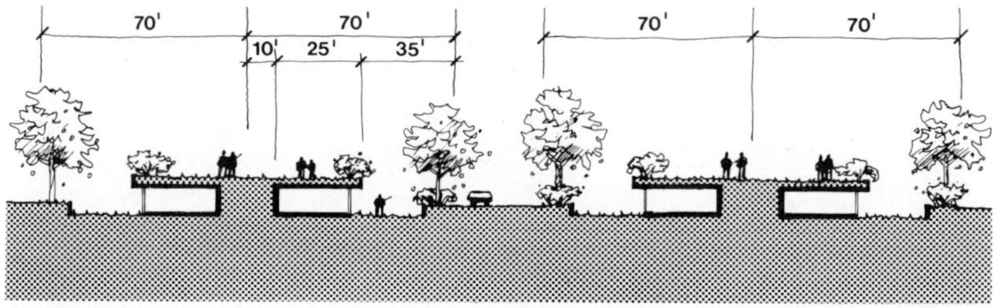
70'
70'
10'
25'
35'
70'
70'

section

5-27: elevational units with multiple orientations

attached units

Lot sizes and densities for single-family detached elevational units are heavily influenced by the size of earth berms and the area needed for proper drainage. Relatively large lots are required unless buildings are set into suitable hillsides, yet slopes are limited to about 20 percent in order to provide direct vehicular access to each unit. These conditions result in some definite density and site selection restrictions. By building attached units, however, many obstacles can be overcome, since all of the units are planned and built together and parking can be clustered. In fact, on more steeply sloping sites (i.e., 30 to 50 percent), attached elevational units may not only be the best solution, but may also make construction possible on slopes normally considered unbuildable.

Units with direct vehicular access attached in groups of four provide a direct comparison to the detached units discussed in the previous examples. Using the prototypical 80- by 20-foot (24- by 6-m), one-level unit (including garage), a density of 3.7 units per acre is achieved on flat land, as shown in figure 5-28. This density is 50 percent greater than the 2.4-units-per-acre density for single-family detached units on flat land. It is important to remember that these density calculations do not include roads or open space, but only the area required for the buildings. Of course, these long, one-story units on flat land with large berms still do not represent very efficient land use. Both sloping topography and the use of two-story units can increase the density considerably. A far greater density of 9.5 units per acre is achieved by the two-story units on a 20-percent slope shown in figure 5-29. Although these 40-foot-long (12-m-long) units are the same size as the one-level units, they require less than half the land area.

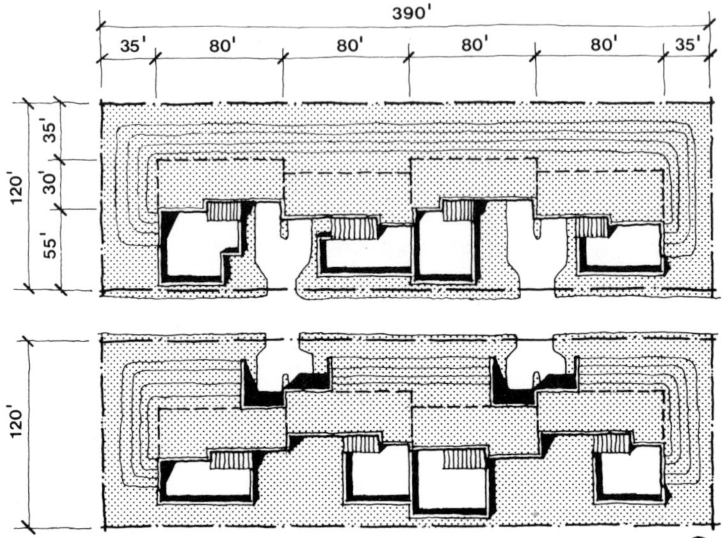
390'
35'
80'
80'
80'
80'
35'
120'
35'
30'
55'
120'

site plan

section

5-28: one-story attached units on flat site

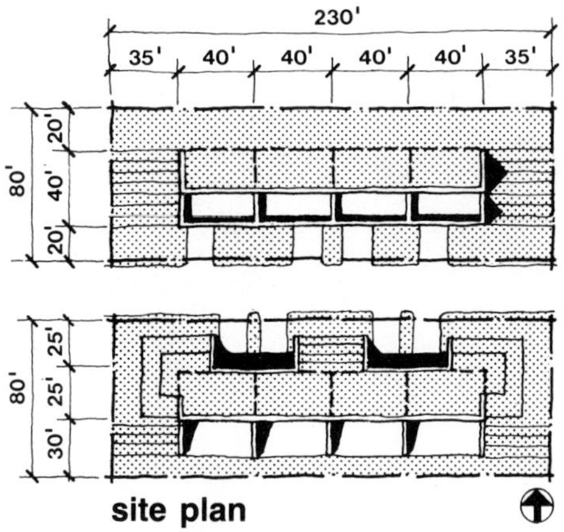
230'
35'
40'
40'
40'
40'
35'
80'
20'
40'
20'
80'
25'
25'
30'

site plan

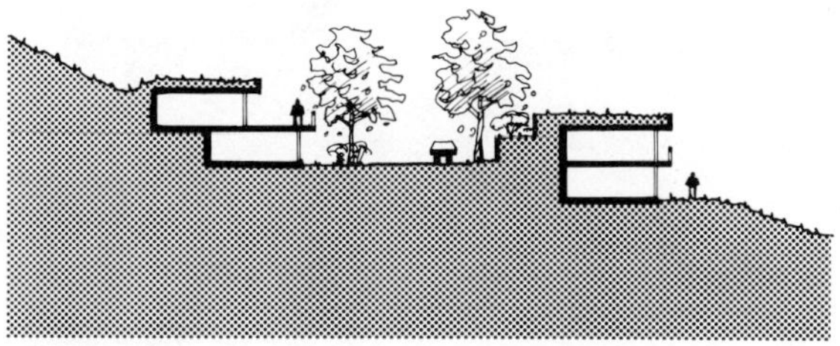

section

5-29: two-story attached units on 20 percent slope

Based on assumptions similar to those already presented for detached units, the lot sizes and densities for attached elevational units on various slopes are summarized in the following chart. These figures are for groups of four units attached in a row.

topography	**lot size (4 units)** (ft)	(m)	**density** (units/acre)
flat	120 × 390	(36 × 118)	3.7
10%, south-facing slope	90 × 370	(27 × 112)	5.2
10%, north-facing slope	160 × 420	(48 × 127)	2.6
20%, south-facing slope (two-story units)	80 × 230	(24 × 70)	9.5

The two clusters of attached units in figures 5-28 and 5-29 illustrate that different site conditions require different architectural responses. For example, one-level units are more suitable on flat sites, whereas two-level units work better on 20-percent slopes. Also in figure 5-29, the units on the north side of the street are stepped back to provide large, private outdoor living areas that are vertically separated from the entry and street below. On the other hand, the units on the south side have a natural separation of entry and yard. The more compact design results from a desire to increase the south yard area while allowing space for the berms on the north. Although site conditions and units differ, the goal is to provide all the houses with equally desirable features.

In designing attached elevational units, a requirement for direct vehicular access for each unit places some definite restrictions on densities and allowable slopes. For any attached housing, reduced paving costs and more flexibility in layout can be provided by placing parking lots and garages further from the units. Remote parking is almost essential in developments of elevational units on steeper slopes (i.e., 20 to 50 percent). Since passive solar collection is virtually impossible on slopes of 20 to 50 percent without proper orientation, only southeast, south, and southwest slopes are usable. If passive solar orientation is not important, then the density calculations can apply to any slope.

In order to illustrate the potential for increased densities on steeper slopes, the distances between one-story elevational units for a variety of slopes are shown in figure 5-30. Road access is ignored, and the spacing is based on maintaining the slope of the land, solar access, and preserving a minimal outdoor space. A similar comparison is shown for two-story units in figure 5-31. For steeper slopes (i.e., those greater than 30 percent), construction of two-story units that are offset would be simpler, resulting both in less retaining and in outdoor areas accessible from both levels. In the illustrations it is assumed that the one-level units measure 60 by 24 feet (18 by 7 m) and that the two-level units are 30 by 24 feet (9 by 7 m) on two levels—areas equivalent to those of the detached units without garages used in the previous examples. No land at the ends of the rows of housing is included in the density calculations; if it were, the densities would be slightly lower. Although many different layouts and densities could be projected from these sections, it appears that densities over 20 units per acre are possible on slopes of 30 percent, and over 30 units per acre on 50-percent slopes.

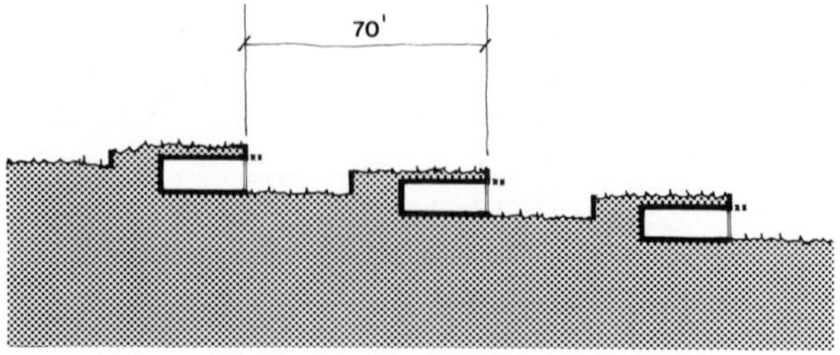
70'

10 percent slope: 16.1 units per acre

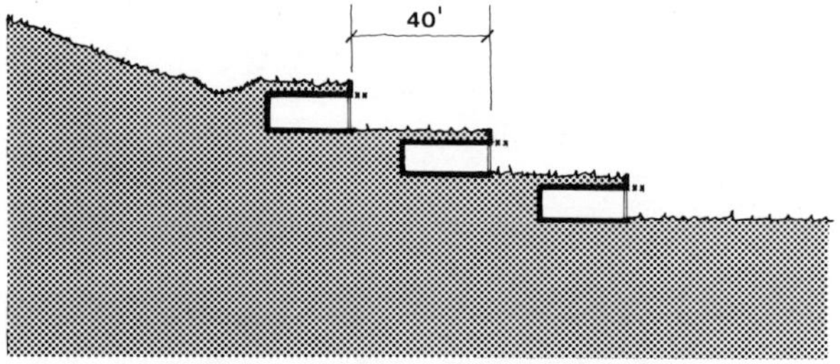
40'

30 percent slope: 24.2 units per acre

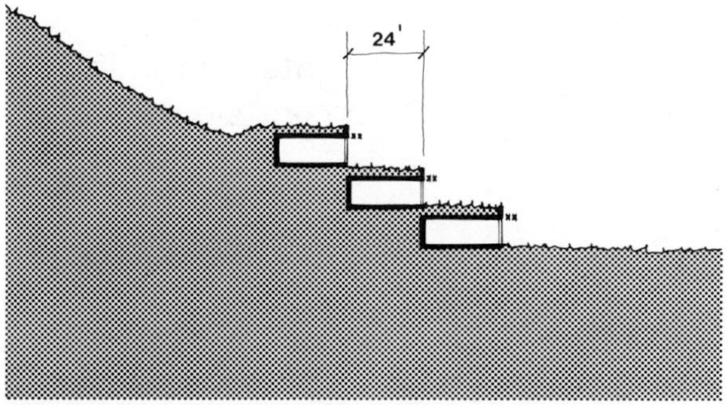
24'

50 percent slope: 36.3 units per acre

5-30: one-story attached units

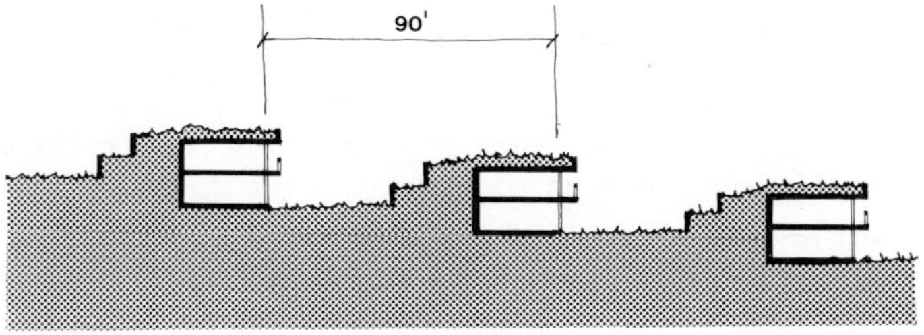
90'

10 percent slope: 10.4 units per acre

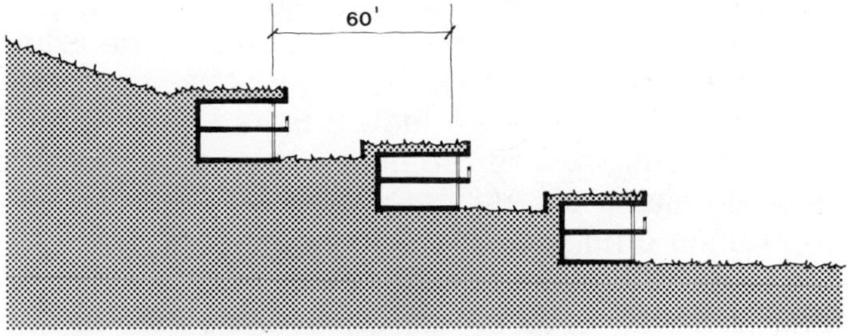
60'

30 percent slope: 18.1 units per acre

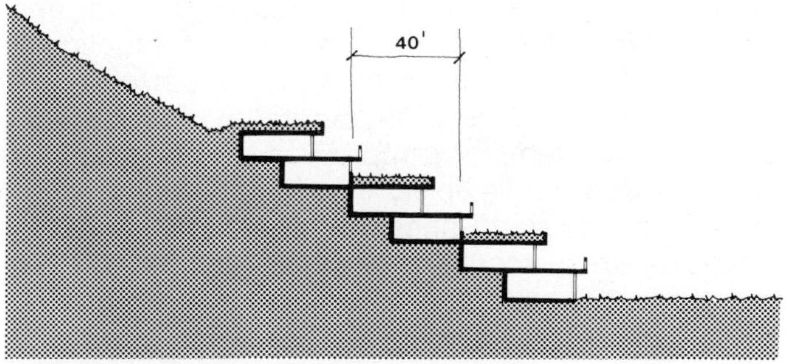
40'

50 percent slope: 30.3 units per acre

5-31: two-story attached units

Although increased densities and the possibility of using steep slopes normally considered unbuildable are certainly significant advantages of attached elevational units, some important limitations must also be considered. Clearly, proper soils are required and the special problems of excavation, construction, drainage, and erosion on hillsides must be understood. Assuming that these difficulties can be dealt with and that in some cases erosion problems can be resolved by building into hillsides, the problems of pedestrian and vehicular access remain. On slopes greater than 20 percent, units can be placed very close together, but some relatively flat areas for roads and parking must be located nearby. Distances from parking to units cannot be excessive, and a distance of more than two flights of stairs to the entry of a unit is usually considered unacceptable unless elevators are used.

The illustrations in figure 5-32 indicate several possible relationships between housing and parking. If elevators are not used, the need for access to the units limits the development to two or three levels at the crest or base of a hill. Under these conditions, a slope could be continuously covered with units only if it was the right length for four to six tiers of units and if parking was available at both the top and bottom of the slope. With elevators designed to service the sloping tiers of units, the number of levels and long slopes that could be developed with access from either the top or the bottom (but not both) would be unlimited. As shown in the last drawing in figure 5-32, such buildings could achieve densities similar to those of conventional high-rise buildings while offering a number of advantages. In addition to using more marginal land, these buildings would have a less massive appearance and would cast no shadows while providing units with privacy, view, increased safety from fire or falling, and perhaps, direct access to the outdoors.

In summary, topography is clearly the most important element in determining lot size and density of development for single-family detached elevational houses with solar orientation. Generally, flat lots for such houses must be at least 0.5 acre (0.2 ha), whereas lots on slopes of 10 percent or more may be reduced to as little as 0.25 acre (0.1 ha). For single-family detached units, slopes of approximately 10 percent are the most flexible for road layouts. It is very important to recognize that the lot sizes in the examples are minimums. Since the prototypical houses are only average in size, the yard spaces are minimal and the houses would have to be designed and built by one party at the same time. Two conclusions about the lot sizes in the examples can be drawn from this information. The first is that densities are likely to be lower than the 2 to 4 units per acre indicated in the examples. Second, so much careful planning and restriction is required for higher densities that attached units appear to be a far better approach to achieving densities of more than 2 units per acre with this type of housing. The greatest potential with regard to elevational units is clearly associated with the use of attached units on slopes of 10 to 50 percent. Not only are the densities relatively high, but on slopes over 15 percent, land that is otherwise unbuildable can be used.

The illustrative layouts of elevational units in this chapter are only diagrams used for density calculations. Nevertheless, they imply a rather rigid structure of east-west streets with direct south orientation for each unit. Although these drawings reflect an optimal situation for maximum and equal solar access, a number of factors may make this rigid type of layout either undesirable or impossible. For example, a more varied topography would require considerable flexibility in orientation and lot size. Actual designs for earth sheltered elevational housing must provide solar access to the units but must do so without creating a rigid and monotonous environment.

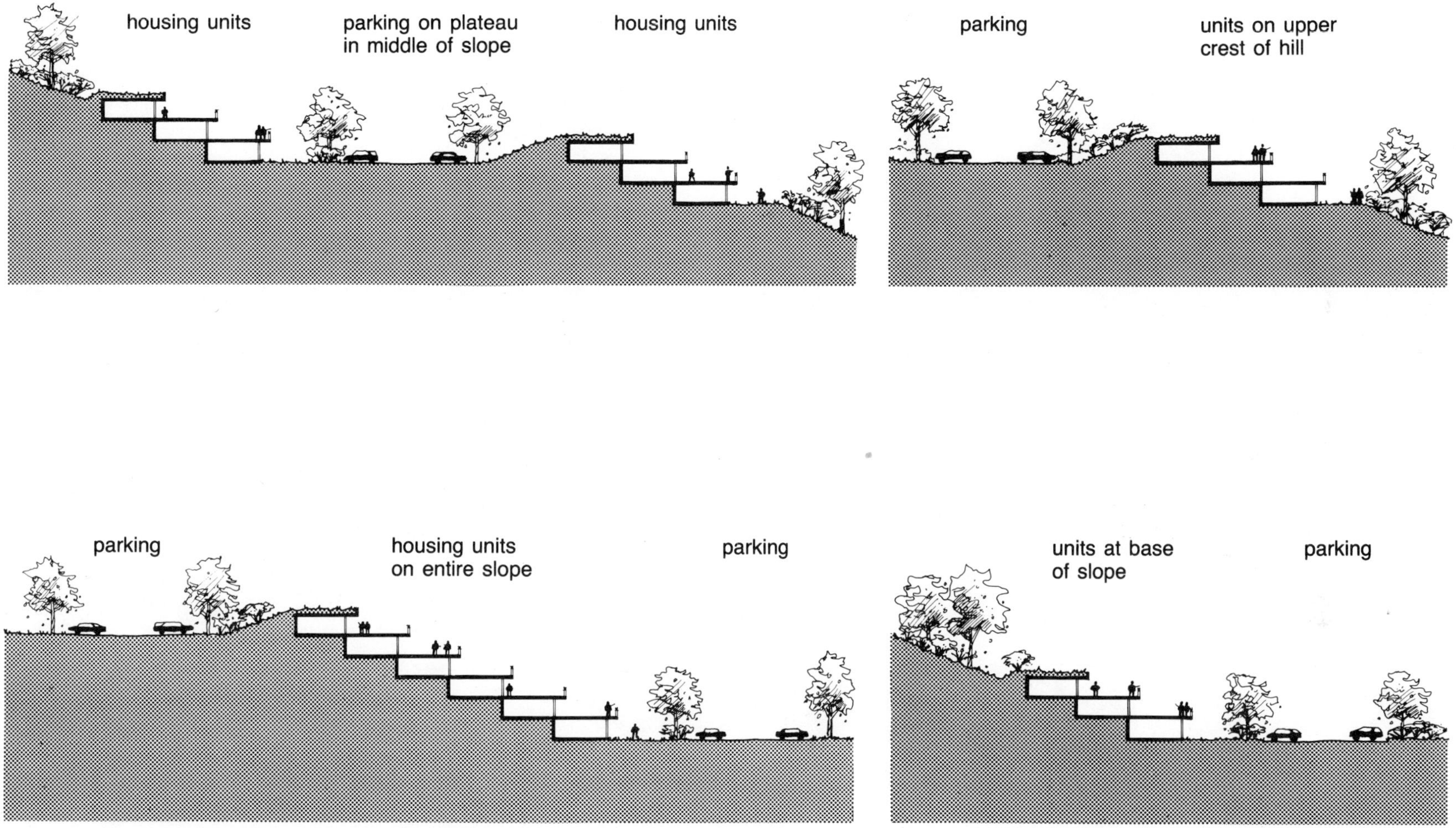
housing units
parking on plateau in middle of slope
housing units
parking
units on upper crest of hill
parking
housing units on entire slope
parking
units at base of slope
parking

5-32: relationship between attached housing and parking

detached units

The size and shape of a single-family detached atrium unit, which can vary considerably, will affect the lot size as well as the depth and manner in which the house is set into the site. As in the previous sections, simple prototypical units in different situations are compared in order to illustrate these effects. In all examples a 60-by 60-foot (18- by 18-m) house with a 20-by 30-foot (6- by 9-m) atrium in the center is used as the basic unit. Although a garage is usually included, a number of variations on its placement are developed to suit the site conditions for each example.

One of the most important factors in determining lot size for atrium houses is the floor level of the house relative to the surface. If the floor level is one full level below the surface, surrounding land for earth berms is unnecessary, although adequate space should be left around the house to permit excavation. Figure 5-33 shows a minimal, 0.17-acre (0.07-ha) lot on a completely flat site. The lot size is based on a 20-foot (6-m) setback from the street and 10-foot (3-m) setbacks on the sides and rear of the lot. Although 10 feet (3 m) is usually not adequate for a rear yard setback, it appears reasonable in this case, since the building is completely below grade and no portions in the rear 30 feet (9 m) of the lot are visible. Two problems with a completely submerged house are access and privacy in the court area. An above-grade structure is part of this design so that an attached garage and pedestrian entry from the street can be provided. The above-grade structure also serves to separate the public street area from the private yard behind and to provide access to the earth-covered roof. This design, in which the roof becomes the yard space for the house, demonstrates an efficient use of land.

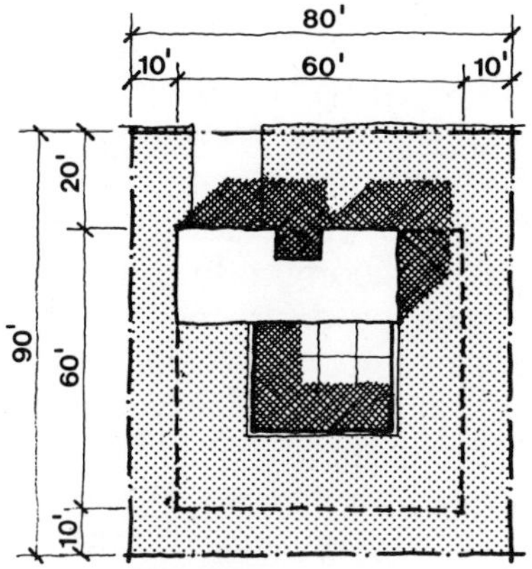
80'
10'
60'
10'
20'
90'
60'
10'

site plan

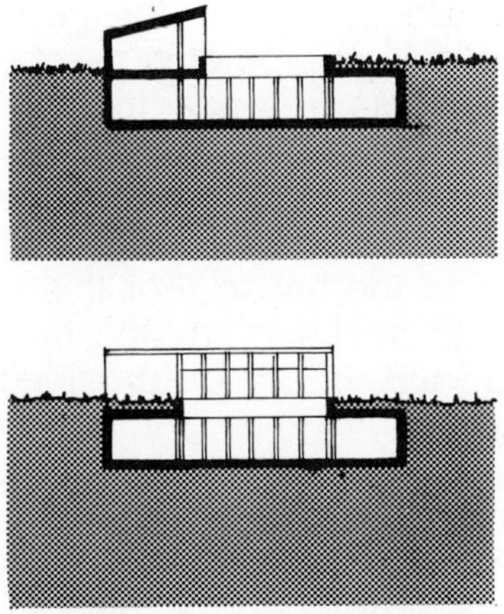

section

5-33: fully recessed atrium house

If the floor level of the house is raised to 4 feet (1.2 m) below existing grade, direct vehicular and pedestrian access to the main floor level of the house are possible. Additional land is required for the berms, resulting in a 0.39-acre or 130- by 130-foot (0.16-ha or 39- by 39-m) lot, as shown in figure 5-34. If the floor level of the house is at grade and berms are placed around the house, a 0.52-acre or 150- by 150-foot (0.21-ha or 45- by 45-m) lot is required to accommodate the berms, as shown in figure 5-35. Because earth must be brought onto the site in this fully bermed example, this is a less satisfactory option than the partially submerged design. The 130-foot-square (39-m-square) lot is used as a basis for the density calculations that follow. The sizes of the berms are based on a 3:1 slope, and 10 feet (3 m) for drainage are provided around the perimeter of the site. The setbacks of 35 and 45 feet (10.6 and 13.6 m) on all sides exceed typical minimum setback requirements.

Although the vehicular and pedestrian access provided in the above examples are acceptable for the bermed atrium houses, other design problems associated with them may be unacceptable. For example, in figures 5-34 and 5-35 a great deal of land is devoted to berms and, except for the atrium, there is very little usable outdoor space. The flat, earth-covered roof is usable but not directly accessible from the house. For this reason an additional yard or court space is created by cutting into the berm. Of course, access can be provided to the rooftop by adding an above-grade portion to the house. One advantage of a bermed house is that the berms form a natural barrier to the rooftop area, thus ensuring more privacy in the courtyard; it may still be necessary, however, to use dense shrubbery or handrails to provide a complete barrier for both privacy and safety. A final concern is that drainage in the courtyard and the entry area must be handled properly.

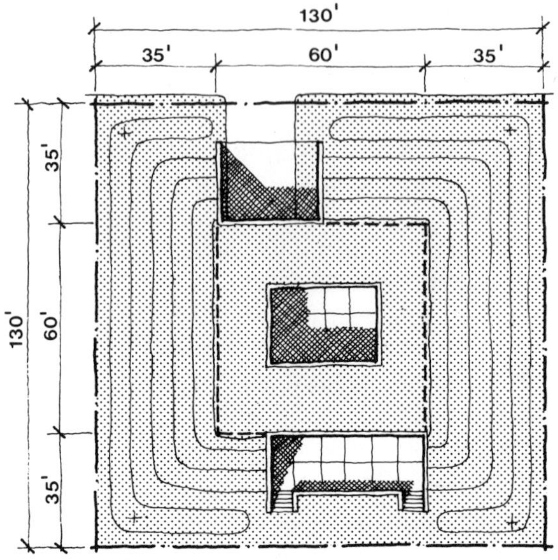

130'
35'
60'
35'
130'
35'
60'
35'

site plan

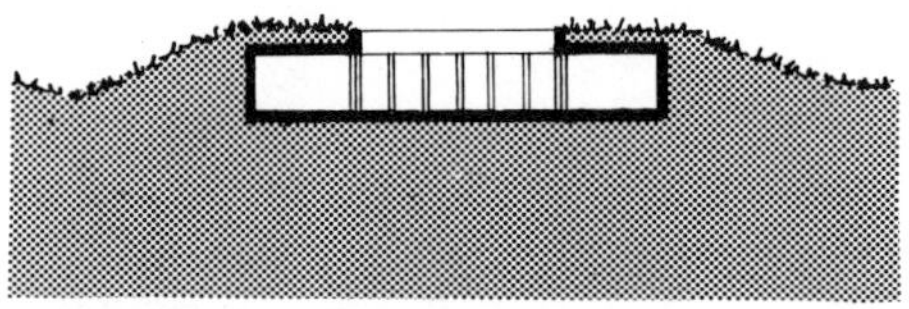

section

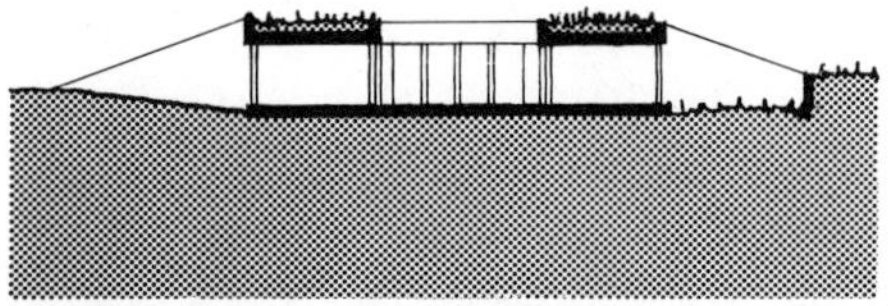

section

5-34: semi-recessed atrium house

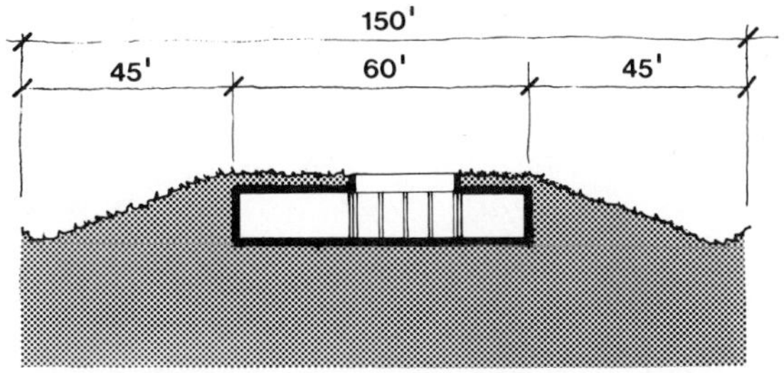
150'
45'
60'
45'

5-35: section—atrium house on grade

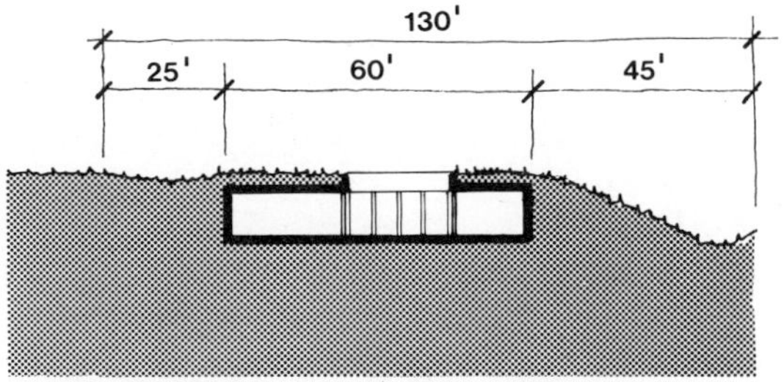
130'
25'
60'
45'

5-36: section—10 percent slope

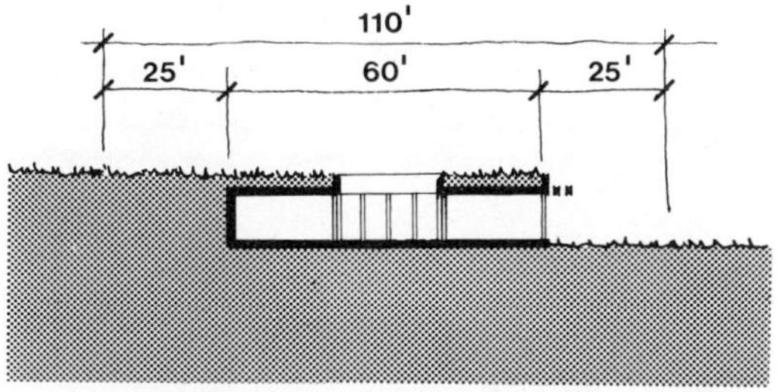
110'
25'
60'
25'

5-37: section—one exposed elevation

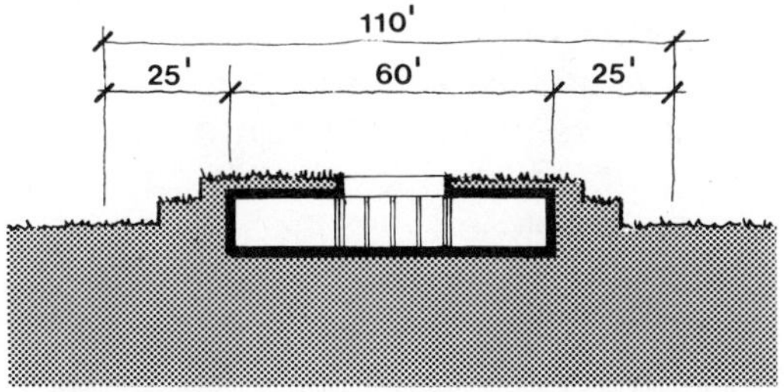
110'
25'
60'
25'

5-38: section—use of retaining walls

Sloping topography has less impact on the lot size and resulting density of single-family detached atrium units than it has on passive solar and elevational houses. An atrium house on a 10-percent slope requires a lot that has approximately the same depth as the 130 feet (39 m) indicated for a half-bermed house on a flat site (fig. 5-36). The width could be reduced somewhat to 110 feet (33 m), however, because less area is required for berms and drainage on the sloping sides of the house. This reduction in lot width results in a lot area of 0.33 acre (0.13 ha). The lot size can be further reduced on a 10-percent slope if the design of the house is modified to expose one entire elevation, as shown in figure 5-37. Atrium units with even one exposed elevation would probably not be built on slopes greater than 10 or 15 percent except for such special designs as those illustrated in the next section.

Variations in the landscape and in architectural design can also help minimize the lot size for an atrium house. As shown in figure 5-38, retaining walls can be used to reduce the land area occupied by berms, resulting in a 0.28-acre or 110-foot-square (0.11-ha or 33-m-square) lot, which has an area nearly 30 percent smaller than the area of the 130-foot-square (39-m-square) lot. This reduction in land area could also be accomplished by simply creating a berm steeper than 3:1 if proper plant materials and soils are used. Like elevational houses, an atrium house could be designed to have earth berms against all the walls and a conventional roof. Again, this type of design would result in a smaller lot, since the height and length of the berms would not be as great.

Like the other housing types—detached as well as attached—earth sheltered atrium designs can be combined in many ways. In fact, they present some unique opportunities, since they have no fixed orientation and have so many possible design variations, all of which can affect layout in some manner. The simple layouts in this section are intended to illustrate relative densities as well as some key design considerations. Because many factors unique to a particular site are not reflected in the layouts, they do not represent prototypical designs.

For single-family detached housing on a flat site, the prototypical lot is 130 feet square (39 m square), which is an adequate land area for a bermed house recessed 4 feet (1.2 m) below grade. This design, explained in the previous section, was selected because it allows for good pedestrian and vehicular access from any direction and for numerous design variations without changing the basic lot size. A simple cluster on flat land is shown in figures 5-39 and 5-40. Ignoring the land required for roads and open space, the density for the housing alone is 2.6 units per acre. For this type of layout, it is unnecessary to assume any particular street orientation.

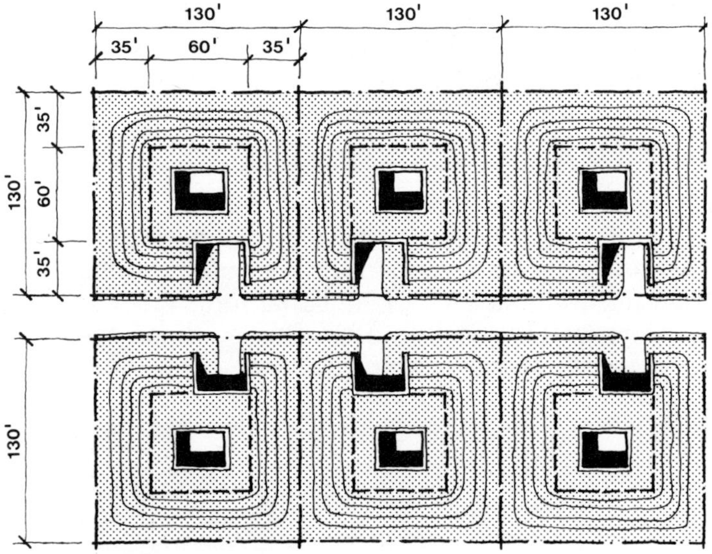

130'
130'
130'
35'
60'
35'
35'
60'
35'
130'
130'

5-39: site plan

As stated earlier, although topography has a limited effect on the density of atrium designs (except in terms of limiting them to slopes no greater than 10 to 15 percent), a number of possible variations and conditions can allow for increased densities and building on slightly steeper slopes. In figure 5-41 atrium units are shown on both a north- and south-facing, 10-percent slope. Building the units on the north slope increases the density from that of units built on flat land (2.6 units per acre) to 3.0 units per acre because a narrower lot width of 110 feet (33 m) is possible on the slope. A development on the south slope could show a similar increase; the south slope here, however, is shown with a density increased to 4.4 units per acre because the units are designed with one exposed elevation facing south for passive solar gain. This layout allows the lots to be shorter, because in this case berms are not required on the south side of the house and the atrium units step down the hill much like typical elevational units.

The concept of combining atrium and elevational designs can be carried further so that units with direct vehicular access can be built on slopes of 20 percent. The increased density of 4.4 units per acre is maintained by the use of two- and even three-level units with exposed south elevations, as shown in figure 5-42. Of course, a similar layout would be undesirable on a north slope, since the units would be exposed to the wind and passive solar heating would be impossible. Therefore, a single unit on a 20-percent north slope is included in this illustration as a possible solution that combines earth sheltering, passive solar, superinsulation, and trees that provide a substantial windbreak.

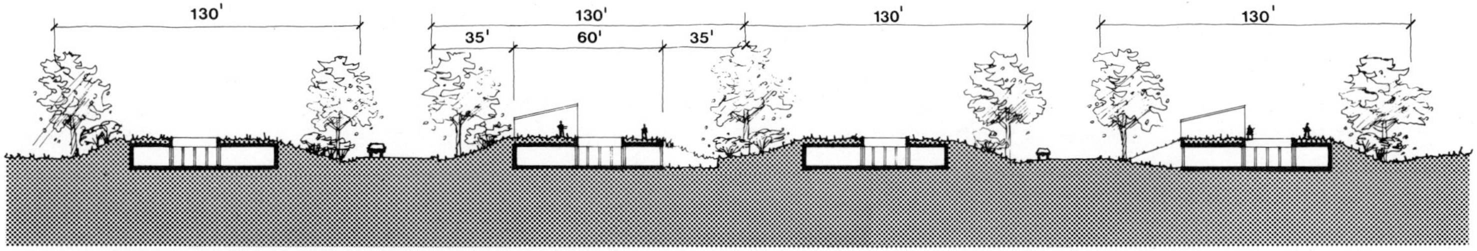
130'
130'
35'
60'
35'
130'
130'

5-40: section—atrium houses on flat site

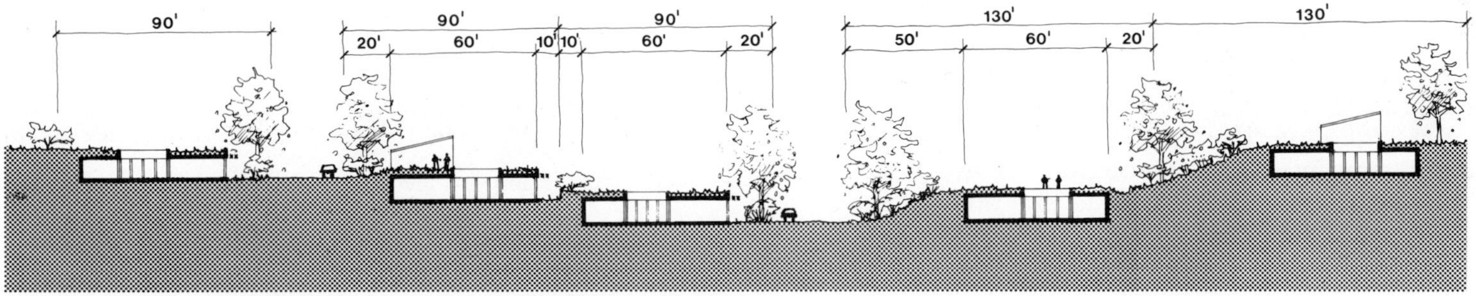
90'
90'
20'
60'
10'
10'
90'
60'
20'
130'
50'
60'
20'
130'

5-41: section—atrium houses on 10 percent slope

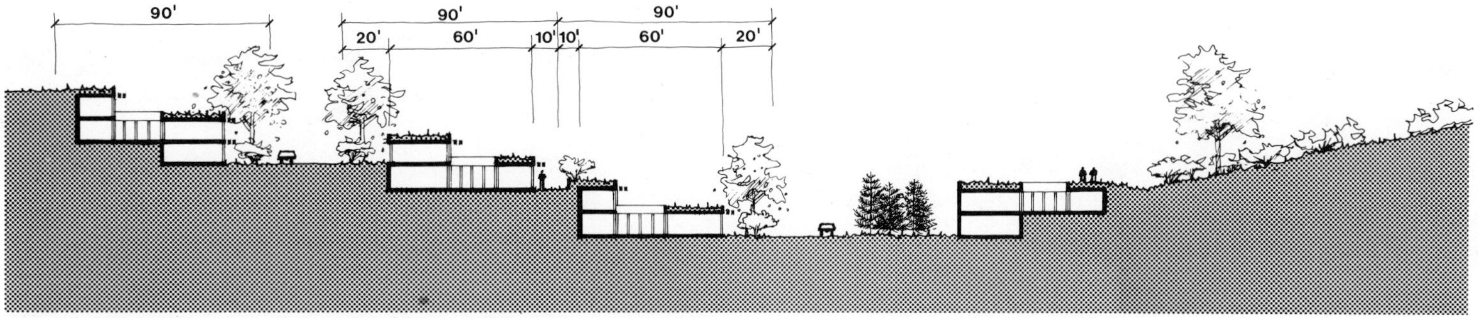
90'
90'
20'
60'
10'
10'
90'
60'
20'

5-42: section—atrium houses on 20 percent slope

One of the main reasons that lots for atrium houses must be relatively large is that a considerable amount of land is required for berms on all four sides of the house. Lot sizes can be reduced for detached units, however, by extending berms across lot lines, as shown in figure 5-43. Here the density is increased considerably, from 2.6 units per acre to 3.6 units per acre. The interior units are 20 feet (6 m) apart—a distance that would satisfy typical setback requirements. Assuming that the land form did not exist, the units would have to be designed and built at the same time. Typical restrictions concerning change in topography and drainage patterns across lot lines need to be adjusted. These units are very similar to completely attached units, which would be simpler and less expensive to build.

Atrium units that are completely below existing grade obviously require no area for berms at all. The reduced lot sizes and increased density—to 4.8 units per acre—are illustrated in figure 5-44. In establishing a reasonable layout for totally submerged houses, it was assumed that an above-grade garage and entry were required for proper access and ample outdoor spaces. These above-grade elements are best located on the north side of the atrium; the units must be spaced far enough apart so that one house does not cast shadows into the atrium of another. The same criteria for passive solar buildings at 40° north latitude presented earlier in this chapter were used, resulting in a layout with solar access for all units. With this type of design, the use of north-south streets is a good technique for providing access to the above-grade portion of the house, which is on the north side of each lot. Lot sizes and densities for detached atrium units on various slopes are summarized on the following chart.

topography	design	lot size (ft)	lot size (m)	density (units/acre)
flat	totally recessed	90 × 80	(27 × 24)	4.8
	semirecessed	130 × 130	(39 × 39)	2.6
10% south-facing	bermed on 4 sides	130 × 110	(39 × 33)	3.0
	open on south side	90 × 110	(27 × 33)	4.4
10% north-facing	bermed on 4 sides	130 × 110	(39 × 33)	3.0
20% south-facing	2-3 levels open on south side	90 × 110	(27 × 33)	4.4

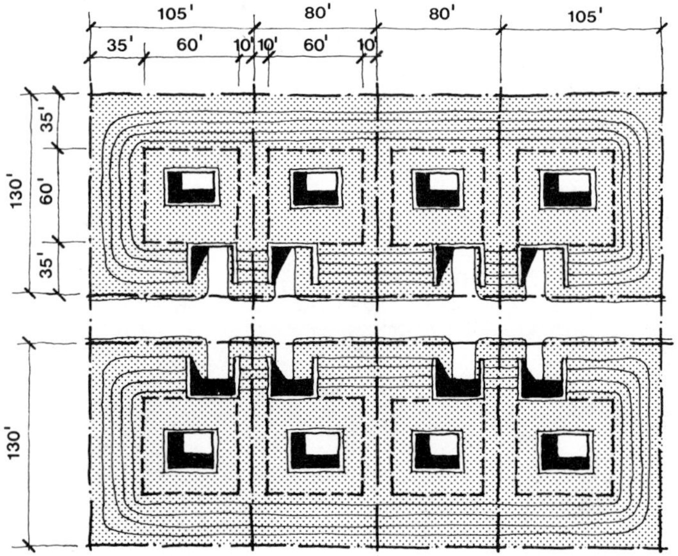

105'
80'
80'
105'
35'
60'
10'
10'
60'
10'
130'
35'
60'
35'
130'

5-43: site plan

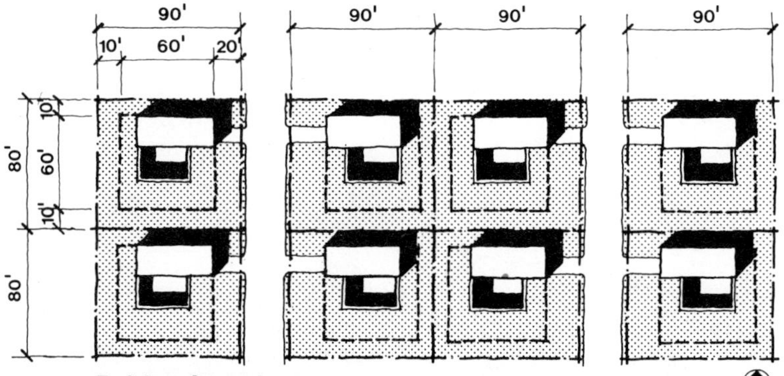

90'
10'
60'
20'
90'
90'
90'
80'
10'
60'
10'
80'

5-44: site plan

attached units

Since atrium units can face in any direction and relate to pedestrian and vehicular access in a number of ways, great variety in configuration of attached units is possible. At the same time, however, the potential densities are limited to a degree by the relatively large area occupied by an atrium unit. If it is assumed that all units must have direct vehicular access and attached garages, the most basic scheme results in single rows of square atrium units with common walls, as shown in figure 5-45. In this example it is assumed that the floor level is 4 feet (1.2 m) below grade, resulting in small berms surrounding each row of units. The density for this configuration is 4.3 units per acre, not including the street area. Attaching atrium units in double rows, as shown in figure 5-46, increases the density to 5.9 units per acre. No specific orientation is implied in either of these layouts, and single or double rows could both work in conjunction with various street patterns.

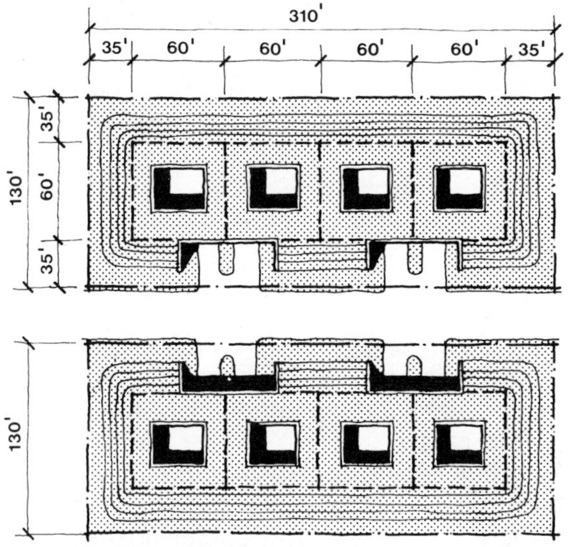

310'
35'
60'
60'
60'
60'
35'
130'
35'
60'
35'
130'

5-45: site plan

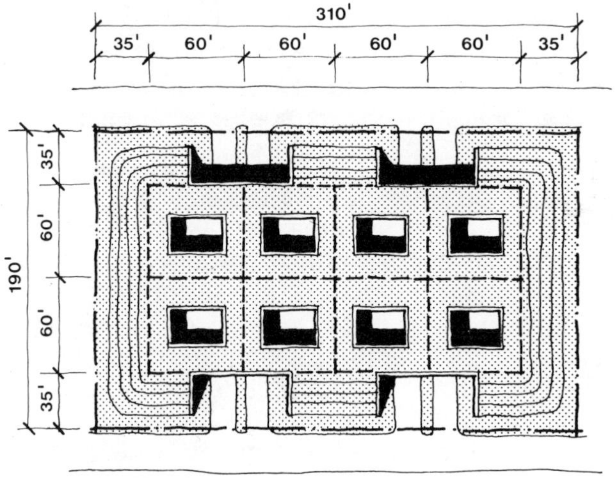

310'
35'
60'
60'
60'
60'
35'
190'
35'
60'
60'
35'

5-46: site plan

These two basic layouts for attached units have the potential drawback of being very monotonous if the rows of units are too long or too regular. On the other hand, if handled properly, such a design could result in a very green, natural, unobtrusive environment. The berms serve to define the private building area and keep outsiders off the rooftops. With a one-level scheme, however, the rooftops—the only usable outdoor space other than the courtyards—are not easily accessible to the residents. Some of the view, access, and other design problems of the scheme shown in figure 5-45 can be solved while maintaining the same cluster of eight prototypical units. Using above-grade spaces, more exposed elevations, additional yard spaces, and greenhouses can increase the variety in the layout (fig. 5-47). The resulting image of the environment, which appears more conventional and less dominated by the earth forms, may have marketing advantages. Increased views and easier access to the rooftops are additional benefits provided by this layout. One important effect of these design changes is the increased window area on one side of the units, making them more like passive solar or elevational units. This arrangement suggests that the rows of attached units should run along the east-west axis and that the exposed elevations should face south, southeast, or southwest in order to benefit from passive gain.

Clusters of attached units can be more efficient and create a more natural environment if attached garages and direct vehicular access are not required for each unit. Eliminating this requirement allows for some additional freedom in arranging units. One possibility is to cluster units around a central parking area, as shown in figure 5-48. The bermed atrium units shown in this cluster benefit from an entry court off the parking area and access to open space on the private side of the house. The overall image of this type of cluster can be very green and natural while still providing variety. The bermed houses simultaneously tend to hide the parking area from the surrounding landscape and separate the public and private areas. A similar layout could provide

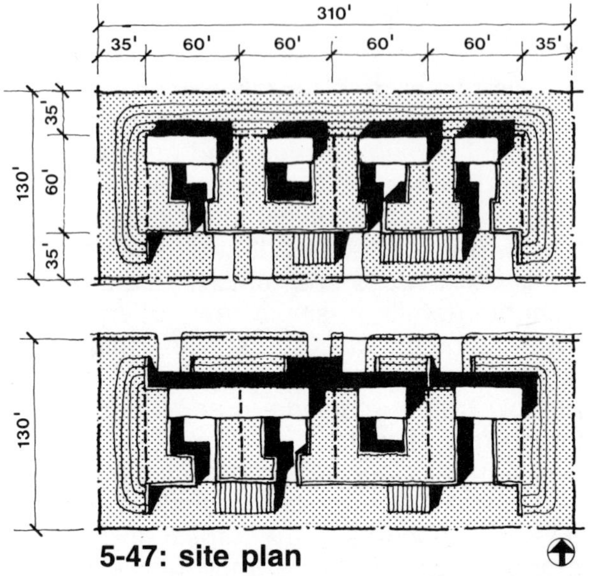
310'
35'
60'
60'
60'
60'
35'
130'
35'
60'
35'
130'

5-47: site plan

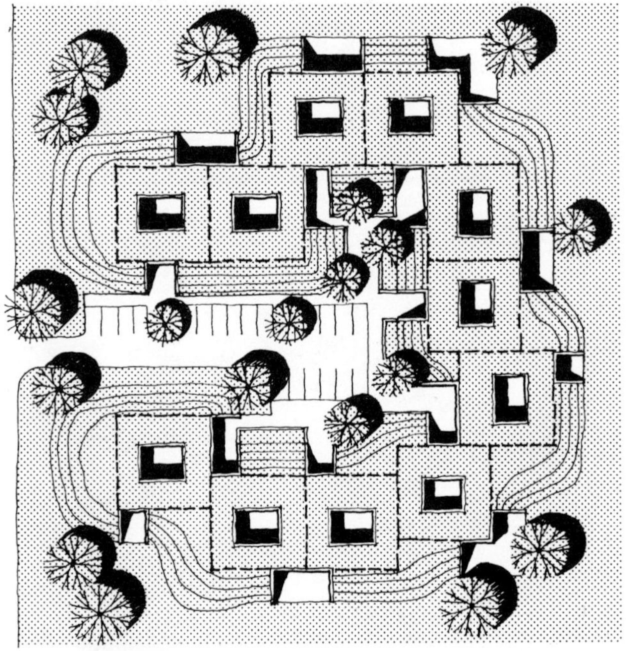

5-48: site plan

the parking and entrances at the periphery of the cluster and an interior community open space. Such a protected open space surrounded by the green earth forms of the houses may be particularly appropriate in a dense, urban setting with no external amenities.

Under certain circumstances densities of attached atrium units that require no direct vehicular access can be increased. If one elevation of the basic atrium unit is exposed, then the units can be placed relatively close together on sloping topography, as discussed earlier for detached units. Ignoring the land required for streets and parking, the density of atrium units on a 10-percent slope would be 7.3 units per acre, as shown in figure 5-49. This density figure is based on the 60- by 60-foot (18- by 18-m) units that are attached in single rows; no land at the ends of the rows is included in the calculation. On a 20-percent slope, the density is increased to 12.1 units per acre (fig. 5-50). Because units cannot be placed any closer together than this, slopes greater than 20 percent cannot be used. Of course, only south-, southeast-, and southwest-facing slopes are appropriate if this type of multiple-unit development is intended to benefit from passive solar heating.

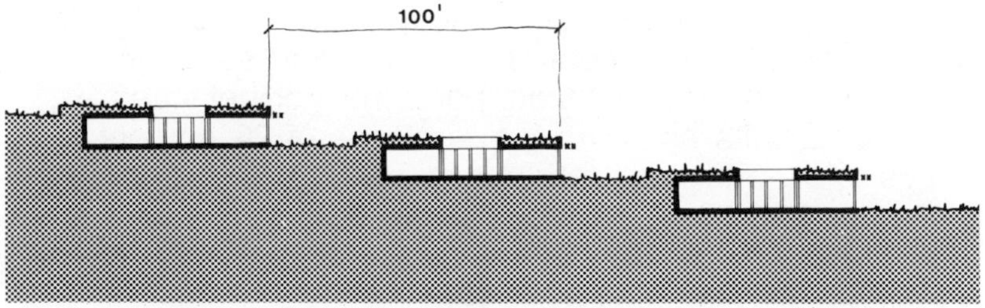
100'

5-49: section—attached units on 10 percent slope

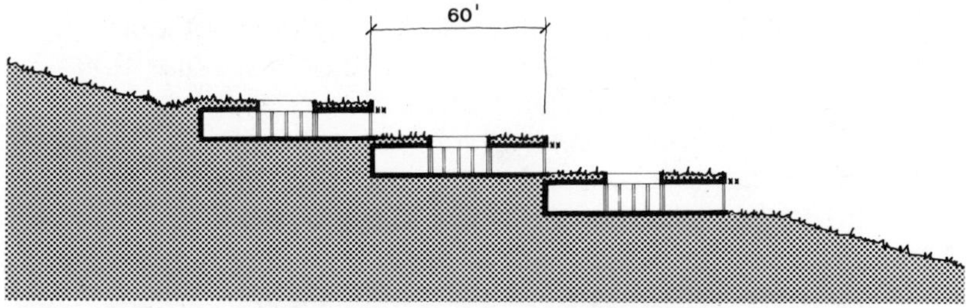
60'

5-50: section—attached units on 20 percent slope

In summary, detached atrium houses require relatively large lots of 0.33 to 0.5 acre (0.13 to 0.2 ha), although fully below-grade atriums can be built on smaller lots of 0.17 acre (0.07 ha) if access problems can be solved. It is important to remember that these lot sizes are minimums based on very tight lots and very simple prototypical units. As with other earth sheltered houses, flexibility in design and in placement on the lot probably requires lot sizes in the range of 0.5 to 1 acre (0.2 to 0.4 ha). For atrium houses lots that are more or less square can be used more efficiently in most cases. Since atrium houses do not rely on specific orientations for solar access, street and lot layouts are relatively unrestricted and could be planned to resemble those for conventional housing.

On sloping land it is most efficient to combine design features of atrium and elevational units so that the houses can be set into hillsides more easily and at increased densities. Nevertheless, atrium units are generally restricted to slopes no greater than 15 percent, although special designs may work on slopes up to 20 percent. As with elevational units, building attached, rather than detached, atrium units has many advantages. In addition to the energy and cost reductions that accrue to any attached units, attached atrium units reduce or eliminate many of the land-use inefficiencies associated with detached atrium units.

summary of comparison

The chart in figure 5-51 indicates some of the key characteristics of earth sheltered, solar, and conventional well-insulated houses. Orientation of the housing unit, allowable percentage of slope and orientation of the land, and ranges of possible densities are listed because they are basic criteria for assessing the feasibility of a certain housing type on a particular site. Earth sheltered housing is actually divided into three categories: elevational houses with passive solar features, elevational houses without passive solar features, and atrium houses.

By definition solar houses and passive solar elevational houses are restricted to southerly orientations. The other alternatives can be oriented in any direction. Although earth sheltered elevational houses without passive solar features can be oriented in directions other than south, these houses are generally limited to predominantly warm climates. Site planning is simpler for conventional and atrium units because of the flexibility of multiple orientations, but the solar and earth sheltered elevational units are the only alternatives designed to make maximum use of the free energy of the sun.

With one important exception, all of the housing types are restricted to land with slopes in the range of 0 to 15 percent. The exception, earth sheltered elevational houses, can be built on slopes up to 50 percent in certain circumstances. While this flexibility is a great advantage for elevational units, it is possible only if other site characteristics—such as soils and access requirements—are favorable. The conventional, atrium, and elevational units without solar orientation can be placed on land that slopes in any direction. Solar houses and elevational units with solar orientation can also be placed on slopes of 15 percent or less that face in any direction, although density on north-facing slopes is reduced. For earth sheltered elevational houses with passive solar exposure, the steeper slopes of 20 to 50 percent generally must face south.

The densities indicated in the chart must be regarded with some caution, since many variables can affect them. These densities are based partly on the examples in this chapter, but they reflect a wider range of possibilities not illustrated here. As with the various cluster layouts in this chapter, the density figures are not gross figures (which include roads and open space), but instead are based on actual lot sizes required for the houses. The higher ends of the ranges do not necessarily reflect recommended or legally allowable densities, but rather what appears to be physically possible in using a particular unit type.

For single-family detached housing, all of the unit types can be built at densities up to 5 units per acre with certain designs. By clustering units quite close together, densities up to 8 units per acre can be achieved for conventional and solar houses. Of course, a very controlled layout is required to reach these densities with solar houses. The density of both earth sheltered elevational and solar houses depends on topography. On a south-facing, 10-percent slope, solar houses could achieve a density of 10 units per acre. For detached elevational units on south-facing slopes of 20 percent, it is possible—with very careful design—to reach a density of 7 units per acre. This density is also possible with special types of earth sheltered units, such as elevational units placed back to back or atrium units that are completely below grade.

With efficient planning conventional single-family attached units can be built at densities up to 20 units per acre. On south-facing, 10-percent slopes, attached solar units can also be built at densities up to 20 units per acre; attached elevational units—which can be built on slopes up to 50 percent—can achieve densities in the range of 20 to 30 units per acre on these steeper slopes. Although attached atrium units appear to be limited to 6 units per acre for most designs, densities with fully below-grade attached units could reach 8 units per acre.

5-51: comparison of energy-efficient housing types

type of housing	orientation of unit	percent and orientation of slope	estimated maximum density (units/acre)		
			single family detached	single family attached	multi-family attached
conventional well-insulated	all	0-15% all slopes	8	20	over 20 (depends on zoning, not physical limitations)
solar: passive and active	south southeast southwest	0-15% south facing preferred	8 on flat land; 10 on 10% south facing slopes	15 on flat land; 20 on 10% south facing slopes	20 on flat land; 25 on 10% south facing slopes
earth sheltered type 1-elevational (with passive solar orientation)	south southeast southwest	0-50% south facing; 0-15% all slopes	3 on flat land; 7 on 20% slopes	5 on flat land; 10 on 10% slopes; 20 on 30% slopes; 30 on 50% slopes	similar to single family attached units
earth sheltered type 1-elevational (without passive solar orientation)	all	0-50% all slopes	5 on flat land; 7 on 20% slopes	7 on flat land; 10 on 10% slopes; 20 on 30% slopes; 30 on 50% slopes	similar to single family attached units
earth sheltered type 2-atrium	all	0-15% all slopes	3 with semi-recessed units; 5 with fully recessed units	6 with semi-recessed units; 8 with fully recessed units	type of structure unfeasible

Very high densities, far exceeding those possible with any of the other building types indicated here, can be achieved with conventional multifamily housing structures. Although low- and even high-rise buildings can be built with solar access for each unit, on flat land their densities appear to be limited to 20 units per acre, which are not much greater than town house densities. On a 10-percent, south-facing slope, a 25-unit-per-acre density can be achieved. Multiple-unit structures similar to conventional low- and high-rise apartment buildings or condominiums are not feasible with atrium earth sheltered units as defined in this study. Elevational units that step down slopes of 30 to 50 percent can be built as multifamily structures, however, and achieve densities up to 30 units per acre.

Earth sheltered houses have two characteristics that affect density comparisons. These are the potentially usable open space on the roofs of earth sheltered structures, and the generally less dense appearance that partly or fully underground buildings may have. Both of these features could be advantages for earth sheltered units over more visible conventional structures. Typical maximum site coverage requirements could be exceeded with buildings that have earth-covered roofs, thereby allowing for greater densities. Although the "feeling" of density is not easily quantifiable and the space on the roof is not always very accessible, these characteristics may, nonetheless, help make earth sheltered units more acceptable than conventional buildings at higher densities.

additional site design considerations

In the preceding comparison of earth sheltered, solar, and conventional well-insulated housing units, a number of energy-conserving strategies and considerations for site design were discussed. Most important were the orientation of each type of unit, pedestrian and vehicular access, the benefits of clustering units together, and the implications of site planning for solar access. Some additional site design considerations were not mentioned, either because they generally apply to all energy-conserving housing types or they are too detailed for a general comparative discussion. These considerations include topography; site elements for wind protection, shading, and natural ventilation; and the impact of ground surface materials on energy use. Although the same elements were discussed in chapter 2 in the context of large-scale planning, they are presented here in the context of detailed site design in order to provide a more complete overview of site design for energy conservation. The techniques and patterns illustrated in this section are intended mainly for designs for cool and temperate climates.

topography

Topography affects air movement and air temperature, both of which are closely related to energy consumption. In addition, varied topography results in areas of increased and decreased exposure to the sun (fig. 5-52). In cool regions building on south- and southeast-facing slopes is the primary pattern that should be followed in site selection and placement of buildings. Higher ridges and hilltops are undesirable, not only because they are exposed to winter winds, but also because they are characterized by lower temperatures created by cold air settling in the valleys. North-facing slopes are usually inappropriate sites because they are exposed to the wind and receive less solar radiation than south-facing slopes. Structures set into the earth on a south-facing slope are particularly effective in providing protection from winds.

In addition to offering wind protection benefits, south-facing slopes have higher ground temperatures due to increased solar radiation. This phenomenon creates a more favorable microclimate in winter and, in effect, results in an earlier spring and later fall than is the case on a north slope. In his book *Design with Climate*, Victor Olgyay calculates the amount of solar radiation received on south-facing slopes for the New York climate. A 10-percent south slope receives 20 percent more solar radiation than a flat surface, while a 20-percent south slope receives 40 percent more solar radiation [5.3].

While there is no doubt that siting on south-facing slopes reduces energy consumption in cool climates, the quantitative effect will vary depending on local climate, exact site conditions, other site features such as trees, and the type of construction used. As a general indication, however, one study compared energy consumption for houses on southern and northern slopes in Syracuse, New York [5.4]. Those houses on the south-facing slopes consumed 10 to 14 percent less energy in winter.

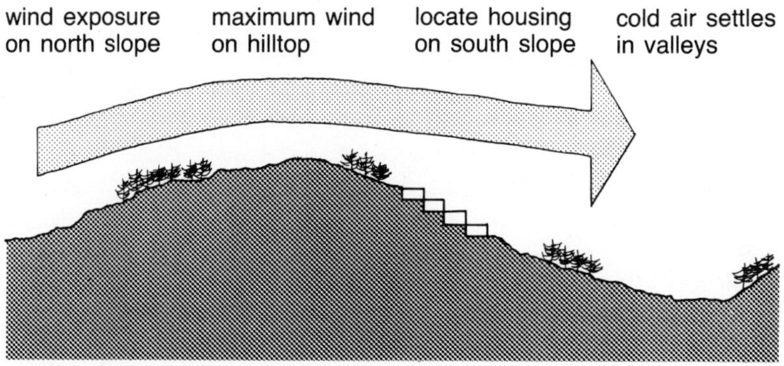
wind exposure
on north slope
maximum wind
on hilltop
locate housing
on south slope
cold air settles
in valleys

5-52: effect of topography

Building on slopes is also sound practice in more temperate climates. In a hot, humid climate, however, the most favorable location would be on hilltops to capture breezes. Conversely, a primary objective in a hot, arid climate is avoiding hot, dry winds; thus, a cooler refuge near the valley floor would be the preferable location.

site elements for wind protection

Existing and new vegetation as well as solid barriers such as fences and earth berms can significantly affect heat loss by preventing wind infiltration into buildings. Existing trees on a site offer potential for substantial energy savings at little or no cost. Windbreaks can be effective in an entire development, a cluster of houses, or individual units. In cooler regions shelterbelts of trees should be located so as to protect clusters from the prevailing northwest winds and extend perpendicular to the winds from the southwest to the northeast, as shown in figure 5-53. The shelterbelt will protect an area up to twenty times the height of the trees in high winds, although the greatest reductions in velocity occur within four to five times the tree height. The shelterbelt should extend so far beyond the houses that accelerated air movement at the ends of the shelterbelt does not direct wind toward some houses.

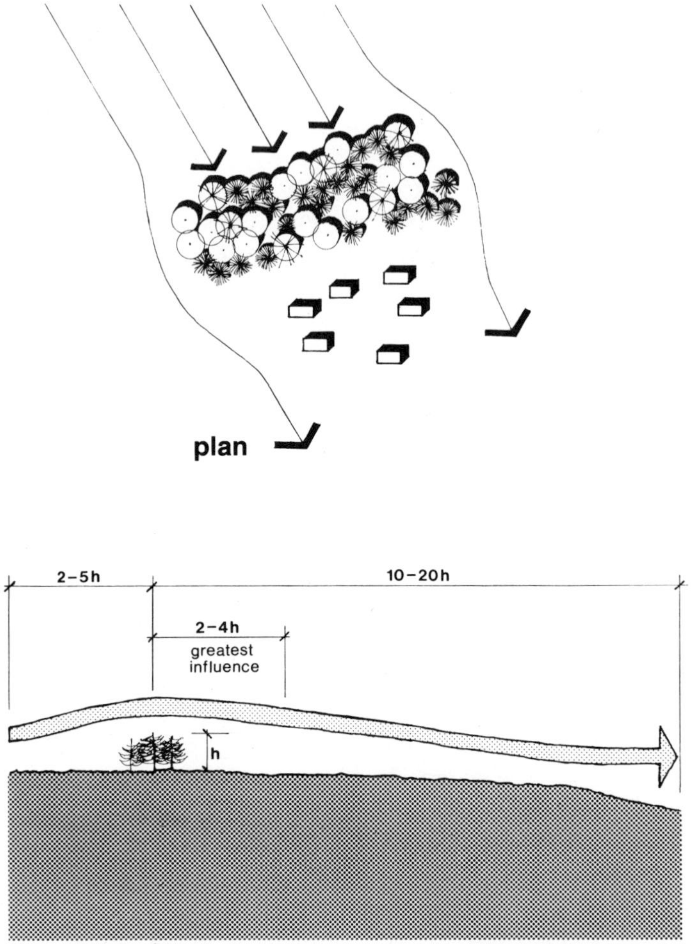
plan
2–5h
10–20h
2–4h
greatest influence
h

5-53: zone of influence of shelterbelt

Closely spaced coniferous trees are the most effective type of windbreak. Deciduous trees mixed with conifers can also be effective, although more rows would be required. In any case multiple rows of staggered trees are superior to a single row. Shelterbelts should include both high trees and low shrubs; otherwise the wind will be accelerated beneath the trees if the lower zone is open. For large-scale windbreaks, vegetation is generally better than solid barriers such as fences, walls, or earth berms. While solid barriers stop the wind almost completely, wind eddies usually result and the wind resumes normal speed very quickly at a distance equal to the height of the barrier. Penetrable barriers, such as trees, do not stop the wind as completely as solid barriers, but their zone of influence is considerably greater. Windscreens composed of coniferous trees and partly open walls and fences are most effective for individual buildings at a distance of one-and-a-half to two times the height of the barriers. Solid walls are most effective at a shorter distance. Other buildings can serve as windbreaks, and earth berms can also be effective for short distances.

Several studies have examined the effects of windbreaks on energy consumption in buildings. At the Lake State Forest Experimental Station in Nebraska, two identical houses, one exposed to the wind and the other protected by dense shrubbery, were compared. A temperature of 70°F (21°C) was maintained in each house. The protected house consumed 22.9 percent less fuel during the winter [5.5]. In a similar study of two identical houses in South Dakota, energy consumption was monitored for one winter month. The house with the windbreak used 40 percent less fuel to maintain the same temperature during that month; the difference between energy use of the two houses for the entire winter was 33.92 percent [5.6].

Eliminating air infiltration through the use of windbreaks can reduce heating energy costs considerably in conventionally constructed buildings, in which air infiltration can account for 25 to 75 percent of the total heat loss. The total amount of infiltration will be far less significant for earth sheltered buildings or above-grade buildings with superbly sealed joints and vapor barriers, however. This observation has some interesting implications for earth sheltered housing, one of which is that windbreaks on-site may not significantly reduce energy use for properly oriented earth sheltered houses. A second implication is that earth sheltered housing may be a more appropriate solution on sites where there is little existing vegetation to provide wind protection.

site elements for shade

The summer cooling load of a structure can be reduced significantly, primarily by the use of trees as shown in figure 5-54, but also by shrubs, walls, and fences that provide shade from the sun. Trees without dense branch patterns that will interfere with solar gain in the winter are preferred. Typically, deciduous trees are located on the south side of the house to provide summer shade. Pruning of lower branches is desirable to allow summer breezes to penetrate the house. Clusters of trees, low hedges, fences, or walls can be used to shade the house from the lower sun on the east and west sides. Vines may be planted to cover and shade walls exposed to the sun and provide cooling by evaporation.

The actual amount of reduction in cooling load due to shading depends on a number of factors, including the type of trees, their shapes, and their location. The most important elements of the building to shade are the windows and the roof. In the summer the east and west walls receive much more direct solar radiation than the south wall. The effect of shade trees is not only to block solar radiation, but also to reduce the temperature of the ambient air around them. On a sunny day, the temperature under a tree has been measured at 5°F (2.8°C) less than the ambient air temperature [5.7].

For houses that are partially or fully earth covered, the grassy berms against the walls and grass on the roof contribute to the cooling effects of the structure and reduce the need for shading these surfaces with other site elements. In addition to using shade trees for protection from the sun, windows and exposed walls may be shaded with overhangs on the south side.

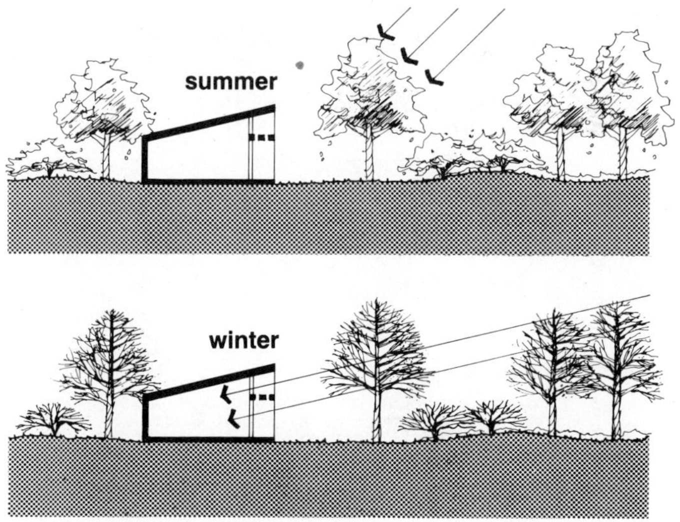
summer
winter

5-54: deciduous shade trees

ground surfaces

The ground surface on a site can have a great influence on the temperature around a building and the reflection of light and heat into buildings. In cool climates it is desirable both to reduce temperatures and reflection of heat in summer and to increase temperatures and reflection of heat into buildings in winter.

For winter heating and increased day lighting, light-colored ground surfaces, such as concrete patios, should be located outside of south-facing windows (fig. 5-55). Any surface with snow cover is an excellent reflector. Grass surfaces and plant materials should be used around buildings for summer cooling to reduce temperatures and to reflect heat and light into buildings.

The light reflected from the ground can represent a significant percentage of light that enters a window. Based on figures from the Illuminating Engineering Society [5.8], 74 percent of the light that strikes new snow is reflected, as compared to 55 percent of the light striking concrete and only about 25 percent of the light striking vegetation.

Grassy surfaces also have more considerable effects on temperature than man-made hard surfaces do. On a sunny day, grass is 10 to 40°F (5.6 to 22.4°C) cooler than exposed soil [5.9]. On the other hand, at an ambient air temperature of 98°F (37°C), the temperature of asphalt has been recorded at 124°F (51°C). Although plants absorb sunlight, the heat gain is reduced because of evaporative cooling and is rapidly dissipated. Man-made materials are far more massive and retain more heat than plant materials.

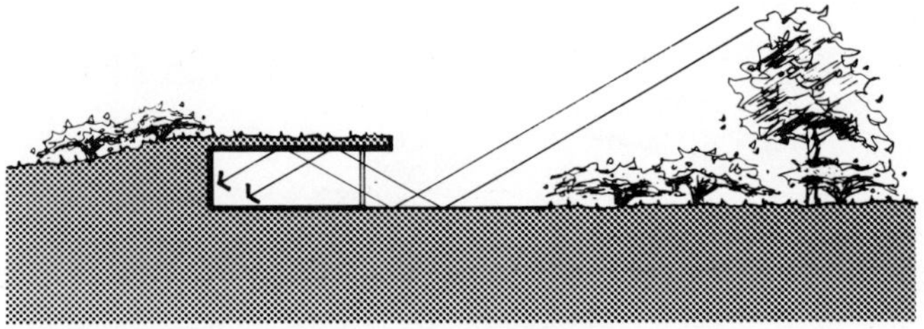

5-55: reflective ground surface

In a cool climate, it would seem preferable to incorporate light-colored surfaces outside of south windows to enhance winter heat gain and light, rather than providing grass surfaces for cooler temperatures and less reflection in summer. Some balance between these two types of features is desirable, however. One solution is to place light-colored patios outside the windows for winter reflection and shade them with deciduous trees in summer to keep the temperature and reflection lower. Another solution is to use vegetation for ground cover as much as possible and allow the snow cover to provide reflection in the coldest parts of the winter.

site elements for natural ventilation

In the same manner that vegetation, earth berms, fences, and walls can be used to reduce cold winter winds, these same elements can be used to channel and even accelerate summer breezes (fig. 5-56). In cooler regions trees, shrubs, fences, walls, and earth berms on the southern side of the house can be located to channel prevailing breezes from the southeast and the southwest through the window openings of the house. Site elements on the north, or lee, side of the house have little effect on summer breezes unless they obstruct the openings or outlets for cross-ventilation. Therefore, winter windbreaks should be placed far enough away from the house to allow some air flow in the summer. In developments where several buildings are clustered together, the structures could be staggered to channel breezes to each building rather than block natural ventilation. Locating housing near bodies of water also enhances natural ventilation in addition to moderating temperatures and providing evaporative cooling in dry areas.

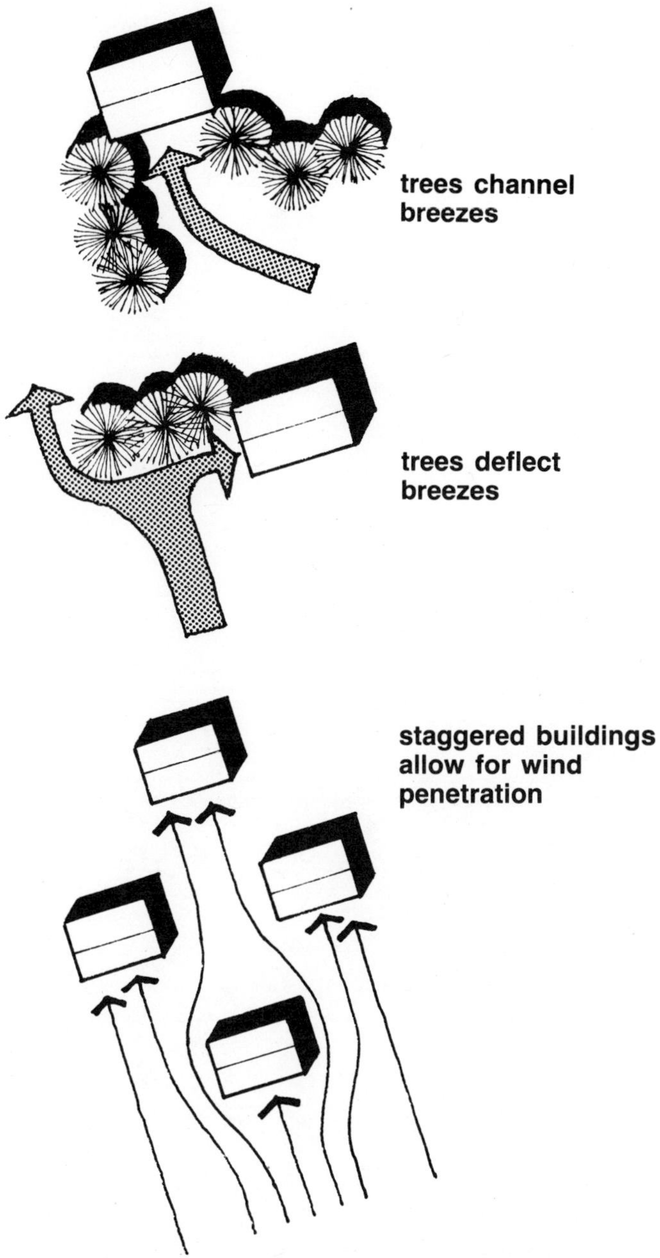
trees channel breezes
trees deflect breezes
staggered buildings allow for wind penetration

5-56: site planning for natural ventilation

Three important points must be considered in using site elements to enhance natural ventilation. First, natural ventilation may be maximized simply by proper orientation of the unit, window placement, and elimination of any obstruction on-site. This implies that site elements for natural ventilation may be unnecessary in many cases but will be particularly desirable in situations where they can correct for poor orientation or help to accelerate meager air flow. A second point to consider is that for houses with a substantial amount of earth contact, which produces cooler temperatures, natural ventilation may not be as necessary to maintain comfort. Finally, the placement of trees to enhance natural ventilation must be coordinated with tree placement for shading and wind protection. In cooler regions, if appropriate coordination cannot be achieved, placement for the winter condition should receive priority.

Design study for prototypical site by Tom Ellison and John Carmody. Drawing by Rick LaMuro.

6 design study for prototypical site

introduction

The preceding chapters of this study have focused primarily on methods of large-scale site analysis and design information for the layout of roads, utilities, and buildings that will result in more energy-efficient, environmentally responsive community planning and housing design. In this chapter the application of the site analysis and the design strategies is illustrated by means of a schematic site design and the design of housing for a portion of the prototypical development site presented in chapter 1. In order to proceed with the schematic site design, all of the site analysis information must be combined into a final energy-efficient development composite. Presented in the first section of this chapter, this composite is based on the analysis of development, suitability, natural systems, and energy-related factors discussed in chapters 1 and 2. This information must then be combined with an analysis of the visual character of the site so that the resulting site design reflects not only the technical considerations of reducing energy consumption and protection of the natural systems, but also the aesthetic potential of the site. The visual character assessment—presented for the prototypical site in the second section of this chapter—is an essential part of the total analysis of a site. Following this section are a presentation of the schematic site design, including a discussion of the basic concepts on which it is based, and a section illustrating the design of several clusters of earth sheltered housing on an appropriate portion of the prototypical site.

final development composite

The final energy-efficient development composite map for the prototypical site, shown in figure 6-1, represents a combination of three composite maps presented in earlier chapters. The three were rated equal in the preparation of the final composite. The maps are:

- the development composite by the traditional process (fig. 1-13)
- the natural systems composite (fig. 1-14)
- the composite of energy-related factors (fig. 2-22)

The final composite distinguishes the areas on the site that should be protected for environmental reasons from the buildable areas. The buildable areas are then subdivided into four levels of energy-related benefits (based on optimizing for the winter) achievable through appropriate design strategies. Optimal areas for energy efficiency are represented by the cross-hatched areas, which are scattered about the site in relatively small parcels totaling 10 acres (4 ha). The dark-toned areas, which comprise 60 acres (24 ha), represent buildable areas with major benefits related to energy efficiency. These two favorable areas—a majority of the site—are predominantly on the south-, southeast-, and southwest-facing slopes on the site. They correspond to the ideal locations in the Minnesota climate for simultaneous maximum exposure to the sun and maximum protection from the winter winds. It should be noted that these areas include both gently and steeply sloping areas. In order to maximize energy efficiency along with land-use efficiency, the proper housing types must be selected and designed in response to the particular slope and orientation of the site area.

Based on this composite analysis, the light-toned areas on the map indicate buildable areas with minor energy-related benefits. This relatively small portion of the site—a total of 4 acres (1.6 ha)—is scattered throughout the site in several parcels, usually adjacent to sites with major energy-related benefits. Although these sites are not rated as highly as those in the previously discussed categories, they should be examined carefully so that buildings in these areas can be located and designed to take advantage of whatever energy-related benefits are available.

The sparse dot pattern located mainly on the northern half of the site represents buildable areas with virtually no energy-related benefits, based on the natural land features. These areas are predominantly north-facing slopes that are exposed to the northwest winter winds. Such slopes present more problems for the development of structures relying on solar exposure for heating. The steepness of the slopes would necessitate increased spacing between the buildings. A number of design strategies can be employed to develop such sites in an energy-efficient manner—e.g., the use of trees for windbreaks and clustering of extremely well-insulated housing.

The white areas on the map represent those portions of the site restricted for building. Because of their physiographic, geologic, vegetative, and hydrologic characteristics, these environmentally sensitive areas should be preserved as open space. These areas include water bodies, wetlands, extremely erodible soils, and soils that have severe limitations for building. Although not suitable for building, these natural areas represent potential visual amenities and some of them could be designed as community recreational areas.

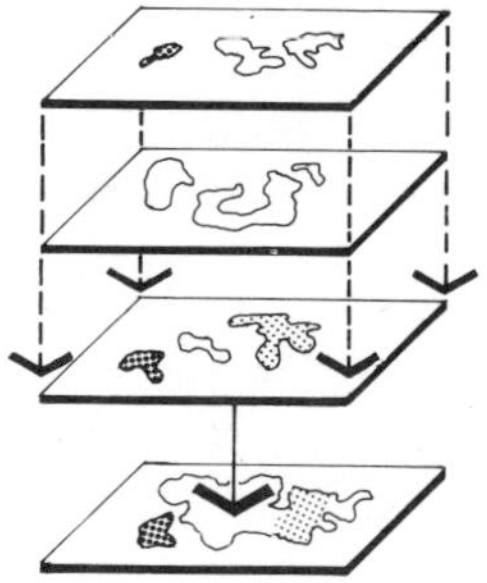

development composite

natural systems composite

composite of energy-related factors

final energy-efficient development composite

optimal buildable areas for energy efficiency, given appropriate siting and design of buildings

buildable areas with major energy-related benefits, given appropriate siting and design of buildings; windbreaks, shade trees and other site design elements may be required

buildable areas with minor energy-related benefits; the less suitable conditions in these areas require careful design to optimize for energy efficiency

buildable areas with no energy-related benefits; all major building and site design strategies are required to achieve energy-efficient design

environmentally sensitive areas that should be protected; all types of building are restricted in these areas

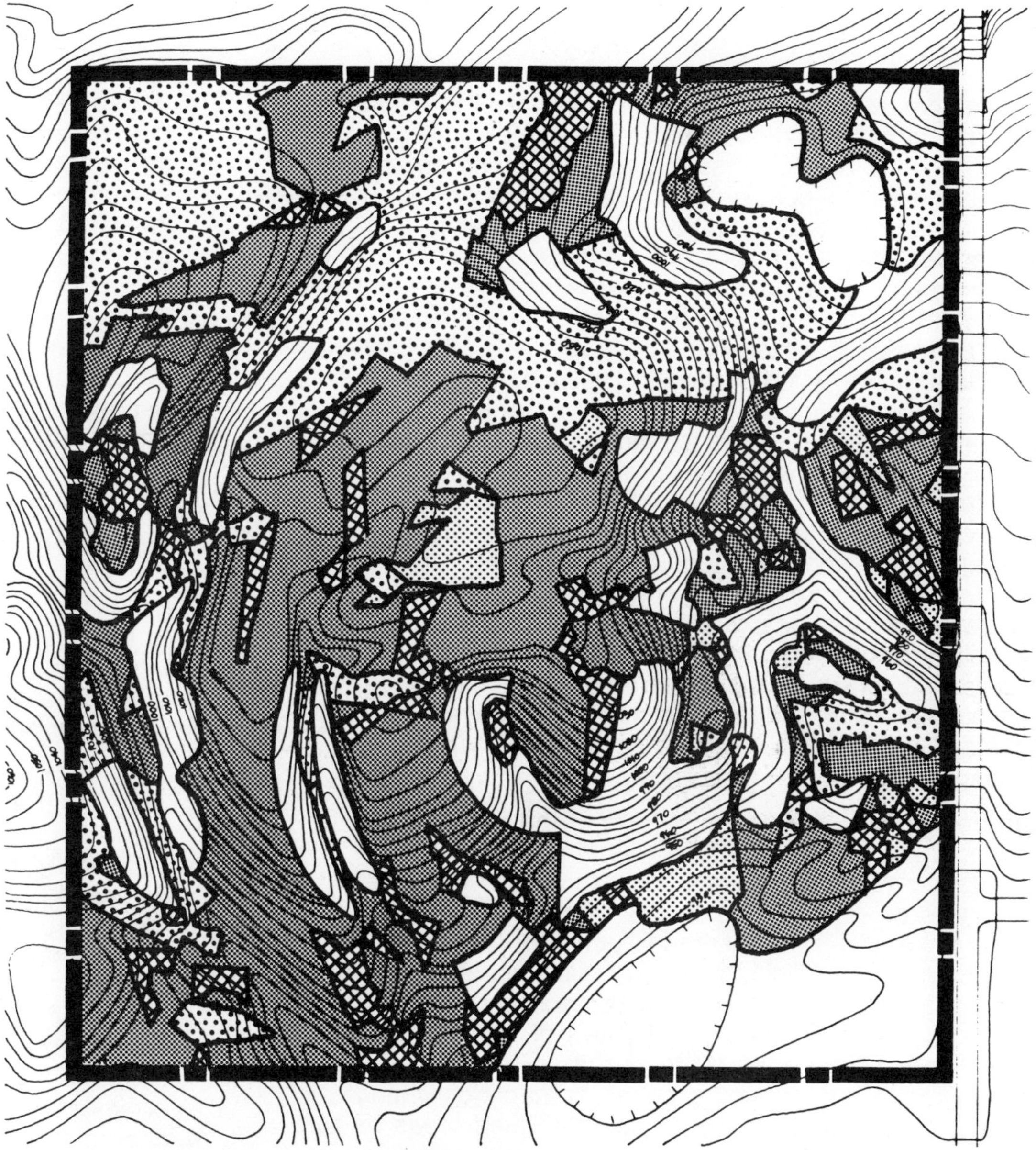

6-1: final energy-efficient development composite

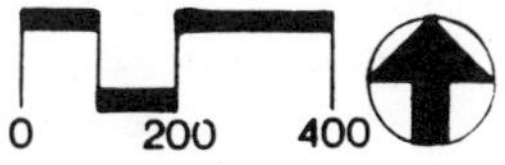
0
200
400

All of the information used to create the final development composite has been technical in nature. In the traditional planning process, the development composite is based on such physical criteria as soil types, percent slope, and hydrological processes. The composite of energy-related factors is based on a technical analysis of recurring microclimatological phenomena, such as sunlight and winds, on the site. The process of creating a composite map for development is not only useful in identifying buildable and unbuildable areas, but also for determining preliminary economic feasibility of development. In addition, by identifying environmentally sensitive areas, the process promotes development that avoids additional construction costs while creating opportunities for open space and recreational areas. Finally, the process identifies opportunities and limitations for building design, particularly with respect to energy efficiency. It is important to emphasize, however, that these technical criteria are only some of the tools to be used by a skilled designer. In order to create a functioning, stimulating, and unique community, the visual design factors must also be considered and included in the design process.

In designing a development, one of the most important components of the total analysis is an assessment of the visual character of the site. An example of this type of analysis on a larger scale, also referred to as an amenity analysis, is shown in figure 6-2 for the prototypical site. This visual analysis illustrates two interrelated concerns—the appearance and character of the site, and the location and views of any amenities. The tones on the map represent three areas of distinct appearance and character based primarily on changes in topography and vegetation. The light-toned areas on the north and south borders of the site represent rolling hills covered with grasses. Steep slopes with coarse, wooded vegetation—represented by the dark-toned areas—are the most dramatic-looking areas on the site. The areas with the sparse dot pattern, located at the top of the hill in the center of the site and around the lake on the east side of the site, represent moderate slopes with sparse, second-growth vegetation. The amenities on the site, indicated by the large asterisks, include two water bodies and the major hill in the center of the site. These features provide significant scenic views available from the site. As indicated by the large arrows, views of the two water bodies from much of the steep, wooded slopes fan out around the hill in the center of the site. This hill is considered a special amenity, primarily because it offers long-distance views of the surrounding land.

Finally, the visual analysis map indicates the land uses adjacent to the site that help establish the character of surrounding area. The entire north and west sides of the site are adjacent to parkland, a golf course is located along the east boundary, and farmland on rolling hills lies to the south. The only likely future change in these land uses is the replacement of the farmland by residential development. In all cases these off-site land uses represent opportunities for attractive views from the steep slopes and the hilltop area of the site.

The visual analysis should not be interpreted as an afterthought or as a supplementary part of the process. Although a site may be suitable for development from a technical point of view, the amenities and appearance of the total community may be the key factors in its marketability. Similarly, site planning and design for energy efficiency in buildings must be achieved in combination with integration of the building forms into the land. One great appeal of earth sheltered buildings is the potential for creating an energy-efficient structure that can be very well integrated with the land forms and visual character of a site.

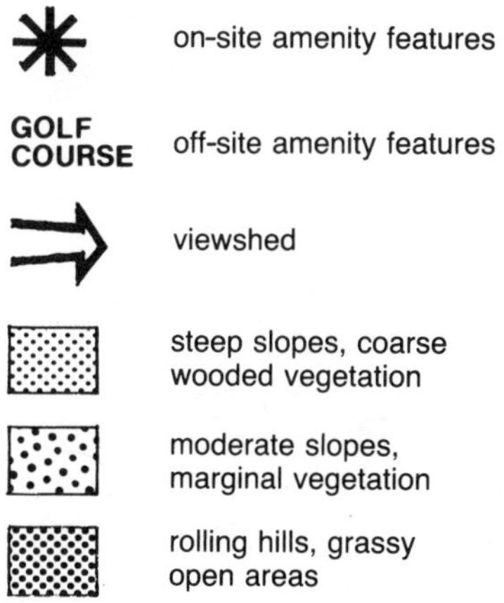
on-site amenity features
GOLF COURSE
off-site amenity features
viewshed
steep slopes, coarse wooded vegetation
moderate slopes, marginal vegetation
rolling hills, grassy open areas

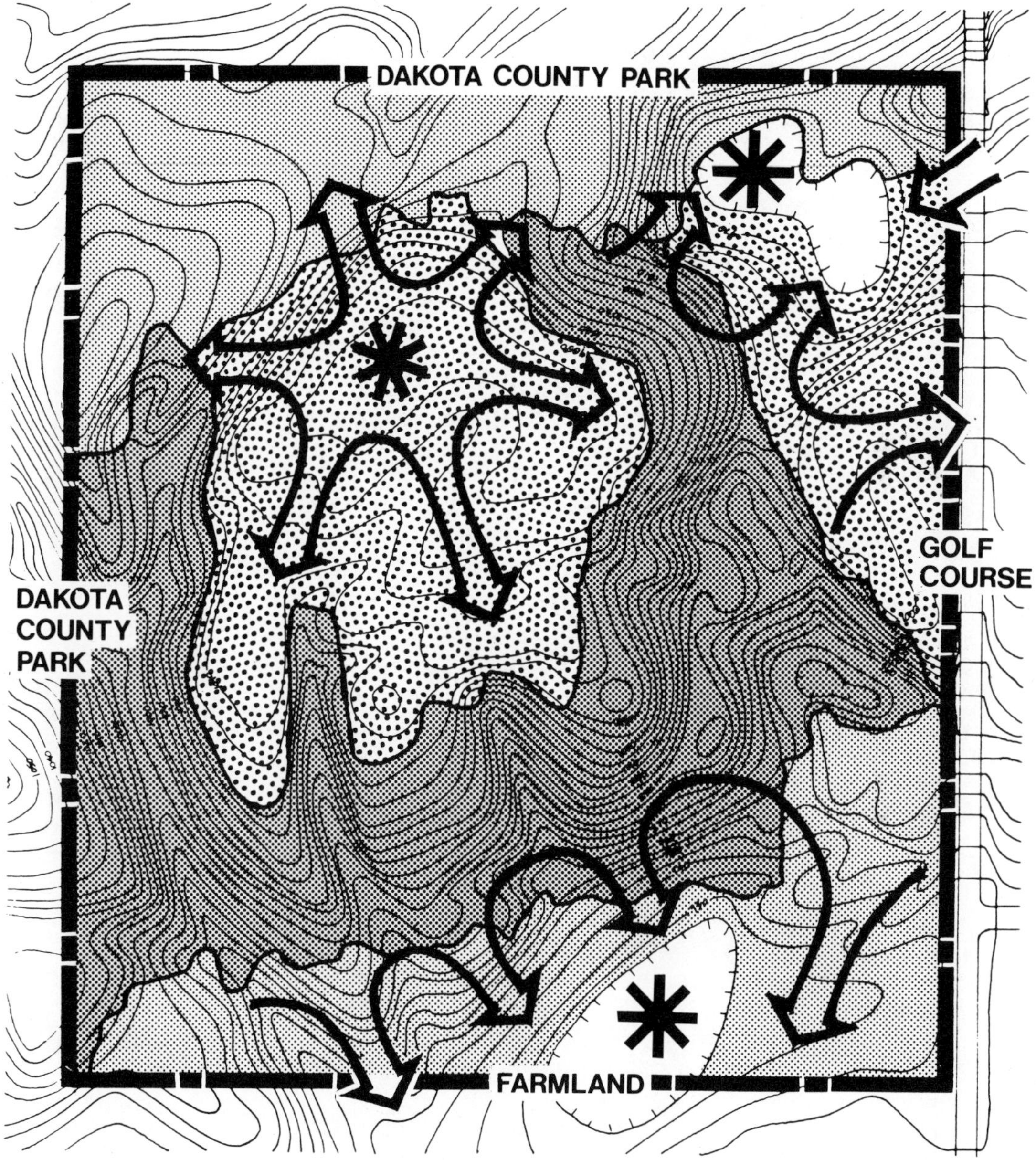
DAKOTA COUNTY PARK
GOLF COURSE
DAKOTA COUNTY PARK
FARMLAND

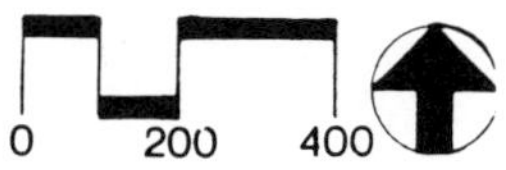
0
200
400

6-2: visual character

After the analysis has been completed for the site, the actual layout and design can begin. A number of options exist at the larger planning scale, as well as in the more detailed scale of road layouts and building design. At the larger scale, decisions concerning allocation of land for particular uses on the site must be made. For example, a site may be exclusively devoted to housing or the housing may be intermixed with other uses. Within a residential development, a certain percentage of the land often must be dedicated for recreational use. Other uses, such as a small commercial area for convenience shopping, may be considered assets to the development and may be energy efficient as well. Many options pertaining to densities and building types are possible within the areas designated for housing. A development may include exclusively single-family detached houses, town houses, or large multiple-unit buildings; or it may have a combination of several housing types. Likewise, with respect to energy-efficient housing types, the concept of the development may include only earth sheltered houses, only above-grade solar houses, or only conventional well-insulated houses. It is, of course, also possible and perhaps more likely to include a variety of energy-efficient housing types.

The decision to select one of these options is based on meeting the general goals of the developer and the community. These goals include efficient land use; energy efficiency; environmental protection; an economic return on investment; and the creation of a unique, marketable, socially stimulating, and aesthetically pleasing community. In order to achieve these goals, a number of specific strategies are applied to help shape the final layout of the development. Because the major emphasis of this study is on designing in response to energy and environmental problems, the conceptual design of the prototypical site discussed below is intended to demonstrate the various strategies examined in previous chapters.

The schematic site plan shown in figure 6-3 represents one conceptual design solution for the prototypical site. The rugged topography, generally dense vegetation, and attractive amenities are very powerful forces in shaping this plan. In order to preserve much of the natural character of the site, the concept for the development integrates the buildings and roads with this natural setting and emphasizes the great potential for outdoor recreation on and around the site. One basis for the plan is the preservation of the environmentally sensitive areas designated by the dark gray tone on the map. These areas, together with the water bodies on-site, represent natural areas that frame the developed areas and provide visual amenities for the housing units. In addition, they form the basis for a pedestrian walkway system throughout the site. The steeply sloping topography would give such a system character while providing pedestrians with a variety of views and experiences. A related concept is to connect the walkways and recreational land on the development site with the parklands adjacent to the site, thus making the parks more accessible and giving the development the appearance of an extension of these completely natural environments.

A very notable feature of this conceptual site plan is the designation of a large area of land at the top of the hill for community use—primarily recreational and possibly agricultural *(AG/REC).* The suitability analysis in chapter 1 indicated that, based on soils and topography, this was the only major area on the site suited for agriculture and types of recreation that require large, flat areas. Leaving this area open for community use has a number of benefits. It creates a central focus for the development and allows the entire community access to one of the greater amenities on the site—the long-distance views in all directions from this hilltop. The potential for agriculture could be increasingly significant in the future, as more people are becoming interested in gardening and on-site food production. The central growing area, accompanying

county road extension

pedestrian trailway

roadway

buildable area

management area

recreational/agricultural potential

environmentally sensitive areas; restricted

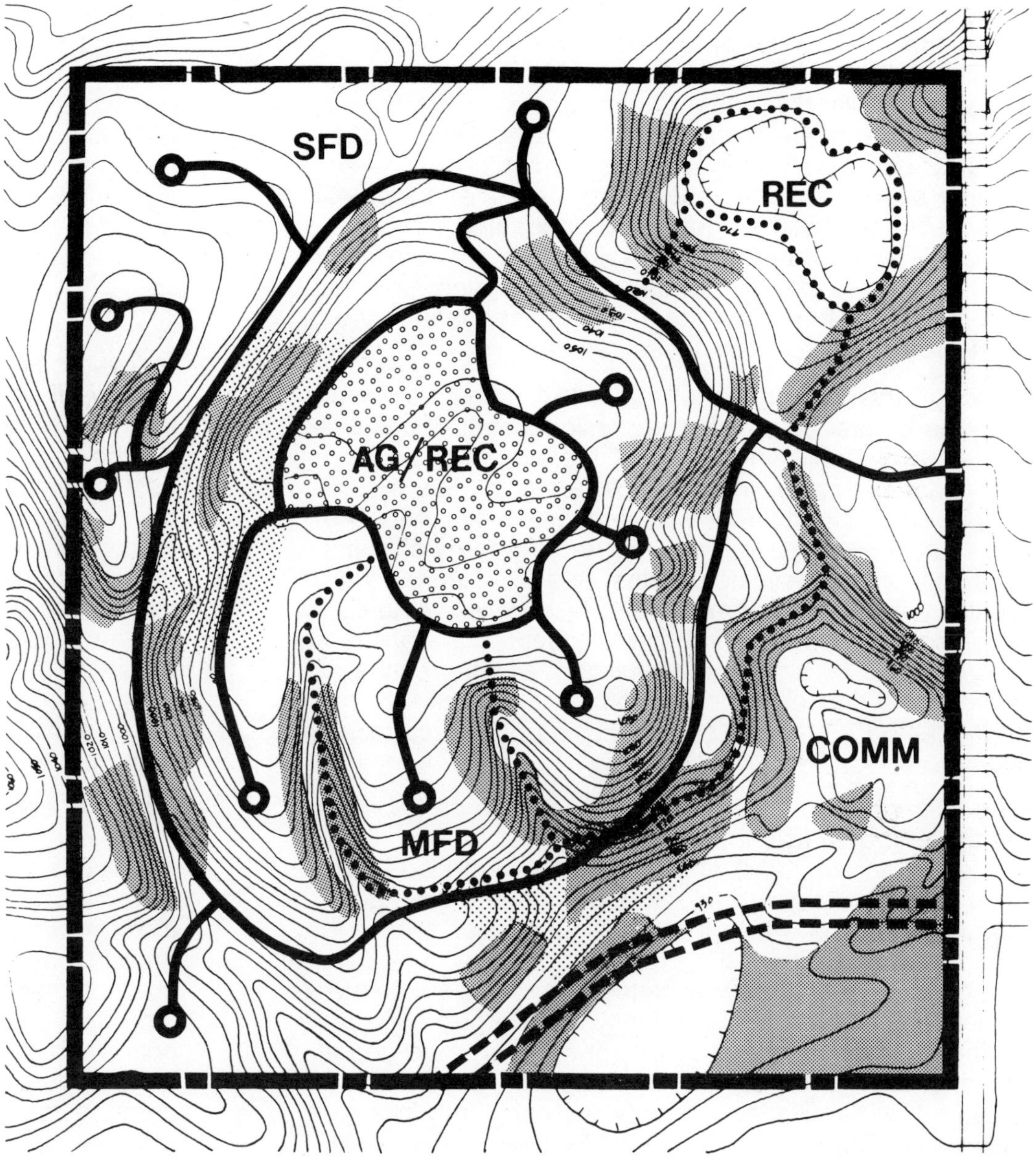
SFD
REC
AG/REC
MFD
COMM

6-3: schematic site design

0 200 400

the dense housing on the surrounding hillsides, will serve the entire community. This area represents a more efficient land-use pattern than would creating larger lots for single-family dwellings in order to accommodate individual gardens. In addition, the preservation of this area for community use allows for a number of on-site energy supply systems that may be feasible in the near future. These systems, described in chapter 3 and appendix A, include wind generators and solar collectors for heat and electricity that could be designed as a community system. This flat, high exposed land is the best area on the site for these systems.

Although the environmentally sensitive areas, combined with the central community recreational/agricultural area, represent a significant portion of the site, this use can be justified if the remaining buildable areas on the site are employed efficiently. More concentrated development in the remaining areas will result in more energy-efficient and economical buildings, roads, and utilities than would be likely if the development were less dense. Actually, a large portion of the environmentally sensitive areas is not very suitable for any type of building; and the central recreational/agricultural area would greatly enhance the marketability and value of the housing on the surrounding slopes.

The schematic road layout shown on the map is based on the energy-efficient strategies for road design discussed in chapter 3 and is a logical response to the rugged topography of the site. One important design feature of the road layout is the single major access to the development from the main road. This access can be designed as a symbolic entrance and thus help create a special identity for the community. The larger loop road at the base of the steep slopes and the smaller loop at the top result in an easily comprehended circulation system that simultaneously provides constantly changing views of the on-site amenities and excellent access to the various buildable areas on the site. This hierarchical road system minimizes cut-and-fill.

Three basic concepts underlie the development of the remaining buildable areas on the site. First, intermixing housing with a small commercial area will create a more diverse community and reduce energy expended for transportation by the residents. The area designated *(COMM)*, located on the east border of the site, is well suited to a small commercial development because it is accessible from the major road, is separated from the housing by a natural buffer, and could be connected to the pedestrian walkway system on the site.

Second, single- and multiple-family housing should be combined on the site, and location of the higher-density structures should be based on greater opportunities for energy-efficient design and access to amenities. Thus, the density should be maximized on the south-, southeast-, and southwest-facing slopes, which have the best potential for energy-efficient design on the site as well as excellent views and proximity to the central community area. On the map, multifamily dwellings *(MFD)* are designated for this general area. Conversely, the buildable areas in the northwest portion of the site are the poorest in terms of the potential for energy-efficient design and are more remote from some of the on-site amenities. Therefore, they are designated for single-family dwellings *(SFD)* so that the lower densities may compensate for the drawbacks of these sites.

The final concept underlying development of this site involves the variety of energy-efficient housing types to be included within it. Rather than a limited development of earth sheltered or solar-oriented houses only, a mixture of housing types allows for the appropriate application of each type in response to various site characteristics and is thus likely to result in more efficient land use. In the next section of this chapter, however, only earth sheltered housing is included in the design of a small portion of the site that is developed in greater detail, because only that type of housing is suitable for that particular area. It is important to stress that the schematic site plan shown in figure 6-3 is only the first step of the design process. As the design process continued, the layout shown here would be refined considerably at a more detailed scale.

housing design study for prototypical site

In order to complete the illustration of the site analysis and design process for an energy-efficient community development, a preliminary design of several clusters of housing was prepared for the prototypical site. The major south-facing slopes on the site were selected because they present the greatest opportunities for energy-efficient development and therefore have been designated for multifamily dwellings, as shown in figure 6-3. Although one of the concepts of this development is to include a mixture of energy-efficient housing types in response to different site conditions, one of the major purposes of this study is to examine and illustrate earth sheltered housing at a multiple-unit scale. Because these south-facing slopes present the best opportunities on the site for earth sheltered housing, that is the only type of structure illustrated in the prototypical design.

On this portion of the site, the relatively steep, south-facing slopes, which are divided by two steep ravines, are the major forces in determining the location and form of the housing to be built here. As shown on the schematic site plan (fig. 6-3), the ravines—which will form part of the pedestrian walkway system—are to be protected. Vehicular access to any housing on the slopes must be from the top of the hills rather than the bottom, since no relatively flat area lies at the base of the hill. The buildable slopes in this area actually can be grouped into two categories: the middle portion and base of the hills, which have a slope of approximately 20 percent; and the upper portion of the hills, which flattens out to a slope of 10 percent. Two types of earth sheltered structures have been designed in response to these two distinct degrees of slope. Two-level attached elevational units stepping down the hillside are located on the steeper slopes, while groups of one-level attached elevational-type houses are located on the gentler slopes.

The fifty-eight two-level units are clustered into three main groups that are divided by the two ravines; their

Design study for prototypical site by Tom Ellison and John Carmody. Drawings by Rick LaMuro.

exact orientation is determined by the topography. The majority of the units have excellent orientation for passive solar gain. The two-level attached units, shown on the following pages, are similar to conventional multifamily structures in that the entrances, garages, and parking are all located in one area at the top of the hill. The buildings are arranged so that one entrance typically serves four units. Both two- and three-bedroom units (1,550 square feet and 1,800 square feet—139.5 ca and 162 ca) are included in these complexes. These multiple-unit hillside structures present the opportunity to maximize densities on what is often considered almost unbuildable land. On these 20-percent slopes, approximately twelve units can be placed on 1 acre (0.4 ha), not including the land required for roads and devoted to open space. On a steeper slope, similar structures could be built at even greater densities. Although the units are attached and the density is relatively high, the development has few of the negative characteristics commonly associated with high-density developments. For example, each unit has extensive exclusive views of the surrounding amenities and little or no view of a neighboring structure except, perhaps, for a grass-covered rooftop.

The one-level earth sheltered structures are attached in groups of three to five units and are generally oriented toward the two ravines—a situation that results in excellent exposure for passive solar heating. The seventeen units all include three bedrooms (1,800 square feet—162 ca) and have attached double garages. The low, flat profile of these one-level units, combined with the earth berms and covered rooftops, would result in very natural, unobtrusive building forms. The scale and density of development would not be apparent when viewed from roads or from the central community area to the north of these housing clusters. Although these elongated one-level earth sheltered units clearly have potential energy-saving and aesthetic benefits, on relatively flat land they are not the best type of unit for maximizing densities. It would be possible to roughly double the density in these flat areas by substituting more conventional two-story town house units that have approximately the same general layout and solar orientation. Some of the same qualities of the more fully earth sheltered houses—e.g., berms around the first level and perhaps earth-covered roofs—could be integrated into the design of more conventional town houses to help them blend into the surrounding landscape and complement the earth sheltered structures further down the hill.

site for housing design study
0
200
400

site plan

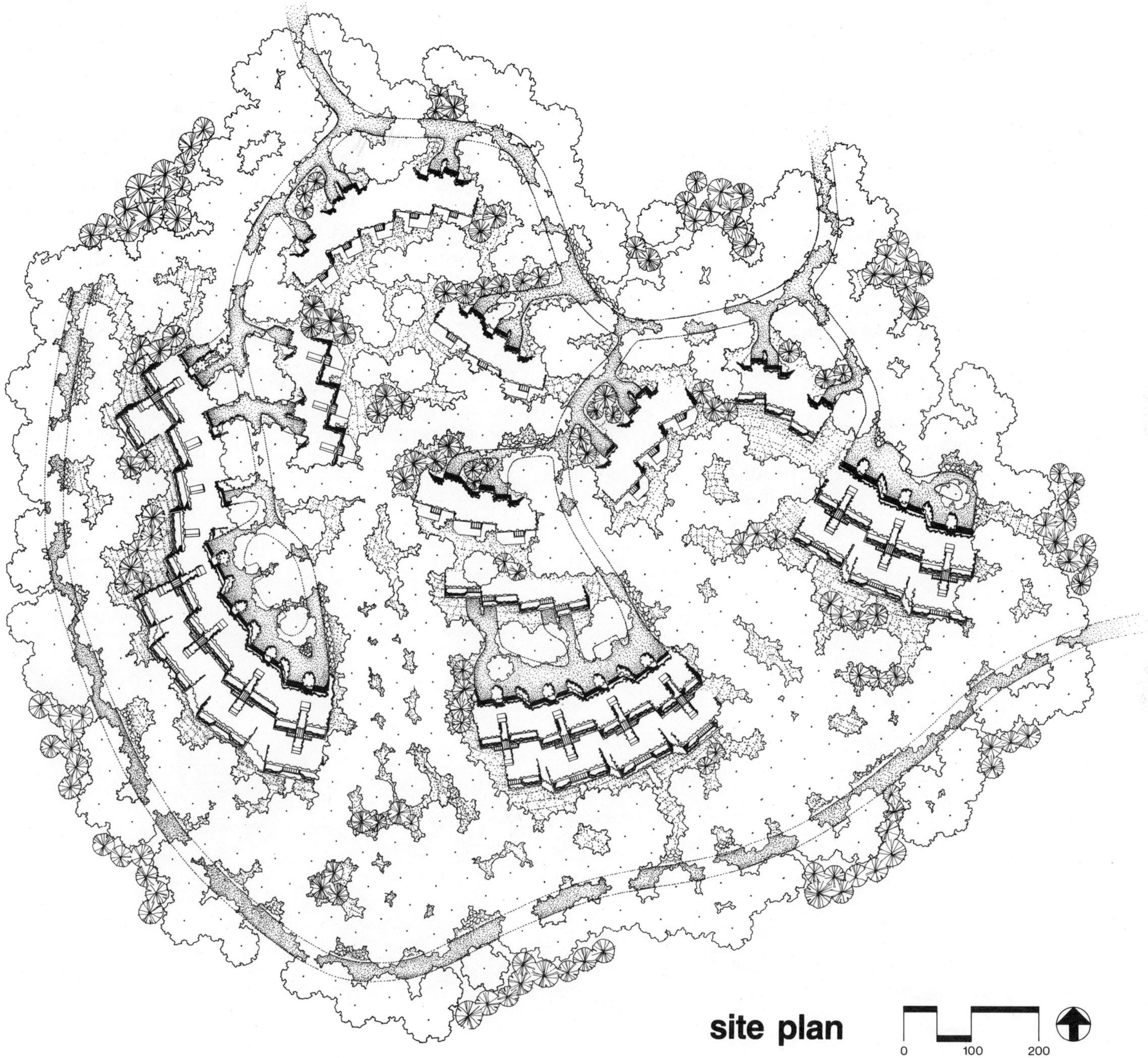

site plan

0
100
200

The entire area shown in this prototypical housing design covers approximately 25 acres (10 ha). This total includes the area of the two ravines, which are considered unbuildable. By building a total of seventy-five units, an overall density of 3 units per acre can be achieved. Although this is not a particularly high density, it must be evaluated in the context of this rugged and somewhat inaccessible site. Even with the fairly efficient land use associated with the two-level earth sheltered units on the steeper slopes, much of the area below and around these structures must remain open. More conventional methods of development applied to this site would undoubtedly result in far fewer units.

By applying the design concepts and strategies from previous chapters of the book to a real site, it becomes apparent that each site has its own particular opportunities and limitations. Hence, generalizations concerning densities and idealized diagrams of optimal layouts must be viewed with discretion. On the site selected for this prototypical design, the location and spacing of the units was strongly dictated by the land forms and the limited access to the site. With the exception of substituting conventional town houses for the one-level earth sheltered houses on the gentler slopes, there were very few possibilities for increasing the number of units. The topography also dictated the orientation of the housing units on this site. Although the majority of the units have excellent southerly orientation, a few are oriented more toward the east or west than to the south. Careful attention must be paid to the detailed design of these units to compensate for this poorer orientation. For example, the large undesirable heat gain from the east and west in the summer must be screened. On this site the extensive vegetation should accomplish much of the required screening. In addition, south-facing skylights or clerestory windows could be used in these units to increase the passive solar gain in winter.

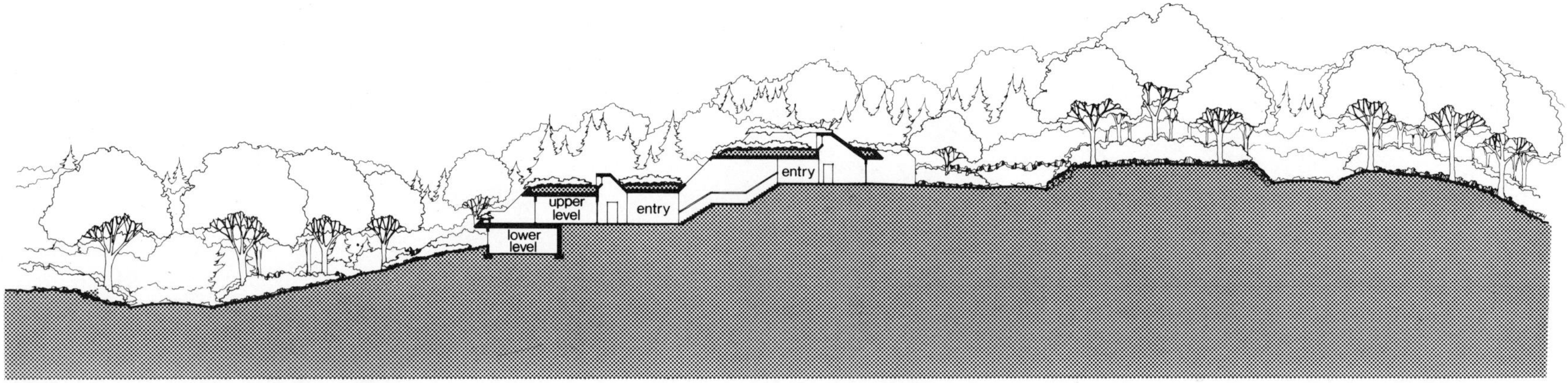
upper level
entry
entry
lower level

section—two level units

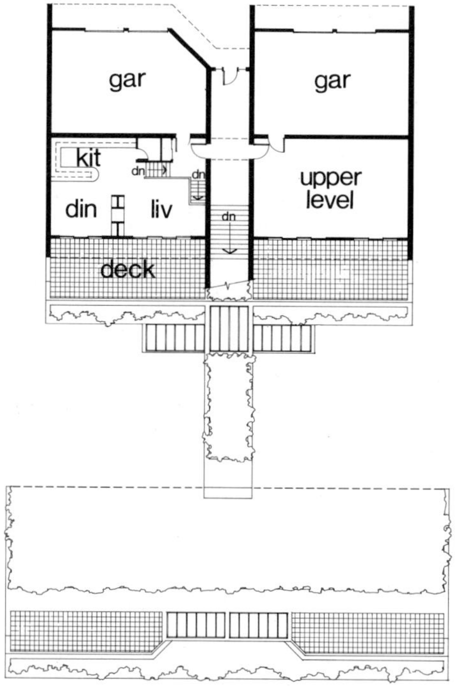
gar
gar
kit
dn
dn
din
liv
upper
level
dn
deck

plan

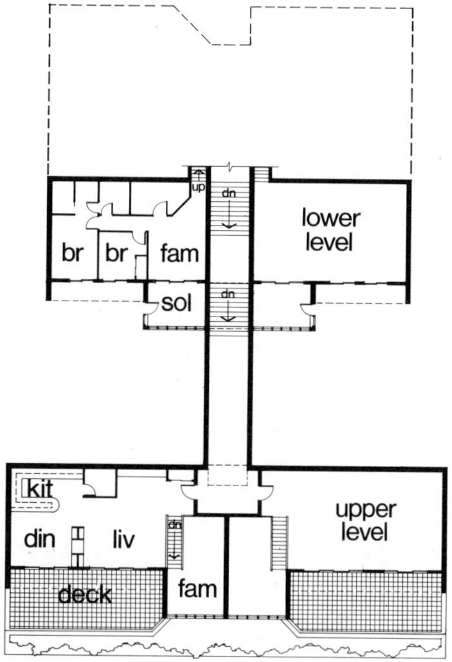
up
dn
br
br
fam
lower
level
sol
dn
kit
din
liv
dn
upper
level
deck
fam

plan

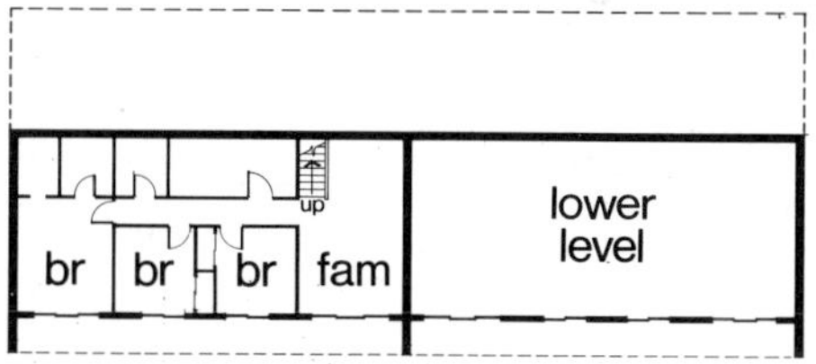
up
br
br
br
fam
lower
level

plan

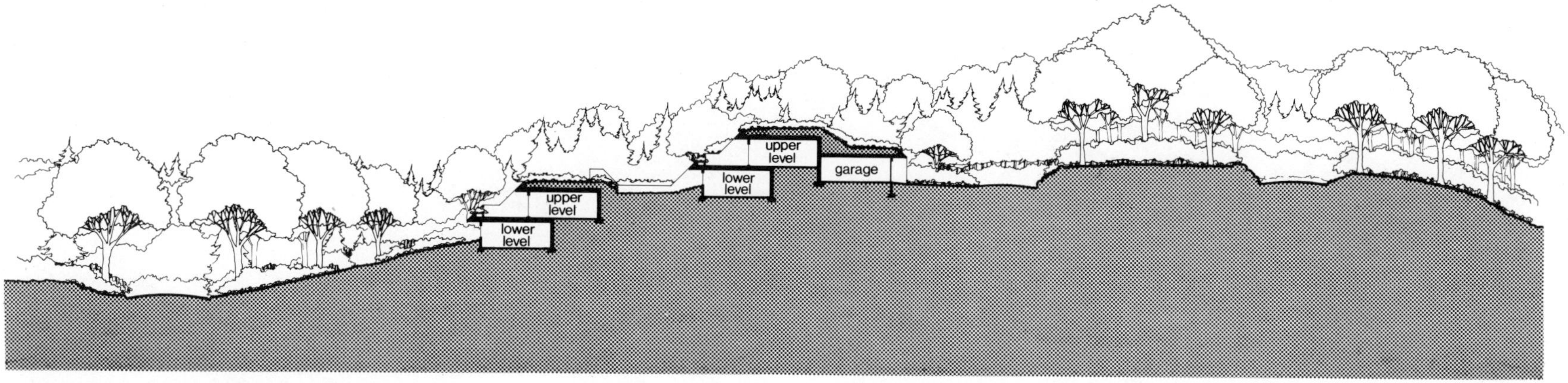
upper
level
garage
lower
level
upper
level
lower
level

section—two level units

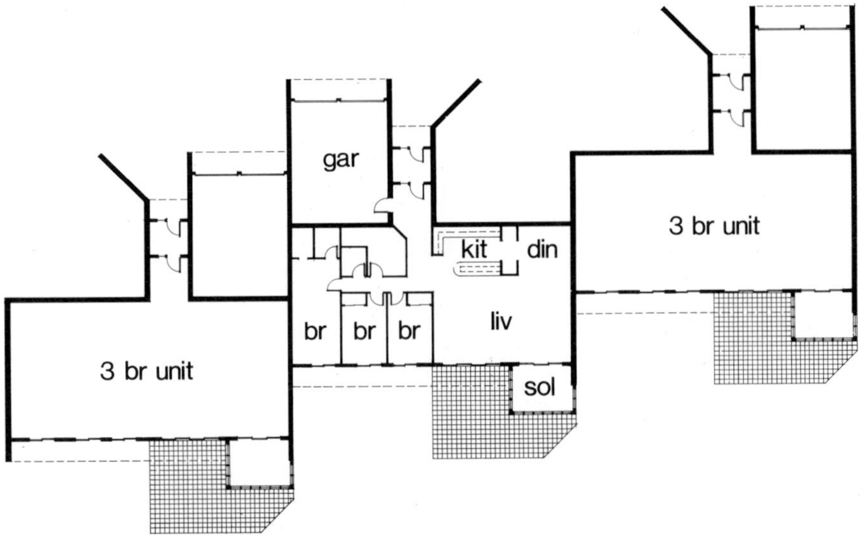
gar
kit
din
3 br unit
br
br
br
liv
sol
3 br unit

plan—one level units

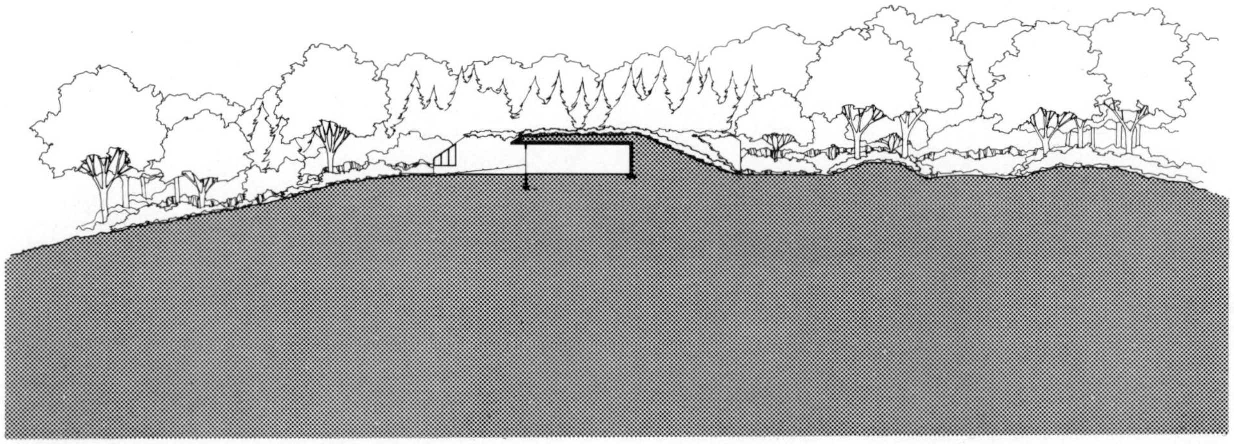

section—one level units

Underground dwellings, Greece.
Drawing by Mark Heisterkamp based on a photograph from *The Prodigious Builders* by Bernard Rudofsky

7 case studies

introduction

This chapter examines several existing and proposed earth sheltered housing projects. Among the few projects in existence today are some notable examples. Included here are two larger developments—Architerra in Nice, France, and Halen Housing in Bern, Switzerland—that may be considered models for more complete energy-efficient communities. Two smaller projects—ten resort condominiums in Mexico and the twelve-unit Seward town house project in Minneapolis, Minnesota—serve as architectural prototypes for multiple-unit projects in differing climates. There are also, of course, historical examples of communities built into the earth that are too numerous to mention here. In ancient civilizations as well as in many developing countries today, the use of earth for shelter has been a natural and inexpensive solution to a wide variety of conditions. A few historic examples are illustrated throughout this study, including the completely underground communities of northern China shown on this page [7.1]. These Chinese settlements are a particularly interesting response to a harsh climate in an area with a soil that is very suitable for hand excavation.

Drawing by Mark Heisterkamp based on a photograph in the book *Architecture Without Architects* by Bernard Rudofsky.

As a result of the increasing interest in earth sheltered housing in recent years, many proposals for visionary underground communities as well as more modest multiple-unit housing structures have been developed. For example, the adjacent drawing of an entire community integrated into a hillside was done by architect Malcolm Wells, one of the first advocates of underground housing [7.2]. The first five proposals presented in this chapter are multiple-unit housing projects for sites in the Minneapolis-St. Paul area. Not only are these proposals well designed and illustrated, but they also demonstrate the great diversity possible with earth sheltered housing designs. The final proposal presented in this chapter is for an earth sheltered community designed by students at the University of Texas in Arlington, which demonstrates some concepts unique to warmer climates.

Drawing by Malcolm Wells from his book *Underground Designs* (see references).

architerra

Architerra homes are unique in that they are based on an unusual structural system that is specifically designed for use on hillsides. Several Architerra complexes have been completed in France and Spain, and the company is seeking developers in the United States. The development illustrated here is a forty-seven-unit complex called Agora, built on a 50-percent slope at St. Pierre de Feric, near Nice, France. Although direct vehicular access to each unit is not provided, the road system does allow for parking relatively close to each unit. Constructed in 1979, this project was designed by Henri Vidal and Yves Bayard and engineered by Archi. These developments serve as an excellent example of how earth sheltering can turn a site considered unsuitable for conventional construction to aesthetic and economic advantage. The Architerra construction system is extremely well suited for developments on steep slopes because of its flexibility and ability to stabilize hillside conditions.

By virtue of the stepped design of the Architerra complexes and the curved glass front walls of the units, all the residents of the development enjoy a 180-degree view of the surrounding landscape. These south-facing glass walls provide natural light, view, and passive solar gain while helping the units appear naturally integrated with the curves of the hillside. In all units the north wall is completely set into the hillside, the end walls are partially covered, and the roof is completely covered with earth. The individual units in the Architerra system can be designed for flexibility in space arrangements. For example, the one- to four-bedroom units can vary from 1,000 to 4,000 square feet (90 to 360 ca) in size, and room sizes can vary depending on the owners' wishes. In most Architerra complexes, each unit has a private garden/courtyard.

The key to the Architerra system is the ability to mold the land and design through a patented construction technique called Reinforced Earth™. The land is first contoured into a series of terraces and excavated for the home sites. Then the Reinforced Earth™ technique, in which long metal strips attached to precast concrete walls are laid between successive layers of backfill, is used to stabilize the backfill. The wall panels, which form the curved rear structural walls of the units, resist lateral earth pressures very efficiently.

Stacking the units stair fashion in slots cut into the hillside imparts a sense of privacy to each unit (e.g., each unit has an unobstructed view of the horizon) while simultaneously permitting a high unit density of over 10 units per acre—a particularly impressive figure considering that all of the units are detached. Surface preservation and use of land that would otherwise be considered unbuildable are obvious environmental benefits associated with this type of development.

Photographs by The Washington Agency

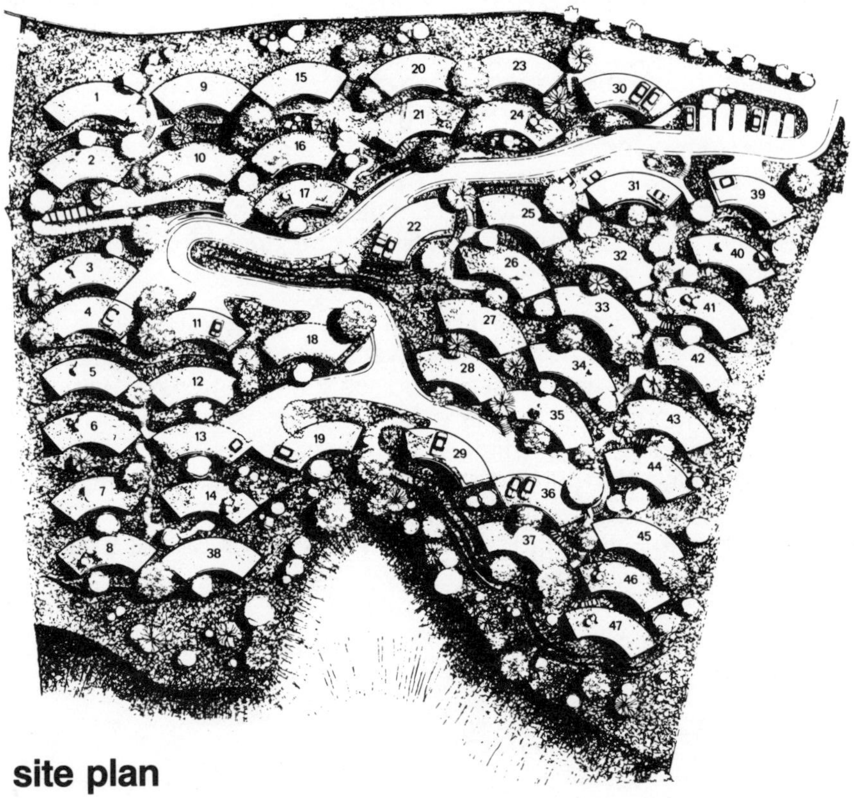
1
2
3
4
5
6
7
8
9
10
11
12
13
14
15
16
17
18
19
20
21
22
23
24
25
26
27
28
29
30
31
32
33
34
35
36
37
38
39
40
41
42
43
44
45
46
47

site plan

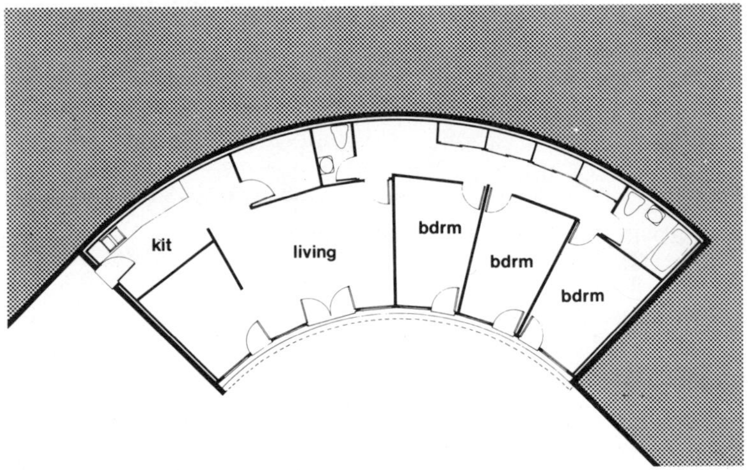
kit
living
bdrm
bdrm
bdrm

unit plan

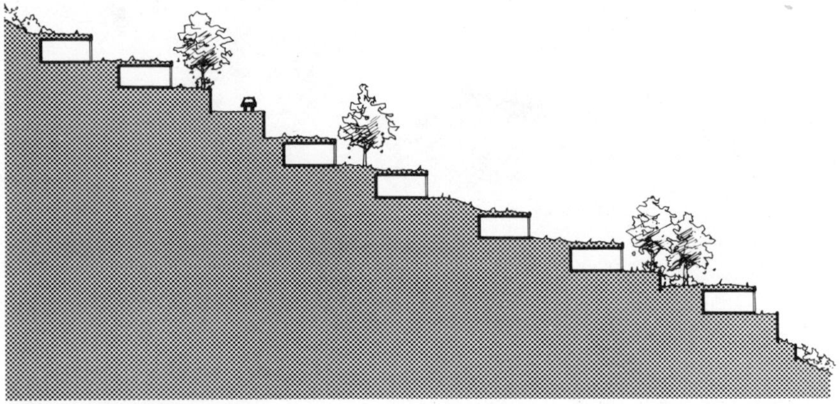

site section

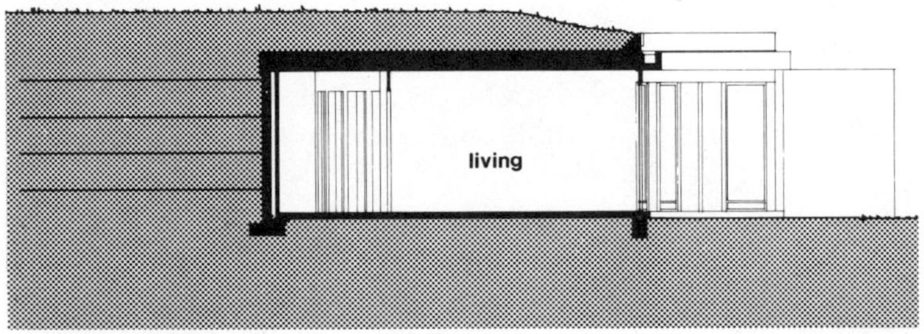
living

unit section

halen housing

The Halen Housing complex near Bern, Switzerland, demonstrates a number of planning and design concepts that result in an attractive, socially stimulating, and efficient project. Designed by Atelier 5, the eighty-one attached housing units set into a south-facing slope surrounded by forest have a magnificent view of the river valley below. The narrow three-level units are arranged in long rows to occupy a 6.2-acre (2.5-ha) site, resulting in a relatively high density of over 13 units per acre.

Although little consideration was given to energy efficiency when the project was completed in 1961, it is an excellent example of town house units designed for passive solar gain. The directly south-facing units step down the 16-percent slope and are covered with earth on the rooftops. This earth covering not only aids in cooling, but also enhances the river view, since only the grass-covered rooftops of the units below are visible. In general, clustering many units close together increases energy savings because many common walls are used, the buildings shelter one another from cold winds, and a central system supplies heat to the entire project. Clustering the housing within such a beautiful natural environment is also an efficient use of the land, as it reduces development costs while actually increasing the impact of the natural amenities.

A sense of community is also evident in this project, partly because of its isolation from surrounding neighborhoods and the cooperative ownership arrangement. This community feeling is enhanced by the design, in which pedestrian walkways lead to a central plaza where a restaurant and a few small shops are located. In addition, a swimming pool and other common facilities are available for all the residents.

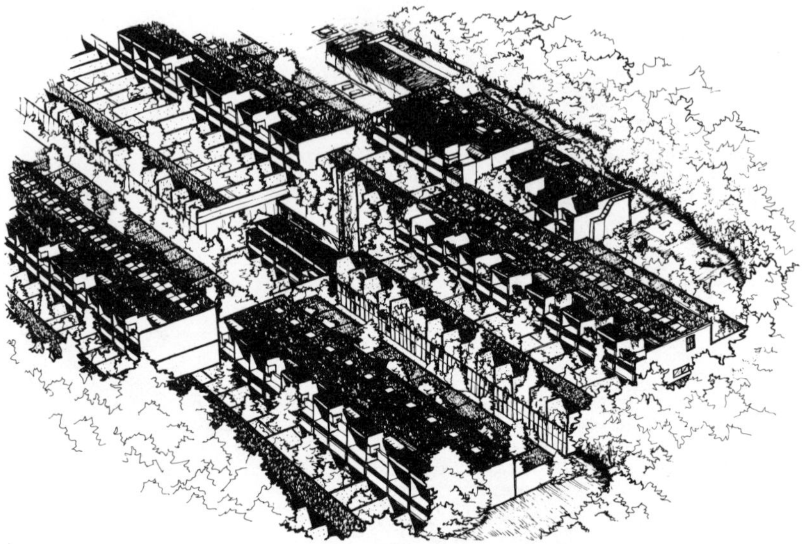

Drawings by Mark Heisterkamp based on photographs and drawings in *Global Architecture Series* published by A.D.A. EDITA Tokyo Co.

Photographs by RETORIA: Y. Futagawa and Associated Photographers.

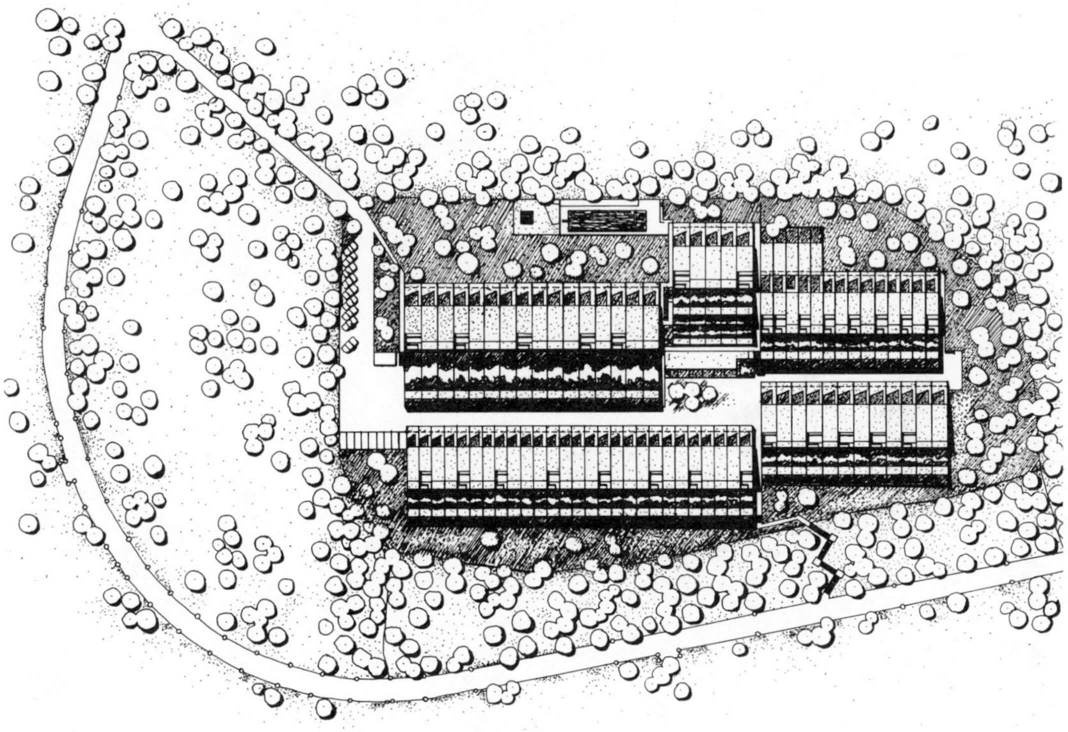

site plan

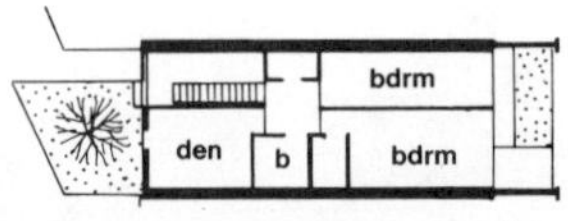
bdrm
den
b
bdrm

upper level plan

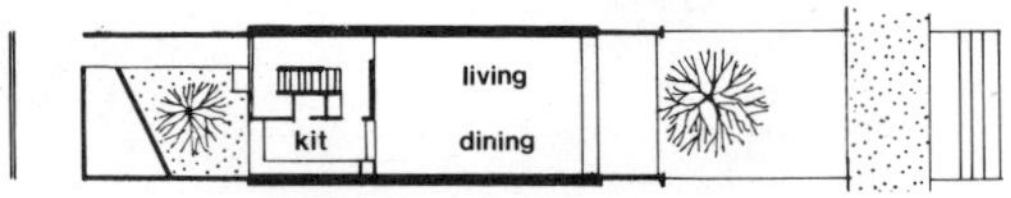
living
kit
dining

middle level plan

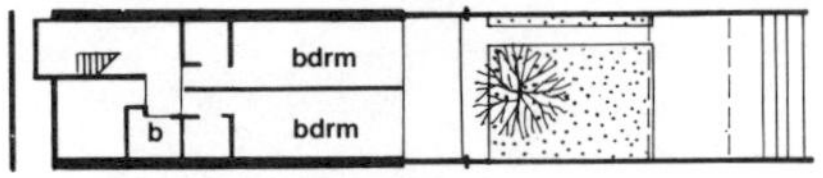
bdrm
b
bdrm

lower level plan

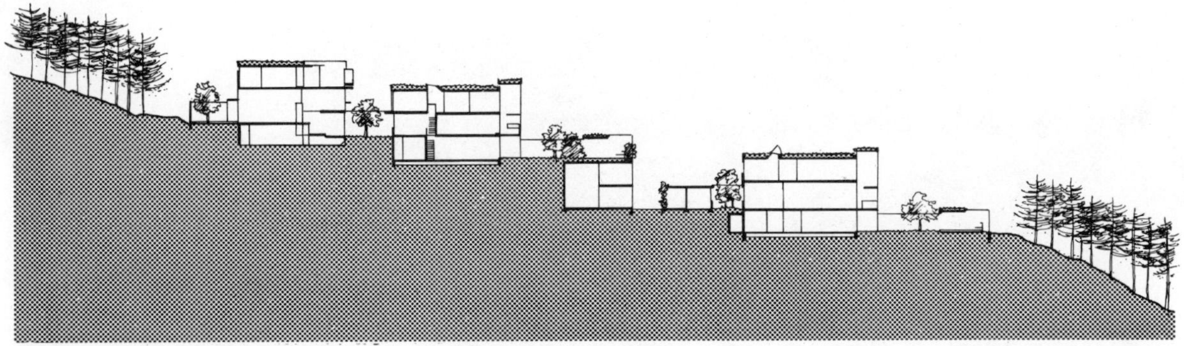

site section

One of the finest examples of multiple-unit earth sheltered housing that has actually been constructed is a ten-condominium project built into the beach at Cabo San Lucas, in Baja California, Mexico, adjacent to the Camino Real Hotel. Designed by Ricardo Legorreta of Legorreta Arquitectos in Mexico, the units are completely underground in order to blend into—and not compete with—the beautiful and powerful forms of the natural landscape. In addition, setting the structures into the earth is a very appropriate means of passively cooling the spaces in this hot, arid climate.

The ten two-bedroom units are recessed into the sloping sand dunes in two rows; the rooftops are completely covered with sand. By setting the units into the slope they can be integrated with the land forms while still opening one side to the ocean to provide an attractive view and to capture natural breezes. Each unit is entered through a sunken courtyard, so that the project is hardly visible from the uphill side. The open courtyards and the ventilating skylights in the bathrooms enhance natural cross-ventilation. Although the units are designed to be two-bedroom condominiums, each unit can also be divided into three separate hotel rooms until it is sold. The retaining walls and courtyards, which are the only exposed architectural elements, are colored to match the sand so as to further blend the structures into the beach. The sand on the rooftops reflects light and heat, thereby increasing the passive cooling of the house. The overall effect of the project is summarized by the architect Ricardo Legorreta, who has written:

> *With the use of the underground elements, the landscape blends with the architecture, giving it strength and personality, and at the same time, the architecture forms part of the landscape. By its lines and volumes, it tries to give man the desired peace and rest that have been lost in most of our cities [7.3].*

Photographs and drawings reprinted from the September 1976 issue of "Progressive Architecture," copyright 1976, Reinhold Publishing. Photographs by Richard Gross.

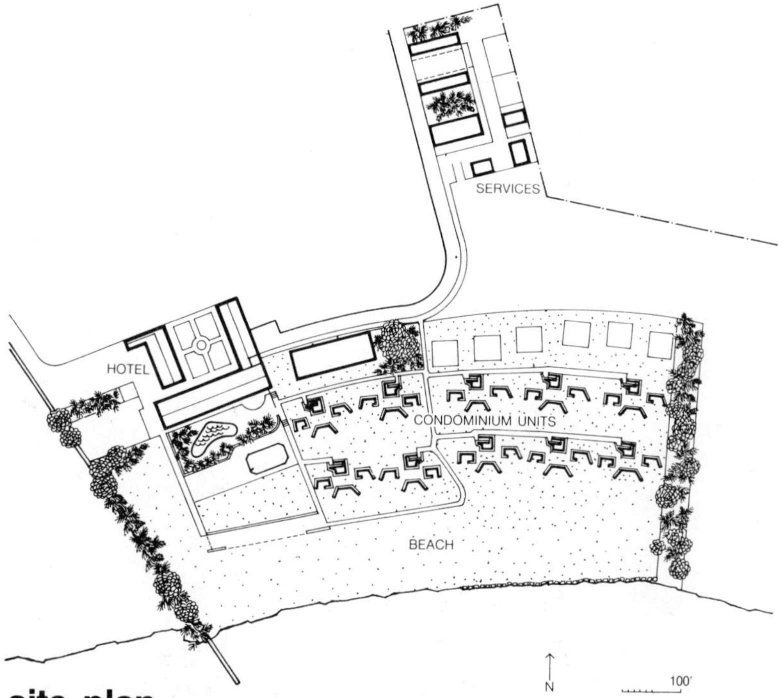
SERVICES
HOTEL
CONDOMINIUM UNITS
BEACH
N
100'

site plan

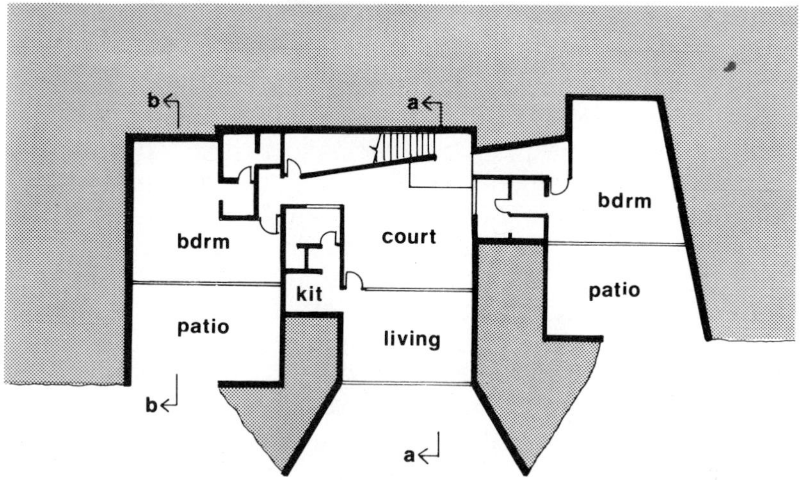
b
a
bdrm
court
bdrm
kit
patio
patio
living
b
a

unit plan

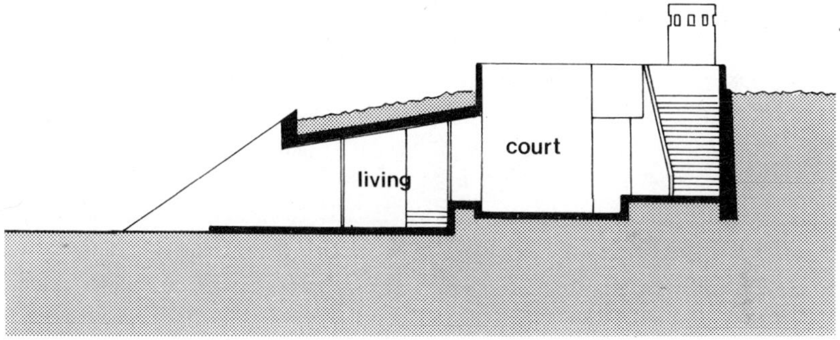
court
living

section a-a

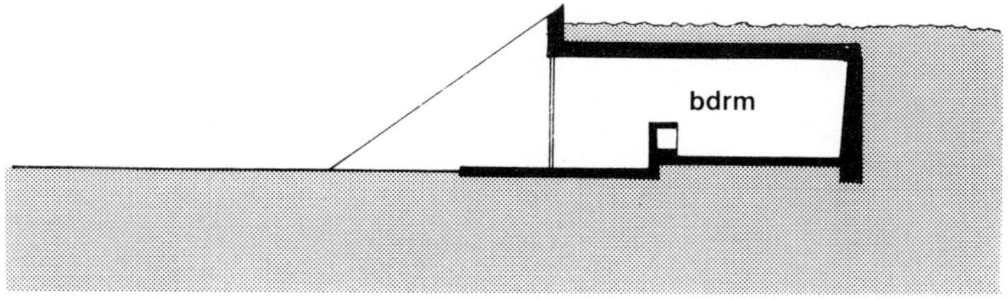
bdrm

section b-b

seward town houses

One of the most innovative and unusual earth sheltered housing projects to date, the Seward town house development in Minneapolis, Minnesota, resulted from a cooperative effort involving the community and the architects. The site, located immediately adjacent to a very busy section of freeway and adjoining a major intersection, had become undesirable to most residential developers. It was slated for use by a major restaurant chain when Seward West Redesign, a nonprofit neighborhood corporation concerned about increasing commercialization of the area, proposed an alternative: an earth sheltered residential complex. The project was designed by architect Mike Dunn of Close Associates, Minneapolis.

The town houses, completed in 1980, demonstrate how a thoughtful, well-planned design can turn normally undesirable site characteristics to advantage through the application of earth sheltering and passive solar techniques. For example, the fact that the noisy freeway is located immediately north of the site dictated that the complex face south—the ideal orientation for passive solar gain. By facing the units south and creating a berm of earth on the north side and both ends of the complex, the architects successfully dampened the freeway noise. The limited size and completely flat topography of the site required a very efficient plan in order to fit twelve units on the 100- by 300-foot (30- by 91-m) site, resulting in a density of 15.8 units per acre. The efficiency in site planning results from the compactness of the two-level units and the use of retaining walls at the site edge to reduce the land area required for earth berms.

The twelve-unit (nine two-bedroom, three three-bedroom) development is completely covered by berms on the three sides; the roof is planted with long natural grasses. The north berm, designed as a continuation of the grassy edge predominant along the freeway, is punctuated by entrances to each of the units. On the south are located the primary entrances and the individual unit courtyards where owners may plant gardens or shrubs. To make the town house units as energy efficient as possible, the architects incorporated both an active solar system and passive solar features into the design.

Photographs by Jerry Mathiason.

STOP

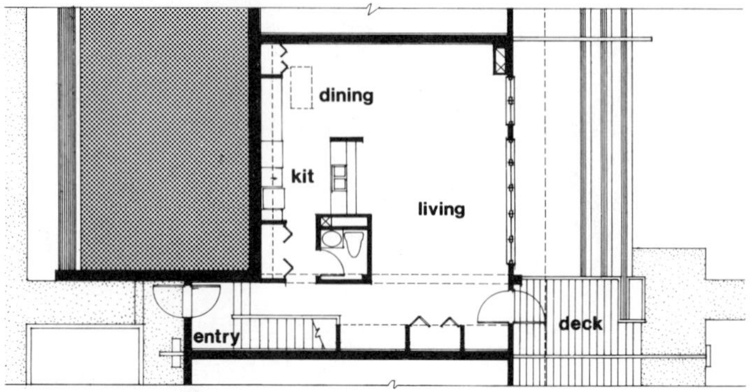
dining
kit
living
entry
deck
upper level plan

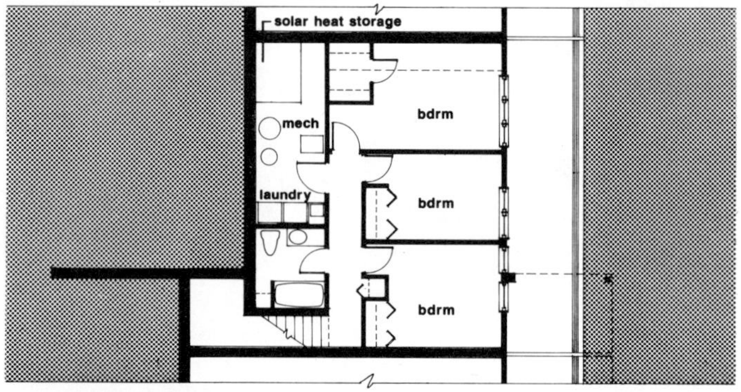
solar heat storage
mech
bdrm
laundry
bdrm
bdrm
lower level plan

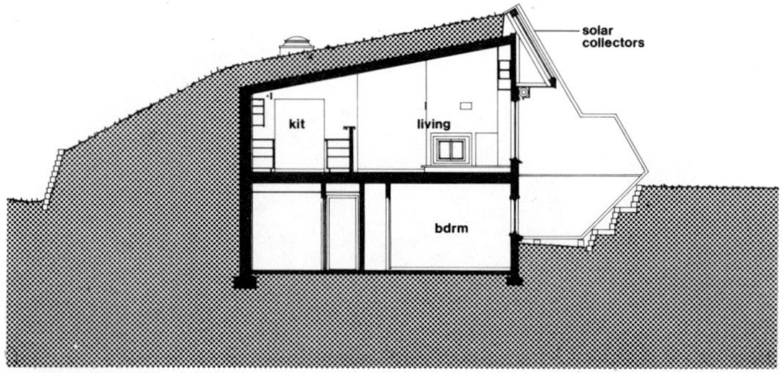
solar collectors
kit
living
bdrm
section

community design competition: 1

To encourage the use of earth sheltered housing in a community setting, the Underground Space Center at the University of Minnesota sponsored a design competition in 1980 for an urban site in Minneapolis. The completely flat and treeless one-block site bordering a park in a residential neighborhood was occupied by a school that was to be abandoned. Essentially, the program called for at least forty earth sheltered housing units on this 8.25-acre (3.4-ha) site. The winning entry in the professional category, shown on the following pages, was submitted by architects Mark Dohrmann and Mike Joyce and engineer Jack Snow, all of the Minneapolis-St. Paul area.

The forty-two earth sheltered homes are planned around the common area, which contains play areas, a grassy field, a garden plot for each home, and an orchard. The earth sheltered community building, in addition to being the energy center for the project, can serve many community needs. The living units are covered with earth; each has an entry with a covered porch facing the street. The low profile and the steady rhythm of gable ends with wood siding relate very well to the existing neighborhood. By stepping the homes back in clusters of three, the designers have relieved feelings of higher density. Parking is designed to avoid the large, asphalt-covered areas common to multiple-unit developments.

The individual units are planned to reduce energy consumption through a combination of earth sheltering, passive solar design, and a shared energy system. Opening through a greenhouse onto a private courtyard, the living area for each unit faces south. The greenhouse collects solar heat during winter days and passes the heat into the house. Earth covers the roofs and north sides of the units. The garages are attached to the north sides of most units to further buffer the homes against north winds, which will be swept over the gently sloping roofs. In addition to the passive solar gain and wood-burning fireplaces in each unit, the homes rely on a central, shared system for heat and hot water. The central heating plant, located in the community building, consists of an array of collectors that will transfer solar energy to a large storage tank below the building, from which the hot water will then be distributed to the individual units.

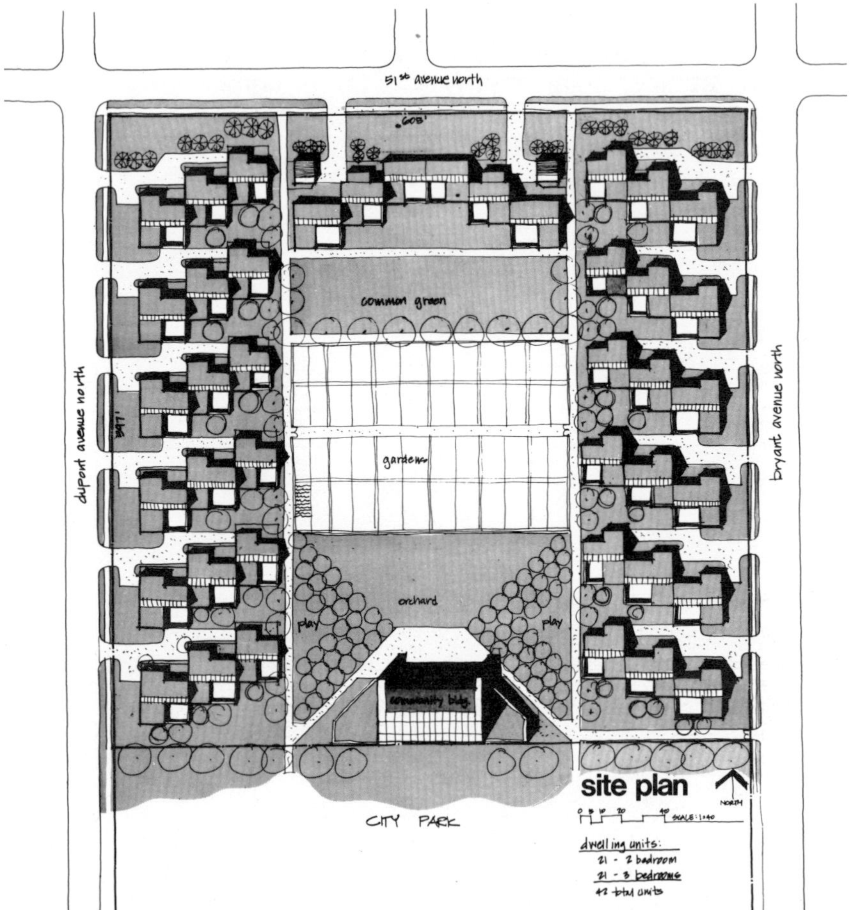
51st avenue north
common green
gardens
orchard
play
play
community bldg.
dupont avenue north
bryant avenue north
CITY PARK
site plan
NORTH
dwelling units:
21 - 2 bedroom
21 - 3 bedrooms
42 total units

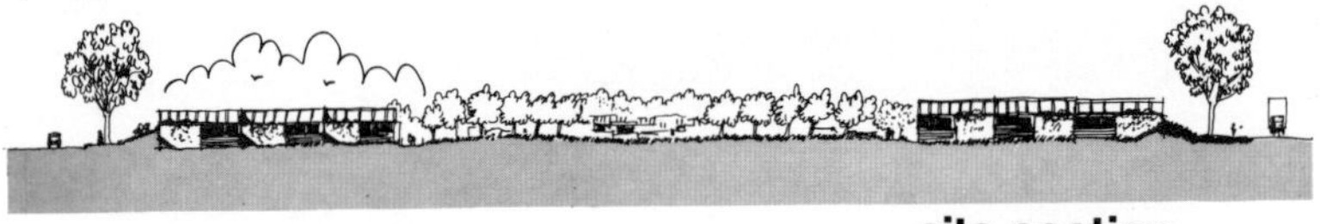

site section

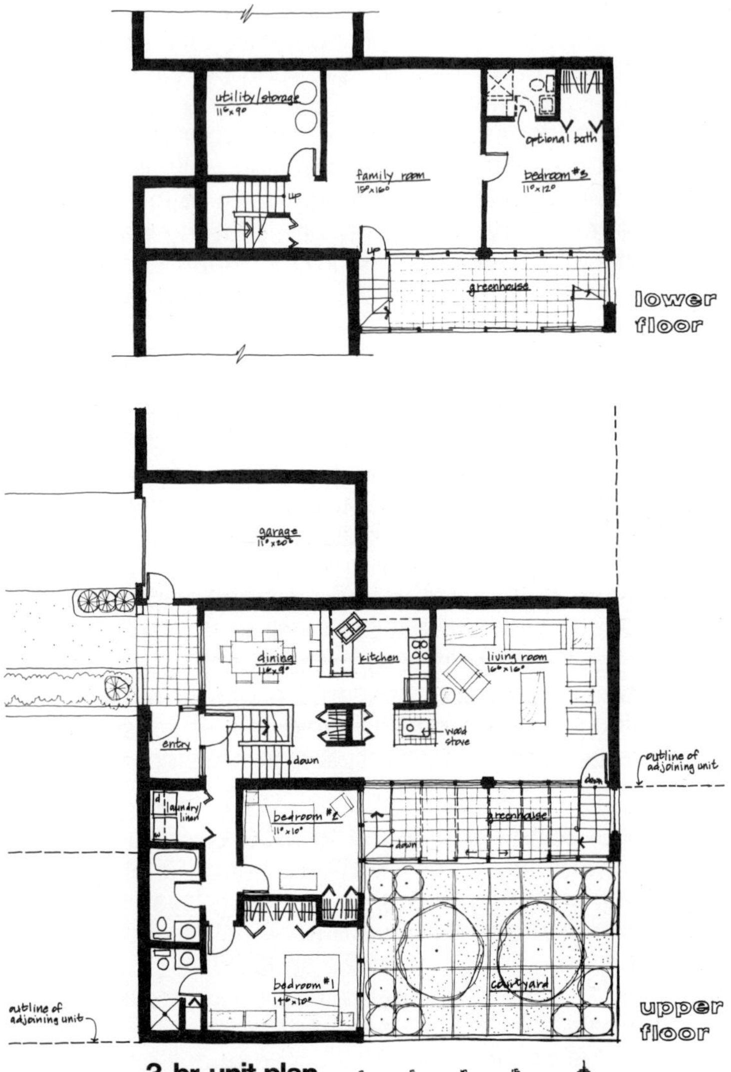
utility/storage
family room
optional bath
bedroom #3
greenhouse
lower floor
garage
dining
kitchen
living room
wood stove
entry
down
outline of adjoining unit
laundry/linen
bedroom #2
greenhouse
bedroom #1
courtyard
outline of adjoining unit
upper floor
north

3 br. unit plan
1596 square feet

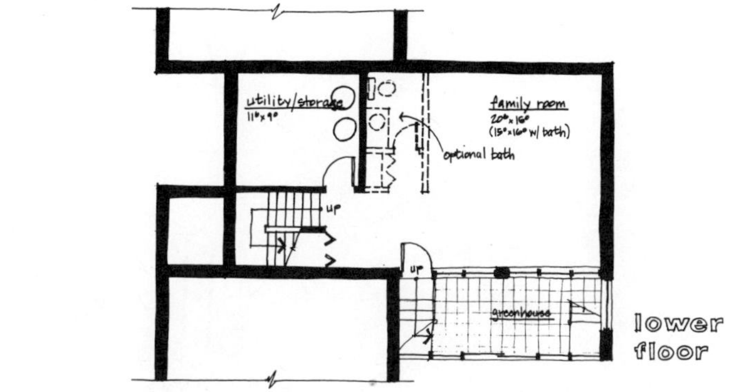
utility/storage
11°x9°
family room
20°x16°
(15°x16° w/ bath)
optional bath
up
up
greenhouse
lower floor

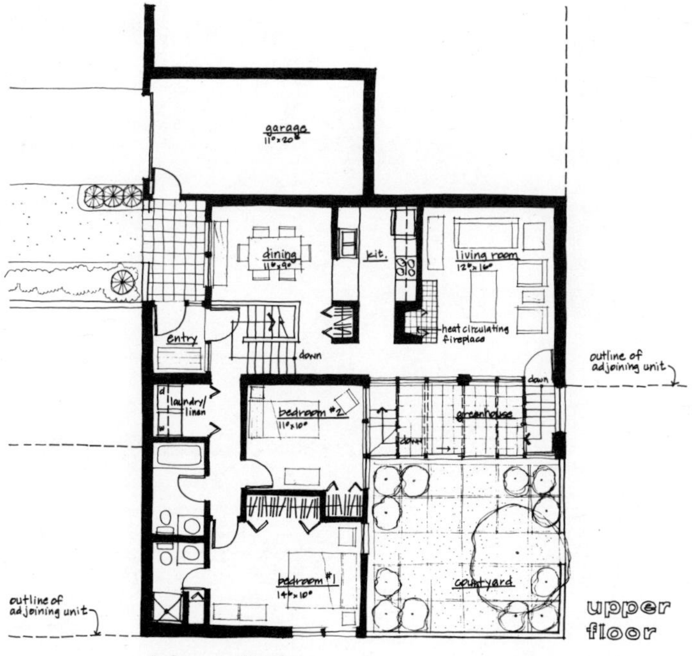
garage
11°x20°
dining
11°x9°
kit.
living room
12°x16°
heat circulating fireplace
entry
down
outline of adjoining unit
laundry/linen
bedroom #2
11°x10°
greenhouse
down
down
bedroom #1
14°x10°
courtyard
outline of adjoining unit
upper floor

2 br. unit plan

1404 square feet

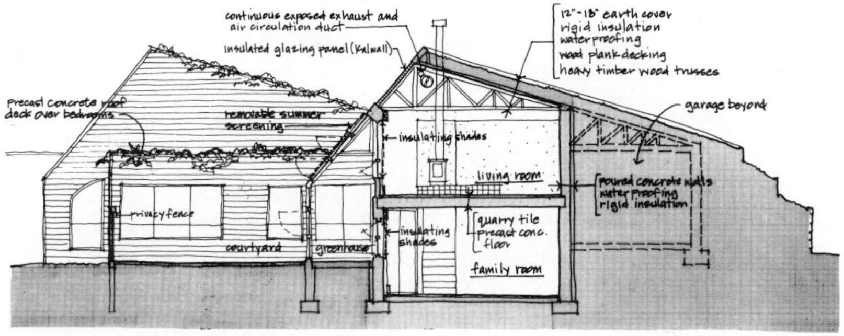
continuous exposed exhaust and air circulation duct
insulated glazing panel (Kalwall)
12"-18" earth cover
rigid insulation
waterproofing
wood plank decking
heavy timber wood trusses
precast concrete roof deck over bedrooms
removable summer screening
insulating shades
garage beyond
living room
poured concrete walls
water proofing
rigid insulation
privacy fence
quarry tile
precast conc. floor
insulating shades
courtyard
greenhouse
family room

typical unit section

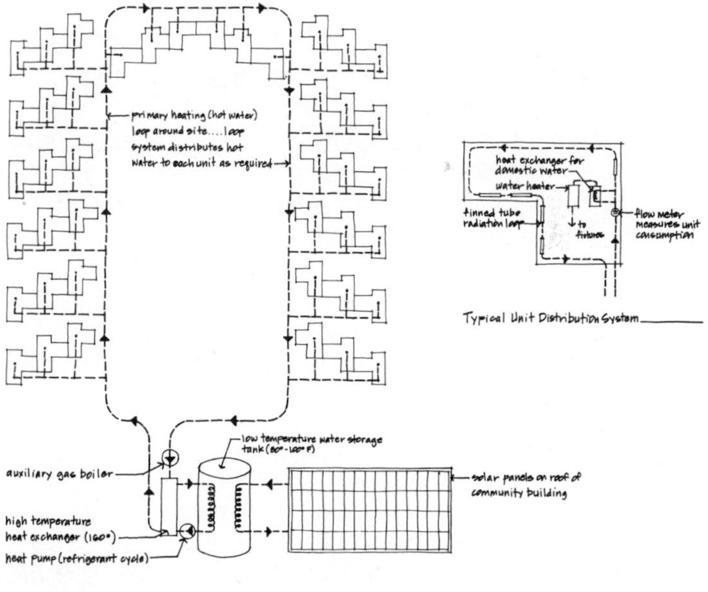
primary heating (hot water) loop around site....loop system distributes hot water to each unit as required
low temperature water storage tank (80°-100° F)
auxiliary gas boiler
solar panels on roof of community building
high temperature heat exchanger (160°)
heat pump (refrigerant cycle)
heat exchanger for domestic water
water heater
finned tube radiation loop
to fixtures
flow meter measures unit consumption

Typical Unit Distribution System

central mechanical system schematic

community design competition: 2

The second prize in the Underground Space Center design competition for an earth sheltered housing community was won by The Architectural Alliance, Minneapolis. The project team consisted of Herb Ketcham, principal-in-charge; Peter Pfister; George Stevens; and Sarah Susanka.

The housing units in this design are arranged in four clusters around a solar pond in the center of the one-block site. The existing school, which has been renovated into a community center, serves as an entry to the project from the park to the south (see site plan). Despite the large amount of space that is devoted to the solar pond, the community center, and large garden areas within each cluster, a density of 7 units per acre has been achieved by placing fifty-seven units on the 8.25-acre (3.4-ha) site. This relatively high density has been accomplished by placing the roads and parking for each cluster underground; community garden space is provided on the roof of each underground garage.

Each housing unit is oriented inward around two courtyards, giving the units a sense of privacy not usually associated with attached housing at this density. The atriums are designed with glass-covered roofs that admit sunlight for passive solar gain in winter and are shaded and opened for natural ventilation in summer. The units are completely below grade and earth covered except for the glass-covered courtyards and some small above-grade portions. The low profile of the development and the quiet, private courtyards are very appropriate to this residential urban setting.

This project is notable in its illustration of a number of innovative energy-conserving systems at the neighborhood scale. Hot water for both space and water heating is distributed to each unit through a central system from the solar pond, which is the primary heat source. The project also includes facilities for food production and storage as well as for recycling solid and liquid wastes.

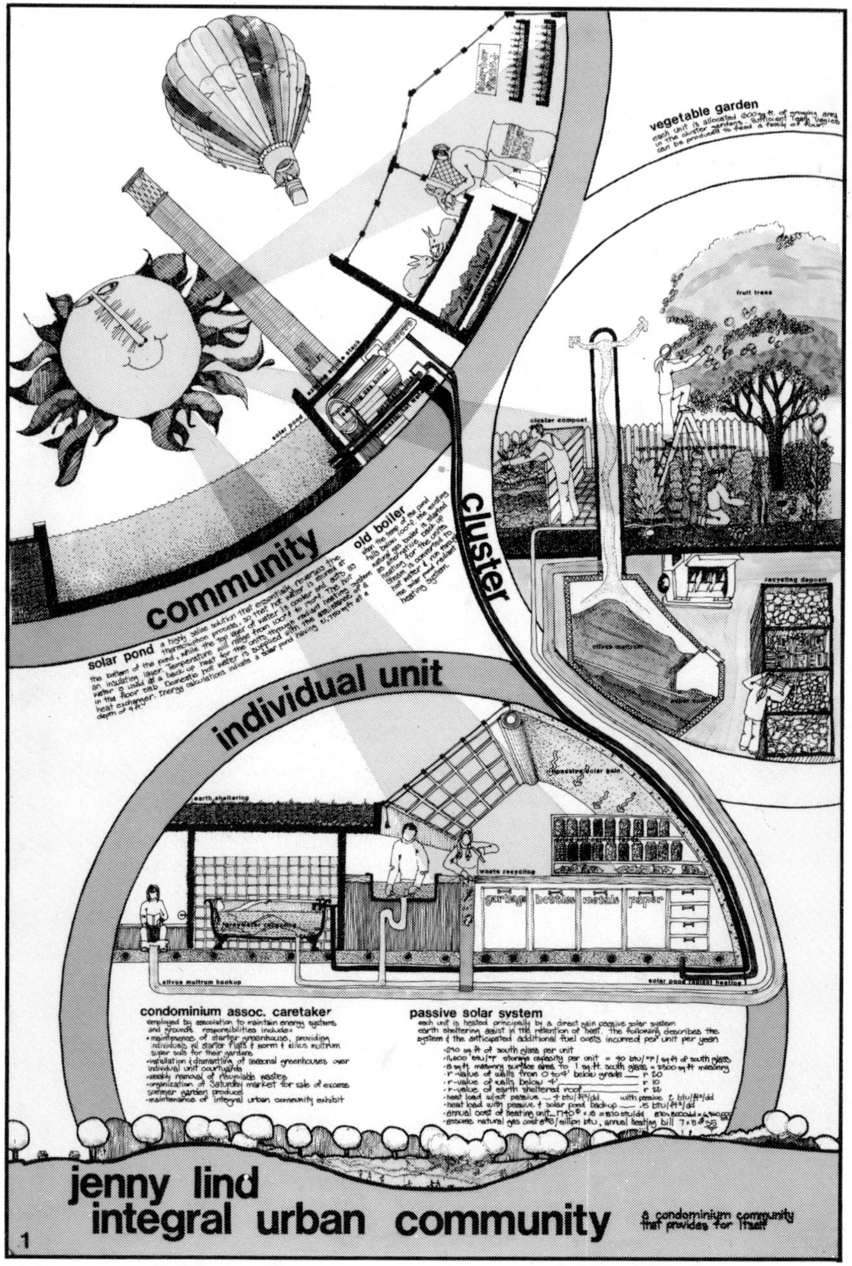
vegetable garden
community
cluster
individual unit
solar pond
old boiler
earth sheltering
waste recycling
garbage
bottles
metals
paper
condominium assoc. caretaker
passive solar system
jenny lind
integral urban community
a condominium community that provides for itself
1

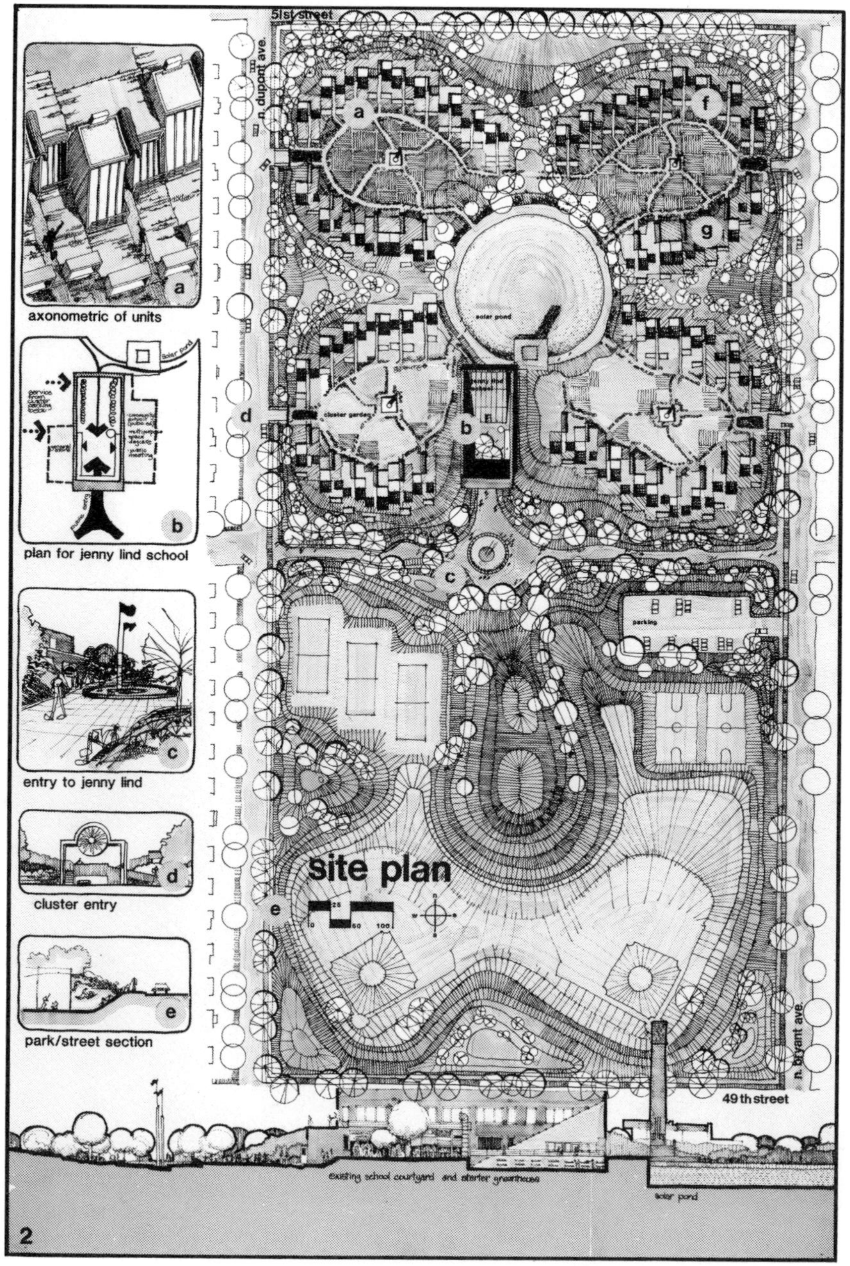
51st street
n. dupont ave.
axonometric of units
plan for jenny lind school
entry to jenny lind
cluster entry
park/street section
site plan
n. bryant ave.
49th street
existing school courtyard and starter greenhouse
solar pond
2

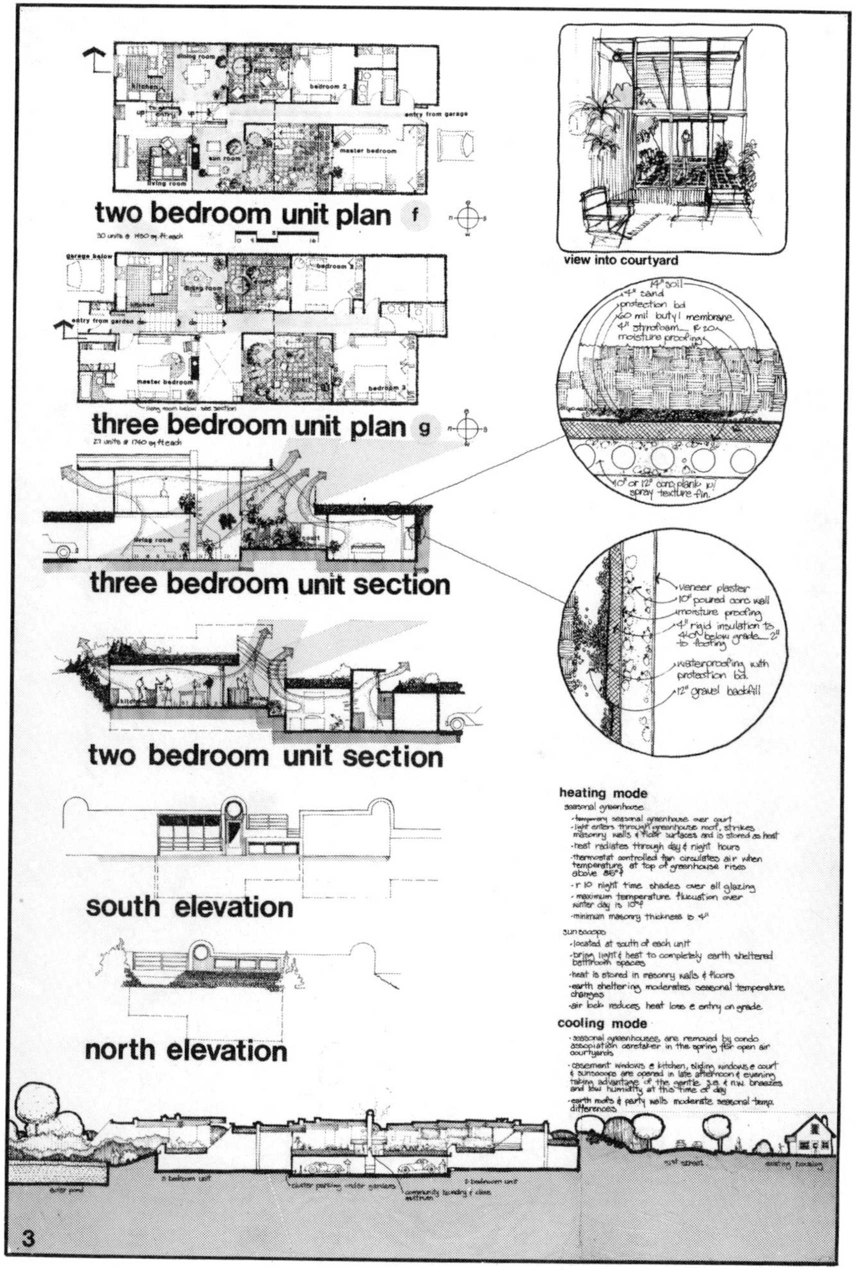
two bedroom unit plan
three bedroom unit plan
three bedroom unit section
two bedroom unit section
south elevation
north elevation
view into courtyard
heating mode
cooling mode
3

multiple-unit housing competition

In 1979 the Underground Space Center at the University of Minnesota sponsored a design competition for single- and multiple-unit earth sheltered housing projects. The winning entry in the latter division was submitted by the architecture firm of Hammel Green and Abrahamson, Inc., of St. Paul, Minnesota. The designers of the project were Mark Dohrmann and Richard Heise.

This project, consisting of eight housing units set into a south-facing hillside, effectively illustrates the use of attached earth sheltered units on a relatively steep 35-to 40-percent slope. The four one-bedroom and four two-bedroom units on either side of an enclosed central corridor make this a true multifamily structure, rare among earth sheltered designs. Although the project is shown on a 1.5-acre (0.6-ha) site—resulting in a density of 5.1 units per acre—much of the site is unused, so that a greater density could easily be achieved with a similar type of building.

All parking is provided on the north end of the site to limit paving and grading as well as to help shelter the structure. A sloping, sod-covered garage roof directs north winds up and away from the units below. The building is linear in design, arranged along a central, stepped corridor. The corridor roof is covered with insulated translucent panels to provide a naturally lighted atmosphere while limiting heat loss. Solar panels for the central water-heating system run along the center of the corridor roof. In summer the corridor will be ventilated naturally as hot air rises to the top and exits through a hinged roof panel.

The living units are planned so that all living rooms and bedrooms face south and have large window areas shaded by a continuous overhang. Because the windows look out over the landscaped roof of the unit below, exterior views are not obscured and a sense of privacy is maintained. Bedrooms open onto a private terrace with access to the surrounding open space. A glass-enclosed sunroom, which will gather sunlight and pass heat to surrounding living areas through sliding glass doors, is planned for each unit. The sunrooms also are built over an insulated rock storage bed that will collect heat and serve as a heat exchange source with the forced-air heating system. All windows, including the sunroom windows, will be equipped with folding insulated shutters to prevent heat loss at night. The sunroom roof will also have a roll-back insulated fabric panel to prevent heat loss. Living unit walls on the north and outer ends are earth sheltered; the roofs are covered with 18 to 24 inches (46 to 61 cm) of soil placed over a drainage bed and insulation.

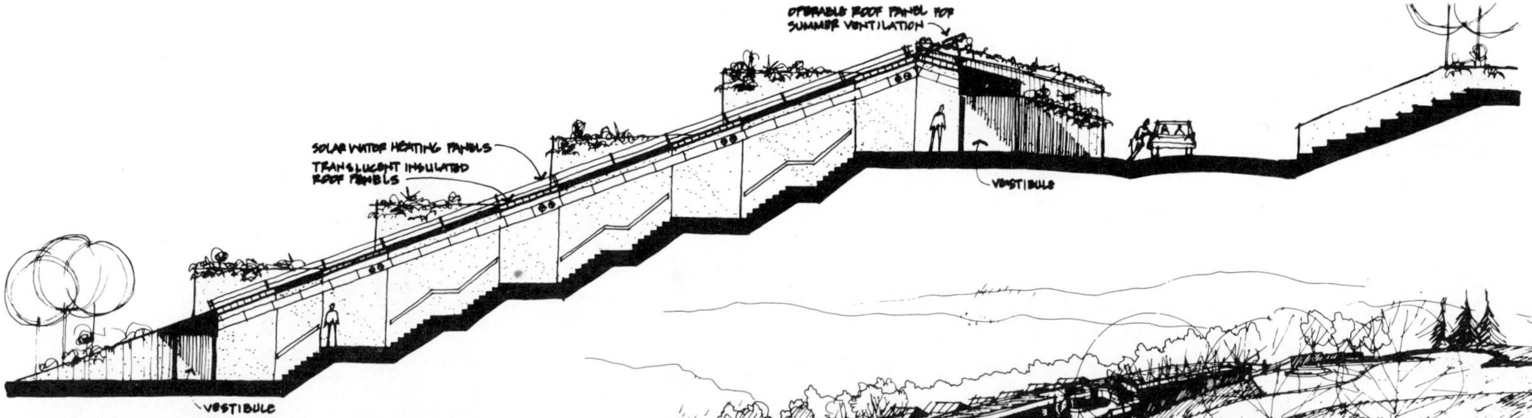
OPERABLE ROOF PANEL FOR SUMMER VENTILATION
SOLAR WATER HEATING PANELS
TRANSLUCENT INSULATED ROOF PANELS
VESTIBULE
VESTIBULE

SECTION THROUGH CORRIDOR

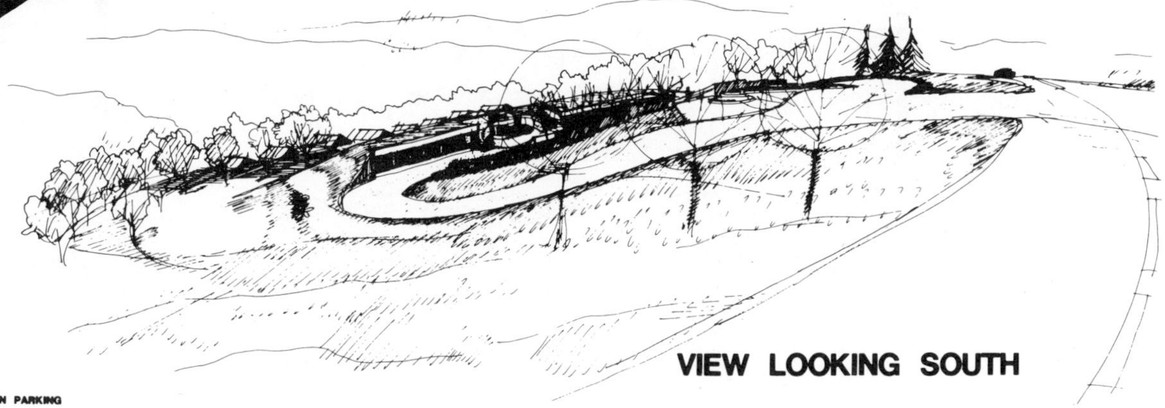

VIEW LOOKING SOUTH

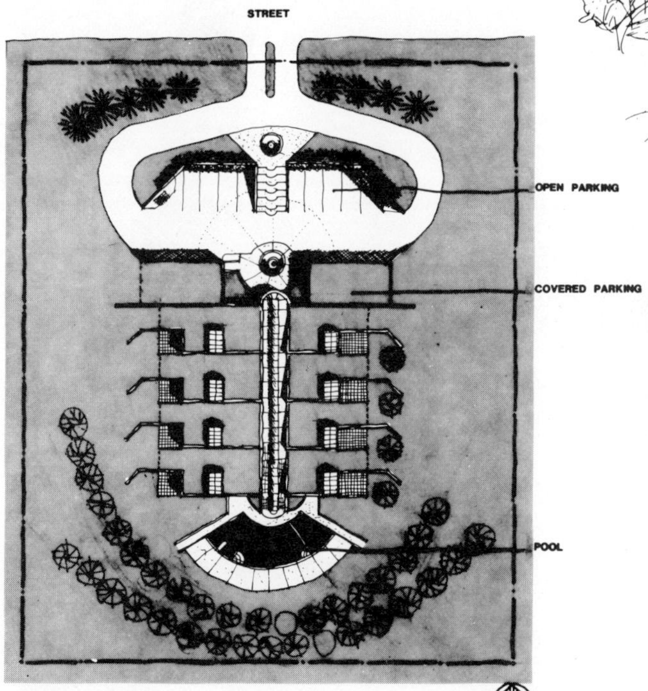
STREET
OPEN PARKING
COVERED PARKING
POOL

SITE PLAN

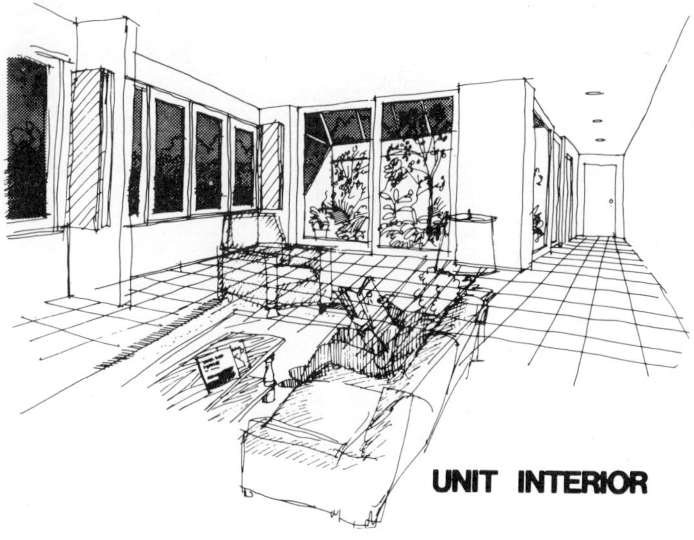

UNIT INTERIOR

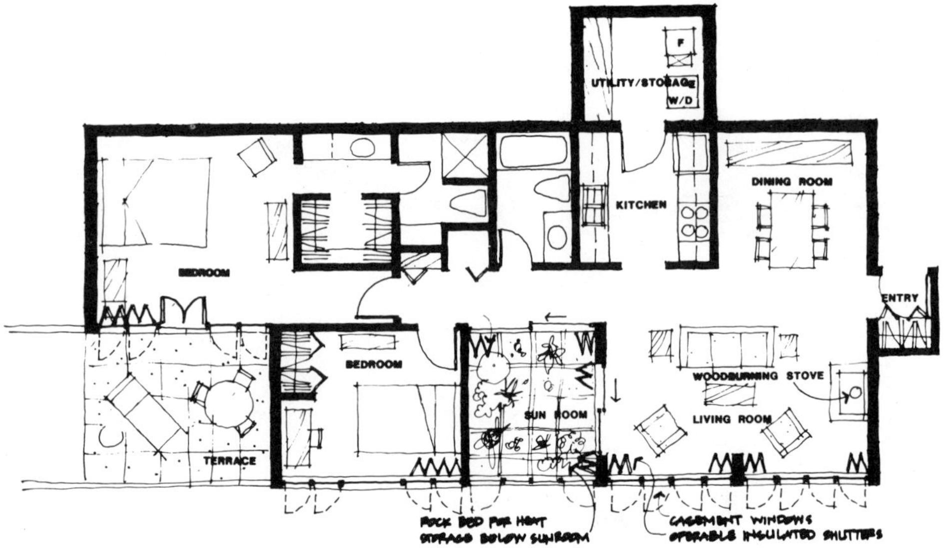
UTILITY/STORAGE
F
W/D
KITCHEN
DINING ROOM
BEDROOM
ENTRY
BEDROOM
SUN ROOM
WOODBURNING STOVE
LIVING ROOM
TERRACE
ROCK BED FOR HEAT
STORAGE BELOW SUNROOM
CASEMENT WINDOWS
OPERABLE INSULATED SHUTTERS

TWO BEDROOM UNIT PLAN (4 THUS)

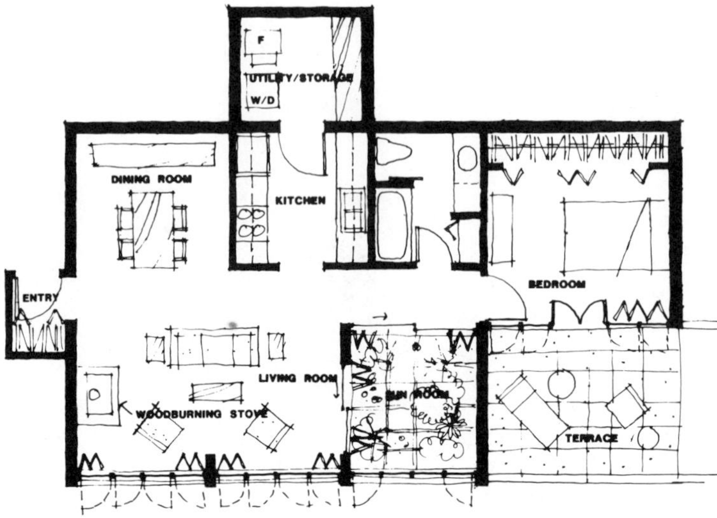
UTILITY/STORAGE
F
W/D
DINING ROOM
KITCHEN
ENTRY
BEDROOM
LIVING ROOM
SUN ROOM
WOODBURNING STOVE
TERRACE

ONE BEDROOM UNIT PLAN (4 THUS)

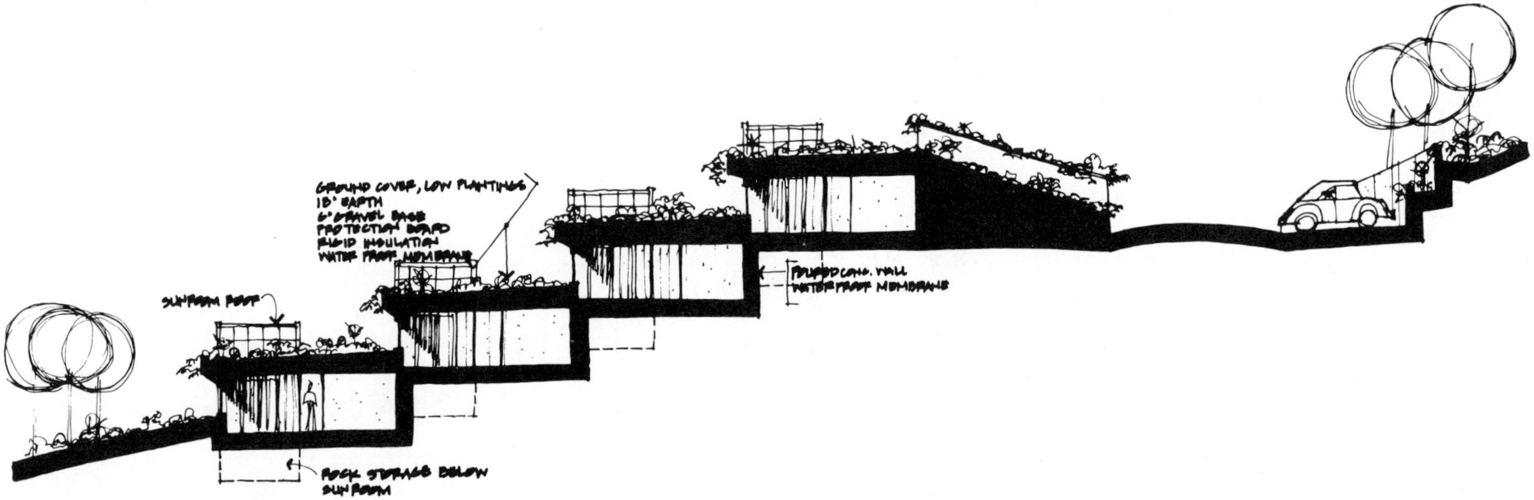
GROUND COVER, LOW PLANTINGS
18" EARTH
6" GRAVEL BASE
PROTECTION BOARD
RIGID INSULATION
WATER PROOF MEMBRANE
SUNROOM ROOF
POURED CONC. WALL
WATER PROOF MEMBRANE
ROCK STORAGE BELOW
SUNROOM

SECTION THROUGH LIVING UNITS

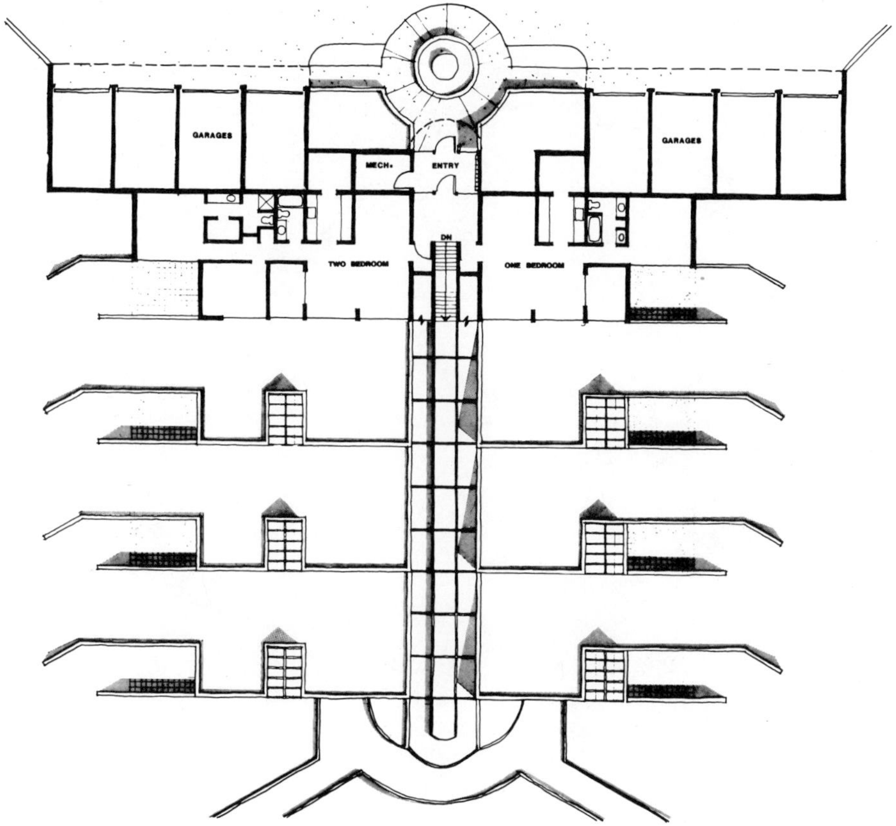
GARAGES
GARAGES
MECH.
ENTRY
DN
TWO BEDROOM
ONE BEDROOM

BUILDING PLAN

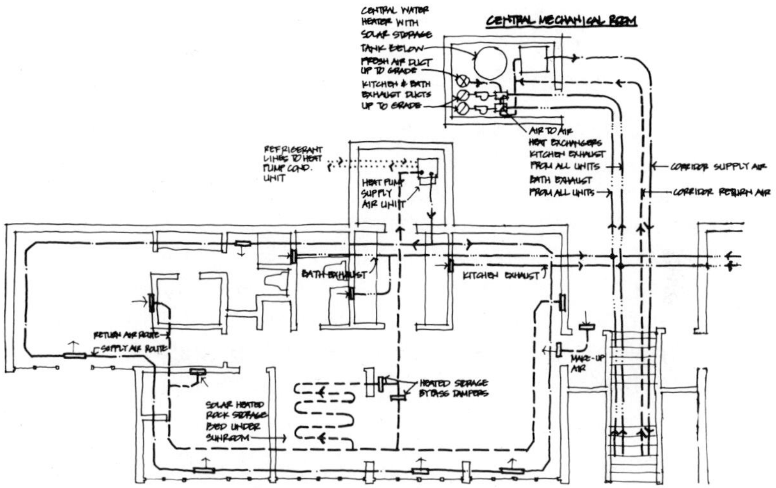
CENTRAL MECHANICAL ROOM
CENTRAL WATER HEATER WITH SOLAR STORAGE TANK BELOW
FRESH AIR DUCT UP TO GRADE
KITCHEN & BATH EXHAUST DUCTS UP TO GRADE
AIR TO AIR HEAT EXCHANGERS
KITCHEN EXHAUST FROM ALL UNITS
BATH EXHAUST FROM ALL UNITS
CORRIDOR SUPPLY AIR
CORRIDOR RETURN AIR
REFRIGERANT LINES TO HEAT PUMP COND. UNIT
HEAT PUMP SUPPLY AIR UNIT
BATH EXHAUST
KITCHEN EXHAUST
RETURN AIR ROUTE
SUPPLY AIR ROUTE
MAKE-UP AIR
HEATED STORAGE BYPASS DAMPERS
SOLAR HEATED ROCK STORAGE BED UNDER SUNROOM

MECHANICAL SYSTEMS SCHEMATIC

(TWO BEDROOM UNIT SHOWN – ONE BEDROOM UNIT SIMILAR)

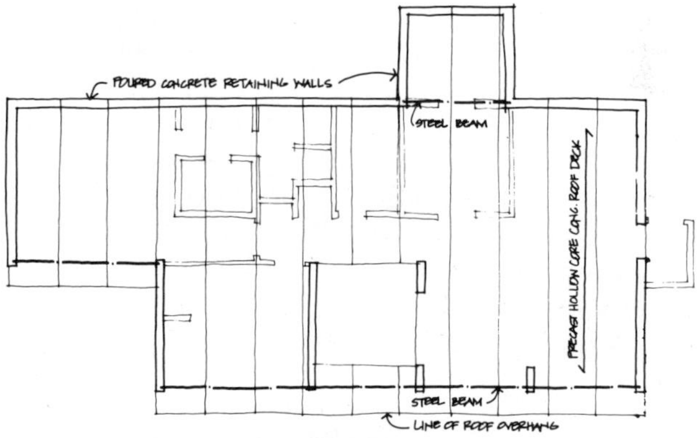
POURED CONCRETE RETAINING WALLS
STEEL BEAM
PRECAST HOLLOW CORE CONC. ROOF DECK
STEEL BEAM
LINE OF ROOF OVERHANG

STRUCTURAL SYSTEMS SCHEMATIC

(TWO BEDROOM UNIT SHOWN – ONE BEDROOM UNIT SIMILAR)

earth sheltered town houses

This proposal for a forty-four-unit town house development on a site in the St. Paul, Minnesota, area illustrates the aesthetic potential of earth sheltered housing while retaining many of the desirable characteristics of more conventional units. The project was designed in 1979 by Gerald Allen of CRITERIA architects, inc. of St. Paul for developer Paulette Bosella.

The 13.25-acre (5.3-ha) site with a wildlife area and pond in the center presents a variety of conditions for solar housing units on both north- and south-facing slopes. Attached units such as these could easily be arranged at densities higher than the 3.3 units per acre shown here. In this case, however, the special character of the site was preserved by leaving one-third of the site completely natural and devoting another third to common recreational areas.

The rows of attached units have completely earth-covered roofs and are fully bermed on the east and west ends. The partially bermed north wall of the units allows for north-facing windows in the bedroom spaces. The units are entered from the north side; the detached garages help protect the structures from the winter winds while creating small entry courtyards. Essentially, the basic unit can be adapted to topography that is flat, sloped to the north, or sloped to the south, as shown in the section drawings. Since not all spaces have south-facing windows, the floor plans can be more compact and similar to those of conventional town house units. The floor plans illustrate the wide variety of room arrangements possible even when a very regular, simple, bearing wall structure is used.

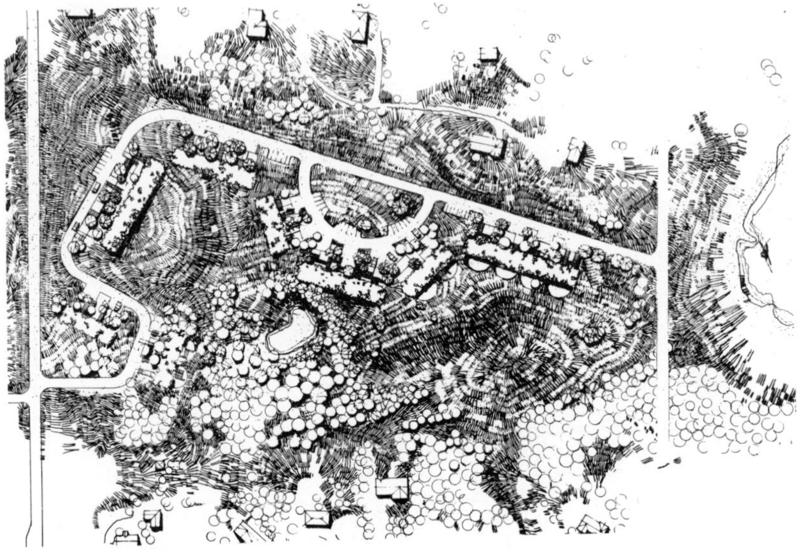

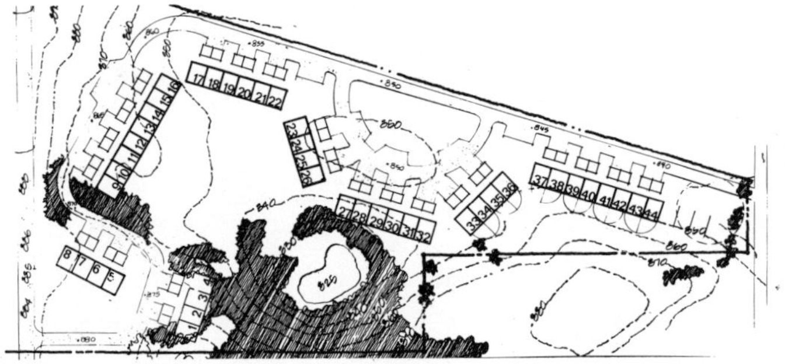

site plan

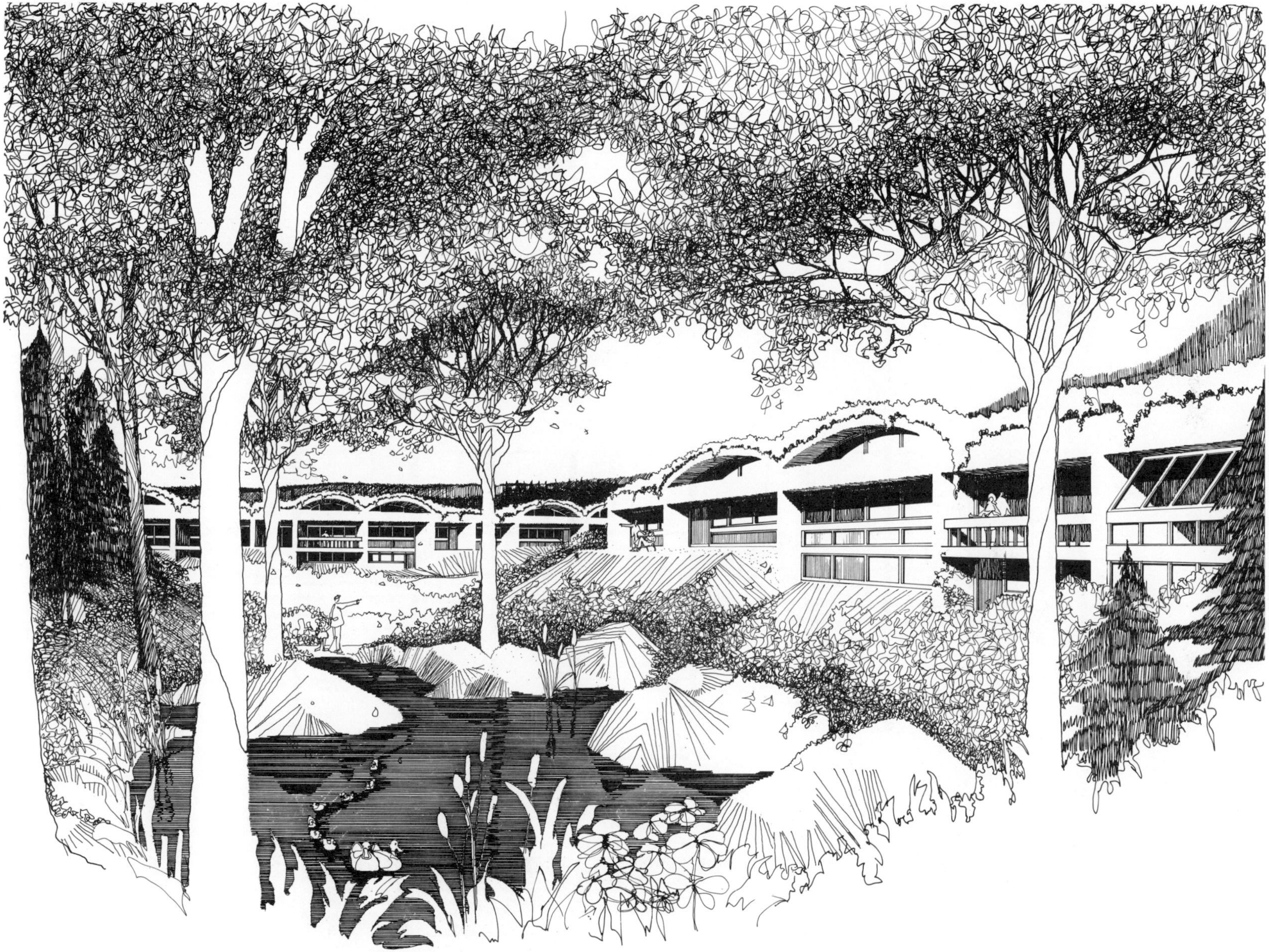

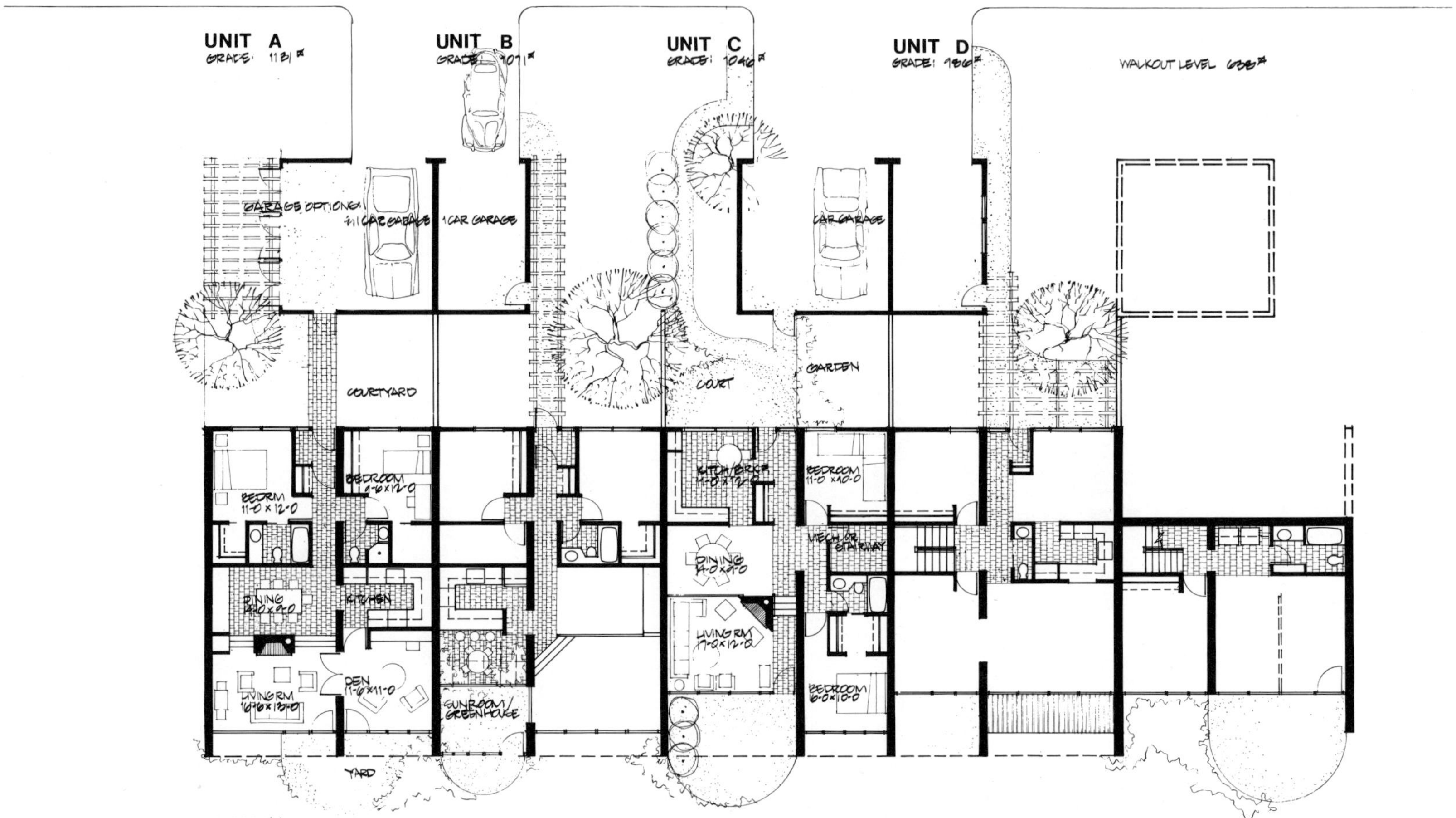
UNIT A
UNIT B
UNIT C
UNIT D
WALKOUT LEVEL
GARAGE OPTIONS
1 CAR GARAGE
CAR GARAGE
COURTYARD
COURT
GARDEN
BEDRM 11-0 x 12-0
BEDROOM 9-6 x 12-0
KITCH/BRKF 11-0 x 12-0
BEDROOM 11-0 x 10-0
MECH OR STAIRWAY
DINING 14-0 x 9-0
KITCHEN
DINING 14-0 x 9-0
LIVING RM 17-0 x 12-0
DEN 11-6 x 11-0
LIVING RM 16-6 x 13-0
SUNROOM/ GREENHOUSE
BEDROOM 16-0 x 10-0
YARD

PLAN 1/8 = 1·0

ELEVATION 1/8 = 1·0

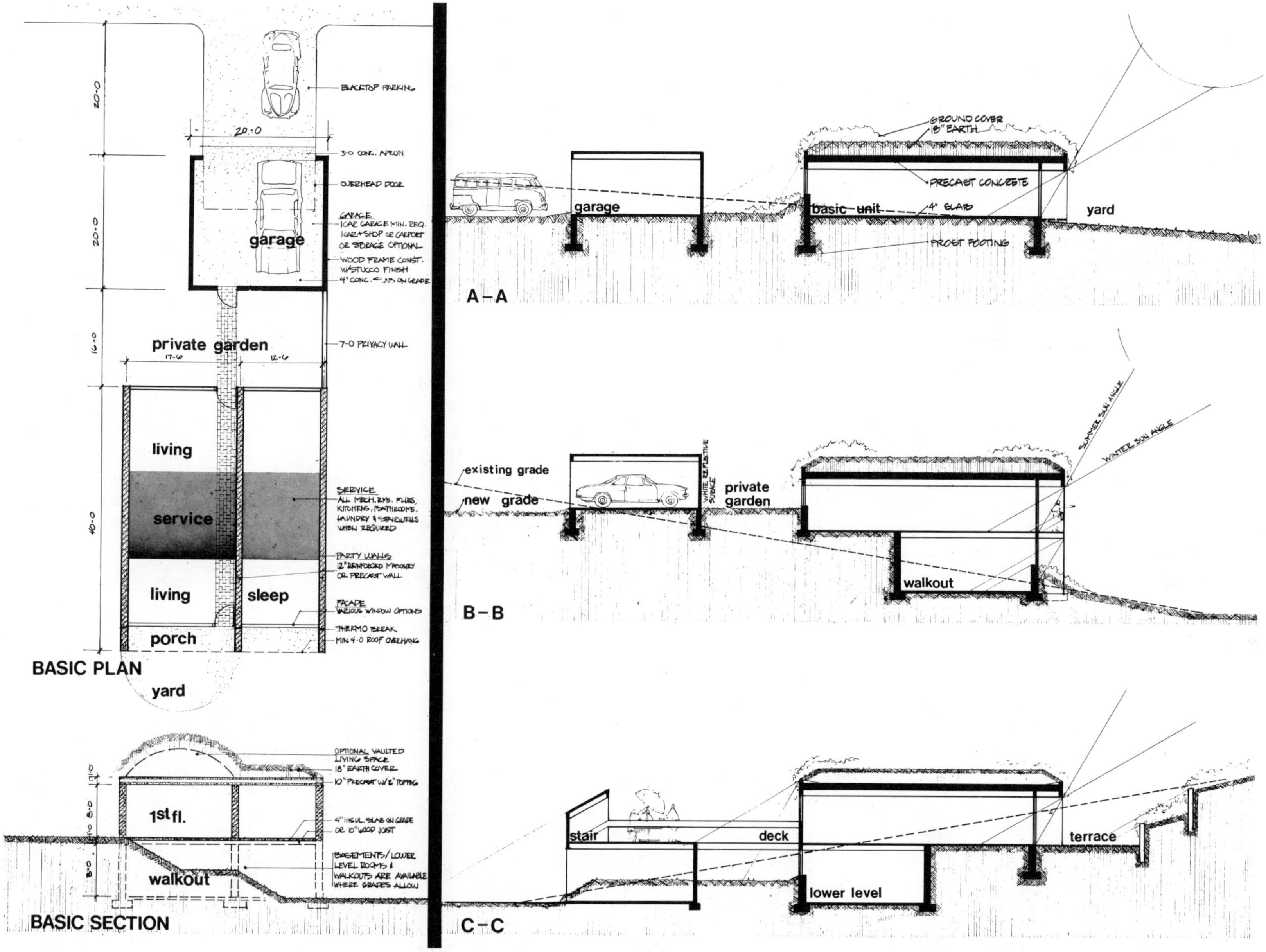

20-0
BLACKTOP PARKING
20-0
3-0 CONC. APRON
OVERHEAD DOOR
garage
GARAGE
1 CAR GARAGE MIN. REQ.
1 CAR + SHOP OR CARPORT
OR STORAGE OPTIONAL
WOOD FRAME CONST.
W/STUCCO FINISH
4" CONC. ON GRADE
16-0
private garden
7-0 PRIVACY WALL
17-6
12-6
living
service
SERVICE
ALL MECH. RMS. FLUES,
KITCHENS, BATHROOMS,
LAUNDRY & STAIRWELLS
WHEN REQUIRED
40-0
PARTY WALLS
12" REINFORCED MASONRY
OR PRECAST WALL
living
sleep
FACADE
VARIOUS WINDOW OPTIONS
porch
THERMO BREAK
MIN. 4-0 ROOF OVERHANG
BASIC PLAN
yard
OPTIONAL VAULTED
LIVING SPACE
18" EARTH COVER
10" PRECAST W/2" TOPPING
1st fl.
4" INSUL. SLAB ON GRADE
OR 10" WOOD JOIST
walkout
BASEMENTS/LOWER
LEVEL ROOMS &
WALKOUTS ARE AVAILABLE
WHERE GRADES ALLOW
BASIC SECTION
GROUND COVER
18" EARTH
PRECAST CONCRETE
garage
basic unit
4" SLAB
yard
FROST FOOTING
A–A
SUMMER SUN ANGLE
WINTER SUN ANGLE
existing grade
new grade
WHITE REFLECTIVE SURFACE
private garden
walkout
B–B
stair
deck
terrace
lower level
C–C

river view condominiums

This twenty-one-unit condominum proposal is another excellent example of earth sheltered units used effectively on a marginal, steeply sloping site. The project, located on a south-facing river bluff in the Minneapolis-St. Paul area, was designed for a developer in 1980 by Jay M. Johnson of Miller Hanson Westerbeck Bell Architects of Minneapolis. The rugged 5-acre (2-ha) site would normally be rejected for conventional one- or two-family detached units because it has so little flat, buildable area for conventional housing. It was estimated that no more than six detached houses could be placed on this site. Building attached town-house-type units that step down the slope achieves a density of 4.2 units per acre, however, and much of the site remains in its natural state.

The south-facing slope is ideally suited for maximum solar gain and the two- and three-level units are designed so that sunlight penetrates into every room. A variety of passive solar heating techniques—such as massive concrete floors and solariums—is employed in the units. Passive cooling through natural ventilation is induced by the stack effect in some of the units and by cross-ventilation in others. The multistory units are almost completely buried on the north side, with only the conventional well-insulated roofs extending above grade.

This project clearly demonstrates a number of energy-efficient strategies and techniques. The housing units are compact and attached in order to reduce heat loss through the exterior. Moreover, they are designed to maximize passive solar gain and earth sheltering. Finally, the siting of the project on marginally developable land represents efficient land use. In addition, this project illustrates some of the major assets associated with building on sloping sites. Although relatively dense, the complex has very little visual impact on the residential neighborhood to the north, and the earth serves to dampen any noise from the road. Each housing unit also has a clear view of the river valley below and a great sense of privacy since no other units are directly visible to the residents of each unit.

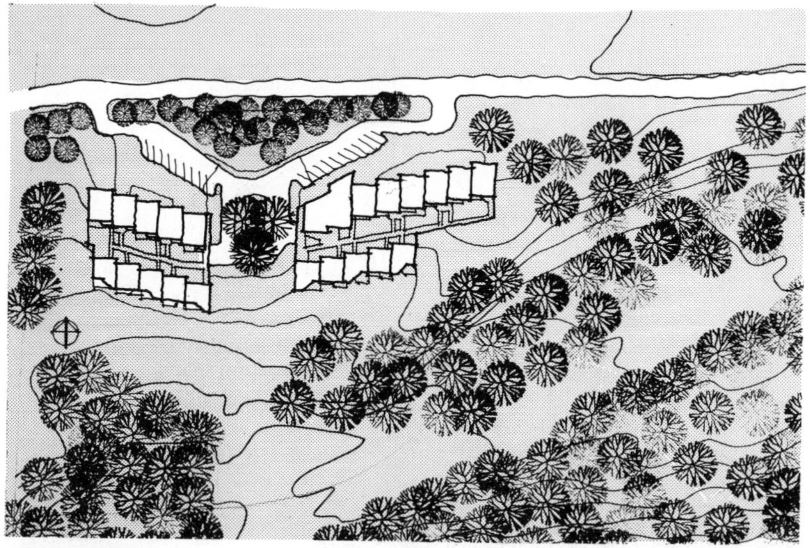

site plan

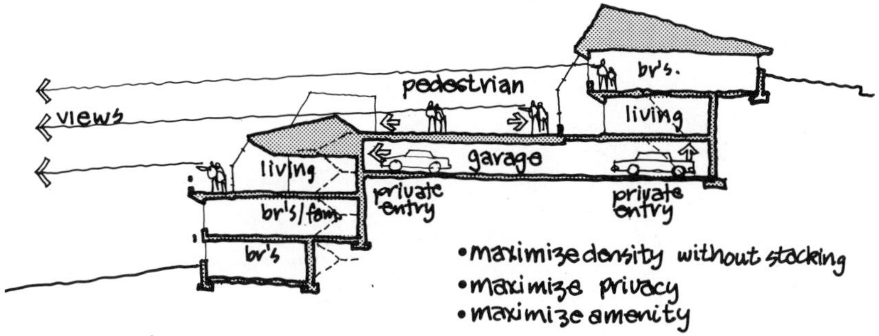
pedestrian
br's.
views
living
garage
living
br's/fam.
br's
private entry
private entry
•maximize density without stacking
•maximize privacy
•maximize amenity

building section

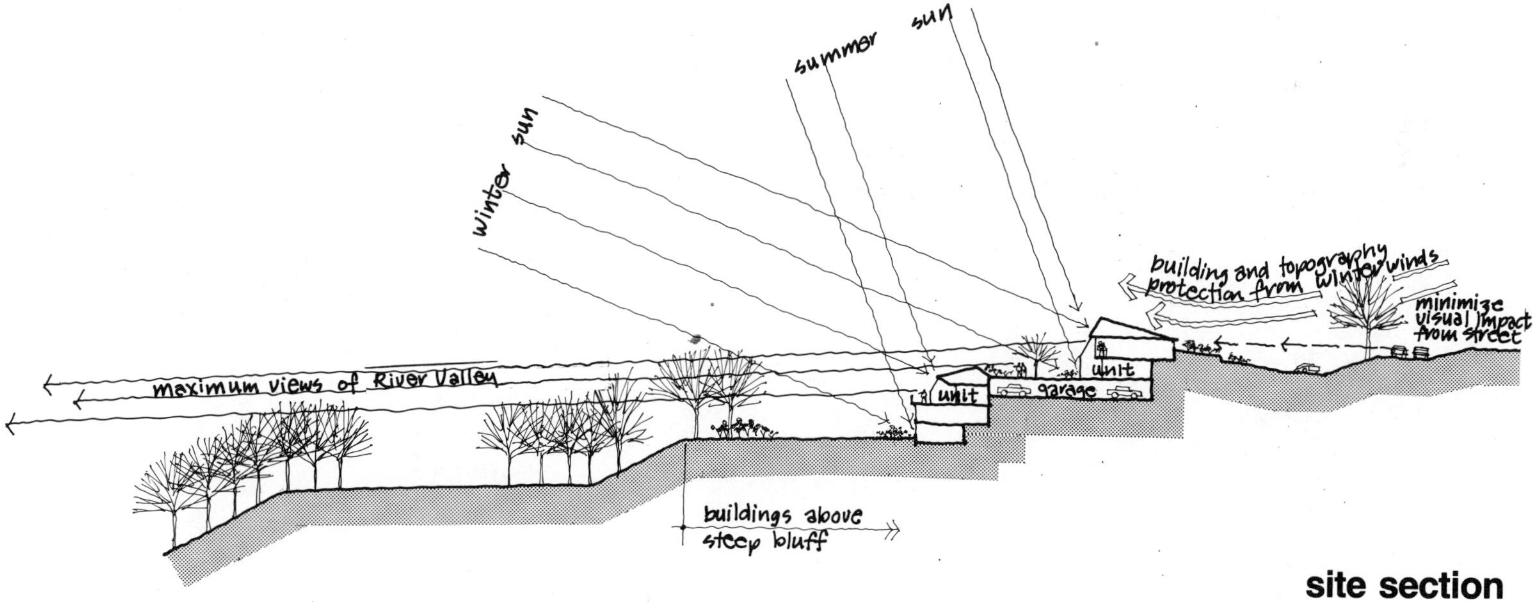
summer sun
winter sun
building and topography protection from winter winds
minimize visual impact from street
unit
unit
garage
maximum views of River Valley
buildings above steep bluff

site section

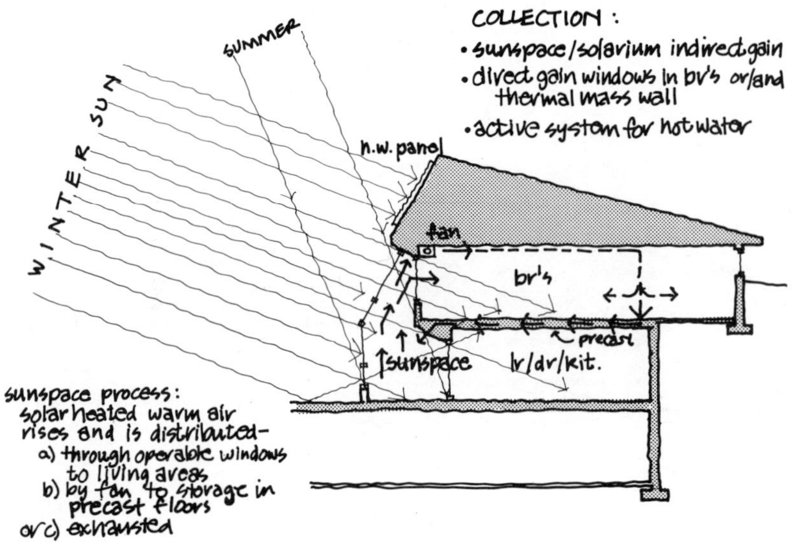
COLLECTION:
• sunspace/solarium indirect gain
• direct gain windows in br's or/and thermal mass wall
• active system for hot water
SUMMER
WINTER SUN
h.w. panel
fan
br's
precast
sunspace
lr/dr/kit.
sunspace process:
solar heated warm air rises and is distributed-
a) through operable windows to living areas
b) by fan to storage in precast floors
or c) exhausted

solar heating

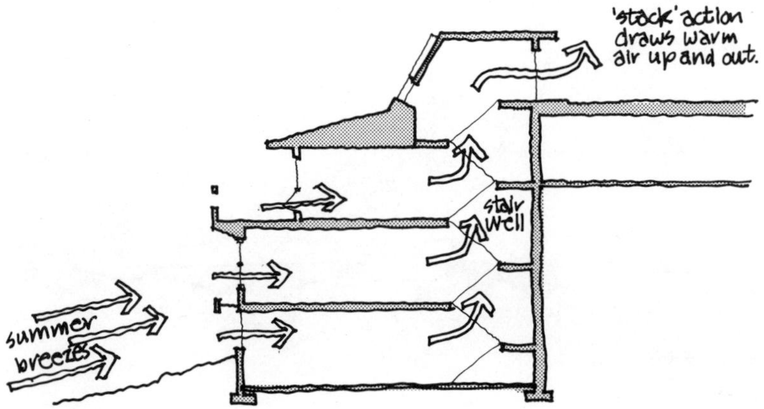
'stack' action draws warm air up and out.
stair well
summer breezes

natural ventilation

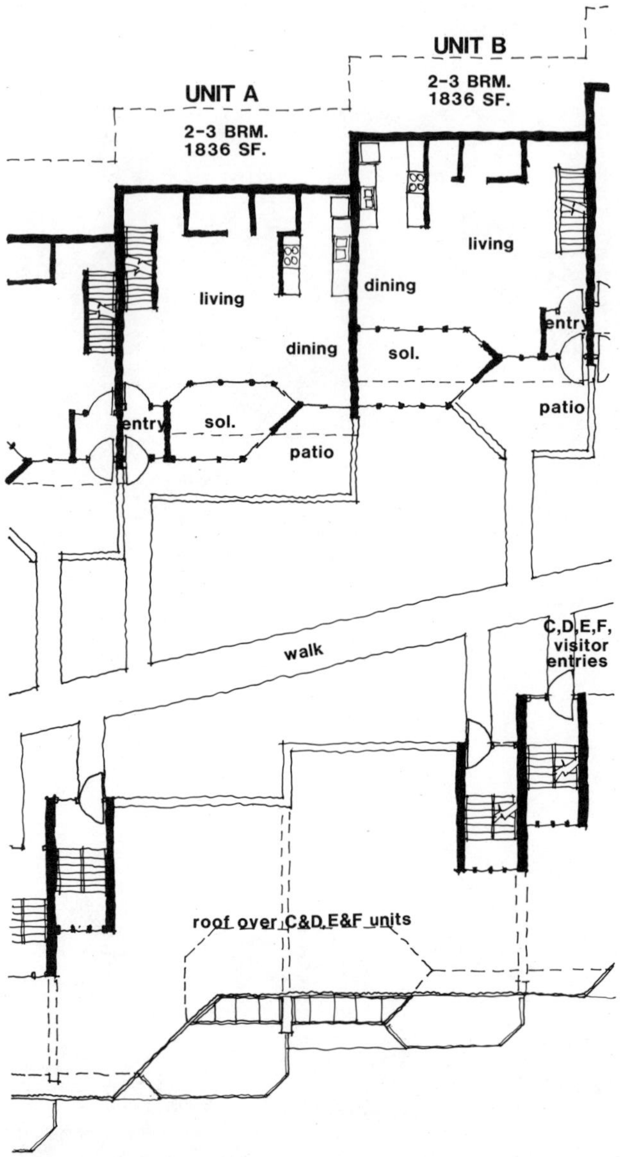
UNIT A
2-3 BRM.
1836 SF.
UNIT B
2-3 BRM.
1836 SF.
living
dining
entry
sol.
patio
living
dining
entry
sol.
patio
walk
C,D,E,F, visitor entries
roof over C&D, E&F units

entry level

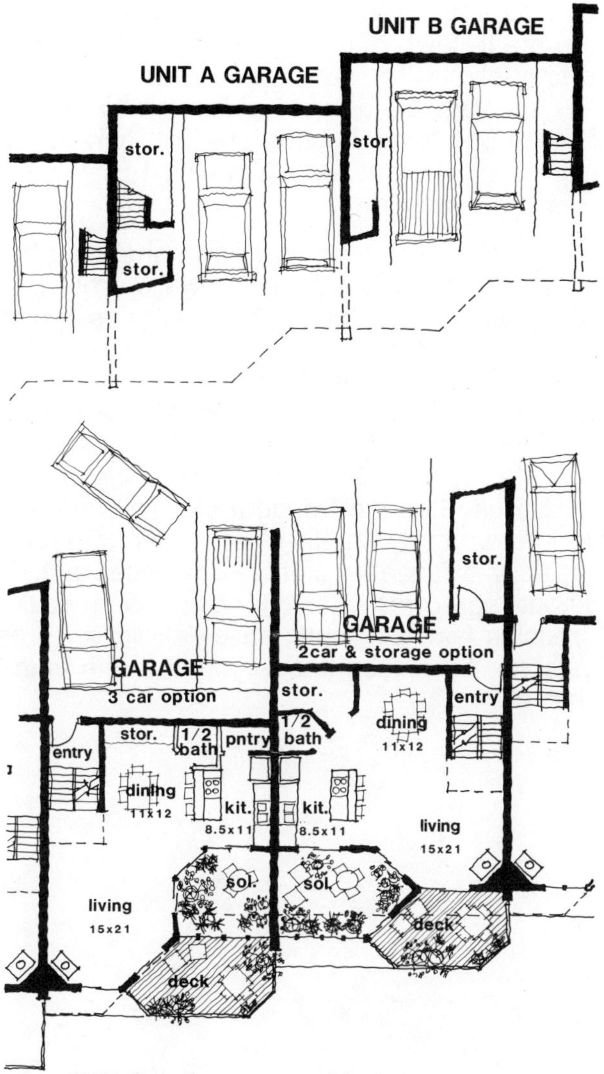
UNIT B GARAGE
UNIT A GARAGE
stor.
stor.
stor.
stor.
GARAGE
2car & storage option
GARAGE
3 car option
stor.
entry
stor.
1/2 bath
pntry
1/2 bath
dining
11x12
entry
dining
11x12
kit.
8.5x11
kit.
8.5x11
living
15x21
sol.
sol.
deck
living
15x21
deck

UNIT C or E

C 3-4 BRM.

E - 2 BRM.

UNIT D or F

D 3-4 BRM. 2262 SF.

F - 2 BRM. 1620 SF.

garage level

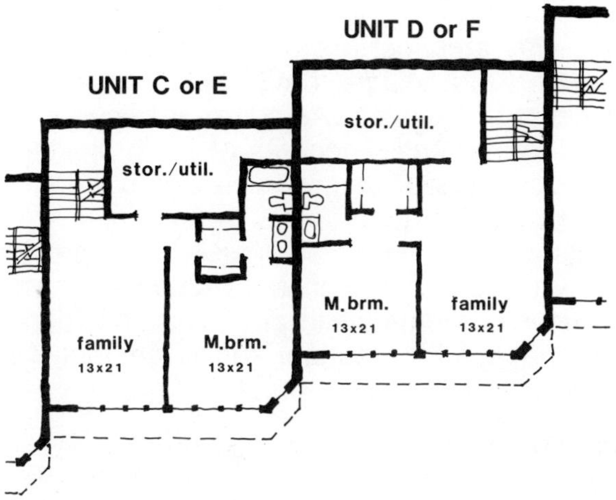
UNIT D or F
UNIT C or E
stor./util.
stor./util.
M.brm.
13x21
family
13x21
family
13x21
M.brm.
13x21

lower level one

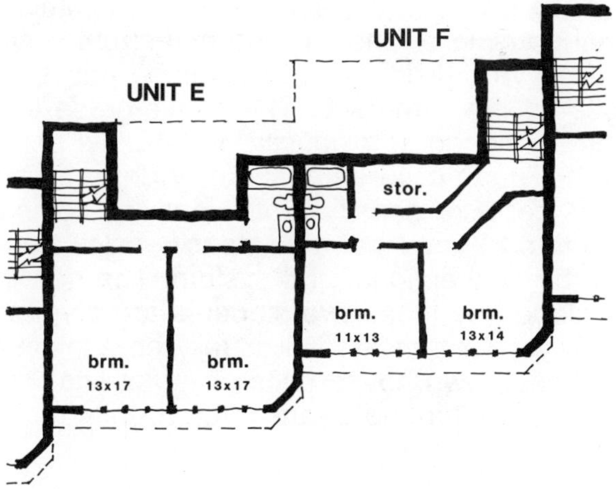
UNIT F
UNIT E
stor.
brm.
11x13
brm.
13x14
brm.
13x17
brm.
13x17

lower level two

urban hill village

One of the first advocates of earth sheltered residential communities was architect Frank Moreland. In examining his research and the designs developed by his students at the University of Texas in Arlington, it becomes apparent that the potential benefits of earth sheltered housing can be realized more completely at a community or neighborhood scale. In particular, developments of earth sheltered housing can provide approximately the same densities as attached town-house-type developments while providing considerably more green space, with resultant social, aesthetic, and ecological benefits [7.4].

The site plan developed in 1977 by students Ronald Horton and Larry Kelso for a site in Fort Worth, Texas, illustrates some of these community development concepts very well. In this case, 210 earth-covered units are placed into man-made hills on a relatively flat 28-acre (11.2-ha) site. Parking is kept at the periphery of the site, resulting in a completely green pedestrian environment in the center. An interesting comparison was then made between the earth-covered community, conventional housing on the existing grid-street system, and an alternative development of attached above-grade town houses on the same site. The above-grade town houses were designed at a density of 7.4 units per acre, while the earth-covered community design resulted in a 7.5-units-per-acre density. Both densities compare favorably to the 4.7-units-per-acre density calculated for housing on the conventional grid system. The density figures developed by these two students are atypical in that a slightly higher density can usually be achieved with conventional town house units on a flat site because the berms around earth-covered units require additional land.

While the densities for this earth-covered community and the above-grade town house alternative are similar, the amount of green space compared to hard-surface space (i.e., buildings, streets, and parking) is quite different. In the above-grade town house development, 69 percent of the land is public and private green space; in the earth-covered alternative, 89 percent of the land is green. Both of these percentages compare favorably to the conventional grid system layout, in which 52 percent of the land is green space.

In addition to demonstrating that earth sheltered housing can be built at reasonable densities while providing maximum green space, this design illustrates two other important points about community design. One is that a better overall design results from creating all of the land forms at one time and setting the houses into them, rather than from building earth sheltered houses separately, i.e., with each having its own berms. This design also illustrates the freedom of layout that is available in a warmer climate where solar orientation of these basically elevational units is not necessary. Siting units without regard for solar orientation is particularly helpful in using land efficiently on a flat site such as this, since units can be placed into all sides of the man-made land forms.

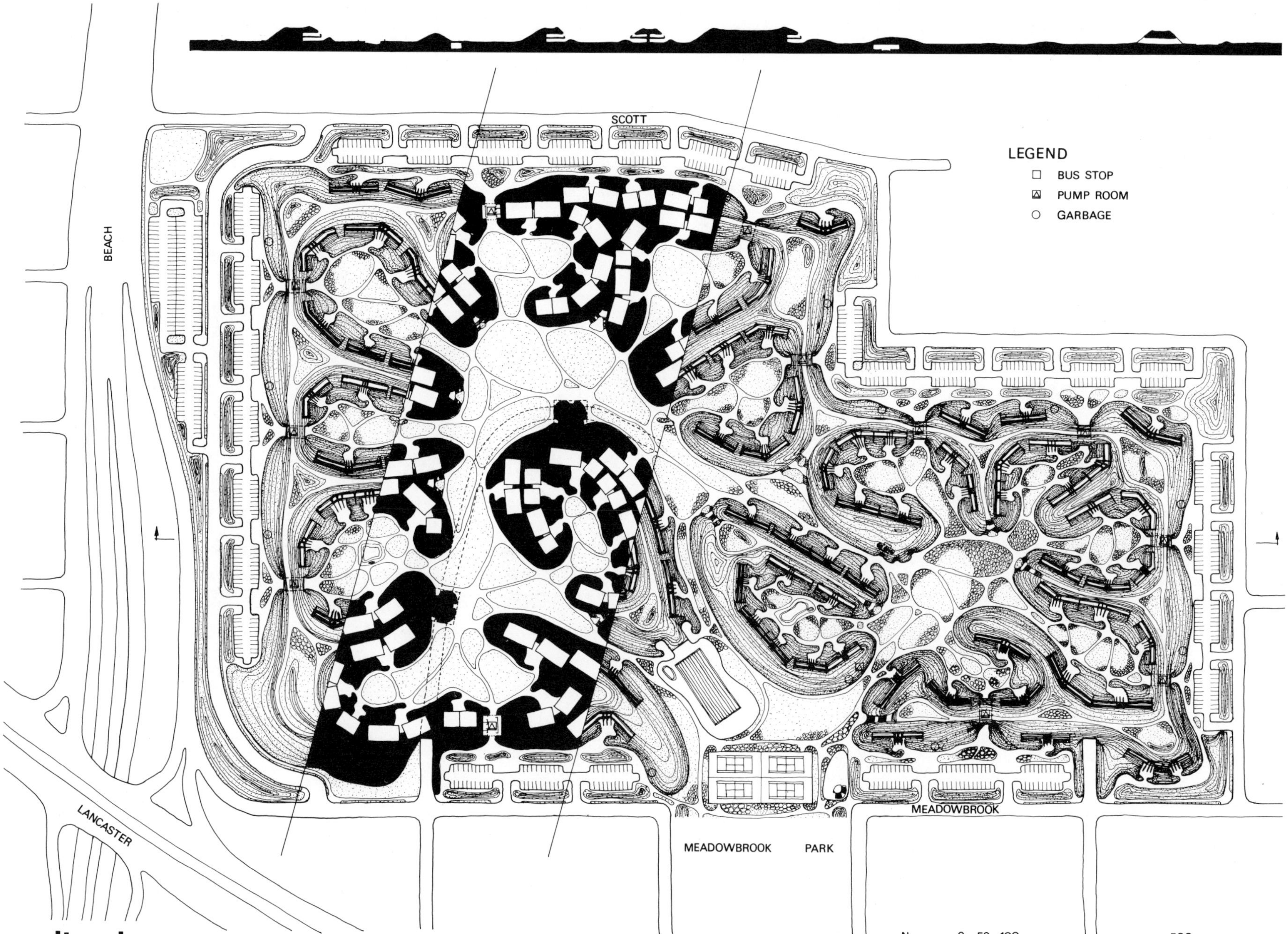

SCOTT
LEGEND
BUS STOP
PUMP ROOM
GARBAGE
BEACH
LANCASTER
MEADOWBROOK
MEADOWBROOK PARK
N
0 50 100 500

site plan

appendices

appendix a: energy supply systems

This appendix presents a more detailed evaluation of the energy supply systems discussed in chapter 3. The supply systems in this section are divided into two general categories: conventional systems and alternative systems. In evaluating both conventional and alternative energy systems, a large number of criteria can be considered. For the purposes of this study, these criteria fall into five general categories:

- energy use characteristics
- technological constraints
- economic feasibility
- environmental impact
- institutional and marketing constraints

The evaluation that follows will focus on the major assets and constraints of various conventional and alternative energy systems. It is beyond the scope of this study to present a detailed technical and economic analysis of these systems. In some cases such an analysis is merely speculative due to lack of information, and for many systems the technical and economic characteristics vary from site to site so that generalizations are not very meaningful. The ultimate goal of this examination is therefore to identify the various likely alternatives for energy supply systems and their characteristics so that physical planning guidelines can be developed.

conventional systems:

fossil fuel heating systems in individual units

Heat is the type of end-use energy required for space heating, hot water heating, cooking, and clothes drying. As discussed in chapter 3, the majority of the total energy use in housing comprises these uses. The main conventional fuel sources for heating are natural gas and fuel oil (electricity, which can also provide heat, is discussed in the next section); a small amount of heat is provided by liquid propane gas and coal, which have similar general characteristics. The conventional system for supply of natural gas consists of major pipeline networks that run from the source of extraction to various regions of the country. The gas is then distributed to individual houses through local or regional pipelines. Fuel oil, which can originate from either domestic or foreign crude oil, is transported from its source by ship and/or pipeline to refineries. Then the oil is distributed to individual houses by delivery trucks and held in a storage tank. In both cases combustion takes place in a furnace or other appliances within the housing unit.

energy-use characteristics: The efficiency of the furnace must be considered in determining the total efficiency of a particular system. Individual furnaces are rated at 80-percent peak efficiency (it is assumed that, in practice, the seasonal efficiency is 60 percent for oil and 70 percent for natural gas). One recent study found an average of only 46-percent efficiency for several furnaces tested, however [A.1]. This figure could be raised significantly with design, operation, and maintenance changes. For example, the latest gas furnace designs report efficiencies exceeding 90 percent. An important basic characteristic of conventional heating systems is that fossil fuels are nonrenewable and, thus, subject to price increases and supply interruptions.

technical constraints: Burning fossil fuels in individual furnaces is a well-known, established technology. The fuels are reliable, durable, and relatively safe. Delivery of fuels by truck offers a great deal of flexibility. Although pipelines are technically capable of running anywhere, they are expensive to change once in place. Fossil fuel systems are shaped by economic rather than technical limitations. Adaptability to future changes in fuel sources is generally a limitation for these systems. Adjustments in or replacement of individual furnaces would be a more complex and massive change than would altering a centralized power plant or district heating plant to use a different fuel. Some alternative fuel sources could, however, be supplied through natural gas pipelines and burned in the same manner. These would include methane gas created from waste material, gasified coal, or various synthetic fuels in gas form.

economic feasibility: The initial investment in the conventional type of system varies from development to development. Because furnaces are mass-produced and inexpensive, the lifetime cost of the total system is dominated by fuel costs rather than initial costs. Monthly fuel rates are subject to rapidly rising fossil fuel costs; deregulation of prices causes even greater increases. An economic advantage of the natural gas pipeline system is that the majority of the system and initial investment is already in place.

environmental impact: Oil-burning furnaces contribute to air pollution, but it is difficult to measure and control on an individual house basis. Pollution from burning natural gas is minimal.

institutional and marketing constraints: There is no obstacle to marketing, since the systems are conventional and well established. These systems may foster negative attitudes, however, simply because the consumer does not have local control and may feel vulnerable to price increases and supply interruptions.

physical planning and design implications: Since fossil fuel delivery systems, particularly for natural gas, are not available on all sites, the existing boundaries of the system may affect the location of the development. Connection of a housing development to natural gas pipelines does not directly affect the physical layout of the development or the units. The use of fuel oil supplied by delivery trucks to individual units requires vehicular access to each unit and an adjacent storage tank.

electrical generation and distribution systems

Electricity is conventionally supplied through relatively large, regional systems that consist of one or more large generation plants and an extensive network of transmission lines. It is typically generated by combustion of coal, oil, or natural gas; by nuclear reaction; or by the conversion of the potential energy of water (hydropower). Electricity is a high-quality form of energy capable of meeting all of the energy needs in housing, including space and hot water heating, but electricity is only essential for lighting and for operating some appliances and devices.

energy-use characteristics: Excluding the efficiency of the end-use device, the system is approximately 25 to 30 percent efficient. Approximately three units of primary fuel are required to generate one unit of electricity; the remaining energy is expelled as waste heat. An additional 10 percent of the electricity generated is lost in transmission through power lines. An important exception to this low overall efficiency is generation by hydropower, which is 70 to 80 percent efficient. Coal, oil, and gas—which account for the majority of the fuel used—are nonrenewable. Although hydropower is renewable, plant sites are quite limited. The nuclear breeder reactor can be considered renewable, since the fuel source is replenishable. The energy embodied in large power plants and transmission lines is relatively high because of the large use of energy-intensive materials and the size of the total system. This is particularly true of nuclear plants, which require complex construction technologies. Conventional fuel sources and typical efficiencies for electricity are shown in figure A-1.

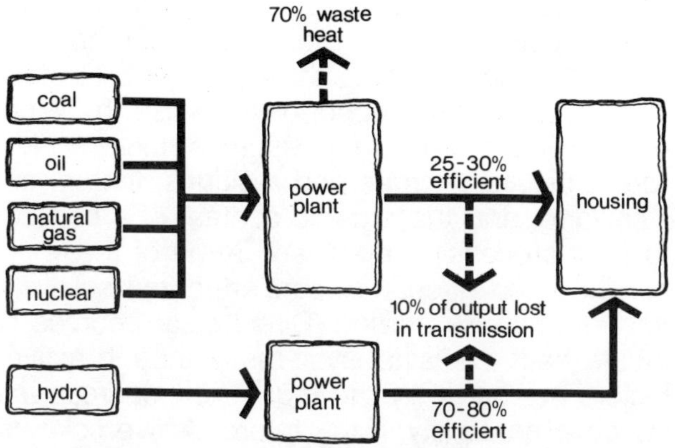

70% waste heat
coal
oil
natural gas
nuclear
power plant
25-30% efficient
housing
10% of output lost in transmission
hydro
power plant
70-80% efficient

A-1: conventional electrical generation

technological constraints: Generally, large-scale electrical generation and distribution networks are a known technology that is reliable and safe, primarily because the system is owned and operated by one company. An exception to this generalization may be nuclear plants, the safety of which is a subject of considerable controversy. Large-scale systems are adaptable in a technical sense to a variety of fuel sources without requiring changes in the delivery system. The capital investment in large plants and the cost of conversion makes adaptability rather expensive and sometimes impractical, however.

economic feasibility: The economics of the electric utility industry are quite complex. The initial investment in the system varies for individual developers. The monthly bills of the customers will reflect rising fossil fuel costs, the huge capital investment of the total system, and any inefficiencies of the total system. One economic advantage of regional-scale systems is that they already exist and much of the initial investment has already been made. This does not necessarily imply further development, however. In fact, the cost of new generating plants is higher than existing ones; consequently, average rates will rise with expansion.

environmental impact: Any burning of large amounts of fossil fuel results in some air pollution; this is a particular concern with coal. The huge amounts of waste heat released into the air or water from power plants also represent a large source of thermal pollution, which is appreciably greater for current nuclear plants than for coal-fired plants of the same size. The environmental impact of a large-scale electrical system on an isolated housing development can be considered minimal, since the undesirable effects of generation are usually far from the site. There is a total environmental advantage to concentrating air pollutants at a few sources located away from centers of population, where they can be controlled and regulated. Nuclear plants present some highly controversial and, perhaps, potentially disastrous environmental effects. Plant operation and radioactive waste disposal must meet nearly perfect standards to be acceptable environmentally.

institutional and marketing constraints: There is no obstacle to marketing, since connection to a large grid is virtually the only accepted supply system at this time for basic electrical uses such as lighting and appliances. Higher prices in comparison to fossil fuels are an obstacle to marketing electric heat. From a community point of view, the negative aspect to large systems is the lack of control or participation in decision making at the local level. People thus tend to feel less self-reliant and more vulnerable to fuel availability and price changes.

physical planning and design implications: In general, because electricity is made available to all buildable sites, it does not represent an absolute restriction on the location of developments. Economics may limit location of the development, however, since the cost of extending service to outlying areas is greater than infilling where the system already exists. Connection of a housing development to an existing utility grid does not directly affect the physical layout of the development or the units. An aesthetic consideration is the placement of lines underground rather than overhead.

alternate systems:

district heating

District heat represents a fundamental change in the location at which heat is generated and the manner in which it is distributed to housing units. Rather than supplying fuel to individual houses and creating heat by combustion within the unit, in a district heating system the fuel is combusted at a central location; the heat is then distributed to the individual units. This operation requires a distribution system of pipes to carry either hot water or steam (hot water is generally preferred because it has several technical advantages). District heating for a housing development can be considered in two ways. As in some European countries, district heating can be supplied by a government or privately owned utility company that generates electricity and heat, which it sells to its customers. This type of system is similar to conventional electrical supply systems. The individual developer can only consider district heating with this type of system if the development is located adjacent to an existing system or heat source, such as a power plant or industry. District heating can also be considered as an on-site centralized heating system that collects or generates heat from a variety of sources and distributes the heated water to the individual units. In this case the system could be privately owned and maintained by the developer, the utility company, or the community itself.

District heating systems can be a medium for distributing heat from either nonrenewable conventional fuels or a variety of renewable sources. Thus the system may represent a fundamental change in fuel source as well as a change in the method of distribution. Obviously, fossil fuels such as oil and natural gas can be burned in a district system, just as they are in individual furnaces. Although coal is also a possibility at the district scale and is preferable because it is more available, pollution control measures and costs are much greater for coal than for gas and oil. In addition to using these conventional fuels, district systems present the opportunity to use the wide variety of renewable biomass fuel sources. Included in this category are agricultural crops and residues, timber, animal manures, sewage, and the organic content of urban solid waste and food processing residues. Some of these sources can be used directly or converted into solid, liquid, or gas fuels that can be burned. Direct solar sources can also contribute heat to district systems. Although active solar collectors are currently the most likely sources, solar ponds may be a possibility in the future. Active solar collectors and solar ponds are discussed below as separate alternative systems of supply.

Many industrial processes release large quantities of unused waste heat, as do conventional electrical generation plants. While these sources are not classified as renewable or nonrenewable because they originate from another process, they nonetheless represent a potential for tremendous improvements in overall efficiency, since heat that would otherwise be wasted can be used. Many of the basic characteristics of district heating systems are the same regardless of the source; however, the high-efficiency characteristics of the cogeneration of electricity and heat in a district system are discussed in the next section.

energy-use characteristics: Based on similar Swedish systems, it is estimated that heat can be generated at efficiencies as high as 85 percent, which is considerably higher than the efficiency rates of individual unit furnaces. Because they are nonrenewable, the fossil fuels are subject to price increases and supply interruptions. Biomass fuels, on the other hand, are completely renewable. The variety of sources for district heat and the general efficiency of the system are shown in figure A-2.

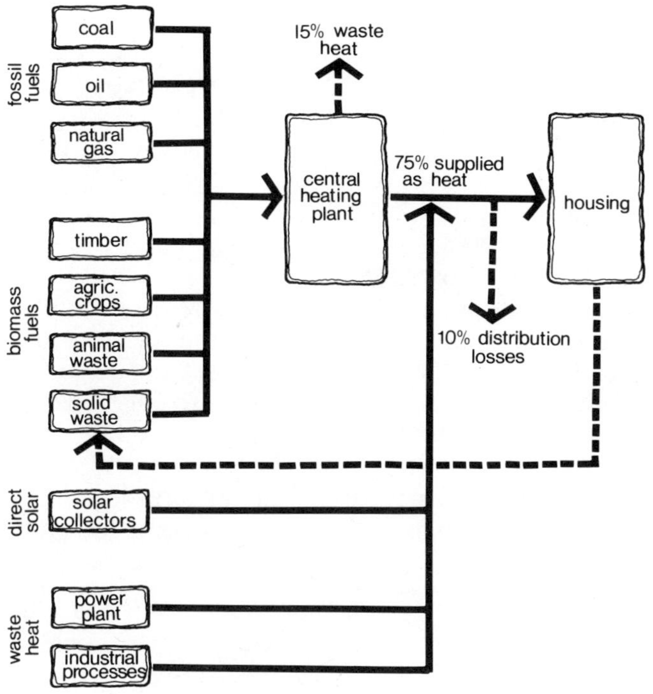
coal
oil
natural gas
fossil fuels
timber
agric. crops
animal waste
solid waste
biomass fuels
solar collectors
direct solar
power plant
industrial processes
waste heat
15% waste heat
central heating plant
75% supplied as heat
housing
10% distribution losses

A-2: district heating

technical constraints: The technology for district heating systems with fossil fuels is well known and well developed in Europe. These systems are at least as reliable, durable, and safe as conventional systems and—since they are better maintained—may even be better. This statement is based on the assumption of professional, skilled operation and maintenance of the boiler. Solid waste has been used extensively in Europe as a fuel source for electrical and steam generation.

There is less precedent for burning some of the other biomass sources, although they should not present great technical problems. Whether on-site systems for generating methane from waste materials could contribute significantly is questionable because of the long time required for conversion and the relatively small quantities of waste materials available. Although they could supplement natural gas supplies, maintenance and reliability of conversion systems may present problems.

Hot water systems are technically superior to steam systems. The maximum length of a hot water line is at least 20 miles (32 km), whereas the length of a steam pipe is limited to about 2 miles (3.2 km). In addition, heat transfer rates are much higher for hot water systems than for steam. Pipes for hot water systems are much smaller, thus reducing capital costs. The hot water provides space heating and hot water heat through a heat exchange device in each unit. The pipes in a district heating system may work in a single loop where the temperature of the water drops with each successive customer on the loop. A superior but more expensive and more complex solution provides a supply and return pipe to each unit; in this case a loop configuration is not implied [A.2]. The pipe sizing is similar to that of a water supply system where the largest pipes are at the central plant and the smallest pipes feed the individual unit.

Although immediate proximity to the plant and high densities with efficient layouts are not technical requirements, they may be dictated by economics. If changes in the system layout are required, underground piping is expensive to tear up. Therefore, flexibility for future layout changes is quite limited. In Sweden systems are developed in a piecemeal fashion, which may correspond to a phased new development in the United States. Each new section is a complete subsystem with a small, sometimes portable, boiler. As new subsystems are added, they can be linked together and supplied from larger central sources, such as electrical generation plants, industrial waste heat, or geothermal energy. Adaptability to changing fuel sources is one of the great assets of district heating systems. Changes can be made at the central plant to heat water with a wide variety of renewable and nonrenewable sources. No change in the distribution system is required to implement such changes.

economic feasibility: In European countries such as Sweden, the feasibility of district heating is based on fuel costs that are higher than those in the United States and almost no sizable fossil fuel resources within the country. Most preliminary studies in the United States have focused on the most cost-effective situations for district heating, namely, areas of high urban densities; areas adjacent to existing electrical generation plants or industry, so that the heat is essentially free; and areas with long heating seasons. Very little investigation has been done for completely new on-site systems associated with medium-density housing.

Compared with purchasing conventional fuels, the economic benefit of using waste heat from industrial sources is obviously great. Similarly, the most positive economic benefits of biomass fuels are related to the use of waste products, which are essentially free and must be disposed of at a cost. The feasibility of using timber, agricultural crops and residues, and other wastes as a fuel source depends on availability of adequate supplies and efficient means of collection and transport. It is unlikely that land within a development would be devoted to biomass production, since the area required would be extensive and other uses for the land would be more cost effective.

Initial construction costs for district heating systems are very site specific. If the piping can be laid with other utilities during street construction, the costs may be reduced significantly. The capital cost per unit depends on:

- density of development
- simplicity of layout
- ease of construction
- total number of units to share plant construction costs
- cost of equipment required

Two items may affect the costs significantly. One item is the ongoing development of flexible pipe, which greatly accelerates construction, thus reducing costs. The second is the heat meters required to measure each unit's consumption. Although such meters encourage conservation significantly, they are expensive ($300 per unit in Sweden). It may also be economically beneficial in a large system to supply water at lower temperatures and then use it as the heat source for heat pumps that work at high efficiencies. In a feasibility study for a proposed system in Switzerland, it was stated that such a low-temperature system allowed the density requirement to be lowered to 8 users per acre in some areas, in contrast to the accepted limit of 40 users per acre for typical systems [A.3]. A final and very critical factor in the economic feasibility of district systems is the amount of energy required by each unit. As various conservation techniques reduce the amount of space and hot water heat required, the capital cost of a district system will be less justifiable.

environmental impact: The major environmental impact of district heating is that the air pollutants from burning fuels are concentrated at one source rather than scattered, as they are with individual furnaces. This concentration of pollutant presents the opportunity to site the plant properly and control the pollution through cleaning devices that are impractical at the unit scale. Measurable improvements in air quality have occurred in Sweden as a result of district heating systems.

institutional and marketing constraints: Since district systems for new developments are not an established concept in the United States, there are likely to be constraints in existing building codes, zoning ordinances for plant siting, financing, and environmental regulations. The required close proximity to a central heating plant could be a negative marketing factor unless the facility is properly designed. Similarly, location of housing near sources of waste heat such as heavy industry may be undesirable from a marketing viewpoint, even if zoning variances allowed for this proximity. Compatible light industry will be required near housing. A marketing asset is that the ability of individuals to own and participate in the operation of a local system may be politically and socially satisfying—especially if the system uses renewable sources available on or near the site.

physical planning and design implications: The key planning implication is the location of the development near a source of waste heat or the inclusion of industrial and commercial uses in the development. Generally, the density of units should be as high as possible and the layout as simple and direct as possible. Exact criteria for density and size of system have not been established. The most economical system would have the central plant near the greatest density and number of units. In addition, hot water lines should be planned so that they can be laid with other utilities during construction. For new developments that are built in phases, the subsystem approach may be the most flexible. Each subsystem is constructed with a small boiler that may be phased out as the system grows and connects to other subsystems.

cogeneration of electricity and heat

Like district heating, the cogeneration of electricity and heat represents fundamental changes in the conventional generation and distribution patterns of energy supply for housing. Cogeneration refers to the combined generation of electricity and heat (steam or hot water) from the same fuel source for district heating. Conventional electrical generation systems using combustion of various fuels can be modified so that steam or hot water is harnessed from the normally wasted heat. Cogeneration can be applied in two different ways in new housing developments. By the first method, heat can be harnessed from existing large-scale power plants and supplied to the housing units. This system is basically the same as the district heating systems described in the previous section. Although the heat and electricity are generated together, the source and pattern of conventional electrical supply are unchanged. The second type of cogeneration occurs completely on-site and is a self-contained energy supply system. Because this represents a departure from conventional electrical supply systems—not only in the smaller scale of generation, but also in the possible ownership and operation by parties other than a public utility—this section focuses on on-site systems. An important component of on-site electrical generation, and one that provides certain advantages, is the connection of the system to the larger public utility grid. In effect, connection to the grid makes an on-site generation system a decentralized power source and, thus, changes the utility company's role from merely that of seller of electricity to that of a purchaser as well.

It is, of course, possible to simply generate electricity by combustion of various fuels on-site without harnessing the waste heat for district heating, but doing so would overlook a prime opportunity to increase overall efficiency while supplying low-temperature heat where it is needed. Because such a system seems unlikely in an energy-efficient development, on-site electrical generation by combustion is not considered here as a separate alternative system, but rather is included with cogeneration. As with district heating systems, on-site cogeneration may represent a change not only from conventional generation and distribution of energy, but also from conventional fuel sources. All of the conventional fossil fuels, as well as the renewable biomass fuels, are potential sources for cogeneration systems.

energy-use characteristics: The major advantage of cogeneration, compared to conventional electrical generation, is that the efficiency of generating useful energy by combustion is increased from approximately 30 percent to 70 percent, based on the first law of thermodynamics, which is concerned with the amount of useful and wasted fuel. In cogeneration, the efficiency of generating electricity is diminished slightly in order to produce the heat at a useful temperature. Cogeneration is not quite as efficient as simply burning fuel for district heating alone when only the amount of useful versus wasted fuel is considered (see fig. A-3). The quality of the energy must also be considered, however. Electricity is a higher-quality form of energy that can be used for a number of essential functions for which heat alone will not suffice. Efficiency is also related to the scale of the system. Although transmission losses are reduced with smaller-scale systems, certain economies of scale are lost; hence, the practical generation efficiencies with smaller systems will be lower. With respect to the fuel sources, fossil fuels are nonrenewable and therefore subject to price increases and supply interruptions, whereas the biomass fuels are renewable.

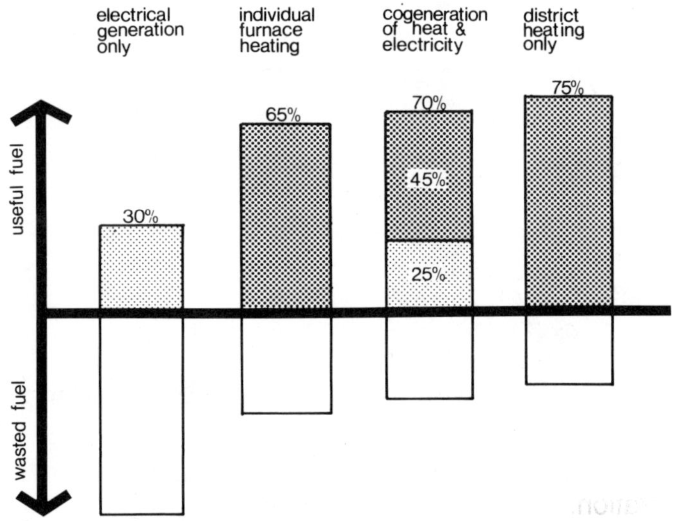

electrical generation only
individual furnace heating
cogeneration of heat & electricity
district heating only
useful fuel
wasted fuel
30%
65%
70%
45%
25%
75%

A-3: efficiency comparison of various systems

technological constraints: Electrical generation and cogeneration by combustion of fuels at any scale is a relatively well-known and safe technology. The reliability of a smaller-scale, community-operated system depends on skilled, professional operation and maintenance. Since large amounts of electricity cannot be economically stored for later use, the power must be generated when the demand occurs. A system must have enough customers so that demands are averaged out and somewhat predictable. By connecting the system to the larger utility grid, backup energy would be provided to help the on-site system run more efficiently, and any excess power could be sold to the company. While this connection could be an asset to the utility if power were supplied at peak times, it would be a drawback if the smaller system required power only at peak times. Utility companies may assess a standby charge to cover the cost of this reserve capacity. Such charges would reduce or offset the value of electricity sold to the utility company. On-site generators and the electrical distribution systems are flexible in layout, as they are with larger systems. The limitations of the district heating portion of the system are more restrictive. As with district heating, one great advantage of an on-site system is the adaptability to future changes in technology and fuel source. Since there is little precedent for small-scale systems, basic efficient and mass-produced sizes of generators are not established. System controls must ensure that the quality of the electricity produced is compatible with the utility's requirements and that controls for isolating portions of the electrical network are coordinated.

economic feasibility: The economic feasibility of on-site systems using conventional or biomass fuels becomes a question of economies related to scale. This question is unresolved, since there is little precedent for these systems; therefore, decisions will have to be made on a case by case basis. In general, smaller systems will have lower distribution and overhead costs, but larger systems will have lower fuel and generation costs.

environmental impact: Burning various fuels to generate electricity at a neighborhood scale can cause major environmental problems. Air pollution from burning coal is the most hazardous type of pollution associated with cogeneration systems. The pollution is concentrated at one plant, however, so it may be controlled more carefully.

institutional and marketing constraints: Location of a small power plant near housing may be a marketing problem unless the design is very carefully handled. On the other hand, a sense of independence and control over a local system may be a marketing asset with some groups. One potential major institutional barrier is related to the willingness of the utility company to connect to and supply backup power for an on-site system if necessary. If the utility company owns and maintains the on-site system, however, marketability might be enhanced, since reliability would be assured.

physical planning and design implications: For on-site cogeneration of heat and electricity, the planning and design implications are the same as for district heating. Densities should be as high as possible and layouts as simple and direct as possible. Electrical distribution is inherently more flexible and imposes no great restrictions on design and layout of a housing development. Since there is so little precedent for on-site generation of electricity, the number of units required per plant for technical efficiency and economic feasibility has not been established. A major complication will be in negotiating the necessary coordination and detailed agreements between the developer and the utility company.

on-site electrical generation by wind power

Another alternative for on-site electrical generation uses the power of the wind to drive turbines. These Wind Energy Conversion Systems (WECS) represent basic changes in the scale and location at which electricity is generated, as well as the source of the energy.

Basically, such a system consists of rotor blades located on top of a tower that are activated by the wind. The blades turn a rotor that, in turn, mechanically generates electricity. Other electrical components that provide alternating current and storage of the energy may be part of the system. WECS can also be used directly to provide mechanical energy for such uses as pumping water. The potential of wind energy deserves attention because it can provide high-quality electrical energy and is suited to small communities or even individual houses. WECS could be owned and maintained by individuals, community groups, the developer, or the utility company.

energy-use characteristics: Wind is a renewable and constantly recurring— although intermittent—source of energy. It provides mechanical motion that is ideally suited for efficient electrical generation, AC or DC. Comparing the actual efficiency of a wind system to electrical generation by burning fossil fuels is irrelevant. Because the source in a wind system is basically unlimited or free, efficiencies are only relevant in terms of comparing the technical or economic benefits of different wind systems with their initial costs. The best way to compare wind with conventional systems is by computing a Fossil Fuel Equivalent (FFE), which is the equivalent of the fossil fuel replaced by the wind systems. In general, the FFE for wind systems will be 3.45 units for each unit of electricity generated. The materials used in the manufacture of WECS—mostly metals and some plastics—have a relatively high energy embodiment.

technical constraints: The technology is well developed in the design of the aerodynamic, mechanical, and electrical parts of small wind energy systems. Some problems related to very large systems are still being researched. The basic unit for residential use has a power output of 1-15kw, which is appropriate for the scale of a single house. At the community scale, larger units are available or several units could be used if the site is appropriate. Power output is greatly affected by wind speed and continuity. Topography, wind direction, height above the ground, and surrounding obstructions all affect the performance of these systems. These characteristics must be analyzed on an individual site basis. Two key determinants of the technical feasibility for a particular site are the average wind speed and, more importantly, the "plant factor," i.e., the percentage of time that the wind is blowing at or greater than the minimum design speed for operation. The critical technical problem with wind energy is that the timing of wind availability does not necessarily correspond to the demand for power. The best solution would be on-site storage, but development of storage systems is slower than development of the WECS themselves. Possible storage systems include pumped hydro, compressed air, flywheels, and chargeable fuel cells. Although chemical batteries can work for an individual house, they are bulky and expensive. Connection to the existing utility grid is another solution for storage, so that the WECS supply excess power to other users and have backup power when the wind is not sufficient. WECS are relatively durable, safe, and simple to maintain; designs must, however, be adequate to provide safety from collapse in high winds.

economic feasibility: WECS produce electricity more expensively than the conventional utility grid. One estimate based on a 1978 study by the Minnesota Energy Agency indicated that costs for wind-generated electricity were twice those of conventional electricity generated with fossil fuels [A.4]. The cost of conventional electricity is likely to increase, however, whereas wind-generated power is likely to decrease in cost with mass production of WECS. The development of storage techniques also will greatly affect the economics of WECS. Community-scale systems may have certain economies of scale when used with shared storage systems. If storage is not used, economic feasibility also depends on the prices at which the utility company is willing to buy and sell power for a wind-generating customer who is connected to the grid.

environmental impact: While wind power is a relatively safe technology that causes no air or thermal pollution, it is associated with some potential environmental problems, such as noise and interference with TV and radio reception. These problems could be reduced by placing wind generators in groups at the windiest locations in the development, rather than scattering them among the housing.

institutional and marketing constraints: The key institutional constraint involves the relationship of individually owned WECS with the power company. Until low-cost storage is developed, the economic viability of WECS will depend on interfacing with a utility company. Prices will probably have to correspond to the time of day power is used, since power during peak demand times is more valuable. There may also be a standby capacity charge by the utility company for providing the backup service. A potential zoning ordinance problem involving the height of wind towers in residential areas may arise, in which case a variance may have to be sought. The appearance of wind towers may be either a negative marketing factor or a positive symbol, depending on the prospective clientele for the development.

physical planning implications: WECS towers must be properly sited to take maximum advantage of the wind. At the scale of a housing development, towers may be concentrated at one area or scattered throughout the site, depending on wind availability. WECS towers may be able to occupy land that is also used for community open space if safety questions are adequately addressed. It appears that when WECS become economically competitive, they will be equally feasible for any scale of development since the components are relatively small and decentralized. Feasibility of WECS will depend on available wind on the particular site. The electrical distribution portion of the system is the same as for other on-site electrical generation systems.

on-site electrical generation by photovoltaic solar systems

Photovoltaics can also represent basic changes in the scale and location of electrical generation, as well as in the source of power. There are actually several known photoelectric and photochemical conversion processes for the direct conversion of solar radiant energy into electricity. Of these processes, the best understood and most technically exploited is photovoltaics. When solar radiation falls on such a photovoltaic device (or solar cell), the photons impart their energy to electrons within the semiconductor from which the cell is made. The semiconductor material most commonly used is silicon. Doping of "p" or "n" material in the surface of the cell permits the electrons to differentially diffuse across the "junction," thereby establishing a voltage or potential across the cell. This potential is maintained as long as the cell remains illuminated. When opposite sides of the cell are connected through an electrical circuit, electric current will flow. Usually groups of these cells are combined in series/parallel array configurations to produce the electrical current desired. As with WECS, the development of photovoltaic systems is very important, since they provide high-quality electrical energy and are suited to small community or individual house applications. Photovoltaic systems could be owned by individuals, community groups, the developer, or the utility company.

energy-use characteristics: Sunlight is a renewable source of energy, although it is not constantly available. In photovoltaic cells sunlight is converted at efficiencies that range from less than 1 to over 20 percent, depending on the material from which the cell is made and the physical characteristics of its manufacture. Most currently available silicon solar cells have efficiencies on the order of 10 to 11 percent. Although additional heat can be recovered from photovoltaic systems if they are combined with thermal active solar systems, the system cannot be optimized for both applications at once. Direct comparison of these efficiencies to a fossil fuel generation system is not appropriate in terms of fuel efficiency, since sunlight is free and renewable, whereas fossil fuels are costly and limited. A Fossil Fuel Equivalent (representing the fossil fuel saved) of 3.45 units for each unit of electricity generated is, however, appropriate for comparison purposes. Photovoltaic cells are mainly made from silicon, which is plentiful; however, most current manufacturing processes for the cells are energy intensive. New techniques of crystal growth and the use of amorphous or polycrystalline silicon offer the very real possibility of substantially less energy-intensive cell manufacture.

technological constraints: Solar cells for the space program have been relatively far advanced for years. Even though the much cheaper cells for large-scale use on earth are at an earlier stage of development, these systems do perform adequately and should be safe and reliable, since they have no moving parts. Because direct current is produced, AC/DC conversion equipment is usually required. The size of the basic unit of power generation is a single cell; an array of cells would be required for a single house. The system is flexible and adaptable to any scale. A major technical problem arises simply because sunlight is not available all the time and therefore the quantity of electricity generated does not necessarily correspond to the demand. Thus, the same two solutions required for wind energy are appropriate for photovoltaics: the use of on-site storage systems (a concept that is not yet adequately developed), or the connection of the system to the existing utility company grid.

economic constraints: At present, the cost of photovoltaic systems—typically, $5 to $10 per peak watt—is considered far too high to be competitive with conventional electricity. In this type of industry, however, technical breakthroughs can occur rapidly and lower costs drastically. Mass production will also have a positive economic effect. Currently, the photovoltaic alternative is far more uncertain with respect to future feasibility than are other alternatives. As with wind, development of storage techniques will affect the economics of photovoltaic systems, particularly at the community scale. Again, like wind systems, it appears that when photovoltaic systems become economically feasible, they will be equally useful for any scale of development because the components are so small and decentralized. Feasibility will also depend on the amount of sunlight available on the site.

environmental impact: Generation of electricity by photovoltaic solar cells has no notable negative environmental impacts. Some of the materials used in the manufacture of solar cells are quite toxic, however.

institutional and marketing constraints: Although the appearance of photovoltaic cells on rooftops may have a negative impact on marketing for some people, this potentially negative appearance may be a positive symbol to others. Good design and integration of the array into the building form are important. As with all on-site generation systems, the ability to connect to the utility company grid represents a potential institutional constraint.

physical planning implications: Provision of solar access for present or future locations of photovoltaic cells is essential. If the system is to be installed on an individual unit basis, then access to each unit must be provided and preserved. With a community system, all of the cells could be concentrated on community land and/or on top of community buildings. The electrical distribution portion of the system is the same as for other on-site electrical generation systems and does not affect design dramatically.

heating with active solar systems

Active solar heating systems convert the sun's radiant energy directly, by the thermal absorption process, into heat that can be used for hot water and space heating. The most common systems for residential use employ flat plate collectors using liquid or air transfer mediums. Active systems are suitable for use on an individual unit-, community-, or district-scale system. When used on an individual housing unit, active solar systems are similar to conventional heating in that the system is owned and operated by an individual. The fundamental difference is that, with an active solar system, the source of heat is renewable and the system depends only on a small amount of electrical energy for control and pumping purposes. Community collector systems, of course, represent changes in the distribution of heat supply as well as a change in the source of energy. The basic characteristics of a community-owned system are discussed in the previous section on district heating. Solar energy for space and hot water heating in houses is an important alternative because it is available on nearly all sites and it supplies the type of low-temperature heat that is very appropriate to these end uses.

energy-use characteristics: The overall efficiency of a collector system depends on climate and the intrinsic efficiency of the collector. In Minnesota collectors can provide an estimated half of the heat for a typical house. This figure would be much higher for warmer climates. The system's performance is also affected by the design of the house and the conservation measures taken by the residents. Since sunlight is intermittent and does not normally correspond to times when heat is most needed, heat storage is important to energy efficiency with this system. In a study done for a medium-density Baltimore neighborhood, it was estimated that solar collectors could provide 40 percent of the heating requirement. If shared storage was used for the neighborhood, however, the solar contribution increased to 70 percent [A.5]. Solar energy is a completely renewable source that is available on nearly all sites and, to a greater or lesser degree, in all climates. Many solar collectors require materials associated with rather high energy embodiment, including metals, plastics, and glass.

technical constraints: Flat plate solar collectors are considered by most sources to be sufficiently developed for application now. Naturally, some problems with reliability exist for any infant industry. The lifetime of the systems is estimated to be twenty to twenty-five years. Collector panels or arrays are quite flexible, in that they can be mounted on rooftops or in open land areas. They must, however, have clear solar access, and the system must include a means of storage. One to three days' storage is typical for individual systems, but long-term storage of several months is currently being studied. Storage systems may use liquid, rocks, or phase change materials. Although centralized storage is more efficient, it is dependent on the overall layout and density of development. Since solar collectors can provide heated water, they can be easily adapted to district heating systems, either to replace or to supplement more conventional sources. Maintenance and adequate control of the functioning of solar systems are important for solar collectors to perform effectively for their anticipated lifespan.

economic feasibility: High-technology solar systems range from $20 to $40 per square foot of collector area, plus additional fixed costs of $2,000 to $3,000 for ductwork and storage. Some lower-technology, site-built systems can be constructed for less than $10 per square foot. A 1978 study by the Minnesota Energy Agency estimated that a system to supply 50 percent of the space and hot water heat for a house in Minnesota would cost between $7,000 and $16,000. The same study indicated that the $20-per-square-foot collector system would have a payback period of twenty-one years to replace electricity and over twenty-five years to replace gas or oil [A.4]. Under current conditions these systems are not economically competitive in Minnesota. It is interesting to note that the payback is reduced to nine years if the system is installed by the home owner. Accurately computing life cycle costs of solar systems is very difficult, however, because economic success depends on a number of variable and uncertain considerations, including:

- initial system cost including storage
- amount of sunshine available on site
- amount of collected heat actually used
- local prices of conventional energy sources
- total cost of providing backup energy
- interest rates, taxes, and subsidies
- performance, reliability, and maintenance costs of the particular system

According to the 1980 "Energy in Transition" study by the National Research Council, solar systems are generally "not economic now and major changes in price of alternatives or government subsidies are necessary for solar to play a role" [A.6]. It should be noted that the economic feasibility of solar systems is quite likely to become more favorable as fuel prices rise. Because solar systems are made up of small, decentralized components, there are no apparent economies of scale except mass-production cost savings for individual systems. Community storage systems would, however, offer some economies of scale.

environmental impact: Solar systems are one of the safest, most pollution-free energy alternatives.

institutional and marketing constraints: Major institutional constraints may be posed by building codes and zoning ordinances. Many codes are currently being adapted to allow for solar systems, however, and zoning ordinances are being altered to preserve solar access rights. Solar access protection is essential to protect the investment in active systems. Marketing may be affected negatively by the appearance and initial cost of collectors, although the effect of the unusual appearance is subjective and may, in some cases, be a positive feature. Likewise, as fuel prices rise costs may become competitive (especially if some incentives are provided). The local or individual control possible and the freedom from the major burden of rising fuel costs may be very positive for marketing, in addition to having beneficial social and political impacts.

physical planning implications: Provision of solar access for present or future location of solar collectors is essential. If the collectors are to be located on rooftops of individual units, then access must be provided for each unit. This need for access affects street layout, lot configuration, density, location of trees, and variations in building heights (see chapter 5 for a detailed discussion of site considerations for solar access). With a community system, all of the collectors can be located on community land or on top of community buildings. This type of layout implies preservation of solar access for these community systems, especially for housing on north slopes or in wooded areas where individual access is not provided.

heating with passive solar systems

Passive solar heating systems are similar to active solar systems in many general ways. In comparison to conventional heating systems, they both represent a fundamental change to a completely renewable heat source. Rather than representing a separate mechanical system, however, passive systems convert the sun's radiant energy into space heat by using parts of the structure of the building or area to be heated as the collector (see chapter 4 for a more complete description of passive solar houses). Because these parts are integrated with the individual structure, passive systems are always individually owned and operated and thus cannot generally be regarded as part of a community system. The importance of passive solar systems as an alternative lies in their availability on nearly all sites and their capacity to supply the type of low-temperature heat that is suitable for home space heating.

energy-use characteristics: Since passive solar systems include a wide variety of techniques, it is difficult to generalize about their performance. For the collection and retention of radiant solar energy to work efficiently in a structure, it is necessary to design for proper orientation, proper window sizing and placement, the use of drapes or shutters, and proper placement of massive materials, such as concrete or brick, for storage. In most climates a number of conservation techniques to reduce the heating load are necessary so that passive systems can then supply a substantial portion of the remaining needed heat.

technical constraints: Unlike active collectors, which are primarily a manufactured product, passive systems result from the design and construction process and vary in almost every situation. Although at present a great deal of experimentation is taking place, the technical barriers are not difficult to overcome. Rather, such experimentation is more a matter of learning to understand the systems better and develop methods to design them with more precision. The simplest systems are called direct gain systems, in which the living space is the collector and there is little change in appearance or construction from a conventional house. Other basic systems include thermal storage walls and roofs, convective loop systems, and sunspaces or greenhouses. All of these systems have been built and operated successfully, although they are not all equally appropriate in all climates.

economic feasibility: It is quite difficult to quantify costs for passive systems because the passive components of the building are difficult to isolate and account for accurately. In addition, the numerous approaches to design are intermingled with conservation techniques. At least in some cases—particularly when the system consists of building components that would be present in normal circumstances—passive solar systems are economically competitive. The great economic advantages of passive systems lie in the long lifetime of the system and the lower nonrecurring fuel costs.

environmental impact: Both passive and active solar systems are among the safest, most pollution-free energy alternatives.

institutional and marketing constraints: The revision of zoning ordinances to ensure solar access is essential for passive systems as well as active. More restrictive ordinances are required for passive systems, since they cannot be placed on rooftops or detached from the house in the same fashion as active collectors.

physical planning implications: As with active solar systems, the provision for present or future solar access is essential. Unlike active systems, however, passive systems require that access always be provided to each unit—and not only to the rooftop, but also to the south wall and yard area. Selection of sites, street layout, lot configuration, density, location of trees, and variations in building heights must all be coordinated to provide clear access (see chapter 5 for a discussion of site design for solar houses).

district heating with solar pond systems

The use of a solar pond to supply a district heating system has potential application to a community housing development. The basic concept is that a large pond with a chemical solution—usually salt—in the water can act as a large solar storage tank. As the water at the surface is heated by the sun, it becomes denser in the salt solution and sinks to the bottom. Thus, the hottest water, at the bottom of the pond, is insulated by the cooler water above. This source of hot water could supplement, or perhaps completely supply, heat for a housing development.

Solar ponds are at an early stage of development; thus, the technical and economic feasibility are unknown at this time. In addition, because most of the early research has been done in warmer climates, the applicability to colder regions at higher latitudes is unknown. There may be some negative environmental aspects to containing a large quantity of highly salinated water on site. Nevertheless, the concept is intriguing and, once additional development and testing takes place, the feasibility of an application to a housing development should be considered. The physical planning implications are quite significant, in that a substantial body of water would have to be integrated into the site and the district heating system.

modifications to conventional systems

In comparing conventional energy supply systems to various on-site alternatives, it is important to recognize that a number of modifications are possible within the existing large systems. Such modifications can affect the basic energy efficiency and economic characteristics of the systems. These include:

- More efficient multiple-stage electrical generating processes using topping cycles (such as gas turbines), which may increase total efficiency from 30 to 40 percent, and magneto-hydro-dynamic and thermionic systems, which have the potential to increase total efficiency to over 50 percent.
- Electrical generation in large plants using biomass fuels, including plant materials, crop residues, garbage, and liquid and gaseous fuels created from wastes. Although it should not be thought of as renewable fuel, peat is sometimes considered in this category.
- Large-scale applications of solar- and wind-driven turbines to generate electricity, as in the "power tower" concept. Photovoltaic solar cell arrays could also supply electricity in a large-scale, centralized system. These applications are most promising in regions with extensive sunshine, such as the southwestern United States.
- Use of wind-driven turbines on a large scale by utility companies. "Wind farms"—that is, groups of much larger generation devices than are normally used for individual houses—could be used at appropriate locations.

- Geothermal, wavepower, and ocean thermal sources of energy to generate electricity.
- Various forms of synthetic and biomass-based fuels, burned in individual furnaces in place of natural gas or oil.

The prospects of increased efficiency and the use of renewable fuel sources may significantly affect future prices and long-term reliability of conventional systems. In addition, the potential environmental effects of air and thermal pollution would be reduced through the use of some of these alternatives. The basic electrical distribution system, its centralized nature and size, and the lack of participation at a neighborhood level would remain the same as with the conventional system, however. The physical planning implications of these modifications for an individual housing development are basically no different than for conventionally generated electricity supplied through a large-scale power grid or for conventional supply of fossil fuels to individual houses for heating.

appendix b: marketability

introduction

The market has been defined as the mechanism that integrates demand—consumers who need a product—with the supply of that product. While the most important function of marketing undeniably is to move—or sell—the product, a market analyst must also assess demand characteristics and convey that information to the developer's organization. For a developer to turn a profit, the product must reflect consumer demand, and production must be synchronized with sales.

Because earth sheltering is a relatively new and often misunderstood concept, good market analysis will be necessary to clarify the image of earth sheltered housing for consumers, identify potential buyers, and provide real estate information that allows comparison of earth sheltered to conventional houses. Such an analysis can help reduce the risks for developers of earth sheltered housing and, in the long run, increase the potential for construction of more earth sheltered homes.

This appendix focuses on the three primary components of the marketing process—the developer's role, the consumer, and the product—as they relate to earth sheltered community designs. These sections are preceded by a brief discussion of general trends in consumer housing and specific characteristics of earth sheltered housing that affect its marketability.

general trends in the housing market

Over the past few years, home buyers have demonstrated an increasing concern with energy conservation. Despite this fact, most homes constructed today reflect the attitudes of the past; consequently, their design is based on the assumption of cheap, abundant fuel supplies. The question for market analysis is whether or not the buying public will assign a value to energy-saving features in homes that is equal to the cost of providing those features.

Within the past several years, potential home buyers have begun to include considerations of energy savings in their decision-making process. Even people with lower incomes have been willing to pay developers more initially to provide additional insulation. In 1978 many home buyers considered paying extra for solar hot water heating and even for solar space heating [B.1]. Figures from 1979 show that consumers were more skeptical about investing in these solar features, perhaps reflecting uncertainty about the efficiency or cost-effectiveness of solar technology, or perhaps because of a lack of accurate information about the availability of these energy-saving options [B.2].

Despite consumers' rather high degree of awareness of energy issues, the uncertainty about the state of the art in energy conservation technologies, together with a lack of available information about them, hinders consumers' ability to make a well-informed decision about the best energy-saving features for their homes. The need for consumers to have access to accurate, up-to-date information is critical, and the dispersion of this information relates directly to the marketability of energy-efficient homes in the future.

Although this interest in energy conservation would appear propitious for growth in the earth sheltered housing industry, it may be offset to an extent by the increasing costs of all types of housing. In some parts of the United States in 1979, up to one-third of a family's income was spent on mortgage payments. Given an investment that requires such a heavy outlay of capital, people are generally cautious about accepting changes in design unless they are assured that such changes will continue to add value to their original investment. This situation, coupled with the fact that, in general, the housing market is quite resistant to change (e.g., the ranch-style house so popular and common today was not fully accepted for approximately twenty years) points up the need for detailed marketing information [B.3].

earth sheltering as an alternative housing solution

Although the merits of building earth sheltered housing units deserve consideration in appropriate situations, successful marketing approaches for this new type of housing have yet to be developed. In preparing marketing strategies for earth sheltered homes, developers will have to take into account the advantageous characteristics of earth sheltered buildings as well as the type of home buyer who has already been sufficiently attracted to the concept to purchase or arrange for the construction of such a home.

To many people earth sheltered housing represents a questionable approach to the solution of energy problems, primarily because of typically negative associations of this type of architecture with dampness, darkness, gloominess, etc. In order to be marketable, then, earth sheltered homes will have to be designed so as to convince house buyers that these qualities need not be present in well-designed earth sheltered dwellings.

Perceptions of earth sheltered houses as odd, extremely unconventional structures have, unfortunately, been exacerbated by the fact that a significant proportion of earth sheltered houses built to date have, indeed, been quite unusual in appearance and design. This situation occurred primarily because many earth sheltered houses have been built by the owner and have thus reflected the owner's idiosyncratic tastes. In addition, these houses generally have been designed neither for resale nor to fit in with the architectural style of the community. The unusual appearance of these homes not only tends to reinforce people's perception of earth sheltering as a faddish type of architecture, but also creates difficulties in using earth sheltered housing as comparable properties for real estate appraisal, since few properties have been resold.

Another "image" problem for earth sheltered homes concerns their lack of visibility. Because nearly all earth sheltered structures are individual houses, often built on rather isolated, rural or suburban sites, they are not normally seen by the general public. If, in the future, earth sheltered houses are built as part of a total community development, some of these image problems and negative perceptions could be alleviated. Furthermore, multiple units would also allow reduced construction costs, in comparison with those of single-family dwellings. The risk to the innovative developer of multiple-unit housing is, however, of course greater than for the developer of a single dwelling.

In addition to the image and design problems associated with earth sheltered housing, data on construction costs and energy performance are rather limited. Particularly in the case of owner-built homes, construction cost information is sketchy and often does not reflect true market costs. Similarly, the generally favorable but subjective data on energy performance make cost-benefit analyses somewhat speculative.

the developer's role in marketing earth sheltered housing

For the purposes of this study, the developer is defined as the person or persons responsible for the whole range of activities associated with land development, including initiating, investing in, and administering all phases of the project. In large developments involving many housing units, the developer's role is essential not only for the sake of cost and management efficiencies, but also, and most importantly, for the purpose of amassing large enough sums of money to construct the entire development as a single project.

risk and return on investment

Because multiple-unit housing development ties up huge sums of money, a developer's willingness to undertake a project depends on his or her perception of the risk involved and ability to secure an adequate return on the investment. Any number of issues affect the developer's perception of the amount of risk in undertaking earth sheltered housing at the community scale. One important consideration is that, in general, housing of any type is a less profitable investment than commercial or institutional ventures. For any new and/or unusual type of housing, the risk is considerably greater than it is for conventional housing.

Another important factor in determining the degree of risk is whether the developer simply prepares the land so that lots can be sold, or whether he or she completely develops the site and builds the units. In the case of earth sheltered housing, it is assumed that the developer is responsible for the total site development, including construction and sale of the housing units. This type of development role represents a larger investment and a less secure type of undertaking than does a more limited involvement. Because the return on investment often is not realized until the last houses are sold, effective sales techniques and sales personnel are critical to the success of a housing development project.

When investors assume responsibility for financing, they must, in a sense, finance the period during which they prepare to meet the planning and negotiating phases of the development process. During the planning process, substantial sums are tied up in the investment, at interest rates that can be considerably higher than normal rates. With new types of housing, more obstacles and delays are likely simply because housing regulations are not always clearly defined with regard to alternative methods of construction; hence, exceptions to standard regulations often must be sought (e.g., with regard to zoning ordinances). Such delays can be quite costly to the developer. Moreover, construction of new housing types is also subject to uncertainty in scheduling, primarily because of a lack of construction experience and the time required to experiment with various techniques and management approaches.

Developers of new housing types are likely to be new to the development business. Not surprisingly, people who have already perfected management of conventional housing developments—so that their return on investment is optimized—are not as likely to be interested in experimenting with innovative housing alternatives. It is sometimes assumed that, because the technologies required for earth sheltered housing construction are, in general, adequately developed and because many of the difficulties and cost inefficiencies associated with single-dwelling construction would be overcome in a larger development, the risk for developers of larger-scale earth sheltered developments would be reduced. New developers are less likely to be familiar with the total planning and construction process, however, and are therefore more likely to proceed inefficiently. This lack of development experience, which also increases the difficulty of assembling a group of investors, contributes to the problems involved in a multiple-unit earth sheltered housing development.

A fundamental concern of the developer in assessing the risk of a housing project is the probability of receiving an adequate return on his or her investment. At times the developer's goals of providing the highest quality living environment while simultaneously receiving the highest possible return on investment may conflict. Ideally, however, the two goals can be successfully pursued in tandem, thus yielding a better quality product which, in turn, will assure that every house is sold.

The packaging of sufficient money at the appropriate times during the development process is one of the developer's major challenges. The term *packaging* refers to the task of forming an appropriate partnership of investors, obtaining money at critical times, and scheduling returns for the money invested. Because earth sheltering involves new construction techniques and information concerning marketability is still quite limited, money for high-risk earth sheltered developments will probably have to come from private investors rather than from lending institutions. Assembling the package with money from private investors is generally more time-consuming and difficult than arranging for financing from lending insitutions.

Federally assisted programs provide an alternative route for financing earth sheltered housing developments. Although the administrative requirements are quite demanding, these federally subsidized projects involve less risk to the developer and less concern with minimizing costs than do private market-funded developments. The protracted administrative procedures associated with federal programs (particularly for unusual projects) tend to discourage many developers from seeking out federal funds for housing projects. According to several developers, however, government involvement is essential to the realization of innovative housing projects.

the consumer

The basic issue with respect to consumer behavior involves determining who the potential buyers of earth sheltered housing are. This information, combined with an understanding of the product, provides a comprehensive view of the marketability of this type of housing. Consumer information is especially important when an entire development, rather than just one house, is being considered, since the breadth of the market must be understood. Since earth sheltered housing has to compete with all other types of housing, knowledge of the kinds of people interested in and capable of buying these types of homes has some important implications.

In general, people building individual earth sheltered houses know the benefits of a secure investment in a house with low maintenance and operating costs and are concerned with curbing inflation. Some of them are planning for retirement. In several regions of the country, a major motivation for building earth sheltered houses is to provide a durable structure that can resist tornadoes and other forms of inclement weather. If these beneficial traits were more clearly described to the public through more extensive marketing efforts, a new and different market demand segment could be created.

In marketing, a profile of demand characteristics is most often compiled by grouping together people who seem to have the same needs and wants for a particular product. These groupings are then identified as a segment. Groups are generally defined in terms of common characteristics that are classified according to such categories as demographics, socioeconomics, personality traits, and life-styles. These categories may be broken down further, as shown in figure B-1.

B-1: typical consumer characteristics for market analysis

type of characteristics	illustrative concept
demographic	age sex geographic location geographic mobility family life cycle race ethnic background
socioeconomic	occupation education income social class (services needed)
personality traits	extroversion venturesomeness self-confidence self-esteem
life-style	activities interests opinions needs values

The following summary of characteristics related to potential buyers of earth sheltered homes is based on several studies of consumer attitudes, some of which deal with all housing, and others which concern earth sheltered housing in particular [B.1, B.2, B.4, B.5].

age: The large 25-35 age group is not only the major buying market for all housing types, but also shows the most interest in earth sheltered housing.

family cycle: The most commonly available earth sheltered house designs, which are small and efficient, are adequate for "empty nesters" (i.e., those couples whose children have left home) and childless couples in the housing market. Because of the difficulty of expanding an earth sheltered house, its appeal to expanding families may be limited unless special design consideration is given to this problem. Given the projected increase over the next decade in the number of couples with children (a result of the post-World War II "baby boom" children starting families of their own), this will be an important segment of the market to consider. Problems of territoriality and the need for flexibility when more than two people are living together will be a challenge in future designs for earth sheltered housing. Closer attention to the programming of spaces will be necessary, including a need to incorporate flexibility of different uses and sizes of spaces within the structure. At present, the biggest attractions of earth sheltered housing are the potential energy savings and low maintenance. These benefits particularly appeal to young couples and older, childless couples.

income: The mean income level of people interested in earth sheltered housing is equal to or slightly lower than that of people interested in the housing market in general. Although current costs of most single earth sheltered dwellings are higher than those for conventional housing, a number of factors may contribute to reducing costs, thus making them affordable by lower-income groups. The development of a large number of houses—particularly attached units—could significantly reduce costs. If lower fuel bills and lower maintenance are included in the assessment of total cost to the home owner, earth sheltered units will look much more competitive in the housing market.

social class and education: Very little information on social class and education of those in the housing market is available, but it appears that, in general, those people interested in earth sheltering are better educated than is the norm for all people in the housing market. Typically, innovators do tend to have higher incomes and be better educated than the general public. Once the product has become less speculative "adapters" (as opposed to the innovators) begin to invest. Thus, earth sheltered housing will need to attract the adapters in order to prove that earth sheltering is a viable, feasible approach to housing and, thus, to encourage developers' willingness to invest in earth sheltered housing developments.

activities and interests: As rising energy costs continue to affect the costs of transportation, the need to provide access to public transit, recreation, and service facilities becomes increasingly important. Earth sheltered housing developments may be an asset in this regard, since they can be built to provide more people with such access without appearing to be as dense as conventional multiple-unit developments. In marketing any new type of design, it should be remembered that people will not want to give up the quality of life they have attained, but rather will seek to better it. Unfortunately, many of the uncertainties and misconceptions associated with earth sheltered housing cause many people to perceive such housing as a step backward. Hence, it is important that design solutions reflect an image of a better life-style.

the product

The third essential component in market analysis is an evaluation of the product—in this case the earth sheltered house. Comparing earth sheltered with conventional homes that are available on today's market can help determine the design features that should be incorporated into earth sheltered designs in order to make them more acceptable to consumers.

This discussion will examine earth sheltered housing in terms of the five most significant factors in selecting a house, as identified in a study prepared for *Housing* magazine [B.6]. In order of importance, these factors—which must be considered in developing any marketing strategy for earth sheltered housing—are:

- layout of rooms
- room sizes
- planning concept
- exterior design
- lot size

In addition, special issues related to earth sheltered housing and community development will be discussed.

layout of rooms

In the *Housing* study, floor plan layout was ranked the most important factor in selecting a house by 70 percent of the people surveyed. Examples of typical floor plans for conventional, solar, and earth sheltered houses are shown in chapter 4. Although a variety of design approaches may be applied to earth sheltered homes, the single exposed elevation is the simplest and most common house design. In this design most of the habitable spaces are placed along the exposed wall in order to meet code requirements for light, ventilation, and fire. The earth sheltered floor plan is not extremely different overall in layout from that of the conventional house.

A design variation that allows more flexibility in the layout of earth sheltered houses is the use of skylights, which can provide both light and ventilation to spaces away from the window wall. The atrium plan provides a dramatically different arrangement of floor space by placing the rooms around an exterior courtyard rather than along a single exposed elevation. Although many people in a survey by Stewart and McKown were interested in the atrium plan, 63 percent preferred the elevational plan over both the atrium and the completely underground plans [B.4].

The *Housing* study reported three other findings that pose some problems related to room layout design in earth sheltered houses:

- a desire for an entryway, front porch, or back porch. Few earth sheltered houses built to date have the traditional entryway or front porches typical of many conventional houses. A conscious effort could be made to provide these features in earth sheltered house designs, however.
- a preference for placement of the garage immediately adjacent to the kitchen. This presents a design challenge to earth sheltered housing since the cost of an underground garage is higher than that of a conventional garage. On the other hand, an above-grade garage may look awkward next to an earth sheltered house.
- a preference for bedrooms located upstairs, because downstairs bedrooms lack a feeling of safety. For two-level earth sheltered structures, placement of the bedrooms may cause a problem.

With regard to number of levels, 43 percent of the people surveyed by *Housing* said that they preferred single-story houses (67 percent of the elderly people preferred this style); 30 percent, two-story homes; and 26 percent, split-level houses.

room sizes

Fifty-eight percent of the people responding to the *Housing* magazine survey ranked room size as a significant factor in choosing a home. According to this survey, the most important room size considerations, in order of importance, are: master bedroom, storage space, kitchen, family room, and master bath. Most people said they would sacrifice space in the den, hallways, and guest bedrooms and, in some regions of the country, the breakfast area. Although the need to align rooms for light access along a corridor tends to create narrower rooms, one consumer analysis of earth sheltered homes found that people living in such homes considered the spatial arrangements to be more than adequate and, in fact, with the exception of the amount of storage space, better than in their previous homes.

Related to room size is the space in the house as a whole. As is true for room sizes, the sizes of earth sheltered houses vary considerably. Cold-climate earth sheltered houses differ significantly from conventional houses in that they do not have unfinished basement spaces. These houses are more like warm-climate house designs, which include utilities and storage space on the main floor. Studies have found that the desired size range for conventional houses is 1,250 to 3,000 square feet (112.5 to 270 ca), with a median size of 1,987 square feet (179 ca); the most preferred size is 2,000 to 2,500 square feet (180 to 225 ca). The small existing stock of earth sheltered houses is mostly in the range of 1,800 to 2,700 square feet (162 to 243 ca).

planning concept

The planning concept was a feature ranked as significant in house selection by 35 percent of the people surveyed by *Housing* magazine. With regard to this concept, the "theme sales" approach has become a powerful sales tool during inflationary periods when many developers are competing for the few eligible home buyers.

The theme concept has been important in attracting buyers for both earlier and more recently built earth sheltered structures. For example, in Oklahoma protection from tornadoes was a major component of the selling approach. More recently, the potential for energy conservation represented by earth sheltered houses has become a primary selling point. This association of earth sheltering with energy savings is so strong that, according to one study, the primary consideration in buying an earth sheltered house was its potential for conserving energy [B.5]. Another analysis has reported that "results show that energy savings were the primary motive in the last five years for the building of earth sheltered houses, rather than storm protection, which has formerly been the reason" [B.7].

Other concepts cited as very significant in terms of consumer interest in earth sheltered designs are freedom from exterior maintenance problems, security from vandalism, reduced insurance costs, and improved privacy. Less significant factors affecting consumer choice are experimentation, noise reduction, improved life-style, and land preservation [B.7].

The presentation of a well-defined theme, which is essential in marketing, should help the consumer to evaluate the potential of the particular type of housing for improving his or her future life-style. Associated with the need for a strongly defined theme is the need to clarify for the consumer the real benefits—and drawbacks—of the style of house being marketed.

exterior design

Ranked as important by 30 percent of the *Housing* magazine group surveyed, design of the house exterior is very difficult to analyze because it is mainly a subjective judgment. Yet it is partly on the basis of the appeal of the house exterior that a banker will decide to finance a development: that is, the house must have a certain "curb appeal" in order to be resalable. Two interrelated elements comprise the exterior design of the house: the architecture of the building and the landscaping (which includes both man-made and natural elements).

Because the exterior design of the building is also related to the internal organization of its spaces, most earth sheltered houses built so far have a single exposed elevation. This type of design has been predominant because it is the simplest layout to construct and it provides direct view and access to the outside, as does a conventional house. A long, uninterrupted facade must be carefully designed, however, to have an appealing and personal, rather than stark and commercial, character. The use of concrete in most earth sheltered houses contributes to their often severe, sterile appearance.

Although many people perceive the design of earth sheltered houses as an opportunity to integrate the building with the surrounding landscape, in practice very few such efforts have proven successful. As a result, many earth sheltered structures provide an even harsher contrast with the surrounding environment than a conventional building would.

Yet another problem in exterior design that results from a house having just one exposed elevation is the lack of separation between the public and private outdoor spaces: that is, earth sheltered houses do not have the sense of entry or privacy achieved in conventional houses with a front and back yard.

These problems are far from insurmountable and have, in fact, been resolved successfully in some earth sheltered structures. The difficulty in measuring the impact of the unconventional exterior appearance of most earth sheltered homes stems from the subjective nature of judgments about exterior design and the lack of information about how such judgments specifically relate to earth sheltered housing.

lot size

In the *Housing* survey, lot size was mentioned as a significant consideration in house selection by 30 percent of the people surveyed. While lot sizes for earth sheltered houses, as for conventional homes, can vary considerably, some physical characteristics of earth sheltered houses can affect the usefulness of the lot as a whole. For example, houses with earth banked against the outside walls may require that a significant percentage of the lot area be devoted to the steeply sloping berms—thereby reducing the amount of land usable as outdoor space. On the other hand, the flat, earth-covered roofs typical of earth sheltered structures may offer additional outdoor space not possible with conventional housing. A detailed examination of lot sizes and layouts for earth sheltered housing is provided in chapter 5.

appendix c: soils criteria

This appendix explains how soils criteria are used in site planning. A fair degree of accuracy in preliminary site planning for housing can be achieved by using soil survey interpretation sheets, which are available in all regions of the country from the Soil Conservation Service. These interpretation sheets provide detailed and quantitative soils information together with assessments of other important parameters. It must be stressed that this information only applies to soils up to a depth of 5 to 6 feet (1.5 to 1.8 m) below ground and hence must be used with caution in assessing foundation conditions for buildings. Many building foundations are located more than 5 feet (1.5 m) below ground, particularly in cold regions and for structures with basements. Nonetheless, the information in the interpretation sheets can be a good planning tool, provided that it is supplemented by deeper borings as the planning progresses.

For the prototypical site, seven soil survey interpretation sheets were obtained from the Dakota County Soil Conservation Service. A map of the site identifying areas where each soil type predominates is shown in figure C-1. Figure C-2 indicates the criteria for conventional housing with respect to each of the seven soil types. Figure C-3 shows an expanded set of criteria that were used to determine suitability of the site for earth sheltered housing. In each case a final column has been added that assesses the overall suitability of the soil for conventional or earth sheltered housing. This assessment was made by summing positive and negative ratings for each soil characteristic and weighting these results according to the importance of each criterion. A negative rating does not necessarily mean that the soil cannot be built upon, but rather that housing built on it necessitates careful design and, usually, more expensive construction. Each criterion is briefly discussed on the following pages for conventional and earth sheltered housing. Finally, a chart indicating the basic classification and properties of all soil types is shown in figure C-4.

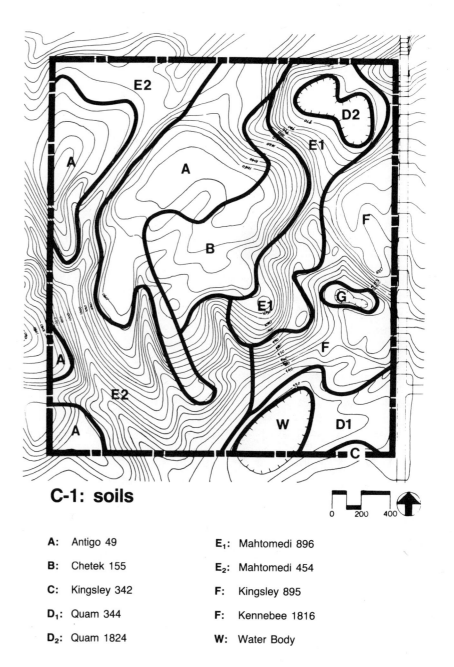

E2
D2
E1
A
A
F
B
G
E1
F
A
E2
A
W
D1
C

C-1: soils

0
200
400

A: Antigo 49

B: Chetek 155

C: Kingsley 342

D_1: Quam 344

D_2: Quam 1824

E_1: Mahtomedi 896

E_2: Mahtomedi 454

F: Kingsley 895

F: Kennebee 1816

W: Water Body

conventional housing

The criteria listed in figure C-2 are restricted to those factors usually examined in planning conventional housing developments. In this table soil properties are combined for all the strata listed within the first 5 feet (1.5 m).

agricultural soil suitability classification: Crop potential is one of the first factors evaluated in planning a conventional site. Areas very suitable for agriculture or recreation are given a strong priority for retention as open space. The number listed in this column indicates the suitability of the soil for various crops or vegetation. Ratings for this classification range from 1 (high potential for most crops) to 8 (very marginal potential). In addition, letters are sometimes used to denote such factors as wet conditions most of the year (W), spring saturation (S), and danger of wind erosion (E).

general drainage description: Well-drained soils are generally preferable to poorly drained soils. The suitability of soil types is indicated in figure C-4, which lists the soils according to their unified soil classification. This classification provides general engineering parameters to be expected for the particular soil type and indicates the general suitability of the soil for building construction.

water table depth: A water table within 5 or 6 feet (1.5 or 1.8 m) of the ground surface is rated negatively. In order to compensate for normal groundwater-table fluctuations, a water table this shallow will generally require extra drainage or structural provisions to be incorporated into the design.

bedrock depth: Bedrock within the planned depth of building foundations is undesirable. Since bedrock was not encountered in any of these shallow borings, no comparative ratings could be made.

erosion potential and frost action potential: These factors are considered together in order to determine the erodibility and stability of the soil types on various degrees of slope. Severe erodibility or frost action potential is a negative factor for slopes at or greater than the percent listed. These two factors applied to the soil map, together with the percent slope data, are responsible for the large areas of the prototypical site deemed unsuitable for conventional development.

ease of basement construction: This factor, which also relates to the steepness of the slope, indicates the relative ease of excavation for a basement, including ease of maintaining the steep sides required for such excavation.

on-site sewage disposal potential: Potential for on-site disposal is poor on the entire site. In the original analysis of the prototypical site, the need for a closed collection system was a factor in the decision to use the land as a park, since adding a development on this site to the existing sewerage network would have been expensive.

pH reaction: The pH level of the soil is used in conjunction with the soil type to select plant materials for the site.

corrosivity: The corrosivity of the soil is important in the design of buried structures and services, although it usually is not as significant as most of the other factors.

general suitability of soils on the prototypical site: This assessment is based on the other data in figure C-2. Only two soil types are considered generally good for conventional development—the Antigo 49 and the Kingsley 895 series. The other soil types, evaluated in conjunction with the slope information, are considered unsuitable for conventional development because they are either too steep or too wet.

C-2: conventional housing criteria

soil type	general drainage description	water table depth	bedrock depth	erosion potential	frost action potential	ease of basement const.	on-site sewage disposal potential	pH reaction	agric. soil class	corrosivity		general suitability on prototypical site
										steel	concrete	
Antigo 49	well drained silty loam	>6′	>60″	erodes easily	moderate	severe on 15+%	poor; perm. 0.6-2.0	4.5-6.5	1, 2, 3e good	moderate	high	good
Chetek 155	well drained sandy loam	>6′	>60″	erodes moderately	low; 15-25% moderate; 25+% severe	good to 15+%	severe; perm. 2.0-6.0	5.1-6.5	3s, 4e	low	high	good in flat areas moderate on steeper slopes poor on very steep slopes
Kingsley 342	well drained sandy loam	>6′	>60″	3-8% moderate; 8-15% severe	low to moderate	moderate 8-15%; severe 15+%	*septic-* severe; *lagoon-* moderate	5.6-6.5 5.6-7.8	—	low	moderate	moderate on flatter slopes poor on steeper slopes
Quam 344 & 1824	very poorly drained silt loam	0-1.0	>60″	erodes moderately	high	severe	severe	6.6-7.8	—	high	low	moderate on flatter slopes poor on steeper slopes
Mahtomedi 896 & 454	well drained loamy sand/ gravel	>6′	>60″	3-8% moderate; 8-15% severe; 15+% very severe	low	0-8% slight; 8-15% moderate; 15+% severe	*septic-* 0-15% severe; *lagoon-* 0-7% severe	5.1-6.5 5.1-7.8	4s	low	high	moderate on flatter slopes poor on steeper slopes
Kingsley 895	well drained silt loam	>6′	>60″	15-25% moderate	low	severe 15+%	*septic-* severe; *lagoon-* landfill	5.6-6.5 5.6-7.8	2e, 3e, 7e	low	moderate	good
Kennebec 1816	moderately drained silt loam	3.0-5.0	>60″	low	high	moderate	severe-wet	5.6-7.3 6.1-7.3	1, 2e	moderate	low	moderate on flatter slopes poor on steeper slopes

earth sheltered housing

An expanded set of criteria is listed for earth sheltered housing in figure C-3. This evaluation relies more on the detailed engineering properties of the soils than does the analysis for conventional housing. The lowest stratum listed (30 to 60 inches—76 to 152 cm—below ground) was examined in the most detail, since it would be the closest to a typical foundation depth for an earth sheltered house. Several of the criteria that would be identical for both earth sheltered and conventional housing were eliminated from figure C-3 for clarity.

unified soil classification: As for the conventional housing analysis, soil types are listed in figure C-4 according to their unified soil classification.

water table: This factor is even more important for earth sheltered than for conventional construction because primary living spaces are included below grade, and even slight leakage must be avoided. A depth greater than the 60 inches (152 cm) indicated may not be sufficient. Additional information for planning purposes could be obtained from test pits, soil borings, or other site records.

bulk density: This property is considered together with the soil type in order to determine whether the soil is loose or dense. In general, the denser soils within each soil type are better for construction purposes.

shrink/swell potential: A low shrink/swell potential is preferable, and a moderate shrink/swell potential was rated negatively for this site; a high shrink/swell potential would require special design measures. Only the lower strata were rated for this potential.

frost action: Although not usually critical for building design, this factor is important for the design and interfacing of roads with buildings. Soils with a high degree of potential for frost action were rated negatively.

percent liquid limit: This parameter is used to determine the moisture content at which silts or clays will pass from a liquid to a plastic state. Higher values of the liquid limit indicate increasing amounts of fine material in inorganic soils. A liquid limit of less than 50 percent is generally considered good; a liquid limit greater than 50 percent indicates a poorer condition for construction. The two soils with the highest liquid limits were given a comparatively negative rating for this site since they approached the 50-percent figure.

permeability: A permeability rate of over 4 inches (10 cm) per hour is considered good; 2 to 4 inches (5 to 10 cm) per hour, medium; and less than 2 inches (5 cm) per hour, poor. Because local drainage provisions would be provided on the prototypical site, this factor was not considered critical for earth sheltered building design.

percent clay: This parameter was considered in conjunction with the soil classification and liquid limit in order to determine suitability for building design. It was also considered in conjunction with the percent organic matter to determine appropriate plantings.

percent organic matter: For building design an organic content of greater than 10 percent was considered poor. For plant specifications the organic matter is considered in conjunction with the soil pH to determine the level of decomposition of the organic matter in the soil.

pH reaction: This factor, together with information about the organic content of the soil, is used to match plant types to the soil condition or to specify soil modifications for planting. This was not an important factor on the prototypical site.

corrosivity of concrete: The corrosivity of concrete was another factor in assessing the suitability of soils for earth sheltered buildings. Soils with high sulphate contents can be particularly damaging to normal concretes.

land-use potential: This factor, which indicates the vegetation type most compatible with the soil conditions, was determined by referring to the most common crop potential of similar soils in the region.

C-3: earth sheltered housing criteria

soil type	general description	unified strata depth	unified soil class	water table depth	moist bulk density (psf.)	shrink swell potential	frost action potential	% liquid limit	perme-ability (in/hr)	% clay	% organic matter	pH reaction	corrosivity to concrete	land use potential	general suitability on prototypical site
Antigo 49	silty loam	0-14"	ML,CL-ML	>60"	1.35-1.55	low	moderate	<25	0.6-2.0	8-15	2-4	4.5-6.0	high	cropland	good
		14-30"	CL		1.50-1.60	moderate		30-45		20-30					
	fine sand and gravel	30-34"	GM,ML,GM-CL		1.75-2.20	low		<25	0.6-2.0	2-15		5.1-7.8	moderate		
		34-60"	SP,SP-SM, GP			low			6.0	1-6					
Chetek 155	sandy loam	0-13"	SM,SM-SC	>60"	1.35-1.70	low	low	<20	2.0-6.0	5-12	2-3	5.1-6.5	high	woodland	good
	loam	0-13"	ML,CL					20-30		7-15					
	sand and gravel	13-18"	ML,CL		1.50-1.60	low		15-31	6.0-20.0	10-18		5.1-6.5	high		
		18-60"	SP,SP-SM							1-6					
Kingsley 342	sandy loam	0-14"	SM	>60"	1.40-1.60	low	low	<20	0.6-2.0	3-10	2-4	5.6-6.5	moderate	marginal cropland, pasture, woodland	moderate
	loam	0-14"	ML					25-35							
	sandy loam	14-34"	SM,SM-SC		1.70-1.82	low		10-20	0.2-0.6	6-18		5.6-7.8	moderate		
		34-60"			1.70-1.85					5-10					
Quam 344 & 1824	mucky, silty clay loam	0-8"	OL	0-1.0'	0.50-1.00	moderate	high	40-50	0.2-0.6	28-35	15-25	6.6-7.8	low	calcareous rushes, sedges	low
		0-8"	OL-ML			low									
		0-8"	CL-ML												
	silty clay loam	8-38"	CL-ML		1.40-1.65	moderate		20-50	0.2-0.6	20-35	6-15	6.6-7.8	low	cropland	
		38-60"													
Mahtomedi 896 & 454	loamy sand		SM SP-SM	>60"	1.40-1.60	low	low	<20	6.0-20.0	2-15	1	5.1-6.5	high	mixed hardwoods, pasture	good
		30-60"	SP-SM		1.45-1.75	low		<20	6.0-20.0	0-10	1	5.1-6.5	high		
Kingsley 895	silt loam	0-14"	ML-CL	3.0-6.0'	1.40-1.60	low	high	20-30	0.6-2.0		2-3	5.6-7.3	high	cropland	moderate
	loam	0-14"	CL			moderate		30-45				4.5-6.5			
	sandy loam	14-34"	CL		1.80-1.90	low		25-40	0.2-0.6	10-17		5.6-6.5	high		
		34-60"	SM,SM-SC					<20	0.6-2.0						
Kennebec 1816	silt loam	0-41"	CL	3.0-5.0'	1.25-1.35	moderate	high	25-45	0.6-2.0	26-30	5-6	5.6-7.3	low	cultivate prairie	low
	silt loam	41-60"	CL-ML		1.35-1.40	moderate		25-45	0.6-2.0	24-38	5-6	6.1-7.8	low		

overall suitability on the prototype site: In great contrast to the analysis of soil conditions for conventional housing, the evaluation for earth sheltered housing rates all but one of the soil types as good or moderate. In fact, when considered in combination with solar orientation and other energy-related factors, this site becomes quite desirable for the development of earth sheltered housing. The potential for erosion on slopes could be lessened by the retaining and terracing effect of earth sheltered construction. The net effect of including consideration of earth sheltered housing in the suitability analysis for the prototypical site is to open up most of it for development rather than limiting it to use as a park.

C-4: classification of soils for engineering purposes

group symbols	typical names	drainage characteristic	frost heave potential	volume change	backfill potential	suggested bearing capacity	range (psf)	general suitability
GW	well-graded gravels & gravel-sand mixtures, little or no fines	excellent	low	low	best	8000 psf	1500 psf to 20 tons/ft^2	good
GP	poorly graded gravels & gravel-sand mixtures, little or no fines	excellent	low	low	excellent	6000 psf	1500 psf to 20 tons/ft^2	good
GM	silty gravels, gravel-sand silt mixtures	good	medium	low	good	4000 psf	1500 psf to 20 tons/ft^2	good
GC	clayey gravels, gravel-sand-clay mixtures	fair	medium	low	good	3500 psf	1500 psf to 10 tons/ft^2	good
SW	well-graded sands & gravelly sands, little or no fines	good	low	low	good	5000 psf	1500 psf to 15 tons/ft^2	good
SP	poorly graded sand & gravelly sands, little or no fines	good	low	low	good	4000 psf	1500 psf to 10 tons/ft^2	good
SM	silty sands, sand-silt mixtures	good	medium	low	fair	3500 psf	1500 psf to 5 tons/ft^2	good
SC	clayey sands, sand-clay mixtures	fair	medium	low	fair	3000 psf	1000 psf to 8000 psf	good
ML	inorganic silts, very fine sands, rock flour, silty or clayey fine sands	fair	high	low	fair	2000 psf	1000 psf to 8000 psf	fair
CL	inorganic clays of low to medium plasticity, gravelly clays, sandy clays, silty clays, lean clays	fair	medium	medium	fair	2000 psf	500 psf to 5000 psf	fair
MH	inorganic silts, micaceous or diatomaceous fine sands or silts, elastic silts	poor	high	high	poor	1500 psf	500 psf to 4000 psf	poor
CH	inorganic clays of medium to high plasticity	poor	medium	high	bad	1500 psf	500 psf to 4000 psf	poor
OL	organic silts and organic silty clays of low plasticity	poor	medium	medium	poor	400 psf or remove	generally remove soil	poor
OH	organic clays of medium to high plasticity	no good	medium	high	no good	remove	—	poor
PT	peat, muck and other highly organic soils	no good	—	high	no good	remove	—	poor

references and bibliography

introduction and chapter 1

references

1.1. Robert Stobaugh and Daniel Yergin, eds., *Energy Future: Report of the Energy Project at the Harvard Business School* (New York:Random House, 1979).

1.2. National Research Council, *Energy in Transition 1985-2010* (San Francisco:W.H. Freeman and Co., 1979).

1.3. U.S. Department of Energy, *Energy Conserving Site Design Case Study—Burke Centre, Virginia* (Springfield, VA:National Technical Information Service, 1980).

1.4. Robert Engstrom and Marc Putnam, *Planning and Design of Townhouses and Condominiums* (Washington, D.C.:Urban Land Institute, 1979).

1.5. City of Apple Valley, Minnesota Planning Department, *City of Apple Valley, Minnesota, Zoning Ordinances* (St. Paul:Minnesota Planning Dept., 1980).

1.6. Duncan Erley, Charles Thurow, and William Toner, *Performance Controls for Sensitive Lands: A Practical Guide for Local Administrators, Parts 1 and 2* (Chicago:American Society of Planning Officials, 1975).

bibliography

Buechner, Robert D. 1971. *National Park Recreation and Open Space Standards.* Washington, D.C.:National Recreation and Park Association.

City of Bloomington, Minnesota, Planning Commission. 1980. *Comprehensive Plan 1980.* Bloomington:City Planning Commission.

Coomber, Nicholas H., and Biswas, Asit K. 1973. *Evaluation of Environmental Intangibles.* New York:Geneva Press.

De Chiara, Joseph, and Koppelman, Lee. 1969. *Planning Design Criteria.* New York:Van Nostrand Reinhold Co.

Denney, Charles H. 1972. *Recreation Planning Guidelines.* Research study for the Dept. of Recreation and Park Administration, Extension Division, University of Missouri-Columbia. Columbia:Univ. of Missouri.

Erley, Duncan; Thurow, Charles; and Toner, William. 1975. *Performance Controls for Sensitive Lands: A Practical Guide for Local Administrators, Parts 1 and 2.* Chicago:American Society of Planning Officials.

Goodman, William I. 1968. *Principles and Practice of Urban Planning.* 4th ed. Washington, D.C.:International City Manager's Association. Pp. 185-207.

Harwood, Corbin C. 1979. *Using Land to Save Energy.* Cambridge:Ballinger Publishing Co. Pp. 90-96, 154-164.

Lynch, Kevin. 1976. *Managing the Sense of a Region.* Cambridge:M.I.T. Press. Pp. 1-79.

McKeever, J. Ross. 1968. *The Community Builder's Handbook.* Washington, D.C.:Urban Land Institute.

Minnesota Metropolitan Council. 1973. *Protecting Open Space: Policy, Plan and Program.* St. Paul:Metropolitan Council.

National Research Council. 1979. *Energy in Transition 1985-2010.* Prepared for the National Academy of Sciences. San Francisco:W.H. Freeman and Co.

Stobaugh, Robert and Yergin, Daniel, eds. 1979. *Energy Future: Report of the Energy Project at the Harvard Business School.* New York:Random House.

U.S. Department of Energy. 1980. *Energy Conserving Site Design Case Study—Burke Centre, Virginia.* Springfield, VA:National Technical Information Service.

University of Illinois, Housing Research and Development. 1974. *Site Improvement Handbook for Multifamily Housing.* Urbana:Univ. of Illinois. Pp. 21-26.

Wallace, McHarg, Roberts and Todd. 1974. *Woodlands New Community: An Ecological Plan.* Philadelphia: Wallace, McHarg, Roberts and Todd.

interviews

Batty, Ron. 1980. Minnetonka Planning Department, Minnetonka, MN.

Clark, Scott. 1980. Brooklyn Park Planning Department, Brooklyn Park, MN.

Geshwiler, Rick. 1980. Senior planner, Department of Community Planning. Bloomington, MN.

Jessen, Marty. 1980. Metropolitan Council Park and Recreation Division. St. Paul, MN.

chapter 2

references

2.1. Charles McClenon, ed., *Landscape Planning for Energy Conservation* (Reston, VA:Environmental Design Press, 1977).

2.2. Rudolf Geiger, *The Climate Near the Ground* (Cambridge:Harvard University Press, 1965).

bibliography

Baker, Donald, and Klink, John. 1975. *Solar Radiation Perception, Probabilities, and Aerial Distribution in the North-Central Region.* North Central Regional Research Publication 225, Technical Bulletin 300-1975, Agricultural Experiment Station, University of Minnesota. St. Paul:Ag. Extension Service, Univ. of Minnesota.

Engstrom, Robert, and Putnam, Marc. 1979. *Planning and Design of Townhouses and Condominiums.* Washington, D.C.:Urban Land Institute.

Geiger, Rudolf. 1965. *The Climate Near the Ground.* Cambridge:Harvard University Press.

Knowles, Ralph. 1974. *Energy and Form: An Ecological Approach to Urban Growth.* Cambridge:M.I.T. Press.

Kuehnost, Earl; Baker, Donald; and Eng, John. 1975. *Precipitation Patterns in the Minneapolis-St. Paul Metropolitan Area and Surrounding Counties.* Technical Bulletin 301-1975, Agricultural Experiment Station, University of Minnesota. St. Paul:Ag. Extension Service.

McClenon, Charles, ed. 1977. *Landscape Planning for Energy Conservation.* Reston, VA:Environmental Design Press.

Metropolitan Waste Control Commission. 1975. *Baseline Environmental Inventory, Twin Cities Metropolitan Area.* Prepared by E.A. Hickok and Associates. Minneapolis:Metropolitan Waste Control Commission.

Olgyay, Victor. 1963. *Design with Climate: A Bioclimatic Approach to Architectural Regionalism.* Princeton: Princeton University Press.

Underground Space Center, University of Minnesota. 1980. *Earth Sheltered Housing: Code, Zoning and Financing Issues.* Prepared for the U.S. Dept. of Housing and Urban Development. Washington, D.C.:Dept. of Housing and Urban Development.

Urban Land Institute; American Society of Civil Engineers; and National Association of Home Builders. 1975. *Residential Storm Water Management: Objectives, Principles and Design Considerations.* Published jointly by the Urban Land Institute, Amer. Society of Civil Engineers, and Natl. Assoc. of Home Builders.

U.S. Department of Energy. 1980. *Energy Conserving Site Design: Case Study—Burke Centre, Virginia.* Prepared for the Dept. of Energy, Office of Buildings and Community Systems. Springfield, VA:National Technical Information Service.

U.S. Department of the Interior, and American Society of Landscape Architects Foundation. 1972. *People/Plants/ and Environmental Quality.* Washington, D.C.:Dept. of the Interior.

Wallace, McHarg, Roberts and Todd. 1974. *Woodlands New Community: An Ecological Plan.* Philadelphia: Wallace, McHarg, Roberts and Todd.

Watson, Bruce. 1975. *Minnesota Weather Almanac 1976.* Minneapolis:Bolger Press.

interviews

Minnesota Zoological Gardens personnel. 1980. Apple Valley, MN.

Northern States Power Company public relations division personnel. 1980. Minneapolis, MN.

Watson, Bruce. 1980. Meteorologist. Minneapolis, MN.

chapter 3

references

3.1. Roger Machmeier, *Minimum Design Standards for Community Sewerage Systems: A HUD Guide* (Washington, D.C.:Dept. of Housing and Urban Development, 1968), p. 7.

3.2. Minnesota State Board of Health, *Minnesota Plumbing Code* (Minneapolis: State Board of Health, 1969), p. 21 (MHD-130-1).

3.3. *Ibid.,* p. 22.

3.4. Health Education Service, Great Lakes-Upper Mississippi River Board of State Sanitary Engineers, *Recommended Standards for Water Works: Policies for the Review and Approval of Plans and Specifications for Public Water Supplies* (Albany:Great Lakes-Upper Mississippi River Board of State Sanitary Engineers, 1976), p. 23.

3.5. Corbin Harwood, *Using Land to Save Energy* (Cambridge:Ballinger Publishing Co., 1977), p. 1.

3.6. Bucks County Planning Commission, *Performance Streets: A Concept and Model Standards for Residential Streets* (Doylestown, PA:Bucks County Planning Commission, 1980), p. 2.

3.7. David A. Bainbridge, *Residential Street Design for Energy Conservation* (Davis, CA:Passive Solar Institute, 1979), p. 5.

3.8. Urban Land Institute, *Residential Stormwater Management: Objectives, Principles, and Design Considerations* (published jointly by the Urban Land Institute, Amer. Society of Civil Engineers, and Natl. Assoc. of Home Builders, 1975), p. 7.

3.9. International Council for Building Research Studies and Documentation, *Energy Conservation in the Built Environment: Proceedings of the 1976 Symposium of the International Council for Building Research Studies and Documentation.* Paper presented by J.B. Chaddock, p. 82.

3.10. Office of Technology Assessment, *Residential Energy Conservation, Vols. 1 and 2* (Washington, D.C.:U.S. Govt. Printing Office, 1979).

bibliography

stormwater

Luthin, James N. 1966. *Drainage Engineering.* New York:John Wiley and Sons, Inc.

Natural drainage: route to lower development costs. *House and Home,* December 1966.

Urban Land Institute. 1978. *Residential Erosion and Sediment Control: Objectives, Principles and Design Considerations.* Published jointly by the Urban Land Institute, Amer. Society of Civil Engineers, and Natl. Assoc. of Home Builders.

__________. 1975. *Residential Stormwater Management: Objectives, Principles, and Design Considerations.* Published jointly by the Urban Land Institute, Amer. Society of Civil Engineers, and Natl. Assoc. of Home Builders.

roads/parking

Bainbridge, David A. 1979. *Residential Street Design for Energy Conservation.* Davis, CA:Passive Solar Institute.

Bucks County Planning Commission. 1980. *Performance Streets: A Concept and Model Standards for Residential Streets.* Doylestown, PA:Bucks County Planning Commission.

Energy Research Group, University of Illinois. 1977. *Energy Use for Building Construction: Final Report, Feb. 1-Oct. 31, 1977.* Springfield, VA:National Technical Information Service.

Interagency Task Force on Energy Conservation. 1974. *Project Independence and Energy Conservation: Transportation Sections, Vol. 2.* Prepared under the direction of the Council on Environmental Quality. Washington, D.C.:Federal Energy Administration.

McGregor, Gloria S. 1976. *Resolution adopting parking standards for the City of Davis, California.* Resolution #1, Series 1976. Davis:Community Development Dept.

Organization for Economic Cooperation and Development. 1973. *Proceedings of the Symposium on Techniques of Improving Urban Conditions by Restraint of Road Traffic.* Paris:Org. for Economic Cooperation and Development.

Proudlove, J.A. 1968. *Roads.* 2nd ed. London:Longmans, Green, and Co. Ltd.

Urban Land Institute. 1974. *Residential Streets: Objectives, Principles, and Design Considerations.* Published jointly by the Urban Land Institute, Amer. Society of Civil Engineers, and Natl. Assoc. of Home Builders.

sewerage

Bowne, W.C., and Ball, H.L. 1981. Pressure sewer system proves effective economics. *Public Works,* March 1981.

Fair, G.M., and Geyer, J.C. 1958. *Elements of Water Supply and Wastewater Disposal.* New York:John Wiley and Sons, Inc.

Hittman Associates. 1978. *Comprehensive Community Energy Planning, Vols. 1 and 2.* Prepared for the U.S. Department of Energy. Columbia, MD:Dept. of Energy.

Jacobs, Lee W., ed. 1977. *Utilizing Municipal Sewage Wastewaters and Sludges on Land for Agricultural Production.* North Central Regional Extension Publication #52. East Lansing:Michigan State Univ.

Machmeier, Roger. 1968. *Minimum Design Standards for Community Sewerage Systems: A HUD Guide.* Washington, D.C.:Dept. of Housing and Urban Development.

Minnesota Department of Health. 1971. *Code Regulating Individual Sewage Disposal Systems.* Minneapolis: Minnesota Dept. of Health.

Minnesota Metropolitan Council. *Minnesota Statutes 1978.* Chapter 473.501-473.549, Metropolitan Waste Control Commission Act. St. Paul:Metropolitan Council.

National Association of Home Builders. 1978. *Alternatives to Public Sewers.* Washington, D.C.:Natl. Assoc. of Home Builders.

National Association of Home Builders. 1980. *Residential Waste Water Systems.* Washington, D.C.:Natl. Assoc. of Home Builders.

water

Health Education Service, Great Lakes-Upper Mississippi River Board of State Sanitary Engineers. 1976. *Recommended Standards for Water Works: Policies for the Review and Approval of Plans and Specifications for Public Water Supplies.* Albany:Great Lakes-Upper Mississippi River Board of State Sanitary Engineers.

Minnesota Department of Health. 1980. *Drinking Water Quality Regulations and Proposals: Summary Chart.* Minneapolis:Minnesota Dept. of Health.

__________. 1979. *Rules Relating to Licensing of Water Well Contractors and Construction of Water Wells.* Minneapolis:Minnesota Dept. of Health.

Minnesota Department of Natural Resources. *Department of Natural Resources Rules for Appropriation of Waters of the State: Minnesota Code of Agency Rules.* St. Paul: Minnesota Dept. of Natural Resources.

__________. 1976. *Elements and Explanation of the Municipal Shoreland Rules and Regulations.* Shoreland Management Supplementary Report #5. St. Paul: Minnesota Dept. of Natural Resources.

__________. 1975. *Procedural Guide for the Implementation of County Shoreland Ordinances.* Shoreland Management Supplementary Report #3. St. Paul: Minnesota Dept. of Natural Resources.

__________. 1976. *Procedural Guide for the Implementation of Municipal Shoreland Ordinances.* Shoreland Management Supplementary Report #6. St. Paul: Minnesota Dept. of Natural Resources.

__________. 1970. *Rules and Regulations of the Department of Conservation Relating to Statewide Standards and Criteria for Management of Shoreland Areas of Minnesota.* Chapter 6, Minnesota State Regulations for Conservation. St. Paul:Minnesota Dept. of Natural Resources.

Minnesota State Board of Health. 1969. *Minnesota Plumbing Code.* Minneapolis:Minnesota State Board of Health.

National Association of Home Builders. 1979. *Home Builders and Water Quality: A Guide.* Washington, D.C.:Natl. Assoc. of Home Builders.

energy supply (see appendix a)

interviews

Apple Valley Planning Corporation personnel. 1980. Apple Valley, MN.

Earth Sheltered Corporation of America personnel. 1980. Wisconsin, Ohio, Illinois.

Geshwiler, Rick. 1980. Senior planner, Department of Community Planning, Division of City Planning. Bloomington, MN.

Honsell, Mike. 1980. Minnesota Pollution Control Agency. St. Paul, MN.

Machmeier, Roger. 1980. Agricultural Extension Service, University of Minnesota. St. Paul, MN.

Minnesota Department of Health personnel. 1980. Minneapolis, MN.

Odde, Raymond. 1980. Metropolitan Waste Commission. Minneapolis, MN.

Preston, Steve. 1980. Department of Natural Resources, Water Planning Division. St. Paul, MN.

Rosene, Bob. 1980. Bonestroo, Rosene, Anderlik and Associates, Inc., consulting engineers. St. Paul, MN.

Seward Redevelopment Corporation personnel. 1980. Minneapolis, MN.

Soil Conservation Service, Water Planning Division personnel. 1980. St. Paul, MN.

chapters 4 and 5

references

4.1. William A. Shurcliff, *Super Insulated Homes and Double Envelope Houses* (Andover, MA:Brick House Publishing Co., 1981).

4.2. Victor Olgyay, *Design with Climate: A Bioclimatic Approach to Architectural Regionalism* (Princeton: Princeton University Press, 1963).

4.3. U.S. Department of Energy, *Passive Solar Design Handbook, Vols. 1 and 2* (Springfield, VA:National Technical Information Service, 1980).

5.1. National Association of Home Builders, *Cost Effective Site Planning: Single Family Development* (Washington, D.C.:Natl. Assoc. of Home Builders, 1976).

5.2. Duncan Erley and Martin Jaffee, *Site Planning for Solar Access: A Guidebook for Residential Developers and Site Planners* (Washington, D.C.:U.S. Govt. Printing Office, 1979).

5.3. Olgyay, *op. cit.*

5.4. U.S. Department of Energy, *Energy Conserving Site Design Case Study—Radisson, New York* (Springfield, VA:National Technical Information Service, 1979).

5.5. Olgyay, *op. cit.*

5.6. S. Robert Hastings and Richard W. Crenshaw, *Window Design Strategies to Conserve Energy* (Washington, D.C.:U.S. Govt. Printing Office, 1977).

5.7. Olgyay, *op. cit.*

5.8. John Kaufman, ed., *IES Lighting Handbook,* 5th ed. (New York:Illuminating Engineering Society, 1972).

5.9. Olgyay, *op. cit.*

bibliography

Erley, Duncan, and Jaffee, Martin. 1979. *Site Planning for Solar Access: A Guidebook for Residential Developers and Site Planners.* Prepared by the American Planning Association for the U.S. Department of Housing and Urban Development. Washington, D.C.:U.S. Govt. Printing Office.

Hastings, S. Robert, and Crenshaw, Richard W. 1977. *Window Design Strategies to Conserve Energy.* Washington, D.C.:U.S. Govt. Printing Office.

Kaufman, John, ed. 1972. *IES Lighting Handbook.* New York:Illuminating Engineering Society.

Labs, Kenneth B. 1979. *Land-Use Regulation of Underground Housing.* American Planning Association Planning Advisory Service Memo 79-5. Chicago:American Planning Association.

Mazria, Edward. 1979. *The Passive Solar Energy Book.* Emmaus, PA:Rodale Press.

Moreland, Frank L.; Higgs, Forrest; and Shih, Jason, eds. 1979. *Earth Covered Buildings and Settlements.* Springfield, VA:National Technical Information Service.

__________. 1979. *Earth Covered Buildings: Technical Notes.* Springfield, VA:National Technical Information Service.

National Association of Home Builders. 1976. *Cost Effective Site Planning: Single Family Development.* Washington, D.C.:Natl. Assoc. of Home Builders.

Olgyay, Victor. 1963. *Design with Climate: A Bioclimatic Approach to Architectural Regionalism.* Princeton: Princeton University Press.

Shurcliff, William A. 1981. *Super Insulated Homes and Double Envelope Houses.* Andover, MA:Brick House Publishing Co.

Thorsen, Gerald W. and Rue, Roger L. 1980. High bank instead of high rise--an earth-sheltered approach to medium density housing. *Underground Space* 5(1980):149-151.

Underground Space Center. 1980. *Earth Sheltered Housing: Code, Zoning, and Financing Issues.* Prepared for the U.S. Department of Housing and Urban Development. Washington, D.C.:Dept. of Housing and Urban Development.

Underground Space Center. 1978. *Earth Sheltered Housing Design: Guidelines, Examples, and References.* New York:Van Nostrand Reinhold Co.

U.S. Department of Energy. 1979. *Energy Conserving Site Design Case Study—Radisson, New York.* Prepared for the Dept. of Energy, Office of Buildings and Community Systems. Springfield, VA:National Technical Information Service.

__________. 1980. *Passive Solar Design Handbook, Vol. 1: Passive Solar Design Concepts.* Prepared by Total Environment Action, Inc. Springfield, VA:National Technical Information Service.

__________. 1980. *Passive Solar Design Handbook, Vol 2: Passive Solar Design Analysis.* Prepared by Los Alamos Scientific Laboratory (J. Douglas Balcomb). Springfield, VA:National Technical Information Service.

Wells, Malcolm. 1977. *Underground Designs.* Brewster, MA:Malcolm Wells. Available for $6.00 postpaid from Malcolm Wells, Box 1149, Brewster, MA 02631.

chapter 7

references

7.1. Bernard Rudolfsky, *Architecture Without Architects* (Garden City, NY:Doubleday, 1969).

7.2. Malcolm Wells, *Underground Designs* (Brewster, MA:Malcolm Wells, 1977).

7.3. Kenneth N. Clark and Patricia Paylore, eds., *Desert Housing* (Tucson:Univ. of Arizona, 1980).

7.4. Frank L. Moreland, Forrest Higgs, and Jason Shih, eds., *Earth Covered Buildings and Settlements* (Springfield, VA:National Technical Information Service, 1979).

bibliography

Boyer, L.L., ed. 1980. *Earth Sheltered Condominiums.* Stillwater:Oklahoma State Univ.

Clark, Kenneth N. and Paylore, Patricia, eds. 1980. *Desert Housing.* Tucson:Univ. of Arizona.

Moreland, Frank L.; Higgs, Forrest; and Shih, Jason, eds. 1979. *Earth Covered Buildings and Settlements.* Springfield, VA:National Technical Information Service.

__________. 1979. *Earth Covered Buildings: Technical Notes.* Springfield, VA:National Technical Information Service.

Morgenthaler, Niklaus. 1973. *Atelier 5* (Vol. 23, *Global Architecture* series). Tokyo:A.D.A. EVITA Tokyo Co., Ltd.

Rudolfsky, Bernard. 1969. *Architecture Without Architects.* Garden City, NY:Doubleday.

Smay, V. Elaine. 1981. Under-hill village tames a plunging slope. *Popular Science,* February 1981, pp. 82-85.

Smith, C. Ray. 1976. Low density in the dunes. *Progressive Architecture,* September 1976, pp. 68-71.

Wells, Malcolm. 1977. *Underground Designs.* Brewster, MA:Malcolm Wells. Available for $6.00 postpaid from Malcolm Wells, Box 1149, Brewster, MA 02631.

appendix a

references

A.1. Craig Conley, "Improving Furnace Efficiency," *Soft Energy Notes,* Feb. 1980, p. 28.

A.2. Craig Conley, "Piping Hot: District Heating Reappraised," *Soft Energy Notes,* June/July 1980, pp. 4-5.

A.3. Steve Meyers, "Cheaper by the Region: Switzerland's Heat Confederation," *Soft Energy Notes,* June/July 1980, pp. 6-7.

A.4. Minnesota Energy Agency, *Energy Policy and Conservation Report* (St. Paul:Minnesota Energy Agency, 1978).

A.5. Steve Meyers, "Debunking the Myth of Solar Sprawl," *Soft Energy Notes,* June/July 1980, pp. 8-10.

A.6. National Research Council, *Energy in Transition 1985-2010* (San Francisco:W.H. Freeman and Co., 1979).

bibliography

Conley, Craig. 1980. Improving furnace efficiency. *Soft Energy Notes,* February 1980, p. 28.

Conley, Craig. 1980. Piping hot; district heating reappraised. *Soft Energy Notes,* June/July 1980, pp. 4-5.

International Council for Building Research Studies and Documentation. 1976. *Energy Conservation in the Built Environment: Proceedings of the 1976 Symposium of the International Council for Building Research Studies and Documentation.* Paper presented by J.B. Chaddock, p. 82.

Meyers, Steve. 1980. Cheaper by the region: Switzerland's heat confederation. *Soft Energy Notes,* June/July 1980, pp. 6-7.

Meyers, Steve. 1980. Debunking the myth of solar sprawl. *Soft Energy Notes,* June/July 1980, pp. 8-10.

Minnesota Energy Agency. 1978. *Energy Policy and Conservation Report.* St. Paul:Minnesota Energy Agency.

__________. 1979. *Energy Policy and Conservation Report.* St. Paul:Minnesota Energy Agency.

Minnesota Environmental Quality Board, Power Plant Siting Advisory Committee. 1980. *Options for Electric Energy Supply.* St. Paul:Minnesota Environmental Quality Board.

Minnesota Solar Energy Association, Inc. 1979. *Statement of Concern and Recommendations for the Development of Renewable Energy Sources in Minnesota.* Minneapolis:MSEA,Inc.

National Research Council. 1979. *Energy in Transition 1985-2010.* Prepared for the National Academy of Sciences. San Francisco:W.H. Freeman and Co.

Office of Technology Assessment. 1979. *Residential Energy Conservation, Vols. 1 and 2.* Washington, D.C.:U.S. Govt. Printing Office.

Okagaki, Alan and Benson, Jim. 1979. *County Energy Plan Guidebook: Creating a Renewable Energy Future.* 2nd ed. Fairfax, VA:Institute for Ecological Policies.

Solar Energy Research Institute. 1979. *Low Temperature Thermal Energy Storage: A State of the Art Survey.* Springfield, VA:National Technical Information Service.

appendix b

references

B.1. "What Home Shoppers Seek in Six Major Markets," *Housing* 54(Oct. 1978):53-76.

B.2. "Home Shopper Survey," *Housing* 56(Nov. 1979):61-84.

B.3. Personal communication with Warner Shippee and Larry Lauka, 1980.

B.4. Cora McKown and K. Kay Stewart, "Consumer Attitudes Concerning Construction Features of an Earth-Sheltered Dwelling," *Underground Space* 4 (1980):293-295.

B.5. Gary Solomonson, Private marketing analysis for Seward town houses (1980).

B.6. "Home Shopper Survey," *op. cit.,* p. 66.

B.7. Lester L. Boyer, Walter T. Grondzik, and Thomas N. Bice, "Passive Energy Design and Habitability Aspects of Earth-sheltered Housing in Oklahoma," *Underground Space* 4(1980):333.

bibliography

The best seller homes of 1979: part II, floor plans. *Automation in Housing/Systems Building News,* May 1980, p. 20.

Boyer, Lester L.; Grondzik, Walter T.; and Bice, Thomas N. 1980. Passive energy design and habitability aspects of earth-sheltered housing in Oklahoma. *Underground Space* 4(6):333-340.

Home shopper survey. 1979. *Housing* 56:Nov. 1979, pp. 61-84.

McKown, Cora, and Stewart, K. Kay. 1980. Consumer attitudes concerning construction features of an earth-sheltered dwelling. *Underground Space* 4(5):293-295.

Solomonson, Gary. 1980. Private marketing analysis for Seward town houses.

Stewart, K. Kay; McKown, Cora; and Peck, Carolyn. 1979. Consumer attitudes concerning an earth-sheltered house. *Underground Space* 4(1):11-15.

What home shoppers seek in six major markets. 1978. *Housing* 55:Oct. 1978, pp. 53-76.

Who's buying townhouses--and why. 1977. *House and Home* 51:May 1977, pp. 72-73.

interview

Shippee, Warner, and Lauka, Larry. 1980. Personal communications.

general bibliography

Burby III, Raymond J., and Bell, A. Fleming, eds. 1978. *Energy and the Community.* Cambridge:Ballinger Publishing Co.

Carpenter, J.D. ed. 1976. *Handbook of Landscape Architectural Construction.* Washington, D.C.:Landscape Architecture Foundation, Inc.

City of Portland, Oregon, Bureau of Planning, Policy Analysis Section. 1978. *Energy Conservation Choices for the City of Portland, Oregon, Vol. 4: Model Local Code Revisions for Energy Conservation.* Washington, D.C.:Dept. of Housing and Urban Development.

Cline, Ann. 1976. City energy planning in a small scale community. Presentation at Community Energy Management Systems Workshop, Energy Planning Division, American Planning Association Conference, Baltimore, Maryland, October 1979.

De Chiana, Joseph, and Kappelman, Lee. 1978. *Site Planning Standards.* New York:McGraw-Hill Book Co.

Energy Research Group, Center for Advanced Computation. 1977. *Energy Use for Building Construction.* Prepared for the U.S. Dept. of Energy. Springfield, VA:National Technical Information Service.

Erley, Duncan, and Mosena, David. 1980. *Energy-conserving Development Regulations: Current Practice.* Chicago:American Planning Association.

Federal Housing Administration. 1961. *Neighborhood Standards.* Land Planning Bulletin #3-24. Minneapolis:Federal Housing Administration.

Goodman, William I., ed. 1968. *Principles and Practice of Urban Planning.* Washington, D.C.:International City Manager's Association.

Hammond, Jonathon; Hunt, Marshall; Cramer, Richard; and Neubauer, Loren. 1974. *A Strategy for Energy Conservation: Proposed Energy Conservation and Solar Utilization Ordinance for the City of Davis, California.* Davis:Community Development Dept.

Jaffe, Martin, and Erley, Duncan. 1979. *Protecting Solar Access for Residential Development: A Guidebook for Planning Officials.* Prepared by the American Planning Association for the U.S. Dept. of Housing and Urban Development. Washington, D.C.:U.S. Govt. Printing Office.

Kalunette, Gary O., ed. 1978. *Options for Passive Energy Conservation in Site Design.* Reston, VA:Center of Landscape Architectural Education and Research.

Landphair, Harlow C., and Klatt, Jr., Fred. 1979. *Landscape Architecture Construction.* New York:Elsevier.

McGregor, Gloria S. 1979. *A New Energy Source: Natural Design for Energy Generation.* Prepared for the Community Development Department, City of Davis, California. Davis:Community Development Dept.

McKeever, J. Ross, ed. 1968. *The Community Builders.* Washington, D.C.:Urban Land Institute.

__________. *Energy Conservation in Urban and Regional Planning: the Davis Experience.* Prepared for the Community Development Department, City of Davis, California. Davis:Community Development Dept.

Minnesota Department of Natural Resources, Division of Waters. 1974. *The Concept of Cluster Development: Explanation and Guidelines for Shoreland Management.* Supplementary Report #4. St. Paul:Minnesota Dept. of Natural Resources.

Minnesota Metropolitan Council. 1978. *Energy and Land Use: A Literature Review.* St. Paul:Metropolitan Council.

__________. 1974. *PUD: Trends and Experience in the Metropolitan Area.* St. Paul:Metropolitan Council.

Minnesota Metropolitan Council, and Minnesota Association of Metropolitan Municipalities. 1979. *Streamlining the Housing Development Approval Process.* St. Paul:Metropolitan Council.

Minnesota State Planning Agency, Office of Local and Urban Affairs. 1979. *PUD: A Special Tool for Special Situations.* St. Paul:Minnesota State Planning Agency.

__________. 1975. *Subdivision Control for Minnesota Communities.* St. Paul:Minnesota State Planning Agency.

National Association of Home Builders. 1969. *Land Development Manual.* Washington, D.C.:Natl. Assoc. of Home Builders.

__________. 1980. *Planning for Housing: Development Alternatives for Better Environments.* Washington, D.C.:Natl. Assoc. of Home Builders.

Okagaki, Alan, and Benson, Jim. 1979. *County Energy Plan Guidebook: Creating A Renewable Energy Future.* 2nd ed. Fairfax, VA:Institute for Ecological Policies.

Ridgeway, James; and Projansky, Carolyn. 1979. *Energy Efficient Community Planning: A Guide to Saving and Producing Power at the Local Level.* Emmaus, PA:The JG Press, Inc.

Seelye, Elwyn E. 1950. *Data Book for Civil Engineers, Vol 1: Designs.* 3rd ed. New York:John Wiley and Sons, Inc.

Williamson, Christine. 1977. *Village Homes: Preliminary Evaluation of Innovations.* Prepared for the Community Development Department, City of Davis, California.

Zehner, Robert B. 1977. *Indicators of the Quality of Life in New Communities.* Cambridge:Ballinger Publishing Co.

index

Italic numbers refer to illustrations

A

B

C

D

E

F

G

P

R

S

T

U

V

W

Z